Quantum Artificial Intelligence

This book explores the transformative potential of quantum computing in artificial intelligence (AI) and its impact on various fields. It delves into the foundational concepts, mathematical frameworks, and algorithmic paradigms, providing a roadmap for interdisciplinary research of quantum computing in AI. With a focus on practical applications and prospects, this book bridges the gap between theory and practice, empowering readers to harness the transformative power of quantum technologies for societal and technological advancement.

Key Features:

- Examines the architecture, foundations, mathematics, algorithms, programming, encryption techniques, predictive data analysis, tools/software, and applications associated with quantum computing in AI.
- Explores the challenges of quantum hardware scalability and stability, and outlines error correction and mitigation strategies in quantum computing.
- Discusses applications in industries like finance, healthcare, cybersecurity, and transportation, offering innovative solutions to complex challenges.
- Provides analysis of quantum encryption methods for enhanced data security in AI systems.
- Offers an evaluation of the cost-effectiveness and practicality of quantum computing solutions.

It is a reference work for academics, scholars, and researchers interested in quantum computing in AI.

Quantum Artificial Intelligence

Technologies, Algorithms, and Programming

Edited by
Deepika Ghai, Suman Lata Tripathi, Ramandeep Sandhu, and
Sardar M. N. Islam (Naz)

CRC Press
Taylor & Francis Group
Boca Raton London New York

CRC Press is an imprint of the
Taylor & Francis Group, an **informa** business
A CHAPMAN & HALL BOOK

Designed cover image: Shutterstock

First edition published 2026
and by CRC Press
2385 NW Executive Center Drive, Suite 320, Boca Raton FL 33431

and by CRC Press
4 Park Square, Milton Park, Abingdon, Oxon, OX14 4RN

CRC Press is an imprint of Informa UK Limited

British Library Cataloguing-in-Publication Data
A catalogue record for this book is available from the British Library

ISBN: 978-1-032-87075-5 (hbk)
ISBN: 978-1-032-87076-2 (pbk)
ISBN: 978-1-003-53080-0 (ebk)

DOI: 10.1201/9781003530800

Typeset in Times
by codeMantra

Contents

Preface

The rapid convergence of quantum mechanics and artificial intelligence (AI) has created an exciting new chapter for human innovation. Computation has moved beyond classical logic, and the rise of quantum artificial intelligence (QAI) now represents a fundamental change in the way data are processed, analysed, and understood. This book intends to develop a comprehensive understanding of QAI, including the basic ideas and principles, algorithmic principles, programming methods, and applications in the real world. The first chapter develops the foundational principles of quantum computing and AI, creating a conceptual link between some of the ideas of quantum theory and machines capable of intelligent behaviour. In the following chapters, we expand on how AI will enhance quantum computational models and how intelligent systems enable quantum optimization, simulation, and decision-making. The discussion then transitions towards the seamless fusion of quantum computing and AI, presenting hybrid architectures, algorithms, and computational paradigms that underpin this evolving discipline.

Further chapters investigate quantum computing's future, identifying future research directions, technical challenges, and worldwide developments in next-generation computation. The mention of quantum encryption and security systems highlights the increasing demand for resilient and adaptive protection of information throughout the quantum era. A detailed exploration of applications and advantages of QAI highlights its potential to transform everything from healthcare to communication and finance to industrial systems. The concluding chapter considers the transformative potential of quantum technologies in the context of e-business, which will redefine trust, transparency, and computing efficiency in a digital economy.

This book represents a collaborative scholarly endeavour by researchers and practitioners from leading academic and industrial institutions. Each contributor offers distinct expertise, thereby ensuring that the content reflects a balanced integration of theoretical depth and practical insight. Collectively, the chapters aim to equip readers with the conceptual clarity, technical knowledge, and visionary perspective required to engage with this rapidly advancing field. As humanity stands at the threshold of the quantum–intelligent era, *this book* seeks to serve as both a foundational reference and a catalyst for further exploration. This book will inspire new research directions, foster interdisciplinary collaboration, and contribute meaningfully to the scientific discourse on the technologies shaping the future of mankind.

About the Editors

Deepika Ghai earned her Ph.D. in Signal and Image Processing from Punjab Engineering College (Deemed to be University), Chandigarh. She did her M.Tech. in VLSI Design and CAD at Thapar University, Patiala, and B.Tech. in Electronics and Communications Engineering from Rayat Institute of Engineering and Technology, Ropar. At Lovely Professional University she is an Associate Professor with more than 8 years of experience in academics. She received the Dr. C.B. Gupta Award in 2021 at Lovely Professional University. She has published more than 50 research papers in refereed journals and conferences. Her area of expertise includes signal and image processing, biomedical signal and image processing, AI, machine learning, deep learning, and VLSI signal processing.

Suman Lata Tripathi is a Professor at Symbiosis Institute of Technology (SIT), Symbiosis International (Deemed University), Pune, with more than 23 years of experience in academics. She earned her Ph.D. in Microelectronics and VLSI Design from MNNIT, Allahabad; her M.Tech. in Electronics Engineering from UP Technical University, Lucknow; and her B.Tech. in Electrical Engineering from Purvanchal University, Jaunpur. She was a remote post-doc researcher at Nottingham Trent University, London, UK, in 2022. She has published more than 181 research papers in refereed Springer, Elsevier, IEEE, and IOPscience journals, conference proceedings, and e-books. She received the "Research Excellence Award" in 2019 and the "Research Appreciation Award" in 2020–2024 at Lovely Professional University, India. She has also received a funded project from SERB DST under the TARE scheme in the area of microelectronic devices. Her area of expertise includes microelectronics device modelling and characterization, low-power VLSI circuit design, VLSI design of testing, advanced FET design for IoT, embedded system design, reconfigurable architecture with FPGAs and biomedical applications, etc.

Ramandeep Sandhu is an Associate Professor at Lovely Professional University with more than 17 years of experience in academics. She earned her Ph.D. in Computer Science and Engineering from Lovely Professional University, Phagwara, Punjab, India, and her M.Tech. and B.Tech. in Computer Science and Engineering from Guru Nanak Dev Engineering College, Ludhiana, Punjab, India. She has published more than 30 research papers in journals and conferences. Her academic and research expertise includes cloud computing, cloud optimization, machine learning, quantum computing, data sciences, opinion mining/sentiment analysis, C/C++, and Python. She has also published two authored books on C++.

Sardar M. N. Islam (Naz), Ph.D., LL.B. (Law), is a Professor at ISILC, Victoria University, Australia. He is also a Distinguished Visiting Professor of Artificial Intelligence, UniSri, and an Adjunct Professor of IT and Business at Armstrong Institute, Melbourne, Australia. He has published 31 authored books, 4 edited books, and about 250 articles, including 60 Q1 and Q2 grade journal articles. He is the Editor-in-Chief of *International Transactions on Artificial Intelligence*—an AI and modelling journal. His area of research includes quantum computing and artificial intelligence.

Contributors

Krishan Arora
School of Electronics and Electrical Engineering
Lovely Professional University
Jalandhar, India

Ajay Kumar Badhan
School of Computer Science and Engineering
Lovely Professional University
Jalandhar, India

Chandani Bhasin
School of Computer Science and Engineering
Lovely Professional University
Jalandhar, India

Abhishek Bhattacharjee
School of Computer Science and Engineering
Lovely Professional University
Jalandhar, India

Ahmed Mateen Buttar
Department of Computer Science
University of Agriculture Faisalabad
Faisalabad, Pakistan

Harpreet Kaur Channi
Department of Electrical Engineering
Guru Nanak Dev Engineering College
Ludhiana, India

Gagandeep Singh Cheema
Mittal School of Business
Lovely Professional University
Jalandhar, India

Sandeep Chouhan
School of Computer Science and Engineering
Lovely Professional University
Jalandhar, India

Arumugam Deepika
Department of Computer Science
Sri Rama Krishna College of Arts and Science
Coimbatore, India

John T. Mesia Dhas
School of Computing
Vel Tech Rangarajan Dr. Sagunthala R&D Institute of Science and Technology
Chennai, India

Kumar Gautaum
Quantum Computing Lab
Quantum Research and Centre of Excellence
New Delhi, India

Deepika Ghai
School of Electronics and Electrical Engineering
Lovely Professional University
Jalandhar, India

J. Viji Gripsy
Department of Computer Science with Cognitive Systems
PSGR Krishnammal College for Women
Peelamedu, Coimbatore, India

Sakshi Gupta
School of Computer Application
Manav Rachna International Institute of Research and Studies
Faridabad, India

S. Sahul Hameed
Department of Information Technology
Syed Hameedha Arts and Science College
Kilakarai, India

Sardar M. N. Islam (Naz)
Institute for Sustainable Industries & Liveable Cities (ISILC)
Victoria University, Melbourne
Australia

Surinder Kaur
Department of Fashion Designing
Guru Nanak Girls College
Ludhiana, India

Natrajan Kavitha
School of Computer Science and Applications
REVA University
Bangalore, India

Ravindran Kiruthika
Department of Computer Science
PSGR Krishnammal College for Women
Peelamedu, Coimbatore, India

Mukesh Kumar
Department of Physics
Lovely Professional University
Jalandhar, India

Raman Kumar
Department of Mechanical Engineering
Guru Nanak Dev Engineering College
Ludhiana, India

Sundaramurthy Manju Priya
School of Computer Science and Applications
REVA University
Bangalore, India

Manjushree Nayak
Department of Computer Science and Engineering
NIST University
Berhampur, Odisha, India

Sadaf Naz
Department of Computer Science
University of Agriculture Faisalabad
Faisalabad, Pakistan

Manorama Patnaik
Department of Computer Science
Amity Institute of Information Technology
Amity University
Jharkhand, Ranchi, India

Sangeeta Prasher
Department of Physics
Kanya Maha Vidyalaya
Jalandhar, India

Narayanan Radha
School of Computer Science and Applications
REVA University
Bangalore, India

Manik Rakhra
School of Computer Science and Engineering
Lovely Professional University
Jalandhar, India

N. Toyaad Kumar Reddy
Department of Computer Science and Engineering
NIST University
Berhampur, Odisha, India

Rita Roy
Department of Computer Science
Gitam Institute of Technology (Deemed to be University)
Andhra Pradesh, India

Ramandeep Sandhu
School of Computer Science and Engineering
Lovely Professional University
Jalandhar, India

Tiyas Sarkar
School of Computer Science and Engineering
Lovely Professional University
Jalandhar, India

Deepak Saroj
Computer Science and Engineering
Baba Farid College of Engineering and Technology
Deon, Bathinda, India

N. A. Sheela Selvakumari
Department of Computer Science
Sri Krishna Arts and Science College
Coimbatore, India

Muhammad Anwar Shahid
Department of Computer Science
University of Windsor
Windsor, Canada

Archana Singh
School of Sciences
Noida International University
Greater Noida, India

Gursewak Singh
Computer Science and Engineering
Baba Farid College of Engineering and Technology
Deon, Bathinda, India

Neetu Singh
Amity Centre for Agricultural Extension Services
Amity University
Greater Noida, Uttar Pradesh, India

Nimisha Singh
Department of Skill Development
Baba Farid College of Engineering and Technology
Deon, Bathinda, India

Suman Lata Tripathi
Department of E & TC
Symbiosis Institute of Technology,
Symbiosis International (Deemed University)
Pune, India

Gopal Usha
Department of Computing Technologies
SRM Institute of Science and Technology
Chennai, Tamil Nadu, India

1 Introduction to Quantum Computing and Artificial Intelligence

Gursewak Singh, Nimisha Singh, Ramandeep Sandhu, Deepak Saroj, and Deepika Ghai

1.1 QUANTUM COMPUTING

1.1.1 Overview of Classical Computing

In many ways, the foundation of modern technology is classical computation. Ever since its conception in the mid-20th century, it has radically changed nearly every field of human life. This method relies on manipulation based on binary digits or bits that may be either one of two states: 0 or 1. Hence, this is called the binary system, which is the basis for all classical computations, from the simplest arithmetic operation to more complex data processing.

Fundamentally, at the base of classical computing are units called transistors, which also function as a switch to either "on" or "off," and are represented with binary 1 or 0, respectively. Modern computer processors contain billions of these transistors, allowing extremely complicated calculations. But there is also an inherent limit to what is possible within classical computing. There are very few problems with the classical algorithms because they involve classical bits in an actual step-by-step procedure to solve computational problems. However, large-scale optimization problems, especially quantum system simulations, cannot be addressed efficiently. Larger portions of the quantum problem require searching multiple possibilities simultaneously.

Indeed, one of the major disadvantages of classical computing is that it scales linearly in computational power, whereas Moore's Law, predicting the exponential growth of transistor density, and thus computational capacity, will shortly reach an end due to quantum effects interfering with its function when transistors are approximately on atomic scales.

The second problem is a consequence of the nature of classical probability: a bit is in one definite state, 0 or 1. This forbids classical systems from solving problems efficiently, involving simulated simultaneous exploration of more than one state. Complex tasks like factoring large numbers, which have applications in cryptography, or simulating quantum systems, which are useful in materials science and chemistry, often face significant computational challenges. For these problems, the required computational resources typically grow exponentially as the problem size increases. As a result, many of these tasks become impractical to solve using classical computers.

Today, most of the infrastructures used in digital architecture are still built on classical computing despite the above limitations. However, its limitations have spurred developments in alternative approaches to computing. Among these is quantum computing, which gained much attention today as it can evade certain basic bottlenecks.

1.1.2 Quantum Computing Basics

Theoretically, quantum computing is revolutionizing the approach to computation, mainly with principles of quantum mechanics being used to approach problems that classical methods cannot. Unlike the classical bits, the bases for the shift in the paradigm of the computational theory lie in the properties of quantum bits or qubits.

a. **The Nature of Quantum Bits (Qubits)**: Classical bits are the two discrete states of 0 and 1, while quantum bits can be simultaneously a 0 and a 1 with probabilities that can change. Because of this facility, quantum computers can calculate multiple possibilities at once, which can lead to an exponential speedup over certain classes of problems. Each method presents distinct advantages and challenges, and ongoing research aims to determine the most effective and scalable approach. Figure 1.1 depicts various ways to physically realize qubits.

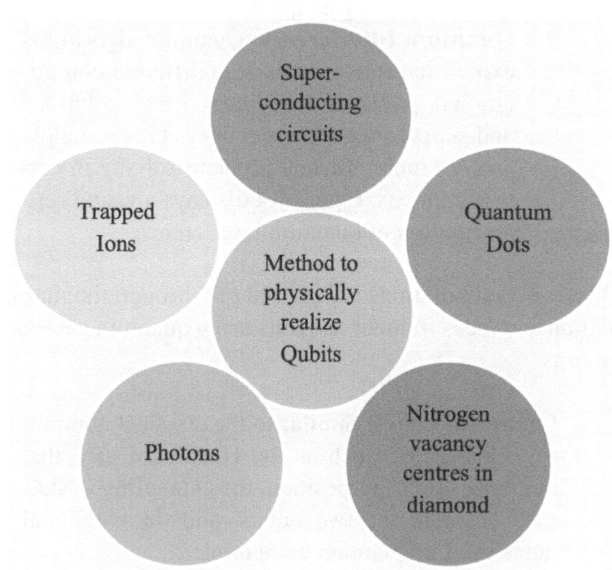

FIGURE 1.1 Various ways to physically realize qubits.

DOI: 10.1201/9781003530800-1

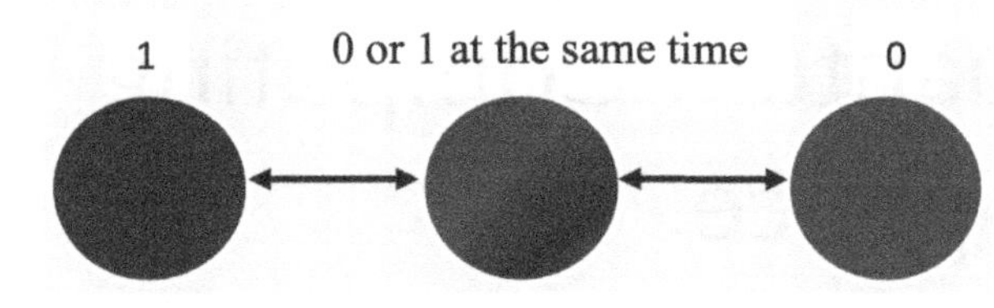

FIGURE 1.2 Superposition.

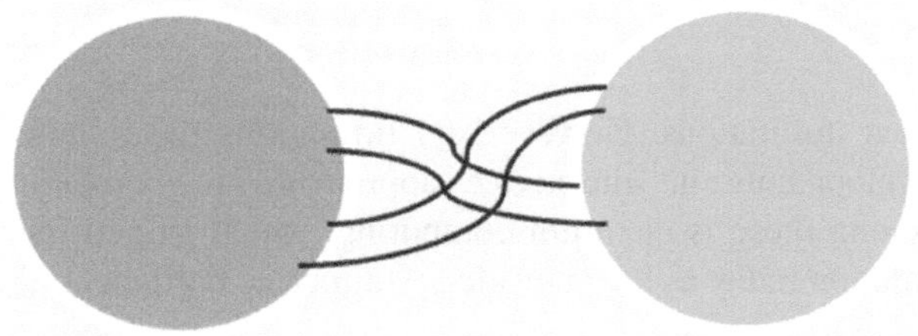

FIGURE 1.3 Quantum entanglement.

b. **Key Principles of Quantum Computing**: Three basic principles of quantum mechanics therefore govern quantum computing:
   1. **Superposition**: This principle allows qubits to exist simultaneously in more than one state; thus, information can be processed in parallel. Hence, some computational problems can be solved more easily than with a classical system. Figure 1.2 gives a visual representation of quantum superposition.
   2. **Entanglement**: Quantum entanglement is the phenomenon in which qubits couple entangles in such a way that the state of one becomes dependent on the other's state. It's an effect that allows quantum computers to process information along pathways classically inaccessible, and it's the basis of a peculiar form of computational power. Figure 1.3 shows two quantum entangled qubits.
   3. **Quantum Interference**: Quantum algorithms exploit interference between different computational paths, amplifying correct solutions and suppressing incorrect ones. This principle enables more efficient problem-solving in certain contexts. Figure 1.4 displays a visual representation of quantum interference.

Quantum computations are carried out through the manipulation and measurement of qubits using quantum gates and circuits:

a. **Quantum Gates**: Similar to the classical computing logic gates, such as the Hadamard gate that demonstrates superposition, the entangling CNOT gate between the two qubits, and the rotational gates used in quantum computing.
b. **Quantum Circuits**: A quantum circuit is a sequence of quantum gate operations on qubits. Quantum circuits execute quantum algorithms. They take the input states of qubits and map them to output states such that, upon measurement, they produce solutions to computational problems.
c. **Measurement**: As qubits are measured, the superposition collapses into a classical state (0 or 1), and the results are probabilistic. The structure of quantum algorithms must deal with this probabilistic nature carefully to obtain useful information. An intrinsic relationship among qubits, quantum gates, quantum circuits, and quantum measurement determines what will be generated at the maturity of quantum computing. Aspects of this kind allow quantum computers to go beyond classical systems for problems of interest in cryptography, drug discovery, and complex system simulation. Table 1.1 shows the comparative analysis of classical computing with quantum computing.

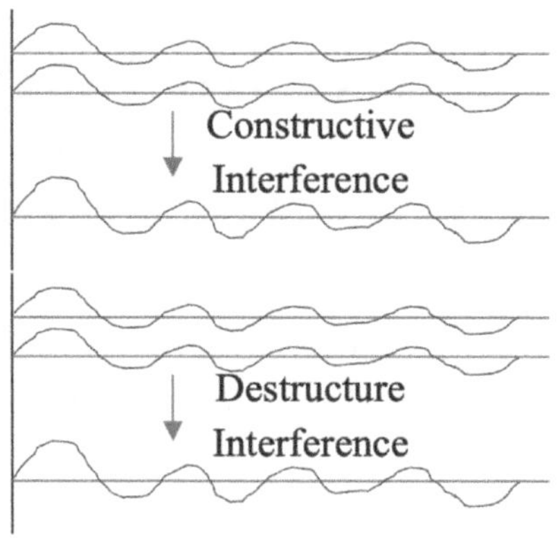

FIGURE 1.4 Quantum interference.

1.1.3 Historical Evolution of Quantum Computing

There has been explosive growth in quantum computing since its conception in the 1980s. This chapter reviews a few of the key developments in the field:

a. Early theoretical foundations
   - **1980**: In 1982, Richard Feynman, in his paper "Simulating Physics with Computers," suggested that computations could be done by quantum mechanical systems. He pointed out a major weakness of quantum simulations, they could not simulate quantum systems and classical computers.
   - **1985**: David Deutsch published a paper titled Quantum Theory, the Church–Turing Principle, and the Universal Quantum Computer, where he established the theoretical underpinnings of quantum computing and outlined the idea of a universal quantum computer that would 1 day supplant the classical computing machine.

TABLE 1.1
Comparison of Quantum Computing with Classical Computing

Parameter	Classical Computing	Quantum Computing
Computational units	Classical bits (0 or 1)	Qubits (0, 1, or both simultaneously due to superposition)
Information representation	Binary logic (definite 0 or 1 states)	Superposition and entanglement (qubits can represent multiple states at once and be entangled with others)
Processing speed	Executes instructions sequentially (bit by bit)	Potential for exponential speedup due to parallelism from superposition and entanglement
Logic gates	Classical gates (AND, OR, NOT, XOR)	Quantum gates (Hadamard, CNOT, Pauli-X, etc.)
Memory requirements	Scales linearly with problem complexity	Scales exponentially; fewer qubits needed to represent more complex states
Error tolerance	Generally low error rates with high stability	More error-prone, requiring quantum error correction mechanisms
Cryptography	RSA, AES encryption based on factorization and complexity of large numbers	Shor's algorithm breaks classical cryptography, but quantum cryptography (e.g., QKD) offers unbreakable encryption.
Optimization problems	Often slow for complex, high-dimensional problems	Quantum algorithms like QAOA offer faster solutions for large-scale optimization.
Applications	General computing tasks, business software, and everyday devices	Used in Cryptography, the discovery of drugs, material science, and complex simulations
Scalability	Easily scalable with classical hardware	Difficult to scale due to qubit coherence, error rates, and quantum hardware limitations
Current status	Fully developed, mature, and widely used	In the early experimental stages, with significant research and development underway

b. Key algorithmic milestones
- **1994**: Peter Shor invented Shor's algorithm and showed that the quantum computer could operate exponentially faster than classical algorithms, thereby threatening current cryptography.
- **1996**: Lov Grover published Grover's algorithm that provided a quadratic speedup for search problems without any special structure, indicating that there is a large area of potential applications for quantum computing.

c. Hardware developments and experimental milestones
- **1998**: Oxford University produces the first 2-qubit quantum computer.
- **2000**: A 5-qubit quantum computer was constructed at the Technical University of Munich.
- **2007**: D-Wave systems produced a processor having 28-qubit quantum annealing that soon created controversy regarding the extent to which the machine was quantum.
- **2016**: IBM opened access to research by making a cloud-based 5-qubit quantum computer.
- **2019**: Google presented its 53-qubit Sycamore processor as part of a solution that would take less time than any known classical machine.

1.2 ARTIFICIAL INTELLIGENCE

1.2.1 Fundamentals of Artificial Intelligence

Artificial Intelligence (AI) refers to a computer science branch that specializes in developing systems capable of performing human practice that demand intelligence. This practice will involve visual perception, speech recognition, decision-making, and other tasks that include language translation, as well as solving problems. The primary aim of AI is to develop machines that may learn and improve from their experiences, making them increasingly competitive with human cognitive ability.

AI beings with human-like intelligence were myths in history. The real formal discipline of AI came about in the middle of the 20th century with great milestones, which are:

- **1943**: Warren McCulloch and Walter Pitts developed the first mathematical model of neural networks.
- **1950**: Alan Turing suggested the Turing Test to test for machine intelligence.
- **1956**: The Dartmouth Conference, organized by John McCarthy and others, was the origin of AI as an academic field of study.
- **1957**: Frank Rosenblatt invented the perceptron, a pioneering neural network model.

1.2.2 Classical AI vs. Modern AI: The Evolution of Algorithms and Machine Learning

It has taken the transition from rule-based and symbolic to data-driven machine learning.

- **Classical AI**: Classical AI probably emerged as the first approach put forth for AI that highly depended on symbolic logic and therefore created very extensive rules to represent knowledge and solve problems. It is such a method that heavily leans on structured, high-level problem-solving techniques. Famous instances of classical AI include expert systems and reasoning that rely on formal logic. Nevertheless, this approach had significant limitations. It fared very poorly when the situation dealt with uncertainty and the messiness of real-world scenarios. Apart from this, classical AI systems could not learn or improve from data, which eventually limited their flexibility and applicability in most practical applications.

- **Modern AI**: The modern AI does not rely on any fixed rules but learns from data and applies statistical methods so that it can learn by experience. Deep learning has had the most fundamental implications on machine learning by using artificial neural networks (ANNs) that caused enormous breakthroughs in such applications and areas as image recognition and natural language processing.

1.2.3 Key Concepts in Artificial Intelligence

a. **Machine Learning**: It is concerned with the development of models that would allow systems to learn through data and thus improve progressively. There are several key types of machine learning methodologies. Supervised learning involves the inductive derivation of patterns from labeled training data to predict outputs. Unsupervised learning, on the contrary, seeks patterns in unlabeled data. Reinforcement learning is a method where the system learns through trial and error, with certain actions being rewarded as correct.

b. **Deep Learning**: Deep learning is surprisingly efficient as a machine learning subfield. Deep learning uses multi-layered neural networks to process and analyze data. Deep learning is capable of learning features automatically from the data without any human interference; therefore, it is especially efficient for such complicated tasks as image and speech recognition. Deep learning computers can understand patterns and characteristics that would be difficult or impossible for people to define or even program.

c. **Neural Networks**: They are a model of computation that is human-brain-inspired and comprises connected nodes or neurons arranged in layers. Their general principle is learned for classification from the given dataset using an input, hidden, and output layer. While the latter adjusts its weight during the learning process, all the connections that information has to go through to come out with a weight are used. Figure 1.5 gives a visual representation of neural network architecture.

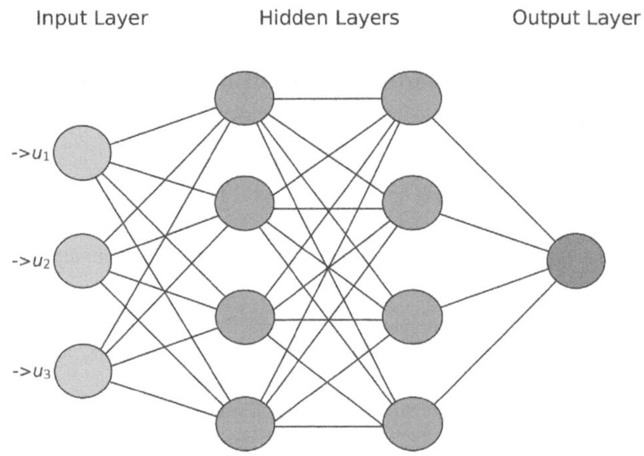

FIGURE 1.5 Neural network architecture representation.

- Neural network types include:
    - **Feedforward Neural Networks**: Simple structure for the input-to-output flow of data.
    - **Convolutional Neural Networks**: Fits image-based tasks.
    - **Recurrent Neural Networks (RNNs)/Long Short-Term Memory (LSTMs)**: These models are particularly suited for sequential data, like text or a time series.
    - **Generative Adversarial Networks**: Generation of new data very similar to the training examples.
- Importance of Large Datasets and Computational Power:
    a. (a) **Large Datasets**: Crucial for training AI systems, large datasets enable AI models to identify intricate patterns, improving generalization and performance. Examples include ImageNet for vision tasks and Common Crawl for natural language processing.
    b. (b) **Computational Power**: Training large-scale AI relies heavily on many computations. Hardware improvements, including the appearance of Graphics Processing Units (GPUs) and Tensor Processing Units (TPUs), are significantly accelerating the training of deep models to start improving experimentation and optimization rapidly.

It's the combination of big data and high-performance computing that has powered many of the recent breakthroughs in AI, exciting remarkably rapid advances in self-driving cars to medical diagnosis, and language translation.

- **Challenges in Current AI Systems**: While AI has achieved remarkable success, several challenges remain.
- **Resource Constraints**: Resource constraints pose significant hurdles, with state-of-the-art AI models requiring massive amounts of computing power available only to large organizations. These ecosystems also raise concerns about high energy

consumption and environmental impact. This also makes the labeled data needed by many AI models, including deep learning, expensive to obtain and thus time-consuming. As more talent tends to flow in, talent has concentrated within just a few tech giants, which further worsens the shortage of talent.

- **Scalability**: It presents another set of challenges. As model size and complexity increase, training, deployment, and maintenance become more difficult. Distributed computing, often necessary for scaling, adds further complexity. AI systems also struggle with transferring knowledge across different domains, limiting their flexibility. Real-time applications face additional challenges in meeting computational efficiency, especially on edge devices.
- **Interpretability and Bias**: Interpretability is a critical concern in the development of AI. Most deep learning models are a black box, and the decision-making processes are partially decipherable. Hence, explainable AI systems are in greater demand where sensitive data is being handled, for instance, in the health and finance sectors. Also, AI systems often inherit the biases present in the training dataset and multiply those biases into unfair or even discriminatory outcomes.
- **Robustness and Reliability**: In all varieties of work, robustness and reliability are required from AI systems. The development of robust and adaptive AI systems is considered key to successfully delivering the application across different domains.

To move AI forward, these barriers must be overcome. Researchers are currently working on improving algorithms, hardware, and AI ethics and developing more transparent, fair, and robust AI systems. Progress in these areas will serve as important stepping stones toward a full range of AI applications through continued research.

1.3 INTERSECTION OF QUANTUM COMPUTING AND AI: QUANTUM AI

1.3.1 Quantum AI

Quantum AI (QAI) is a new emerging subject that links quantum computing with AI and machine learning techniques. It is targeting to gain from the strange principles of quantum mechanics to increase and accelerate the power of AI and even solve complicated problems faster and efficiently than ever before.

1.3.2 Quantum Computing and AI

It also consists of computing – quantum computing – based upon the principles of quantum mechanics, the part of physics describing how the smallest particles in the universe, such as electrons and photons, behave. Whereas the former works with bits – 0s and 1s that represent information – the latter, the quantum computer, works using quantum bits, or qubits. Another characteristic that qubits possess is superposition, that is, they can be 0, 1, or both simultaneously. As a result, the quantum computer would handle mind-boggling information in parallel rather than serially, as does a conventional computer.

1.3.3 Working with Quantum AI

QAI puts all these quantum properties together to elevate AI and machine learning models. In classical AI, conventional computing machines are used to process big data and run algorithms; however, when the information becomes extremely large or the problem highly complex then the computation can become slow and inefficient. QAI solves this by putting the power of computation for quantum computers into AI algorithms.

- **Superposition** enables QAI to explore several possible solutions to a problem simultaneously, instead of one by one, as in classical AI. This can drastically speed up the decision-making process, especially for optimization tasks.
- **Entanglement** allows quantum systems to process and relate data in a more interconnected way, potentially offering deeper insights from complex datasets.
- **Quantum interference** helps in refining and improving the accuracy of AI predictions, as quantum computers can enhance the likelihood of correct outcomes while minimizing errors.

1.3.3.1 Key Elements of Quantum AI

- **Quantum Data**: The data is represented and processed using quantum states; hence, exponentially more information is stored than is offered by the ability of classical bits.
- **Quantum Algorithms**: They employ quantum principles to yield more performance or efficiency in solving a problem than classical algorithms.
- **Hybrid Quantum-Classical Systems**: These provide the benefits of both quantum and classical computing.
- **Quantum-Highlighted Machine Learning**: It utilizes quantum methods to enhance the majority of the ML operations, such as optimization, feature extraction, and classification.

1.3.4 The Quantum Computing Potential to Revolutionize AI

This creates the possibility of an active paradigm shift in AI. Here's how:

- **Exponential Speedup**: Quantum algorithms possess exponential speedup of classical algorithms for specific problems, allowing machines to learn much better on extremely large data sets.

- **Advanced Optimization**: AI, specifically deep learning, uses extremely complex optimization challenges. Quantum algorithms, in general, and specifically under the class called Quantum Approximate Optimization Algorithm (QAOA), have results that greatly outperform the classical way.
- **Improved Feature Spaces**: Quantum systems can natively perform better in high-dimensional feature spaces than classical ones and may provide a much more powerful model of machine learning.
- **Quantum Sampling**: Quantum computers can generate samples from complex distributions more effectively, benefiting AI tasks like generative modeling and probabilistic simulations.
- **Quantum-Inspired Algorithms**: Although fully realized quantum computers are still far from practical availability, a quantum driver has inspired new classical algorithms that often outperform traditional methods.
- **Quantum Simulations**: Quantum computers will simulate quantum systems, for instance, in materials science, where interaction at the quantum level is important. This will give QAI the ability to solve problems that are currently not solvable for classical AI and open up new avenues of research for AI applications.

1.3.5 Quantum AI Theoretical Framework

Quantum machine learning encompasses all the ideas of machine learning and quantum computing in new forms of developing AI. Two of the relatively established subfields in QML are, for the sake of this paper, variational quantum algorithms (VQAs) and quantum neural networks (QNNs).

a. **VQAs**: It is the most encouraging development in quantum computing, especially in connection with existing quantum hardware, namely, VQAs. These hybrid algorithms typically merge quantum circuits with classical optimization methods, and they set a proper stage to approach many computational problems. The basic idea of VQAs is based on the following: It is a parameterized quantum circuit, or ansatz, coupled with the proper cost function measuring the quality of the output of the quantum circuit. A classical optimization loop iteratively adjusts the circuit's parameters to improve performance. The most well-known examples of VQAs are QAOA, VQE, and the Quantum Variational Classifier.
b. **QNNs**: They are another very important development of quantum computing since the quantum version of their classical cousins, that is, neural networks. These networks are therefore designed to process quantum data and exploit quantum properties to achieve performance superiority.

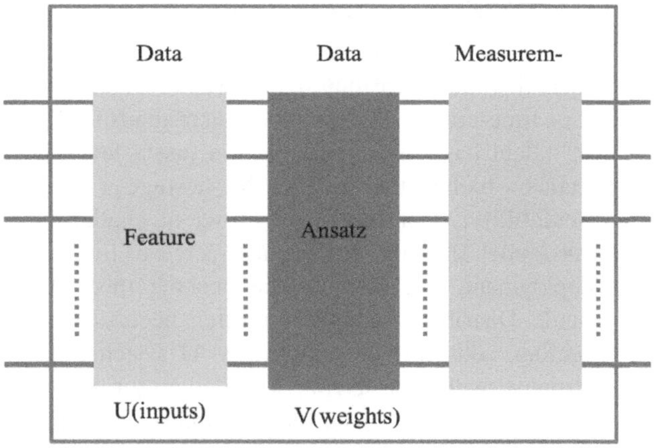

FIGURE 1.6 Quantum neural network.

In addition to all the networks, QNNs are unique for having quantum layers that involve parameterized unitary transformations and nonlinear quantum measurements between the layers. The QNN block diagram is shown in Figure 1.6.

1.3.6 Quantum Optimization Techniques in AI

Quantum computing employs many techniques that are likely to prove better than the optimizations traditionally used by traditional AI.

- **Quantum Annealing**: It is applied to minimize the cost function, taking advantage of quantum fluctuations. It is consequently adapted for combinatorial optimization problems. This is commercially implemented by systems like D-Wave.
- **QAOA**: It potentially tackles optimization problems similar to MaxCut or the traveling salesman problem.
- **Quantum Adiabatic Algorithm**: This method leverages the adiabatic theorem to find the Hamiltonian ground state, useful in both optimization and quantum simulation.
- **Quantum-Inspired Classical Algorithms**: Classical algorithms that are inspired by quantum computing principles, such as tensor networks, offer enhanced performance in specific areas even without quantum hardware.

These quantum optimization techniques could outperform classical methods, especially in problems involving complex constraints or large search spaces. The side-by-side evolution of various quantum machine-learning models is shown in Table 1.2.

1.3.7 Potential of Quantum AI

It opens several rather important areas of scientific research, such as drug discovery and cryptography, and analysis of

TABLE 1.2
Quantum Model Comparison

Model	Applications	Computational Efficiency	Challenges
Quantum neural networks (QNNs)	Pattern recognition, image classification, deep learning, quantum control systems	Potentially more efficient than classical neural networks for large-scale problems due to quantum parallelism	Quantum noise and scalability issue
Quantum approximate optimization algorithm (QAOA)	Optimization problems such as MAX-CUT, job scheduling, logistics	Provides approximate solutions faster than classical optimization techniques, especially for large datasets	Requires precise control of quantum gates, struggles with noise in current quantum hardware
Quantum support vector machines (QSVMs)	Classification tasks, data analysis, fraud detection, medical diagnosis	Quantum speedup in large-scale classification tasks by handling high-dimensional data efficiently	Data loading into quantum systems is slow; it requires robust error correction for scalability
Quantum Boltzmann machines (QBMs)	Generative modeling, probabilistic inference, quantum-inspired data generation	Potential exponential speedup in solving complex generative tasks and sampling	Training challenges require quantum annealers or advanced quantum hardware.
Variational quantum Eigen solver (VQE)	Chemistry simulations, molecular modeling, optimization	Efficient at approximating ground states of molecules, useful in drug discovery	Requires classical-quantum hybrid architecture, prone to errors in noisy environments
Quantum *k*-means (*Qk* means)	Clustering tasks, image compression, and recommended systems	Quantum speedup in clustering large datasets with high dimensionality	Loading classical data into quantum systems remains a bottleneck

very large data. QAI will make an incredibly groundbreaking difference in drug discovery and materials science due to very precise molecular simulations.

This will have the possibility of quantum algorithms helping to solve problems in the field of protein folding for drugs. In materials science, QAI could facilitate the design of materials with specific properties, such as superconductors, by accurately simulating atomic interactions.

Quantum cryptography can provide unbreakable encryption, which is bolstered by methods such as quantum key distribution. As quantum computing becomes a threat to classically encrypted data, scientists develop algorithms resistant to quantum attacks, hence providing security. In addition, quantum-enhanced AI is envisioned to further make anomaly detection through cybersecurity systems in ways whose implementations surpass those compared above.

In the domain of large-scale data analysis, QAI holds great promise. Quantum algorithms can potentially perform dimensionality reduction methods more effectively. Quantum enhancements may accelerate computations in clustering and classification tasks, leading to improved data classification and pattern detection. Moreover, QNNs could train a much larger dataset in a much faster time. So, this would make it a pretty sophisticated model.

1.4 RELATED WORK

Rapid advancement and convergence of AI with quantum computing have opened a new interdisciplinary field called QAI [1]. It applies tremendous computing capabilities from quantum computing to enhance the typical algorithms within AI to solve various problems from other fields.

This literature review provides an analysis of recent research from 15 academic papers focused on key themes such as theoretical advancements, algorithmic innovations, real-world applications, and the challenges that remain in QAI [1–24]. Each study offers insight into the evolving landscape of QAI, highlighting both its transformative potential and the obstacles to further development [2].

In Tsapa [11], the core principles of QAI are discussed, particularly delving into quantum computing elements like qubits and quantum gates, emphasizing the key quantum principles of superposition and entanglement. These principles are highlighted for their ability to significantly accelerate AI algorithms. A QAI example is Tsapa. The most crucial early applications of QAI come particularly in problems of quantum machine learning and optimization; these represent how AI models will develop at the stage of quantum technology.

The work of Taghavi [23] pays specific attention to the mathematical uplift quantum computing brings to AI in optimization problems that are NP-hard for classical algorithms. The paper traces how QAOA improves upon the ability to handle large-scale optimization challenges in AI. Such analysis gives a clear perspective on how quantum approaches could speed up machine learning models' training whenever such regimes use large sets. Taghavi underscores the potential of quantum techniques in improving computational efficiency and reducing the time required for AI-driven tasks. Figure 1.7 depicts the flowchart of QAOA.

In the paper presented by Martín-Guerrero et al. [7], one will find a discussion on several of the quantum algorithms at the simplest level, including Quantum support vector machines and QNNs. This paper addresses concerns

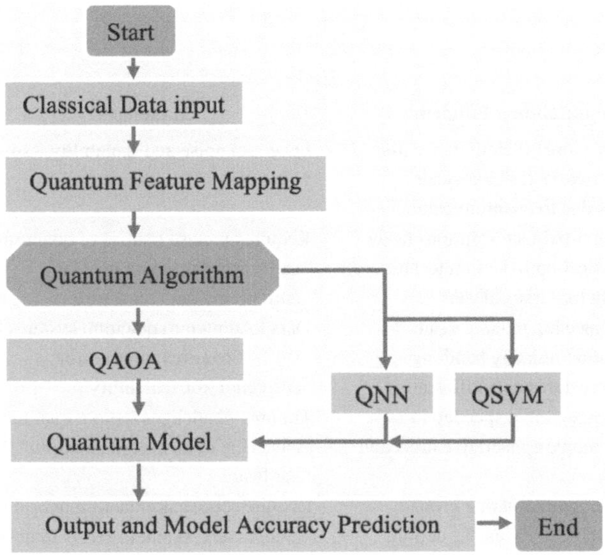

FIGURE 1.7 Quantum approximate optimization algorithm.

around the explainability of quantum models, which is an increasingly important topic as the field of QAI develops.

Alipour and Gulliver [3] facilitate simulations of large quantum systems and enable strong predictive capabilities. Applications that are commonly cited include extremely powerful AI systems requiring the simulation of real-world objects; for example, applications in data-intensive fields like modeling complex systems and predicting the outcome with greater precision.

Qamar et al. [8] examine how quantum computing can optimize AI tasks by improving computational efficiency and performance. It critically evaluates how quantum algorithms, particularly those that require intensive resources, can revolutionize existing AI trends by enhancing both speed and accuracy in real-world AI applications.

Wang et al. [12] discussed the practical applications of QAI in smart city infrastructure. Their research demonstrates how quantum-enhanced AI algorithms can streamline urban planning, traffic management, and energy distribution. A key focus is the integration of quantum-powered AI analytics with IoT devices to enable more accurate predictive analysis and efficient resource allocation in the development of smart cities.

Weinberg and Faccia [13] discussed how quantum algorithms can be useful for anti-financial crime purposes. They look into the use of quantum machine learning models in fraud detection and transaction monitoring. This paper indicates the vast improvement made by algorithms that process complex financial data, which could provide solutions for improving financial system security.

Wu et al. [15] proposed a Quantum Inference Engine capable of handling large-scale decision-making processes. The paper laid out a map for future development that would allow designing advanced AI systems to run steadily in a quantum environment.

Tripathi et al. [9] formulated an improved version of LSTM in the research article of the year 2024, with a specific improvement of its quantum effectiveness for upgrading the domain of cyber threat effectiveness in cyberspace. The authors have tried to prove the feasibility of quantum-enhanced RNNs compared to their classical counterparts in detecting patterns that are difficult to identify in cybersecurity data. When the authors tap into the quantum potential of LSTM models, they demonstrate that their method performs significantly better than other cybersecurity models, especially when those models fail on high-dimensional data.

Tripathi et al. [10] proposed a sequel work of the earlier group of papers from the same authors on quantum cybersecurity. This paper deals with QNN in their implementation to elevate the capability of threat detection. They contend that, due to principles such as quantum entanglement and superposition, QNNs can identify threats much more quickly and precisely, as threats are usually located in a very large, high-dimensional data space that represents the environment. This paper beautifully argues for the future of quantum-enhanced cybersecurity systems.

Klusch et al. [6] suggested an overview of the status quo in QAI. This paper gives an overview of the development of quantum algorithms that have been applied across various sectors, especially their use cases. The authors also describe their impact on machine learning or any other areas of AI. It gives newcomers solid ground on these matters and highlights the role that quantum algorithms may play in overcoming the computational limits of classical AI. It particularly points to the needs still to be met by researchers, such as scaling up and hardware constraints. Thus, it is a very valuable source of information to understand what has been achieved so far in the subject and what remains unexplored.

Bangroo et al. [4] presented research at the intersection of quantum machine learning and toxicology. The research uses techniques of quantum computing for the simulation and deciphering of signatures of toxicity, thus providing a new approach to the analysis of biochemical data. Quantum algorithms are therefore applied in demonstrating the potential that quantum simulations can bring about in the accurate, rapid assessments of toxicology in biomedical research and the development of drugs.

Wichert [14] provides a well-researched and comprehensive treatment addressing QAI in detail by using IBM's Qiskit framework for representing quantum computing. To put it simply, at the basics, the book covers how quantum circuits and quantum gates create the foundation of describing how those elements may be formed into AI models. The text is intended for both developers and researchers and provides very practically useful knowledge for the use of Qiskit to implement QAI models – such as an effective resource to probe the practical aspects of QAI.

Potter and Stilinski [16] provided an overview of quantum machine learning. With such a focus, the experts could explain how quantum computing was going to revolutionize applications in the field of AI. The authors explain how a quantum system learns to manipulate information from large datasets that are intrinsically intractable for the classical computer. The work serves as a foundational contribution outlining the theoretical basis of QML across various AI domains in its scope throughout various AI domains.

Kumar et al. [17] introduced the term "Quantum Intelligence," which mentions that the integration of AI with quantum computing can produce computational capabilities much superior to the current generation of computation. The authors illustrate in great detail how the principles that underpin the theory of quantum mechanics may be applied to improve a whole range of algorithms in AI, which will trigger breakthroughs in optimization, machine learning, natural language processing, and much more. This clearly refers to the transformative power that synergies can create in real-world problems.

Raparthi [18] discussed the quantum computing technique in designing neural networks in a very scholarly way. The authors bridged together the architectures of high-performance quantum-influenced ones into ANNs and quantum mechanics. The results hint that more adaptation of the principles found in quantum, like superposition and entanglement, into even better and more powerful models for neural networks may give revolutions in deep learning and image recognition.

Kumar et al. [19] demonstrated the potential of QAI in smart power grids. In this study, the authors demonstrated the possibility of potential energy distribution optimization, strengthening of security in grid systems, and overall efficiency in power management systems by combining these. Their work, in this sense, constitutes a living example of how, in the very deepest of senses, QAI-based technologies may 1 day reshape power and lead to much more sustainable and resilient power systems.

Rawat et al. [20] formulated various possible impacts and possibilities that quantum computing and AI may bring about. The writer's comment on possible social and technological implications given these technologies sets the stage for research directions and practical applications in different sectors. Their work can be seen to be providing readers with a definitive look at what the long-term effects of QAI could mean for industries, scientific research, and everyday life.

Mangini et al. [21] formulated ANNs on quantum computing models, proving that the principles of quantum can truly be exhibited and applied in the architectures of a neural network. The architectures may well be able to develop efficient and powerful AI systems. Their work gives an expansive technical insight into the realization of QNNs, challenges, and opportunities existing in this up-and-coming area. This puts the theoretical concepts of quantum computing into practical scenarios in AI.

Ramezani et al. [22] formulated quantum computing machine learning algorithms. The authors introduce several different quantum machine learning algorithms, comparing them with their classical counterparts, and point out exactly where the quantum ones shine.

Tripathi et al. [24] discussed the healthcare applications of QAI with special application to cardiovascular. This paper presents a scenario that portrays the data simulation and analysis by quantum-enhanced AI models for early disease detection and predictive diagnosis, ultimately aiming to improve healthcare outcomes. This paper is a valuable contribution to the growing interest in QAI's role in healthcare innovation.

The further exploration of QAI is pushing forward innovative solutions across various sectors – from cybersecurity and healthcare to financial services and smart city infrastructure. However, the main issues are hardware limitations and scalability. Yet, integration with AI is promising, as more computing power and efficiency can unleash new levels of performance and problem-solving abilities in many industries [24–27].

1.5 FUTURE PROSPECTS AND CHALLENGES IN QUANTUM AI

Continuing to grow, QAI might shape both AI and computing. This chapter will outline such future directions in QAI research as well as the challenges that will arise when deploying quantum-enhanced AI systems and the ethical as well as security issues accompanying such mighty technology.

1.5.1 Future Directions for Quantum AI

Future applications for quantum computing will deeply improve deep architectures in the world of learning model designs. Quantum deep learning, which is emerging as a field of research into which interest is growing at an incredible rate, now continues to absorb principles from quantum mechanics into AI models.

Quantum convolutional neural network algorithms are designed to be much faster than their classic analogs in processing high-dimensional data. A fully realized makeover could change the world in image processing and signal recognition. Quantum RNN algorithms, which are expected to be particularly strong in natural language processing and time series, even permit the capture of complex temporal patterns, which are largely too complex to process with classical methods. Quantum generative adversarial networks algorithms will invoke quantum superposition and, in return, transform generative models.

Another exciting development is quantum reinforcement learning, which could improve decision-making in complex environments, such as robotics and autonomous systems. By utilizing quantum principles like superposition, quantum reinforcement learning may learn optimal policies more quickly by exploring multiple states simultaneously.

Other than these, many more breakthroughs are expected to come from quantum-enhanced AI. Quantum Kernel Methods may map classical data to quantum feature spaces, which potentially upgrades the ability to find patterns beyond the complexity, generally overlooked by the usual algorithms. New algorithms for future AI might be possibly better than those used nowadays from the concepts of quantum computing inspired by quantum algorithms. Hybrid models taking the advantages of both quantum and classical systems are also expected to have practical, powerful applications in AI.

1.5.2 Breakthroughs in Quantum Hardware

Exactly what quantum hardware enhances shall be realized by the QAI potential. The closest to the wire, as of now, with potential improvements are scalable architectures for qubits, quantum error correction, and QAI accelerators. The ability to stabilize and scale qubit architectures will be critical to running advanced quantum systems, while robust quantum error correction techniques are required for ensuring the reliability of quantum computation.

With optimized QAI accelerators that will speed up AI tasks at an orders-of-magnitude larger rate than classical AI did during the previous AI increase, quantum memory and quantum random access memory advances are supposed to significantly improve QNNs.

1.5.3 Challenges in Implementing Quantum AI

The biggest challenge when developing QAI is to overcome numerous technological limitations. Quantum systems are noisy and decohering; that is to say, quantum states lose coherence, resulting in computation errors. Such effects need to be overcome to make a success of QAI.

First of all, error correction is necessary for reducing the effect of errors without making it overly computational. Robust methods for error correction would have to be implemented for quantum computation to be considered reliable. Noise-resistant algorithms would have to be devised to run on existing quantum devices, which are noisy by design. This area remains a focal point of ongoing research.

In addition, it improves coherence time, that is, the duration vital for executing more complex QAI algorithms. Lastly, enhancing quantum gate fidelity, or the accuracy of quantum operations, is fundamental to the reliable implementation of quantum circuits. Another significant challenge for QAI is the scarcity of resources, particularly in terms of high costs and limited qubit availability. Quantum computers require substantial resources to operate, and scaling them for widespread use presents several difficulties.

One major constraint is the cost involved in the high infrastructure needed for maintenance, which requires costly cooling in controlled environments. Additionally, limited qubit availability is a pressing issue, as current quantum computers possess far fewer qubits than what is necessary for executing many practical QAI tasks. The field also faces a shortage of specialized expertise in quantum physics and AI, a key factor in the further development of QAI. Energy consumption is a critical issue, and devices based on superconducting qubits are extremely energy-hungry. This would introduce innovation on both hardware and software levels and increase investment in infrastructure as well as talent development.

1.5.4 Ethical and Security Considerations in Quantum AI

The development of QAI brings a good deal of new ethical issues. Among the most salient of these is algorithmic bias, a quantum enhancement of capabilities that potentially introduces new biases within datasets, which, under those circumstances, might lead to unequal and discriminatory decisions. Moreover, the transparency and explainability of QAI decisions pose challenges. The first is privacy. While QAI can process huge volumes of data at unprecedented rates, one can derive details about the users, and thereby, violations of privacy will occur. Increased efficiencies in QAI implementation may accelerate automation jobs and cause sharp disturbance to economic systems and massive job loss, since many tasks will be automated through quantum technologies. Therefore, careful handling of such ethical concerns will be needed for the responsible and fair development of QAI.

1.6 CONCLUSION

QAI is an emerging technology, available for wide-ranging industries and problem-solving methodologies by integrating quantum computing principles and AI, more specifically, deep learning; however, these superpositions and entanglements are a way to go beyond classical algorithms in many domains. The algorithms of QAI can possibly and strongly be applied in real-world applications, including drug discovery and climate prediction. Generally, QAI has a transformative impact that can be seen in accelerated drug discovery and advances in personalized medicine; improvement in risk evaluation and fraud detection in finance; breakthroughs in the design of new materials and catalysis research material science; better predictions of resource allocation in climate and environmental modeling; and expanded capability through quantum key distribution and quantum security. Other applications include, but are not limited to, logistics, agriculture, aerospace, energy, and solving complex optimization problems and high-throughput computing needs. QAI will hopefully be an advance on AI by itself, providing faster architectures in the case of neural nets and better paradigms for machine learning. More significant challenges would include overcoming quantum decoherence, qubit scalability, and infrastructure cost. Full potential can only be achieved with support in developing the algorithm, error correction, benchmarking, and workforce training. It is in the actualization of the technology of QAI within the organizations that industry leaders are called to do. Policymakers should address mechanisms for funding, regulatory systems, and workforce development initiatives. Educators and entrepreneurs go hand in hand in encouraging innovation and practical experience in QAI for future practitioners. Other than this, there are several ethical considerations such as bias mitigation for AI, decision-making transparency in processes of quantum models, and implications for cryptographic security, which will impact the development and implementation of QAI responsibly. Combined with sharp insight and responsible innovation, great research, and collaborative efforts, the scientific community will build QAI capable of responding to some of the world's most monumental challenges on unprecedented scales that could revolutionize nearly every field and create opportunities to further enhance computing power and problem-solving capacities.

REFERENCES

1. Arora, C., & Sandhu, R. (2024, January). Adoption of quantum NLP for improved healthcare system. In: *International Conference on Computation of Artificial Intelligence & Machine Learning,* Jaipur, India (pp. 51–59). Springer, Cham.
2. Sandhu, R., Ghai, D., Tripathi, S. L., Kaur, R., Rawal, K., & Dhir, K. (2024). Machine learning for cognitive treatment planning in patients with neuro disorder and trauma injuries. In: D. Jude Hemanth (Ed.), *Computational Intelligence and Deep Learning Methods for Neuro-rehabilitation Applications,* Kidlington, England (pp. 165–193). Academic Press.
3. Alipour, P. B., & Gulliver, T. A. (2024). QF-LCA dataset: Quantum field lens coding algorithm for system state simulation and strong predictions. *Data in Brief*, 57, 110789.
4. Bangroo, I. S., Del Cid Hernández, M. F., & Kumar, R. (2024). Decoding toxicological signatures through quantum computational paradigm. *Optical and Quantum Electronics*, 56(4), 545.
5. Klusch, M., Lässig, J., & Wilhelm, F. K. (2024). Quantum computing and AI. *KI-Künstliche Intelligenz*, 38, 251–255.
6. Klusch, M., Lässig, J., Müssig, D., Macaluso, A., & Wilhelm, F. K. (2024). Quantum artificial intelligence: A brief survey. *KI-Künstliche Intelligenz*, 38, 257–276.
7. Martín-Guerrero, J. D., Lamata, L., & Villmann, T. (2024). Quantum artificial intelligence: A tutorial. In: *European Symposium on Artificial Neural Networks, Computational Intelligence and Machine Learning,* Bruges, Belgium.
8. Qamar, R., Zardari, B. A., & Khang, A. (2024). Quantum computing AI: Artificial intelligence and quantum computing applications. In: A. Khang (Ed.), *Applications and Principles of Quantum Computing* (pp. 146–161). IGI Global.
9. Tripathi, S., Upadhyay, H., & Soni, J. (2025). A quantum LSTM-based approach to cyber threat detection in virtual environment. *The Journal of Supercomputing*, 81(1), 142.
10. Tripathi, S. M., Upadhyay, H., & Soni, J. (2023, December). Quantum neural network classification-based cyber threat detection in virtual environment. In: *2023 International Conference on Computational Science and Computational Intelligence (CSCI),* Las Vegas, USA (pp. 391–396). IEEE.
11. Tsapa, J. A. (2024). Quantum synergies: Pioneering the frontier of enhanced artificial intelligence. *International Journal of Science and Research*, 13(5), 1108–1111.
12. Wang, S., Wang, N., Ji, T., Shi, Y., & Wang, C. (2024). Research progress of quantum artificial intelligence in smart city. *Intelligent and Converged Networks*, 5(2), 116–133.
13. Weinberg, A. I., & Faccia, A. (2024). Quantum algorithms: A new frontier in financial crime prevention. arXiv preprint arXiv:2403.18322.
14. Wichert, A. (2024). *Quantum Artificial Intelligence with Qiskit.* CRC Press.
15. Wu, N., Song, F., Zhang, W., & Li, X. (2024, June). Quantum inference engine: An architecture for quantum artificial intelligence. In: E. Donkor and M. Hayduk (Eds.), *Quantum Information Science, Sensing, and Computation XVI* (Vol. 13028, pp. 55–63). SPIE.
16. Potter, K., & Stilinski, D. (2024). Quantum machine learning: Exploring the potential of quantum computing for AI applications. *EasyChair Preprints.* https://easychair.org/publications/preprint/bb78/download.
17. Kumar, S., Simran, S., & Singh, M. (2024, March). Quantum intelligence: Merging AI and quantum computing for unprecedented power. In: *2024 International Conference on Trends in Quantum Computing and Emerging Business Technologies,* Pune, India (pp. 1–7). IEEE.
18. Raparthi, M. (2022). Quantum-inspired neural networks for advanced AI applications: A scholarly review of quantum computing techniques in neural network design. *Journal of Computational Intelligence and Robotics*, 2(2), 1–8.
19. Kumar, M. S., Krishna, R. V. V., Satyanarayana, V., & Rao, A. P. C. (2024). Enabling smart power grids through quantum computing and artificial intelligence. In: C. Ananth, T. Ananth Kumar, and O. I. Khalaf (Eds.), *Real-World Challenges in Quantum Electronics and Machine Computing* (pp. 58–78). IGI Global.
20. Rawat, B., Mehra, N., Bist, A. S., Yusup, M., & Sanjaya, Y. P. A. (2022). Quantum computing and AI: Impacts & possibilities. *ADI Journal on Recent Innovation*, 3(2), 202–207.
21. Mangini, S., Tacchino, F., Gerace, D., Bajoni, D., & Macchiavello, C. (2021). Quantum computing models for artificial neural networks. *Europhysics Letters*, 134(1), 10002.
22. Ramezani, S. B., Sommers, A., Manchukonda, H. K., Rahimi, S., & Amirlatifi, A. (2020, July). Machine learning algorithms in quantum computing: A survey. In: *2020 International Joint Conference on Neural Networks (IJCNN),* Glasgow, UK (pp. 1–8). IEEE.
23. Taghavi, M. (2024). *Mathematical Optimization in Artificial Intelligence and Machine Learning.* Iran University of Science and Technology. doi:10.13140/RG.2.2.24185.48482.
24. Tripathi, S. M., Upadhyay, H., & Soni, J. (2024). Advanced cardiovascular health in a quantum AI-driven healthcare framework. https://www.techrxiv.org/users/761734/articles/738757-advanced-cardiovascular-health-in-a-quantum-ai-driven-healthcare-framework.
25. Ghai, D., Tripathi, S. L., Saxena, S., Chanda, M., & Alazab, M. (Eds.). (2022). *Machine Learning Algorithms for Signal and Image Processing.* John Wiley & Sons.
26. Ghai, D., Saxena, S., Dhingra, G., & Tripathi, S. L. (2024). A comprehensive review on performance-based comparative analysis, categorization, classification and mapping of text extraction system techniques for images. *Multimedia Tools and Applications*, **84**(5), 2327–2484.
27. Sandhu, R., Channi, H. K., Ghai, D., Cheema, G. S., & Kaur, M. (2024). An introduction to generative AI tools for education 2030. In: R. Doshi, M. Dadhich, S. Poddar, and K.K. Hiran (Eds.), *Integrating Generative AI in Education to Achieve Sustainable Development Goals* (pp. 1–28). IGI Global.

2 Role of Artificial Intelligence in Quantum Computers

A New Era of Advancements

Sandeep Chouhan, Ramandeep Sandhu, and Chandani Bhasin

2.1 INTRODUCTION

The convergence of quantum computing (QC) and artificial intelligence (AI) is initiating an era of technical innovations that could transform and revolutionize industries and reshape problem-solving. As AI progresses, applications are proliferating in many areas, such as healthcare, finance, and transportation, allowing machines to analyze large datasets and make predictive proposals and decisions at scale and at an unprecedented speed and accuracy [1–5]. However, traditional ML algorithms often rely on classical computing structures that are unable to manage the complexity and scale of information being created in today's technologies. This constraint has highlighted the urgent need for innovative computational solutions that can keep pace with the demands of modern AI applications [6]. Figure 2.1 describes various limitations that exist in classical computing environments, along with a better task management system of AI.

Figure 2.2 represents some of the quantum computing systems. Quantum computing provides a paradigm-breaking option that utilizes the quantum mechanics to overcome such

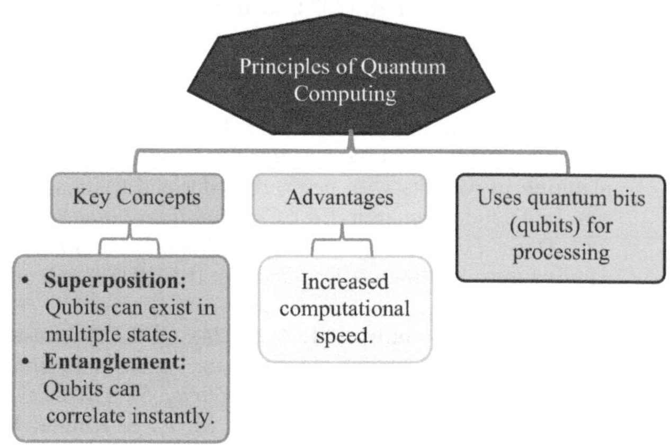

FIGURE 2.2 Principles of quantum computing.

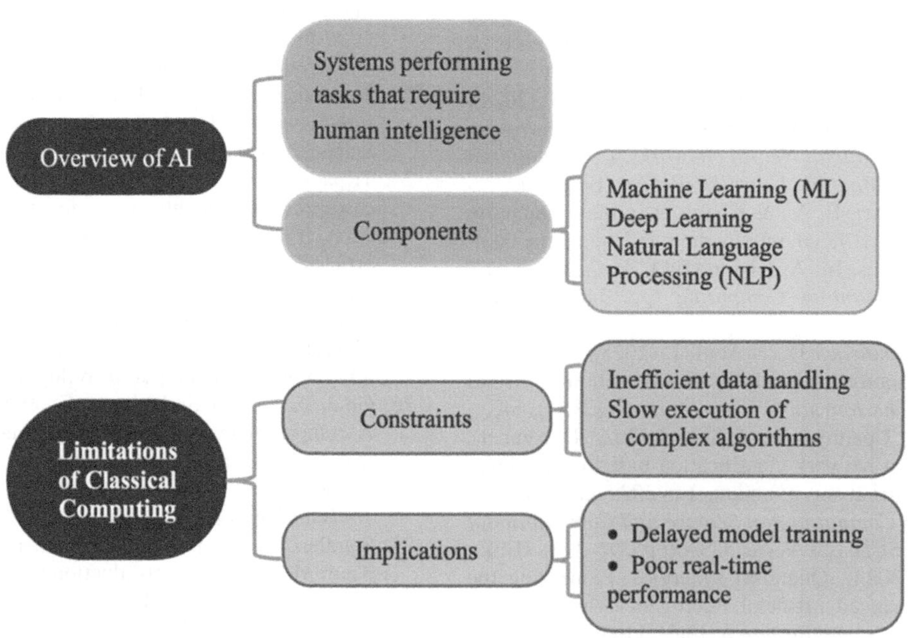

FIGURE 2.1 Overview of AI and limitations of classical computing.

DOI: 10.1201/9781003530800-2

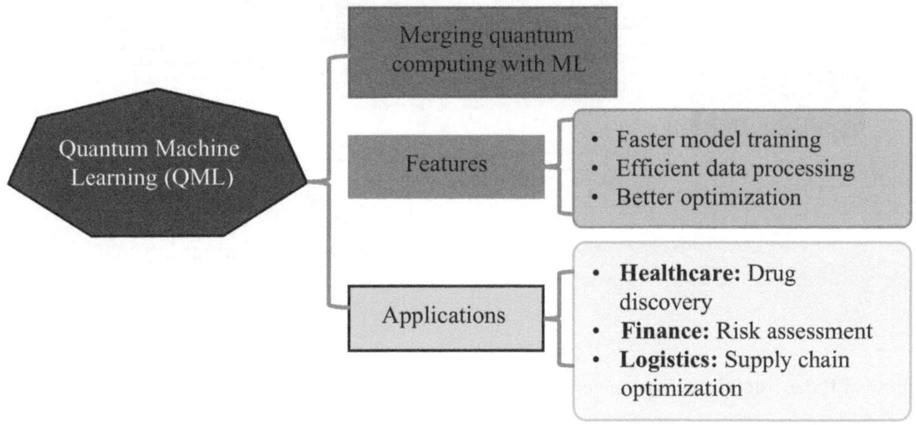

FIGURE 2.3 Emerging field of quantum machine learning.

limitations. Unlike the classical bits, on which information is encoded in binary (0 or 1), the quantum bits (qubits) can be in multiple states simultaneously, such as superposition and entanglement [7]. This allows the quantum computers to compute at breathtaking velocities, thus putting them in the best position to solve the intricate issues that face AI systems [8–10].

The newly evolving field of quantum machine learning (QML), depicted in Figure 2.3, exemplifies the possibilities of leveraging quantum computing capabilities. QML integrates quantum computing with traditional machine learning (ML) algorithms, leading to much faster data analysis [11–14]. That is to say, QML can dramatically cut down on the time it takes to train AI models and help give scientists and researchers the ability to work with more complex experiments involving larger datasets and more complex algorithms. This is critically important for hiring the strongest AI tools for fields like drug discovery, where fast simulations of molecular interactions can lead to new therapeutic compounds faster than traditional methods.

Additionally, the potential collaboration between AI and QC creates new possibilities for complex optimization problems, typically viewed as difficult by classical computers. In the finance domain, QML can assist in optimizing investment portfolios through an in-depth look at many variables and scenarios at once, and may enhance risk assessment and decision-making management. In the logistics domain, QML can help with real-time supply chain management beyond merely providing data, and also allowing adaptation and strategy through dynamic modeling. As progress is made, it is clear that AI has many opportunities for future collaboration with quantum computers [15]. There are many challenges ahead, including the ability to produce stable quantum systems, the need to move toward scaled solutions with scaled algorithms, and determining how to apply QML to actionable solutions for the many benefits. While challenges will remain, the opportunities are significant across many domains, and it should be clear that this partnership allows ML to take advantage of speed and execution, leveraging technology to fundamentally rethink what is possible for people. One way or another, we are entering a new era of new and innovative products, which will have a significant and revolutionary impact across many aspects of the domain. The beginning of the next transition is starting QML, which will be very impactful! This is captured by developments in the current area, as shown in Figure 2.4.

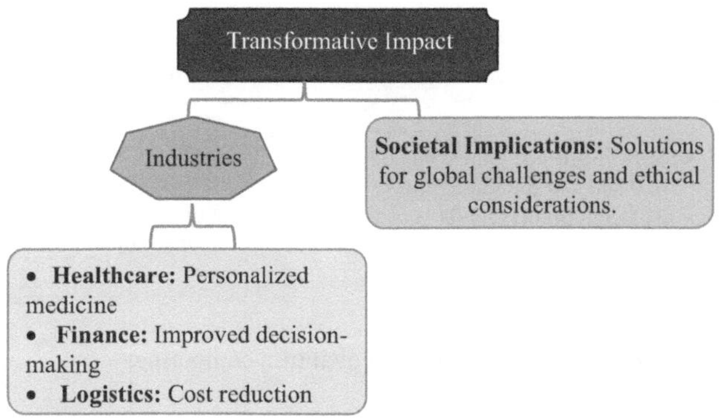

FIGURE 2.4 Transformative impact of QML.

2.1.1 Understanding AI in Quantum Computing: A Unique Perspective

The intersection of AI and QC signifies a game-changing moment in computing technology. AI, which focuses on enabling machines to learn from data and make intelligent decisions, has traditionally relied on classical computing systems. The overview of the AI era is shown in Figure 2.5.

These systems process data in binary form 0s and 1s, limiting their ability to process large and intricate data sets efficiently. As there is increasing complexity in AI applications, these limitations are more apparent, particularly in real-time processing or dealing with high-dimensional problems [16]. Quantum computing, in contrast to classical systems, uses quantum bits (qubits), which can exist in many states simultaneously through superposition, as illustrated in Figure 2.6. This allows quantum computers to make multiple calculations at once, with a dramatic

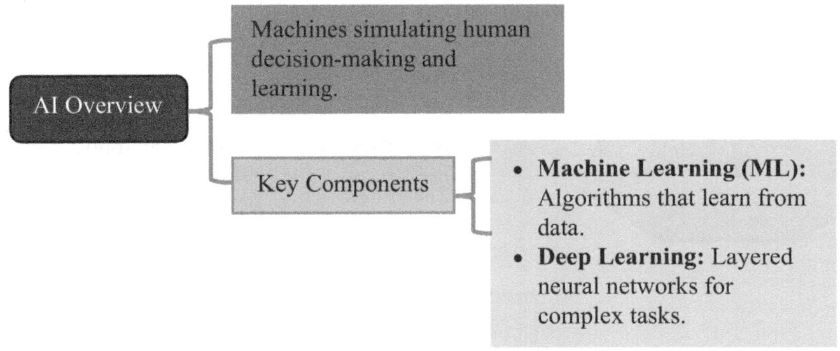

FIGURE 2.5 Overview of the artificial intelligence era.

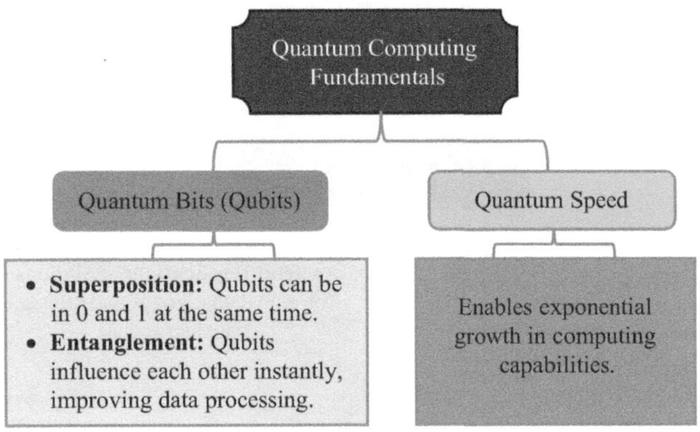

FIGURE 2.6 Fundamentals of quantum computing.

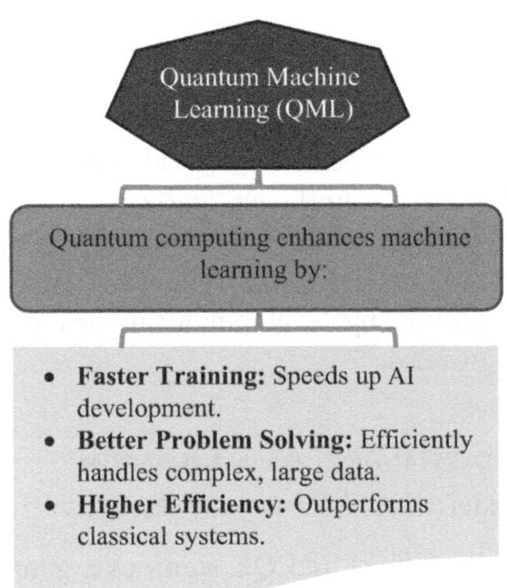

FIGURE 2.7 Benefits of quantum machine learning.

improvement in computational capacity. Additionally, entanglement, a quantum property, allows qubits to influence each other instantaneously, further improving computational efficiency.

Incorporating quantum computing into AI, particularly in QML, as shown in Figure 2.7, opens up new possibilities for processing and analyzing massive datasets. Quantum algorithms have the potential to:

- **Accelerate AI Model Training**: By leveraging the parallelism of qubits, quantum computers can process data exponentially faster than classical machines.
- **Solve Complex Optimization Problems**: Many AI applications rely on optimization, such as refining models to achieve better accuracy. QC's ability to explore multiple solutions simultaneously allows faster and more effective problem-solving.
- **Handle Large-Scale and High-Dimensional Data**: Quantum systems can manage complex data structures that overwhelm classical systems, enabling more accurate predictions and insights [17–20].

The implications of integrating AI with quantum computing are profound. In healthcare, for example, QML can rapidly analyze medical data to improve diagnoses and accelerate drug discovery, as shown in Figure 2.8. In finance, it can optimize investment strategies by quickly processing vast amounts of market data. While quantum computing is still in its developmental stages, its collaboration with AI promises to revolutionize industries by tackling computational challenges that were previously deemed insurmountable [21].

2.1.2 Implementation Strategy

2.1.2.1 Phase 1: Define the Problem and Data Pipeline

- **Problem Definition**
  - Identify a domain-specific problem where classical computing struggles, such as optimizing

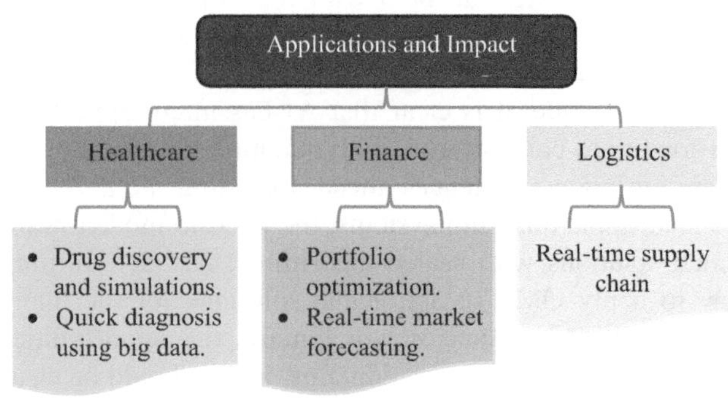

FIGURE 2.8 Applications of quantum machine learning.

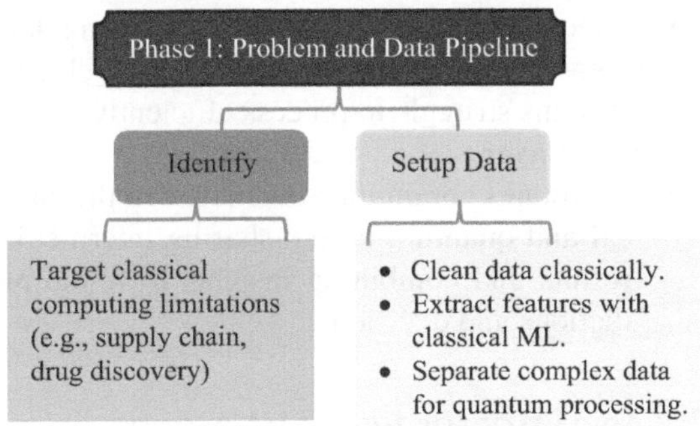

FIGURE 2.9 Problem and data pipeline.

a large-scale supply chain or drug discovery, as shown in Figure 2.9.

- **Data Pipeline Setup**
  - Start with data preprocessing in the classical layer – filter, clean, and prepare data for both classical and quantum tasks.
  - Utilize classical ML for initial feature extraction and simpler predictive modeling.
  - Partition the dataset so that complex data segments (high dimensionality or large volume) are passed to the quantum layer [22–24].

2.1.2.2 Phase 2: Implement Hybrid Quantum-Classical Workflows

- **Classical Training**
  - Train the classical ML model on simpler tasks such as regression, classification, and basic anomaly detection.
- **Quantum-Assisted Optimization**
  - For the high-dimensional data subset, implement quantum algorithms (e.g., Grover's search for optimization and quantum neural networks).
  - Use quantum computers to optimize the models faster and more efficiently.
- **Hybrid Synchronization**
  - Use the hybrid layer to combine the classical insights (e.g., feature importance) with quantum outputs to refine predictions and handle decision-making processes, as shown in Figure 2.10.

2.1.2.3 Phase 3: Model Testing and Validation

- **Model Testing**
  - Run multiple scenarios with varying data sizes to evaluate model performance, as shown in Figure 2.11.
  - Use classical benchmarks and quantum-enhanced benchmarks to compare results.
  - Optimize hyperparameters in both layers for the most accurate and efficient performance.
- **Quantum Error Correction**
  - Implement error correction protocols to ensure that the quantum layer's outputs are reliable, given the current limitations of quantum hardware [25–27].

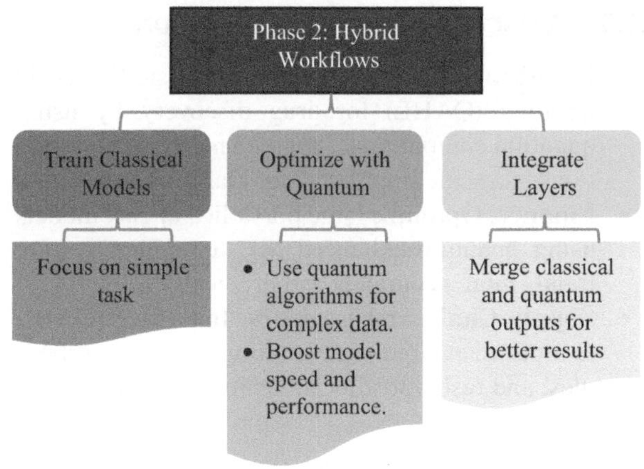

FIGURE 2.10 Hybrid workflows.

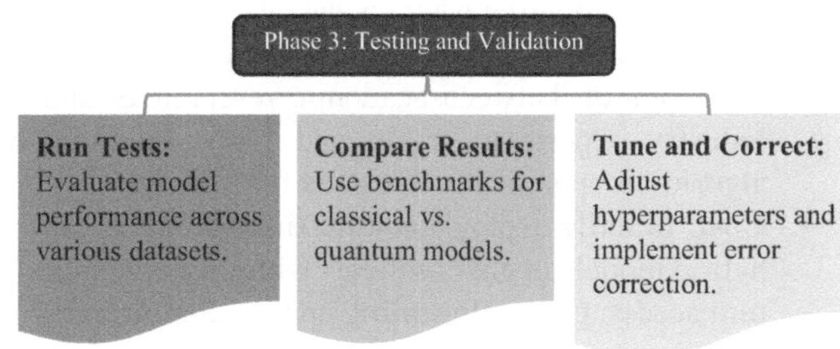

FIGURE 2.11 Testing and validation.

2.1.2.4 Phase 4: Scaling and Deployment

- **Scaling**
  - As quantum hardware becomes more powerful, it gradually shifts more tasks from the classical layer to the quantum layer for increased efficiency.
- **Deployment**
  - Build a hybrid cloud platform that allows for real-time decision-making.
  - Use application programming interfaces (APIs) to integrate the quantum layer with existing AI systems for businesses, such as financial modeling platforms or healthcare diagnostic systems, as shown in Figure 2.12.

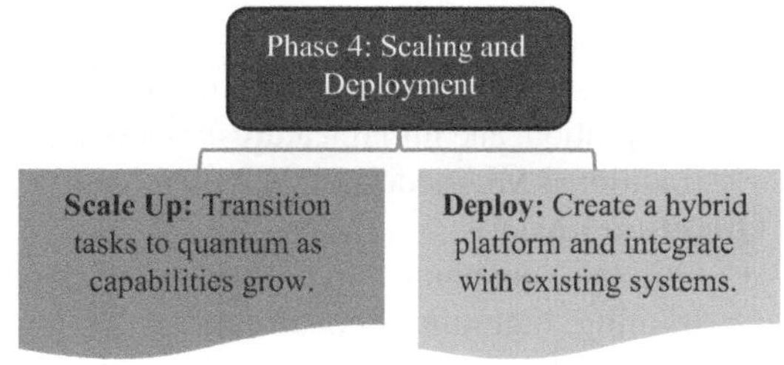

FIGURE 2.12 Scaling and deployment.

2.1.3 Applications of the QAHL Model

- **Healthcare**: Apply quantum-assisted hybrid learning (QAHL) for drug discovery by using quantum computing to simulate molecular interactions at a scale impossible for classical computers.
- **Finance**: Optimize large portfolios or risk models using quantum-enhanced ML to predict market trends more accurately and efficiently.
- **Supply Chain and Logistics**: Implement QAHL to optimize large-scale routing, delivery schedules, and resource allocations in real-time [10].

2.2 CHALLENGES AND MITIGATION

- **Quantum Hardware Limitations**: Develop hybrid models that can shift computational tasks based on available quantum resources, leveraging classical computing where necessary.
- **Quantum Algorithm Development**: Encourage collaboration between academic researchers and industry experts to create and refine quantum algorithms specifically designed for ML tasks.
- **Cost**: Initially deploy quantum simulations or use hybrid models in environments with limited quantum access, gradually scaling up as quantum technology matures [28,29].

2.3 PROPOSED APPROACH

In the proposed approach, QAHL framework is used for better healthcare with quantum artificial intelligence involvement.

2.3.1 Overview of the QAHL Model

The QAHL framework is designed to combine the computational advantages of QC with traditional ML. The goal is to create a system where classical ML algorithms handle simpler tasks, and quantum computing handles more computationally intensive operations, such as optimization and data analysis at large scales.

2.3.2 Model Components

Figure 2.13 provides various components of the proposed model.

- **Classical Layer**
  - Handles preprocessing of data, basic pattern recognition, and initial feature extraction using traditional ML models.
- **Quantum Layer**
  - Utilizes quantum algorithms for model training, high-dimensional data analysis, and optimization.
  - Executes complex tasks like handling large datasets with many variables that classical systems struggle to process efficiently.
- **Hybrid Layer**
  - Facilitates communication between the classical and quantum layers, sharing intermediate results and combining insights to refine predictions and decisions.

2.3.3 Advantages of the QAHL Model

- **Faster Model Training**: The quantum layer accelerates the training of deep learning models through high-dimensional data training, faster than classical methods.
- **Scalable Data Processing**: The model is optimized to grow with the complexity of the data, improving performance with larger datasets.
- **Optimization**: The hybrid framework allows the quantum layer to solve difficult and complex optimization tasks that cannot be solved using classical computing on its own.

2.4 KEY PARAMETERS FOR OPTIMAL QML PERFORMANCE

2.4.1 Quantum Circuit Design

- **Depth and Width**: Optimize the depth (number of layers) and width (number of qubits) of the circuit to carry out quantum algorithms with maximum efficacy.
- **Gate Use**: The fewer gates employed will reduce error rates and execution time.

2.4.2 Qubit Coherence Time

- **Coherence Time**: Increasing the coherence time of qubits can hold a quantum state before decoherence and keep those calculations reliable.
- **Error Correction**: Using methods to offset the effects of noise and decoherence on qubit behavior.

2.4.3 Feature Mapping

- **Good Mapping**: Using the best methods to map classical data into quantum states provides more expressivity for quantum models.
- **Reducing Dimensions**: Reduction of input dimensions can potentially increase efficiency and lower overfitting.

2.4.4 Algorithm Selection

- **Selecting Algorithms**: Use nominal methods of algorithms in the quantum setting that best

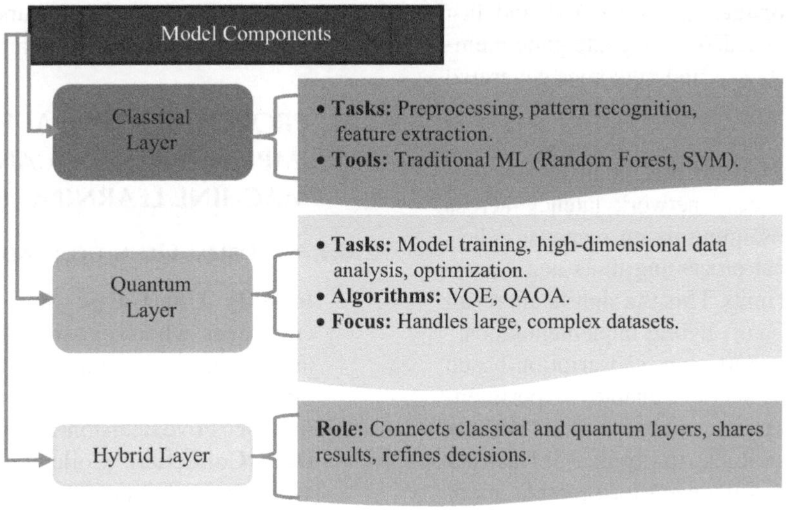

FIGURE 2.13 Proposed model components details.

match the specifications of the problem area (e.g., Quantum Support Vector Machine (QSVM) for any classification-type task).

- **Hybrid Solutions**: Hybrid models represent the best of both opposite settings by taking advantage of properties of both quantum and classical.

2.4.5 Hyperparameter Optimization

- **Tuning Levels**: Tune hyperparameter levels of quantum models to improve performance.
- **Cross-Validation**: Ensures that any validation process is robust and ensures generalization, and avoids overfitting.

2.4.6 Hardware Optimization

- **Quantum Hardware**: Use appropriate quantum hardware (e.g., superconducting qubits and trapped ions), depending on the application and scaling required.
- **Parallel Learning**: It provides quantum computers with the ability to take advantage of parallel processing in order to train and carry out execution significantly faster.

2.4.7 Data Quality and Quantity

- **Data Processing**: Spend dedicated time to clean, organize, and transform your data before running it to the fullest capability.
- **Data Count**: Ensure that you have enough training data and a variety of training data to improve its ability to generalize [30–34].

2.4.8 Integration with Classical Systems

- **Hybrid Gaming**: Create a seamless interface between quantum and classical processing systems to bring data onto both systems seamlessly, integrating it into the decision-making process you design.
- **System API**: Create a modular API that could be unidirectional between the quantum processor and classical ML workflows, but more than likely multipurpose in that it would be bidirectionally and sequentially capable.

2.5 ESSENTIAL HARDWARE AND SOFTWARE REQUIREMENTS FOR QUANTUM MACHINE LEARNING

2.5.1 Hardware Requirements for QML

1. Quantum Computing Devices
   - **Quantum Processors**: Investigate quantum-accessible devices such as superconducting qubits, Ion traps, and photonic systems that can perform quantum computations.
   - **Control Electronics**: High-precision control electronics are required for performing awe-inspiring quantum gates and controlling qubit states.
2. Classical Computing Infrastructure
   - **Functionally Superior Processing Units**: High-quality CPUs and GPUs are required for processing the data up until closest point possible, both before releasing it to classical ML activities and after connecting to quantum outputs.

- **RAM and Storage**: Enough RAM and fast storage will be needed to give adequate memory for large data sets and outcomes generated by the QML experiments.

3. Networking Solutions
   - **Low Latency Networking**: High-speed communication reduces network latency across both connections, minimizing response delays between classical processing units and quantum processing units. This is a significant result for the future use of hybrid implementations.
   - **Cloud Access**: Offering subscription-based cloud computing services enables experimentation with quantum computations without requiring direct access to physical infrastructure and supports the need for scalable quantum computational resources.

2.5.2 Software Requirements for QML

1. Quantum Programming Languages
   - **Qiskit**: A free tool created for quantum computing that allows users to easily build, run, and analyze quantum circuits.
   - **Cirq**: A Python library created to develop quantum algorithms and implement those on various quantum processors.
2. ML Frameworks
   - **Scikit-Learn**: A complete classical ML library that can be used before quantum algorithms in preprocessing and initial modeling tasks.
   - **TensorFlow Quantum**: An extension of TensorFlow specifically designed to connect quantum computing and ML and allow the user to create QML models.
3. Simulation Software
   - **Quantum Simulators**: Include tools like Qiskit Aer that enable quantum circuits to be simulated on classical hardware, making it easier to test quantum algorithms before executing them on the actual device.
4. Data Processing and Management Tools
   - **Pandas and NumPy**: Libraries that should be used for data manipulation and numerical computation, providing support to preprocess data for QML.
   - **Database Solutions**: Ideal systems for using databases for large amounts of data and systems that provide easy access for QML applications.
5. Development Environments
   - **Integrated Development Environments**: Tools like Jupyter Notebooks or PyCharm support in coding, testing, and visualizing the results of QML projects.
   - **Version Control Systems**: Ensuring version control with systems like Git can be helpful to manage code changes and develop certain collaboration in research and development.

2.6 PROPOSED APPROACH FOR IMPLEMENTING QUANTUM MACHINE LEARNING (QML)

2.6.1 Problem Definition and Data Acquisition

- **Identify Use Cases**: Start by identifying specific areas where classical ML has famous limitations such as complex optimization problems, high-dimensional data transformations, or time-sensitive decision-making.
- **Data Collection**: Collect relevant datasets from as many different data sources as possible and make sure the datasets remain representative of the problem space in which you are working. Furthermore, attempt to use the best-quality data that is structured (such as tabular forms), meaning the data will be able to be incorporated into classical and quantum settings. Refer to Figure 2.14, which shows the problem and the data acquisition.

2.6.2 Data Preprocessing and Classical Modeling

- **Data Cleaning and Normalization**: Perform thorough data preprocessing, including cleaning, normalization, and feature engineering. This step ensures that the data is ready for analysis and modeling [35–39].
- **Classical Baseline Models**: Develop classical ML models (e.g., decision trees, support vector machines) to establish baseline performance metrics. This provides a reference point for evaluating the effectiveness of QML approaches. Figure 2.15 provides data preprocessing and modeling.

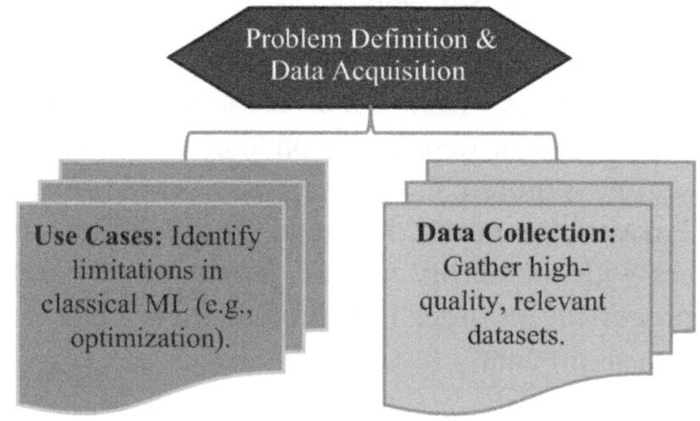

FIGURE 2.14 Problem and data acquisition.

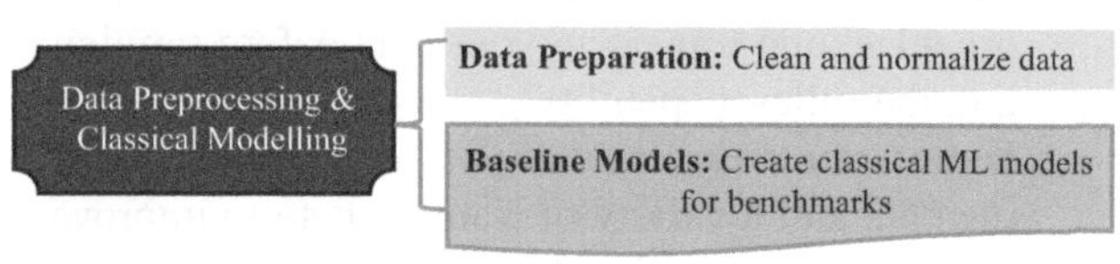

FIGURE 2.15 Data preprocessing and modeling.

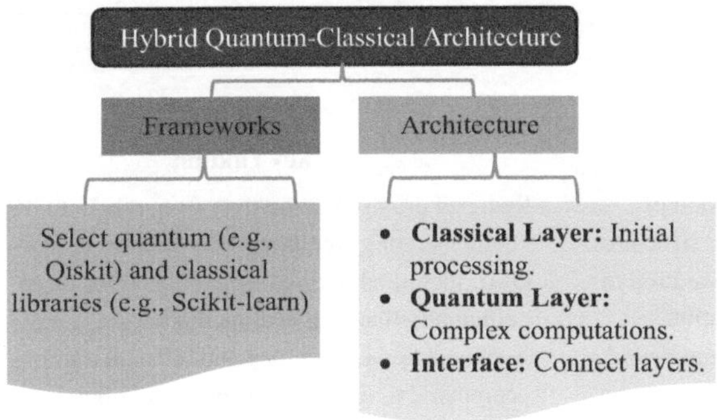

FIGURE 2.16 Hybrid quantum architecture.

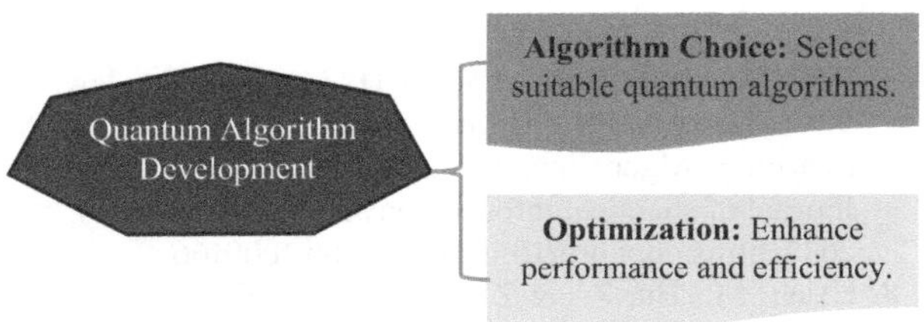

FIGURE 2.17 Quantum algorithm development.

2.6.3 Hybrid Quantum-Classical Architecture Design

- **Framework Selection**: Choose appropriate quantum programming frameworks (e.g., Qiskit, Cirq) and classical ML libraries (e.g., Scikit-learn, TensorFlow) to facilitate the integration of quantum and classical components.
- **Layered Architecture**: Design a hybrid architecture comprising the components shown in Figure 2.16:
  - **Classical Layer**: Responsible for initial data processing and simpler modeling tasks.
  - **Quantum Layer**: Executes complex computations using quantum algorithms for optimization and high-dimensional data processing.
  - **Hybrid Interface**: Facilitates communication between the classical and quantum layers, sharing intermediate results and refining predictions.

2.6.4 Quantum Algorithm Development

- **Algorithm Selection**: Identify suitable quantum algorithms for the specific tasks at hand. This may include quantum versions of classical or novel quantum-specific approaches.
- **Algorithm Optimization**: Fine-tune quantum algorithms to enhance performance, focusing on minimizing qubit usage and maximizing computational efficiency. Figure 2.17 provides a Quantum Algorithm.

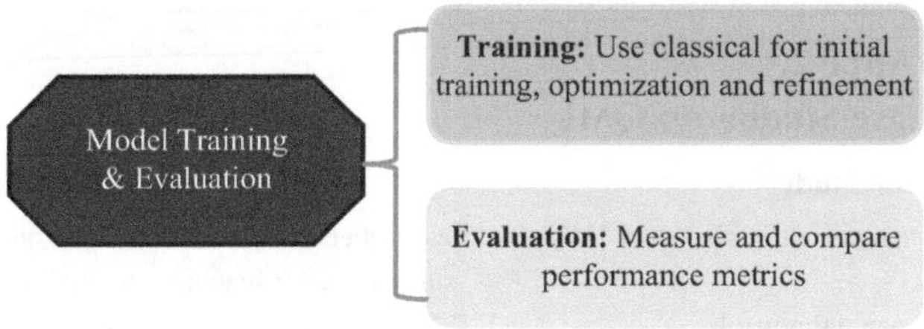

FIGURE 2.18 Model training and evaluation.

2.6.5 Model Training and Evaluation

- **Training Process**: Train the hybrid model by leveraging the strengths of both classical and quantum layers. Utilize the classical layer for initial model training and the quantum layer for refining and optimizing results [35–39].
- **Performance Evaluation**: Assess the model's performance using established metrics. Compare results against classical models to evaluate improvements, as shown in Figure 2.18.

2.6.6 Scalability and Deployment

- **Scaling Strategy**: Develop a plan for scaling the quantum component as quantum hardware advances. Gradually transitioning more tasks to the quantum layer to exploit its full potential.
- **Deployment Environment**: Create a user-friendly platform that allows for seamless integration with existing systems. This could involve cloud-based solutions that provide real-time access to quantum computing resources.

2.6.7 Continuous Improvement and Feedback Loop

- **Iterative Refinement**: Implement a feedback loop to continuously monitor model performance and update algorithms based on new data and insights.
- **Research and Development**: Stay abreast of advancements in QC and ML to integrate new techniques and improve the model further.

2.7 CASE STUDIES

Various case studies on QML are illustrated in Table 2.1.

2.8 CONCLUSION

The synergy of AI and QC is marking the beginning of a paradigm shift in computer science through QML. In a way, QML tackles and embodies not only the principles of ML but also the principles of quantum mechanics, allowing greater computational ability to get around classical computing limits, enabling faster computations and learning from larger sets of complicated data. Not only will the processes enhance the reliability of predictive models, but also

TABLE 2.1
Case Studies on QML

Case Study	Description	Key Finding
Quantum drug discovery [30]	Researchers at Xanadu utilized a quantum version of support vector machines to analyze molecular structures.	Reduced drug screening time from weeks to days, demonstrating significant acceleration in discovery.
Financial portfolio optimization [31]	D-Wave Systems partnered with a financial institution to apply QML for investment portfolio optimization.	QML identified optimal asset allocations more efficiently than classical methods.
Quantum image recognition [32]	The University of Waterloo developed a quantum neural network for image classification tasks.	Achieved higher accuracy and reduced training time compared to traditional neural networks.
Natural language processing (NLP) [33]	IBM Research explored quantum circuits to enhance sentiment analysis of text data.	Improved classification accuracy for sentiment analysis compared to classical models.
Quantum computing for climate modeling [34]	A collaborative study utilized QML to analyze climate-related datasets for better modeling.	Enhanced predictive accuracy for climate patterns, aiding in climate resilience planning.

enable new solutions in previously unexplored avenues of health care, finance, logistics, etc. That being said, there are obstacles to be overcome in realizing the full potential of QML in AI. These efforts include tackling quantum noise in prototype QML frameworks, correcting errors, and developing robust hybrid architectures as initial steps toward realizing the full potential of AI with quantum computing. This also involves collaboration between researchers and industry practitioners to develop strong frameworks that harness information for both quantum and classical systems. The evolution of quantum technology is evolving as is its use in AI, if applied properly, we will be able to rethink what it means to solve problems and uphold great achievements previously thought impossible. If we combine concrete research, proper community development, and interdisciplinary practices, we will accomplish a great deal of good, and the world will be able to advance its computational science about real-world complex tasks and problems.

REFERENCES

1. Cheng, N., Wang, S., Zhao, L. et al. (2025). Quantum-enhanced beetle swarm optimized ELM for high-dimensional smart grid intrusion detection. *Discover Applied Sciences*, 7, 837. https://doi.org/10.1007/s42452-025-07506-z.
2. Rafi, S., Maisam, R. M. A., Zahid, A., Yaqoob, M. H., Ajmal, S., & Azam, A. (2023). Synergy between quantum computing and machine learning in quantum neural network. *Central Asian Journal of Mathematical Theory and Computer Sciences,* 4(8), 95–101. https://cajmtcs.casjournal.org/index.php/CAJMTCS/article/view/505.
3. Farhi, E., Goldstone, J., Gutmann, S., & Neven, H. (2017). Quantum Algorithms for Fixed Qubit Architectures. arXiv preprint: arxiv.org/abs/1703.06199.
4. Cerezo, M., Arrasmith, L., Cincio, S. M. B., & Coles, P. J. (2021). Variational quantum algorithms. *Nature Reviews Physics,* 3(9), 622–635.https://arxiv.org/abs/2012.09265.
5. Pérez-Ramírez, D.F. (2024). Variational Quantum Algorithms for Combinatorial Optimization. ArXiv, abs/2407.06421.
6. Farhi, E., Zhang, R., & Li, W. (2023). Quantum algorithms for fixed-qubit architectures. *Physical Review A,* 107(4), 042310. https://doi.org/10.48550/arXiv.1703.06199.
7. Batra, K., Zorn, K. M., Foil, D. H., Minerali, E., Gawriljuk, V. O., Lane, T. R., & Ekins, S. (2021). Quantum Machine Learning Algorithms for Drug Discovery Applications. Journal of chemical information and modeling, 61(6), 2641–2647. https://doi.org/10.1021/acs.jcim.1c00166.
8. Hsieh, M., Hu, Z., & Zhou, T. (2021). Quantum machine learning on near-term quantum computers. arXiv Preprint arXiv:2103.03424. https://doi.org/10.48550/arXiv.2103.03424.
9. A., Sharma, N., Marriwala, N. K., Panda, S., Aruna, M., & Kumar, J. (2024). Quantum machine learning with Qiskit: Evaluating regression accuracy and noise impact. *IET Quantum Communication,* 5(4), 310–321.
10. Arora, C., & Sandhu, R. (2024). Adoption of quantum NLP for improved healthcare system. In: *International Conference on Computation of Artificial Intelligence & Machine Learning,* Jaipur, India (pp. 51–59). Springer.
11. Liu, J., Liu, M., Liu, J., Ye, Z., Alexeev, Y., Eisert, J., & Jiang, L. (2023). Towards provably efficient quantum algorithms for large-scale machine-learning models. *Nature Communications,* 15.
12. Lloyd, S., Mohseni, M., & Rebentrost, P. (2013). Quantum algorithms for supervised and unsupervised machine learning. arXiv:1307.0411.
13. Ladd, T. D., Liu, M., & Zhang, R. (2022). Quantum computing with superconducting qubits. *Nature,* 547(7663), 204–208. https://doi.org/10.1038/nature22378.
14. Rawat, B., Mehra, N., Bist, A. S., Yusup, M., & Sanjaya, Y. P. A. (2022). Quantum computing and ai: Impacts & possibilities. *ADI Journal on Recent Innovation*, 3(2), 202–207. https://doi.org/10.34306/ajri.v3i2.656.
15. Zhao, R., & Wang, S. (2021). A review of quantum neural networks: methods, models, dilemma. arXiv preprint arXiv:2109.01840.
16. Wiebe, N., Kapoor, A., & Svore, K. M. (2014). Quantum deep learning. arXiv preprint arXiv:1412.3489.
17. Cerezo, M., Verdon, G., Huang, H. Y., Cincio, L., & Coles, P. J. (2022). Challenges and opportunities in quantum machine learning. *Nature Computational Science*, 2(9), 567–576. arXiv:2303.09491.
18. McClean, J. R., Romero, J., Babbush, R., & Aspuru-Guzik, A. (2016). The theory of variational hybrid quantum-classical algorithms. *New Journal of Physics*, 18(2), 023023. arXiv:1509.04279.
19. Liu, D., Wu, Y., Kang, Y., Yin, L., Ji, X., Cao, X., & Li, C. (2023). Multi-agent quantum-inspired deep reinforcement learning for real-time distributed generation

control of 100% renewable energy systems. Engineering *Applications of Artificial Intelligence*, 119, 105787. https://doi.org/10.1016/j.engappai.2022.105787.
20. Ribeiro, P., Xu, Y., & Zhang, L. (2021). The role of quantum computing in artificial intelligence. *Computing Research Repository*. https://doi.org/10.48550/arXiv.2102.05451.
21. Abbas, A., Sutter, D., Zoufal, C., Lucchi, A., Figalli, A., & Woerner, S. (2021). The power of quantum neural networks. *Nature Computational Science*, 1(6), 403–409. arXiv:2011.00027.
22. Singh, A., & Soni, V. (2023). Recent advances in quantum machine learning. *Journal of Machine Learning Research*, 24(51), 1–30.
23. Farhi, E., Goldstone, J., Gutmann, S., & Neven, H. (2017). Quantum algorithms for fixed qubit architectures. arXiv preprint arXiv:1703.06199.
24. Ullah, U., & Garcia-Zapirain, B. (2024). Quantum machine learning revolution in healthcare: a systematic review of emerging perspectives and applications. *IEEE Access*, 12, 11423–11450. DOI: 10.1109/ACCESS.2024.3353461.
25. Biamonte, J., Wittek, P., Pancotti, N., Rebentrost, P., Wiebe, N., & Lloyd, S. (2017). Quantum machine learning. *Nature*, 549(7671), 195–202. arXiv:1611.09347.
26. Gharehchopogh, F. S. (2023). Quantum-inspired metaheuristic algorithms: comprehensive survey and classification. *Artificial Intelligence Review*, 56(6), 5479–5543. https://doi.org/10.1007/s10462-022-10280-8.
27. Nguyen, T., Sipola, T., & Hautamäki, J. (2024). Machine learning applications of quantum computing: A review. arXiv preprint arXiv:2406.13262.
28. Sandhu, R., Ghai, D., Tripathi, S. L., Kaur, R., Rawal, K., & Dhir, K. (2024). Machine learning for cognitive treatment planning in patients with neurodisorder and trauma injuries. In: D. J. Hemanth (Ed.), *Computational Intelligence and Deep Learning Methods for Neuro-rehabilitation Applications* (pp. 165–193). Academic Press.
29. Sandhu, R., Channi, H. K., Ghai, D., Prabha, C., & Kaur, H. (2024). From stress to success: Optimizing brain performance with resilience. In: S. Saluja, J. Kukreja and S. Sharma (Eds.), *Building Organizational Resilience with Neuroleadership* (pp. 194–214). IGI Global.
30. Jia, Z. A., Yi, B., Zhai, R., Wu, Y. C., Guo, G. C., & Guo, G. P. (2019). Quantum neural network states: A brief review of methods and applications. *Advanced Quantum Technologies*, 2(7–8), 1800077. arXiv: 1808.10601.
31. Carrascal, G., Hernamperez, P., Botella, G., & del Barrio, A. (2023). Backtesting quantum computing algorithms for portfolio optimization. *IEEE Transactions on Quantum Engineering*, 5, 1–20. DOI: 10.1109/TQE.2023.3337328.
32. Dunjko, V., & Briegel, H. J. (2017). Machine learning\& artificial intelligence in the quantum domain. arXiv preprint arXiv:1709.02779.
33. Kjaergaard, M., Schwartz, M. D., Braumüller, J., & Gambetta, J. M. (2020). Superconducting qubit technology. *Annual Review of Condensed Matter Physics*, 11(1), 369–395. https://doi.org/10.1146/annurev-conmatphys-031119-050605.
34. Zhou, M. G., Liu, Z. P., Yin, H. L., Li, C. L., Xu, T. K., & Chen, Z. B. (2023). Quantum neural network for quantum neural computing. *Research*, 6, 0134. https://doi.org/10.34133/research.0134.
35. Ghai, D., Saxena, S., Dhingra, G., & Tripathi, S. L. (2024). A comprehensive review on performance-based comparative analysis, categorization, classification and mapping of text extraction system techniques for images. *Multimedia Tools and Applications*, 83, 1–158.
36. Sandhu, R., Channi, H. K., Ghai, D., Cheema, G. S., & Kaur, M. (2024). An introduction to generative AI tools for education 2030. In: R. Doshi, M. Dadhich, S. Poddar and K. K. Hiran (Eds.), *Integrating Generative AI in Education to Achieve Sustainable Development Goals* (pp. 1–28). IGI Global.
37. Ghai, D., Tripathi, S. L., Saxena, S., Chanda, M., & Alazab, M. (Eds.). (2022). *Machine Learning Algorithms for Signal and Image Processing*. John Wiley & Sons.
38. Kumar, S., Ghai, D., Jain, A., Tripathi, S. L., & Rani, S. (Eds.). (2023). *Multimodal Biometric and Machine Learning Technologies: Applications for Computer Vision*. John Wiley & Sons.
39. Soewu, T., Kaur, H., Sandhu, R., Sandhu, P., Ghai, D., Dhir, K., & Tripathi, S. L. (2025). Machine learning models for text and image processing. In: S. L. Tripathi, V. E. Balas, M. Mahmud and S. Banerjee (Eds.), *Machine Learning Models and Architectures for Biomedical Signal Processing* (pp. 153–177). Academic Press.

3 Navigating the Fusion of Quantum Artificial Intelligence Paradigm Principles and Algorithms

Ahmed Mateen Buttar, Muhammad Anwar Shahid, and Sadaf Naz

3.1 INTRODUCTION

In some significant issues, such as factoring big integers, quantum computing's non-classical computation is superior to classical computation. Classical computer represents information using bits (0 & 1; up and down; ON and OFF). Quantum computer uses qubits, in which the state may be 0,1. $\Delta x \Delta p \geq \hbar/2$. Δx=position, Δp=momentum= mass× velocity=1.05×10^{-34} Joule-second. For an electron, if the uncertainty in velocity is approximately $\Delta v \approx 10$m/s, then the uncertainty in position is about $\Delta x \approx 10\mu$m, as governed by the Heisenberg Uncertainty Principle. Furthermore, certain quantum algorithms exhibit polynomial-time complexity (e.g., $O(N_3)$), making them computationally tractable [1].

3.1.1 Brief Overview of Quantum Computing

D-Wave Systems sold DWave One, the first commercially successful quantum computer, for US$10 million in 2011 [2]. IBM said that it was required to develop a semiconductor that remained constant and sufficient to grasp the potential of quantum computing's (QC's) impending arrival in popular fields and businesses. The initial descent of quantum systems will be commercially available in 10 or 12 years from the time this book was published, which is foreseeable [3]. Therefore, QC represents a significant improvement over predictable computing. For instance, a quantum computer with 30 qubits corresponds to a deterministic processor operating at ten teraflops of performance. Comparing this to modern computers, which operate at gigaflop (i.e., Giga Floating-Point Operations Per Second) speeds. From an applied standpoint, challenges with carnal provision data distribution, quantum algorithm design, and quantum structures are of particular note [4]. Carnal provision is a silent and difficult issue. The following prerequisites must be met for quantum computation to be valid:

1. The system must be ready, which means we must begin from a recognized and knowledgeable state.
2. To remain talented in recreating any additional plausible logic gate, it must be probable to operate qubits competently, with processes that comprise a global set of logic gates.
3. Throughout the trial, the quantum structure must preserve its quantum consistency.
4. It is essential to be able to deliver the system's concluding state following a calculation.
5. The structure needs to be climbable so that more qubit containers can be added to take on issues with higher computing demands.

The qubit container, however, is in a linear mixture of the two fundamental states, recognized as a quantum superposition state as shown in the equation (Eq. 3.1).

$$|\varphi\rangle = \alpha_0 |0\rangle + \alpha_1 |1\rangle \tag{3.1}$$

The amplitudes 0 and 1 in the overhead equation are restricted by the following:

- Complex numbers make up the breadths: $\alpha_0, \alpha_1 \in C$
- The probabilistic nature of quantum mechanics: $|\alpha_0|^2 + |\alpha_1|^2 = 1$

3.1.2 Formalism of Quantum Computing

Since it was assumed that the theory would guide the real structure, the physics of the device was often not mentioned in the classical theory of computation. The development of QC began with the discovery of a relationship between two ostensibly unrelated domains of computation and quantum mechanics [5].

Qubits, which are the building blocks of quantum computing, must be operated in agreement with the rules and constraints of quantum physics. Consequently, before exploring this novel computing example further, it is essential to review the important ideas and terms of the quantum method, but from an additional strict standpoint. The elementary unit of evidence in the traditional perfect of multiplication is the bit, which has the two values 0 and 1. A bit, from a formal standpoint, is a part of the set (Eq. 3.2):

$$V = \{0,1\} \tag{3.2}$$

It is possible to think of a cable with n bits as a part of Cartesian production (Eq. 3.3):

$$V^n = V \times \cdots \times V \tag{3.3}$$

Any information can be described by a cable of bits if we start a coding tool. From a correct vantage point, we can

DOI: 10.1201/9781003530800-3

state that an algorithm estimates Boolean functions since it is a tool for manipulating cables of bits [6,7]. As a result, the algorithm adjusts the inventive cable to produce an alternative cable of n bits Boolean function by the equation (Eq. 3.4):

$$V^n \rightarrow \frac{V^n}{f}(\alpha) = \beta \quad (3.4)$$

3.1.3 Systems of Qubits

The direct superposition of two components of the origin results in the most widely applicable standardized one-qubit that can be constructed (Eq. 3.5).

$$| x\rangle = \alpha_0 \,| 0\rangle + \alpha_1 \,| 1\rangle ; \alpha_0, \alpha_1 \in C; \; | \alpha_0 |^2 | + | \alpha_1 |^2 = 1 \quad (3.5)$$

A qubit can exist in the two states – as previously discussed – as well as in middle states, or states that are a linear blend of $|0\rangle$ and $|1\rangle$. So, for instance, an electron's spin (Eq. 3.6) could be as follows:

$$\Phi = \left(\tfrac{1}{2}\right) | 0\rangle + \left(\tfrac{\sqrt{3}}{2}\right) | 1\rangle \quad (3.6)$$

We establish that a qubit is a vector space course (Eq. 3.7):

$$V = L\left(|0\rangle, | 1\rangle\right) \quad (3.7)$$

V is a compound Hilbert space that renders to quantum mechanics (Eq. 3.8) and contains:

$$B = \left[|0\rangle, | 1\rangle\right] \quad (3.8)$$

where singular vectors represent the states and form an orthonormal origin. The following states of a qubit (the quantities labeled amplitudes; Eq. 3.9) are thus possible:

$$| x\rangle = \alpha_0 \,| 0\rangle + \alpha_1 \,| 1\rangle ; \alpha_0, \alpha_1 \in C; | \alpha_0 |^2 + \alpha_1 |^2 = 1 \quad (3.9)$$

Let's start with a straightforward illustration and say $n=2$ denotes the rotation of a structure of two electrons. Each electron's rotation has two possible states. Once the two-qubit system is formed, it generates the combined four states: $|00\rangle$, $|01\rangle$, $|10\rangle$, and $|11\rangle$. Figure 3.1 denotes the sphere-shaped synchronization.

The space measurement and 2² space origin for these two-qubit (Eq. 3.10) are as follows:

$$| x_i\rangle \oplus | v_j\rangle = | x_i, v_j\rangle = | x_i v_j\rangle \quad (3.10)$$

This equation's relations allow us to describe the four-dimensional space's derivation (Eq. 3.11) as follows:

$$\left\{|0\rangle \oplus |0\rangle, |0\rangle \oplus |1\rangle, |1\rangle \oplus |0\rangle, |1\rangle \oplus\rangle \, |1\rangle\right\} \quad (3.11)$$

This can be reproduced in the same way (Eq. 3.12):

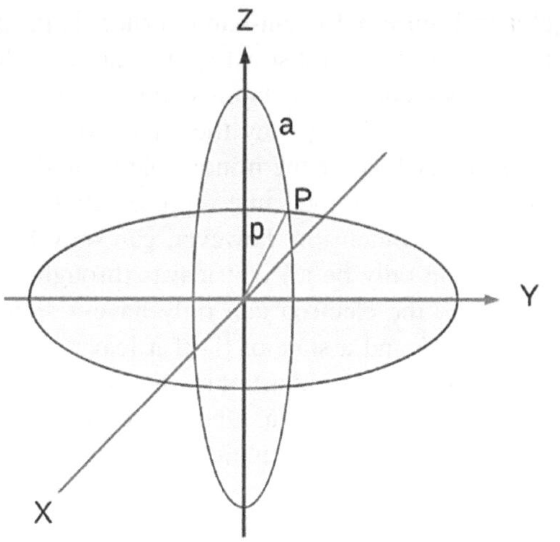

FIGURE 3.1 Sphere-shaped synchronizes.

$$\left\{|00\rangle, |01\rangle, |10\rangle, | 11\rangle\right\} \quad (3.12)$$

3.1.4 Qubits and Measurement

We will now discuss the issue of measuring qubits. Let's assess the probabilities for trying to portion the ensuing qubit (Eq. 3.13):

$$\varphi = (1/2) \,| 0\rangle + \left(\sqrt{3/2}\right) | 1\rangle \quad (3.13)$$

We'll utilize the apparatus in Figure 3.2 to create the dimension. The magnetic field that the electron experiences when it passes through the hole causes it to take a different course depending on its spin until it ultimately succeeds in passing one of the two hovels in the second barrier. We have the electron pass through one of the two holes in another wall, which is where the pure single qubits are located in the leftward portion of Figure 3.2. The spin of the electron is not taken into account if it moves into the center of these holes.

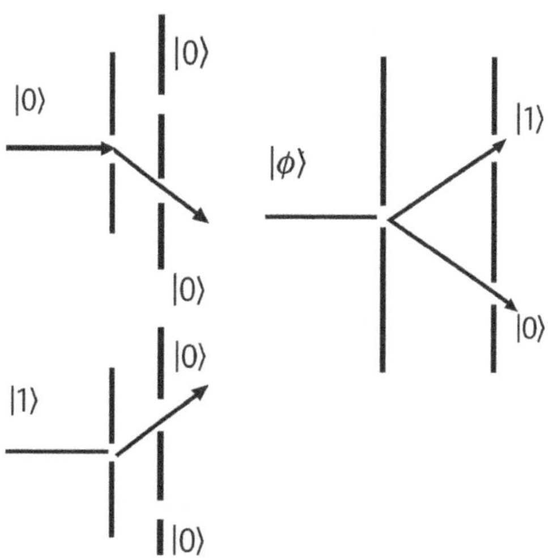

FIGURE 3.2 Probability lower holes greater than zero do not have a clearly defined spin.

The qubit in Figure 3.2 (right-hand corner) is in an intermediate state and lacks a distinct spin because of this. The electron in this scenario may bounce upward or downward.

Let's attempt to clarify why the choice of the electron to exit the higher hole or the minor hole is predetermined [8]. Figure 3.2 denotes the same representation. The electron's spin after dimension, however, can only be half of its state and can only be $|0\rangle$ if it leaves through the lower hole. Similarly, the electron can only have a spin after a dimension of +½ and a state of $|1\rangle$ if it leaves through the higher hole. The qubit is adjusted by dimension in addition to elastic missing information. One of the two states of the basis must be chosen by the qubit due to the dimensioning procedure [9].

After investigating one qubit dimension subjectively, it makes sense to explain the complete process quantitatively. As a result, the qubit in the example will have a final value of $|0\rangle$ with possibility P0 of ¼ and $|1\rangle$ with possibility P1 of ¼ ¾. It describes how to measure a qubit. If the final state is $|0\rangle$ or $|1\rangle$ individually, the measurement will provide the predicted bit 0 or 1.

We can equal either the first or the second qubit in a two-qubit system. We start by measuring the initial quantum bit. The procedure is illustrated by the following example given in the equation (Eq. 3.14):

$$\varphi = \left(1/\sqrt{3}\right)|00\rangle + \left(1/\sqrt{3}\right)|01\rangle + \left(1/\sqrt{3}\right)|10\rangle \quad (3.14)$$

3.1.5 Putting It All Together

Entanglement is a specific and counterintuitive example of a quantum system, as we have already shown. The presence of entangled quantum state means that it is not always possible to describe the ideal state of a quantum system by describing its constituent parts. If a quantum state of n qubits cannot be articulated as the tensor product of the states of all n fundamental qubits, it is said to be entangled. Let's examine two qubits, denoted by the terms $|x\rangle$ and $|y\rangle$, as shown in the equations (Eqs. 3.15 and 3.16) respectively:

$$|x\rangle = \alpha|0\rangle + \beta|1\rangle \quad (3.15)$$

$$|y\rangle = c|0\rangle + d|1\rangle \quad (3.16)$$

So that $\alpha, \beta, c, d \in C$. The two-qubit is created by the tensor product of these two qubits (Eq. 3.17):

$$\begin{aligned} |x\rangle \oplus |y\rangle &= |x, y\rangle = (\alpha|0\rangle + \beta|1\rangle) \oplus (c|0\rangle + d|1\rangle) \\ &= \alpha c|0,0\rangle + \alpha d|0,1\rangle + \beta c|10\rangle + \beta d|1,1\rangle \end{aligned} \quad (3.17)$$

If a system of two qubits cannot be articulated in the manner of the earlier equation, it is said to be entangled (Eq. 3.18). Therefore, the system:

$$\alpha c = +1/2;\ \alpha d = 1/2;\ \beta c = 1/2 \quad (3.18)$$

3.1.6 Constructing Algorithms with Qubits

A procedure is a tool for controlling n qubits in the quantum model of multiplication. Creating portions of qubits and converting a preliminary state $\varphi 1$ obsessed by its equivalent concluding state $\varphi 2$ are two approaches to accomplishing this. If the function of $V^n \to V^n$ is represented by U in such a way that (Eq. 3.19):

$$U\varphi_1 = \varphi_2 \quad (3.19)$$

The application follows from quantum mechanical assumptions: U is linear and turns states into states, or conserves the average. Because of this, U can only be a particular conversion of a lined operator whose adjoint is reversed, and the succeeding conditions hold (Eq. 3.20):

$$U^{+}U = I \quad (3.20)$$

However, no quantum computer has the skill to carry out a generic unitary transformation. As a result, it must be classified as a series of fundamental unitary changes made through quantum gates. Two restrictions must be evaluated to define quantum algorithms. The starting state, which must always be the same and is $\varphi_1 = |0\rangle$, is disturbed by the first limit. The incompatibility of quantum gates with quantum dimensions is the second restriction.

3.2 MAJOR CONTRIBUTIONS AND CHAPTER ORGANIZATION

This chapter makes substantial contributions to the field of QC by thoroughly analyzing foundational concepts such as qubits, superposition, and entanglement, which set QC apart from classical approaches. It discusses the formalism of QC, systems of qubits, and measurement techniques that underpin this field. Additionally, this chapter covers practical applications, demonstrating the impact of QC in areas such as optimization and quantum simulation. It also addresses current challenges and suggests future research directions, with an emphasis on advancements in error correction techniques and scalable quantum hardware.

This chapter is organized as follows: Section 3.3.1 lays down the background to quantum computing, giving a brief description of what it is, what it is based on, and the basics of this division. Section 3.3.2 provides the literature background, highlighted researches on quantum mechanics, linear algebra, and postulates of quantum theory. In Section 3.3.3, different techniques are discussed authors used to analyze quantum supremacy and several computational paradigms such as sampling and optimization. Section 3.3.4 includes examples, proofs of concept, actual uses of QC technologies, their potential nowadays, and an overall discussion about their efficiency. Finally, Section 3.3.5 sums up the work done in the chapter, laying out the main conclusions and directions for further development of the topic.

3.3 RELATED WORK

3.3.1 Quantum Mechanics

Quantum mechanics provides the most accurate and thorough account of the known universe. It also provides the basis for considering quantum information and quantum multiplication. To comprehend quantum mechanics, there is no prerequisite. Quantum physics is easy to learn, despite being a difficult subject. The standing stems from the complexity of some submissions, such as comprehending the assembly of challenging compounds, which are not crucial to knowing the topic; thus, we won't be discussing them. Only having a working knowledge of fundamental linear algebra is required for compassion [10]. Even someone who has never studied the subject before can begin to solve simple problems in a few hours with this foundation.

3.3.2 Linear Algebra

Learning of vector spaces (VC) and linear processes on individuals is known as linear algebra. A strong command of elementary linear algebra is a prerequisite for a decent understanding of quantum mechanics. In this segment, we examine several fundamental perceptions in linear algebra and identify the common representations context of quantum mechanics research. Table 3.1 presents these concise notations with the linear algebraic report in the right column and the quantum representation in the left column. We believe that the substantial body of linear algebraic concepts necessary to implement the quantum mechanical hypotheses, rather than the hypotheses themselves, is the main obstacle to their integration. When combined with the uncommon Dirac representation that physicists adopt for quantum mechanics, it might give the notion a (falsely) impressive appearance. Aimed at these details, we advise the bookworm unfamiliar with quantum mechanics to skim finished the quantifiable that shadows, stopping primarily to think about taking into account the overall fundamentals of the representation in use. Then move on to a careful examination of the chapter's primary topic, the quantum mechanical hypotheses, making sure to regularly study the more complicated notations and principles of required linear algebra [11].

A usual of vectors $|v_1\rangle,\ldots,|v_n\rangle$ exists on both sides of the setting for a vector space, slightly vector $|v\rangle$ in the VC container to be expressed as a direct mixture $|v\rangle \sum_i a_i |v_i\rangle$ of the vectors in that usual [12]. For the vector space C_2, an instance of a usual with elements on both sides is the set (Eq. 3.21):

$$|v_1\rangle \equiv \begin{bmatrix} 1 \\ 0 \end{bmatrix}; |v_2\rangle \equiv \begin{bmatrix} 0 \\ 1 \end{bmatrix} \tag{3.21}$$

The following vector (Eq. 3.22):

$$|v\rangle = \begin{bmatrix} a_1 \\ a_2 \end{bmatrix} \tag{3.22}$$

can be expressed in C_2 as a direct mixing of the vectors $|v1\rangle$ and $|v2\rangle$, where $|v\rangle = a_1|v_1\rangle + a_2|v_2\rangle$. The vectors $|v1\rangle$ and $|v2\rangle$ are said to span the vector space C_2. In general, there may be numerous differences on both sides of sets in a vector space. For the vector space C_2, a second on either side of a set is the set (Eq. 3.23):

$$|v_1\rangle \equiv \frac{1}{\sqrt{2}}\begin{bmatrix} 1 \\ 1 \end{bmatrix}; |v_2\rangle \equiv \frac{1}{\sqrt{2}}\begin{bmatrix} 1 \\ -1 \end{bmatrix} \tag{3.23}$$

TABLE 3.1
Quantum Mechanical Notations for Linear Algebraic Concepts: Dirac Notation

Notation	Description	References
$\|\psi\rangle$	Vector to $\|\psi\rangle$ known as a *bra*.	[13]
$\|\psi\rangle$	Vector known as a ket.	[14]
z^*	The complex conjugate of the z. $(1+i)^* = 1 - i$.	[15]
A^*	Complex conjugate A matrix.	[16]
$\|\phi\rangle\|\psi\rangle$	Abbreviated tensor product of $\|\phi\rangle$ and $\|\psi\rangle$.	[17]
$\phi \mid \psi$	Inner product vectors $\|\phi\rangle$ and $\|\psi\rangle$.	[18]
$\phi \| A \| \psi$	Inner product $\|\phi\rangle$ and $A\ \|\psi\rangle$.	[18]
$\|\phi\rangle \otimes \|\psi\rangle$	Tensor product $\|\phi\rangle$ and $\|\psi\rangle$.	[19]
$A^\dagger$	Hermitian conjugate or adjoint of the A matrix, $A^\dagger = (A^T)^*$. $\begin{bmatrix} a & b \\ c & d \end{bmatrix}^\dagger = \begin{bmatrix} a^* & c^* \\ b^* & d^* \end{bmatrix}$.	[20]
A^T	Transpose A matrix.	[21]

3.3.3 Postulates of Quantum Mechanics

A measured foundation for the creation of fundamental notions in quantum theory is provided by quantum mechanics. Although quantum mechanics does not provide the specific laws that every physical system must follow, it offers the mathematical and theoretical background for establishing such regulations. After a long process of experimentation, refinement, and corrections—with substantial debate and uncertainty among early physicists—the quantum mechanical postulates were eventually formulated. Be prepared if the motivation behind the basic quantum mechanical theories seems unexpected, even to experts, as this is not uncommon. In the following sections, you can anticipate gaining a firm understanding of the hypotheses, including when and how to use them.

3.4 METHODOLOGY

3.4.1 Quantum Supremacy

The phrase primarily used by Preskill in 2012 mentions computing work containing the creatively completed procedure of a quantum computer without the aid of modern, expertly rigged classical supercomputers [22]. We point out that this relates to any computational activity that confronts the standards, not unavoidably a meaningful task, as the strong term supremacy can lead to misunderstandings. The method used to demonstrate such dominance only needs to be capable of operating effectively on a quantum processor in contrast to a traditional computer where the set of rules is rigid. Popular in this segment, we review the issues that researchers are considering as they try to demonstrate quantum dominance [23]. Regardless of the particular issue raised, quantum supremacy is a significant accomplishment in physics and computer science.

3.4.2 Random Circuit Sampling

One of the most common issues to prove quantum superiority is sampling from a quantum circuit's output delivery. A quantum computer performs this process by naturally evolving the quantum state, while the unitary operators are physically implemented. The number of qubits is often scaled exponentially by traditional techniques for building quantum circuits. For example, there are 2^n possible configurations in the wavefunction an n-qubit system, especially when the system is in a fully entangled, universal state.

The wavefunction's breadths are typically complex values that need the storage of two real floating-point numbers for every length. The wavefunction requires a total memory size of 2^n breadths, 2 real numbers per amplitude, and 2^3 bytes per tangible number 2^n+4 byte, which is less than these assumptions. Remember that 2^{10} bytes equals one kilobyte, 2^{20} equals one megabyte, etc. The most advanced supercomputers have petabytes to exabytes of RAM. We may calculate the top bound of a quantum circuit reproduction for any given classical system based on our prior disagreement about the memory sources of storing wavefunctions [24].

3.4.3 Quantum Simulation

Currently, new molecular mixes are modeled on powerful classical computers. This work aids researchers in developing new sources, unique medications, and mixes for other requests [25]. We will possibly have new capabilities in this area, due to quantum computers.

3.4.4 Sampling from Probability Distributions

In several requests, including pattern acknowledgment and probabilistic implication, we use distribution samples. We can sample from a much broader circulation using a quantum CPU. As we declare later in this section, this is one of the reasons why the circulation sample is presently used to prove quantum reign.

3.4.5 Linear Algebra Speedup with Quantum Computers

In the business world, linear algebra has various uses. A mutual method called matrix capsized can be used, for instance, to compute electromagnetic shapes and create a projection. One approach that might work well for these applications is the Harrow-Hassidim-Lloyd (HHL) methodology that we discussed in the chapter.

3.4.6 Optimization

Distribution automobile steering, connected ad order plans, and combinations of various elements for electric automobile battery construction are all common optimization applications in the sector [26]. It is alluring and obvious that these kinds of systems can be improved by using quantum computers.

3.4.7 Tensor Networks

The request for quantum computation to Tensor Networks is an important and growing area of research. The online version of this book includes introductions to several excellent summaries of Tensor Networks. Many tensor network structures – multi-scale entanglement renormalization ansatz, matrix product states, tree tensor networks, and projected entangled pair states – have been shown to be valuable tools for addressing physics problems and for applications similar to deep learning networks. Many organizations have also developed a variety of tensor network submissions.

3.5 QUANTUM ALGORITHMS

What types of calculations can be performed using quantum circuits? How does that time frame relate to the calculations that can be performed using traditional logical circuits? Could a quantum computer be able to perform a task more efficiently than a classical computer? This unit discusses these problems, explains how to do classical computations on quantum computers, offers some examples of challenges where quantum computers perform better than classical computers, and gives a brief synopsis of the current quantum algorithms [27].

3.5.1 Classical Computations on a Quantum Computer

Is it possible to use a quantum circuit to implement it on a traditional logic circuit? The answer to this query must be verified. Given that scientists hope to use quantum physics to eventually understand every aspect of our environment, including classical logic circuits, it would be surprising if this were not the case [28]. Since many classical logic gates, such as the NAND gate, are integrally irrevocable, whereas unitary quantum logic gates are integrally revocable, quantum circuits cannot be used to efficiently mean classical circuits. Figure 3.3 provides a clear circuit representation of the same.

3.5.2 Quantum Parallelism

Quantum parallelism is a key component of many quantum algorithms. Quantum parallelism heuristically supports the notion that quantum computers instantly assess a function $f(x)$ for a large range of x values, at the risk of oversimplifying. In this section, we review how quantum parallelism and what are its drawbacks.

Assume that $f(x)$: $\{0,1\} \rightarrow \{0,1\}$ has a province and range of one bit, namely 0 and 1. This state is likely to be transformed into $|x, y \oplus f(x)$, which implies $\oplus$ accumulation modulo 2; the first catalog is known as the "statistics" catalog, and the additional catalog is the "goal" catalog, with the right arrangement of logic gates. The second qubit's final state is the value f if $y=0, f(x)$.

Assume we study the function on $(|0\rangle+|1\rangle)/2$ and associate U_f with a Hadamard gate on the data catalog [29].

Input			Output		
a	b	c	a'	b'	c'
0	0	0	0	0	0
0	0	1	0	0	1
0	1	0	0	1	0
0	1	1	0	1	1
1	0	0	1	0	0
1	0	1	1	0	1
1	1	0	1	1	0
1	1	1	1	1	1

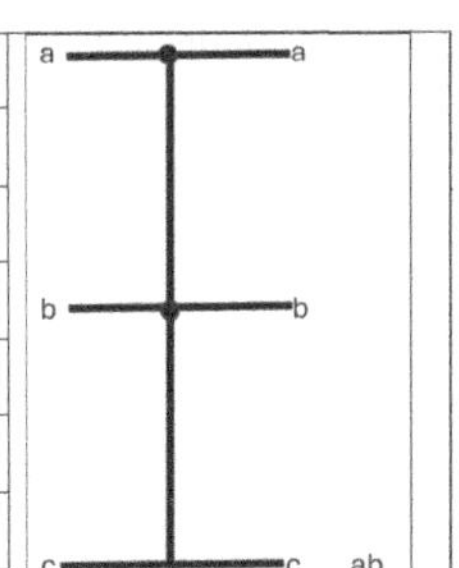

FIGURE 3.3 The Toffoli gate's truth table and its circuit representation.

The outcome state will be given in the equation (Eq. 3.24): if we run U_f with $y=0$.

$$\frac{|0, f(0)\rangle + |1, f(1)\rangle}{\sqrt{2}} \tag{3.24}$$

3.5.3 Deutsch's Algorithm

The spirits of the Deutsch algorithm are given below. Start a black box with the following two inputs, x and y, which have revenue values of "0," "1," and a goal (Eq. 3.25):

$$\alpha : \{0;1\} \rightarrow \{0;\ 1\} \tag{3.25}$$

We decide to make an effort to be constant or balanced, drawing attention to the version that.

1. α is constant if and only if $\alpha(x)=\alpha(y)$.
2. α is balanced if and only if $\alpha(x)\neq\alpha(y)$.
   - α_1: $x=0, y=1$: $\alpha_1(\text{x})=0, \alpha_1(y)=0 \rightarrow \alpha_1(\text{x})=\alpha_1(y)$ $\rightarrow\alpha_1$ is constant.
   - α_2: $x=0, y=1$: $\alpha_2(\text{x})=0, \alpha_1(y)=1 \rightarrow \alpha_2(\text{x})\neq\alpha_2(y)$ $\rightarrow\alpha_2$ is balanced.
   - α_3: $x=0, y=1$: $\alpha_3(x)=1, \alpha_1(y)=0 \rightarrow \alpha_3(x)\neq\alpha_3(y)$ $\rightarrow\alpha_3$ is balanced.
   - α_4: $x=0, y=1$: $\alpha_4(x)=1, \alpha_1(y)=1 \rightarrow \alpha_4(x)=\alpha_4(y)$ $\rightarrow\alpha_4$ is constant.

Using the formula above, we obtain the following outcomes (Eq. 3.26) if the input is 0:

$$\alpha_1(0)=0; \alpha_2(0)=0; \alpha_3(0)=1; \alpha_4(0)=1 \tag{3.26}$$

And if the input is 1, we have the following outcomes (Eq. 3.27):

$$\alpha_1(1)=0; \alpha_2(1)=1; \alpha_3(1)=0; \alpha_4(1)=1 \tag{3.27}$$

3.5.4 Deutsch–Jozsa Algorithm

One of the earliest algorithms considered to benefit from quantum computer was the Deutsch–Jozsa Algorithm (D-JA). The D-JA is more structured than classical counterparts because it is based on the principles of quantum superposition and interference.

The function in the D-JA problem is a black box expected output created by an input bit. If all of the outputs are either 0 or 1, then the function is a continuous. If the outputs are evenly split between 0 and 1, then the function is stable. Verifying whether it is constant or balanced is the task at hand, which we accomplish by perceiving outputs after suckling the black box with inputs [1–4,30–38]. These are input ranges [1–4] and dataset ranges. These ranges [30–38] refer to specific subsets of data being used in the context of the Deutsch–Jozsa Algorithm. The values within these ranges are tested as inputs to the black-box function to determine whether it is constant or balanced.

Let U_{DJ} to generalize Deutsch's method (Eq. 3.28) as follows:

$$U_{DJ} \mid x\rangle \mid y\rangle \rightarrow \mid x\rangle \mid y\rangle \mid y \oplus \alpha(x)\rangle \quad (3.28)$$

As observed above, $|x\rangle$ is a string made up of n zeros and ones. For instance, $|x\rangle$ may $|1, 1, 0, 0, 1\rangle = |11001\rangle \equiv |25\rangle$, if $n=5$. For estimating $\alpha(x)$, the following arrangement is advantageous (Eq. 3.29):

$$U_{DJ} \mid x\rangle \mid 0\rangle \rightarrow \mid x\rangle \mid 0 \oplus \alpha(x)\rangle = \mid x\rangle \mid \alpha(x)\rangle \quad (3.29)$$

3.6 TAXONOMIES RELATED TO QUANTUM COMPUTING

Table 3.2 provides a detailed classification of the QC landscape, highlighting various aspects such as software, hardware components, quantum communications, and security [35,36]. It organizes the field into primary and secondary classifications, including key tags and business categories. This taxonomy serves as a structured guide for understanding the diverse technologies, applications, and stakeholders involved in the QC industry.

TABLE 3.2
Taxonomies Related to Quantum Computing

Primary Classifications	Software	Hardware Components	Quantum Communications & Security	Quantum Computer	Quantum Sensing & Imaging	Other Quantum
			Classifications (here you can read and explore our main taxonomies)			
	Multiple software offerings	Components and cooling systems	Quantum encryption	Superconducting	Quantum dots	Consultancy
	Quantum computing applications	Other hardware	Quantum communications & security hardware	Trapped ion	Quantum wells	Private research company
	Quantum computing algorithms	Lights and lasers	Post-quantum encryption	Neutral atoms	Quantum sensing & imaging hardware	Education
Secondary classifications	Development toolkits	Multiple hardware offerings	Multiple security solutions	Silicon	None	None
	Simulators	Processors and chips	None	Photonics	None	None
	Firmware and enablers	Control hardware	None	Topological qubits	None	None
	Other software	None	None	NV diamond	None	None
			Tags (Here you can explore and familiarize yourself with our tags)			
Logistics	Advance materials	Quantum Key Distribution (QKD)	Quantum computing	Atomic Clocks	Cloud access	Leasers
	Control electronics	Consulting	Cryogenics	Graphics rendering	Quantum measurement	Quantum Random Number Generator (QRNG)
	Superconducting	Amplifier	Compiler	Microwave	AI / ML	Blockchain
Life science	Quantum realm	Quantum inspired	Quantum algorithm	Vacuum equipment	Quantum microscopy	Online news
	Quantum clock	Software	Agriculture	Media	Optimization	Telecoms
	Ion traps	Quantum dots	Quantum simulation	Machine learning	Quantum accelerator	Quantum positioning
Finance	Magnets	Quantum clock	Quantum annealing	Quantum optics	Quantum internet	Data science
	Lidar	Navigation	IoT	Material science	Workshops	On-premise
	Advertising	Full platform	Quantum networking	Key distribution	Sensing devices	Photonics
Business tags	Private company		Corporate division		Listed corporate division	
	Listed company		Public company		Non-profit	
Investor types	Accelerator	Corporate	Family office	Venture capital	SPAC vehicle	Angel investor
	Corporate VC	Government office	Investor network	Diversified investor	Listed vehicle	University investor

3.7 IBM QUANTUM CASE STUDIES

3.7.1 ExxonMobil × IBM Quantum: Taming the Monster of Maritime Logistics

- ExxonMobil works to transport the fuel with the cleanest burn around the globe, which is a conundrum that needs a quantum solution.
- ExxonMobil claims that a sizeable section of the world's population encounters daily obstacles to getting access to energy, which has an effect on public health and prevents many people from reaching their full potential. With the world's increasing population from 7.5 billion people now to a predicted 9.2 billion people by 2040, energy difficulties will only get worse [5–11].

3.8 CONCLUSION

We anticipate that both hardware and software will advance at a slow rate in this area, and that more universities and businesses will begin to understand how these developments can affect their work. As the field advances, we encourage the student to visit the volume's online companion site for additional resources and information. The industrial titan Honeywell said this week that it had developed the fastest quantum computer ever, surpassing its main competitors IBM and Google in a race for technological mastery that might produce value for the global economy worth trillions of dollars [31]. By utilizing lasers to target atoms ejected in absolute-zero temperatures, Honeywell brought the world closer to a quantum future that might offer enormous breakthroughs across fields, including healthcare, computing, banking, and mobility, especially security. Leading international technology security and policy professionals recently gathered to discuss the strategic cybersecurity issues raised by quantum technology as part of the World Commercial Opportunity Centre for Cybersecurity's Future Series [32]. Two crucial competitive circles must be jointly won by the global municipality. QC can undermine encryption, which is used to safeguard data in the majority of ideas, digital organizations, and economies. Public key cryptography is inherently vulnerable, as it is designed in a way that could be broken by a sufficiently powerful and error-corrected quantum computer, threatening the security of many critical digital systems and operations today. Key connections, encryption, and digital signatures are employed by all devices used for secure communications, e-commerce, identity, and electronic voting to protect financial transactions. These devices would no longer be able to operate if this were to occur. The geopolitics of the area may prevent quantum technology from realizing its full potential. Unlocking the transformative potential of quantum technology may face substantial difficulties due to national security concerns about gaining and keeping control of the intended capability. There is a significant risk that such concerns could hinder international collaboration and deepen existing gaps in security and industrial capability. Quantum technology has the potential to fundamentally alter national security and the information race. The development of self-governing quantum knowledge and abilities is a priority for national governments, and several nations have previously added quantum knowledge to their lists of measurable goods.

3.9 FUTURE WORK

- How did this adventure begin, though? The first QC in the cloud was introduced in 2016, and Qiskit, an open-source software expansion equipment for managing these QC, was unveiled in 2017. We revealed our growth strategy, which included our plans for making quantum computers a commercially viable technology, in 2020 [33]. We unveiled the IBM Quantum System One, the first hybrid QC system, in 2019.
- By incorporating threads into the Qiskit Runtime in 2023, the speed of quantum programs will be preserved. This will allow us to use parallelized quantum processors and mechanically reject irrelevant parallelizable tasks. We will integrate error explanation and destruction methods into the Qiskit Runtime in 2024 and 2025 so that users can concentrate on improving the caliber of the outputs generated by quantum hardware. The foundation for quantum error correction will be built using these methods in the future.
- Given that Musk himself had warned that the technology may become civilization's "greatest existential threat" if governments don't control it, the scandal surrounding AI is not shocking. However, the world has already lured a different, equally harmful AI demon, regardless of whether or not computers ever get human-like aptitude. As a result of governments and businesses using AI extensively to survey public spaces, monitor social media, produce deepfakes, and deploy autonomous lethal weapons, it is undoubtedly dangerous for humankind [34]. This is because modern AI is little more than an instinctive, silly system for systematizing decisions using algorithms and other technologies that, in reality, use exceptional amounts of data.
- The risk associated with the lack of any AI rules is a combination. Instead, bizarre technology firms like Google and Meta have anticipated the roles of panel and justice in all things AI. They are stifling oppositional voices, including those of their engineers who warn of the dangers.

3.10 DOING PHYSICS WITH QUANTUM COMPUTERS

One of the most intriguing possible uses of QC is the investigation of unsolved physics-related issues. Due to the Anti-de Sitter/Conformal Field Theory (AdS/CFT). division agenda. Susskind and others have staked their careers on employing quantum computers to identify this split. Although we are still far from developing quantum computers that can perform these experiments on a large scale and with minimal errors, progress in this direction would allow us to observe these states and, as a result, we can ask about their dynamic forces. We are not just exhibiting an entangled or superposition state and directing it from a traditional computer.

REFERENCES

1. A. Khrennikov, "Roots of quantum computing supremacy: superposition, entanglement, or complementarity?," *Eur. Phys. J. Spec. Top.*, vol. 230, no. 4, pp. 1053–1057, 2021, doi:10.1140/epjs/s11734-021-00061-9.
2. A. A. Zhahir, S. M. Mohd, M. I. M. Shuhud, and B. Idrus, "Quantum computing and its application," *Int. J. Adv. Res. Technol. Innov.*, vol. 4, no. 1, pp. 55–65, 2022, doi: 10.55057/ijarti.2022.4.1.7.
3. V. Mavroeidis, K. Vishi, M. D. Zych, and A. Jøsang, "The impact of quantum computing on present cryptography," *Int. J. Adv. Comput. Sci. Appl.*, vol. 9, no. 3, pp. 405–414, 2018, doi:10.14569/IJACSA.2018.090354.
4. V. Silva, *Practical Quantum Computing for Developers: Programming Quantum Rigs in the Cloud Using Python, Quantum Assembly Language and IBM Qexperience.* Apress, 2018. doi:10.1007/978-1-4842-4218-6.
5. A. Mateen and H. Amir, "Enhancement in the effectiveness of requirement change management model for global software development," vol. 28, no. 2, pp. 1161–1164, 2016. https://arxiv.org/abs/1605.00770.
6. V. Moret-Bonillo, S. Magaz-Romero, and E. Mosqueira-Rey, "Quantum computing for dealing with inaccurate knowledge related to the certainty factors model," *Mathematics*, vol. 10, no. 2, 2022, doi:10.3390/math10020189.
7. V. Moret-Bonillo, *Adventures in Computer Science: From Classical Bits to Quantum Bits.* Springer, 2017. doi:10.1007/978-3-319-64807-1.
8. M. Gong et al., "Genuine 12-qubit entanglement on a superconducting quantum processor," *Phys. Rev. Lett.*, vol. 122, no. 11, 2019, doi:10.1103/PhysRevLett.122.110501.
9. P. Chawla, A. Kumar, A. Nayyar, and M. Naved, *Blockchain, IoT, and AI Technologies for Supply Chain Management.* CRC Press, 2023. doi:10.1201/9781003264521.
10. V. Moretti, *Spectral Theory and Quantum Mechanics: With an Introduction to the Algebraic Formulation.* Springer, 2013. doi:10.1007/978-88-470-2835-7.
11. A. M. Buttar, M. Bano, M. A. Akbar, A. Alabrah, and A. H. Gumaei, "Toward trustworthy human suspicious activity detection from surveillance videos using deep learning," *Soft Comput.*, vol. 0123456789, 2023, doi:10.1007/s00500-023-07971-x.
12. M. A. Nielsen and I. L. Chuang, *Quantum Computation and Quantum Information.* Cambridge University Press, 2012. doi:10.1017/cbo9780511976667.
13. P. Kok, *Bra Vectors and the Inner Product.* LibreTexts, 2002. Accessed from https://phys.libretexts.org/Bookshelves/Quantum_Mechanics/Advanced_Quantum_Mechanics_(Kok)/06%3A_Evolution_of_Open_Quantum_Systems/6.3%3A_Bra_Vectors_and_the_Inner_Product.
14. E. W. Weisstein, *Ket from MathWorld,* 2024. Accessed from https://mathworld.wolfram.com/Ket.html.
15. U. Mathematics, *Complex Conjugate,* 2009. Accessed from https://undergroundmathematics.org/glossary/complex-conjugate.
16. A. P. Problems, *Complex Conjugate of a Matrix,* n.d. Accessed from https://www.algebrapracticeproblems.com/complex-conjugate-of-a-matrix/
17. Mathematics. *Tensor Product and Cartesian Product,* 2014. Accessed from https://math.stackexchange.com/questions/724186/tensor-product-and-cartesian-product.
18. Wikipedia, *Inner Product Space,* 2024. Accessed from https://en.wikipedia.org/wiki/Inner_product_space.
19. T. Product, *The Tensor Product, Demystified,* 2018. Accessed from https://www.math3ma.com/blog/the-tensor-product-demystified.
20. A. Corinne and T. D. Manogue, *The Geometry of Linear Algebra,* 1992. Accessed from https://books.physics.oregonstate.edu/LinAlg/book-1.html
21. M. Khurma, *Transpose of a Matrix.* Ceumath, 2022. Accessed from https://www.cuemath.com/algebra/transpose-of-a-matrix/
22. H. L. Huang, D. Wu, D. Fan, and X. Zhu, "Superconducting quantum computing: a review," *Sci. China In. Sci.*, vol. 63, no. 8, pp. 1–21, 2020, doi:10.1007/s11432-020-2881-9.
23. J. D. Hidary, *Quantum Computing: An Applied Approach.* Springer, 2021. doi:10.1007/978-3-030-83274-2.
24. A. Mateen, M. A. Anwar, S. Afsar, Q. Nawaz, Q. Yasin, and R. Odinaev, "Performance analysis on automatic number plate recognition system and methods," *Int. J. Adv. Trends Comput. Sci. Eng.*, vol. 10, no. 2, pp. 1289–1295, 2021, doi:10.30534/ijatcse/2021/1131022021.
25. B. Zygelman, *A First Introduction to Quantum Computing and Information.* Springer, 2018. doi:10.1007/978-3-319-91629-3.
26. A. Ajagekar and F. You, "Quantum computing for energy systems optimization: challenges and opportunities," *Energy*, vol. 179, no. 607, pp. 76–89, 2019, doi:10.1016/j.energy.2019.04.186.
27. P. Wittek, *Quantum Machine Learning: What Quantum Computing Means to Data Mining.* Academic Press, 2016.
28. M. Nivelkar and S. G. Bhirud, "Modeling of supervised machine learning using mechanism of quantum computing," *J. Phys. Conf.* Ser., vol. 2161, no. 1, 2022, doi:10.1088/1742-6596/2161/1/012023.
29. J. D. Whitfield, J. Yang, W. Wang, J. T. Heath, and B. Harrison, "Quantum computing 2022," 2022, *arXiv preprint*, pp. 1–13. https://arxiv.org/abs/2201.09877.
30. IBM, *ExxonMobil x IBM Quantum*, 2022. Accessed from https://www.ibm.com/case-studies/daimler/.
31. D. Herman et al., "A survey of quantum computing for finance," 2022, *arXiv preprint*, https://arxiv.org/abs/2201.02773.
32. M. D. Cavelty and A. Wenger, *Cyber Security Politics.* Routledge, 2022. doi:10.4324/9781003110224.
33. S. S. Gill et al., "Quantum computing: a taxonomy, systematic review and future directions," *Softw. Pract. Exp.*, vol. 52, no. 1, pp. 66–114, 2022, doi:10.1002/spe.3039.

34. U. Awan, L. Hannola, A. Tandon, R. K. Goyal, and A. Dhir, "Quantum computing challenges in the software industry. A fuzzy AHP-based approach," *Inf. Softw. Technol.*, vol. 147, p. 106896, 2022, doi:10.1016/j.infsof.2022.106896.
35. Taxonomy, *All Quantum Technology Data Points The Quantum Inside.* Taxonomy, 2022. Accessed from https://app.thequantuminsider.com/taxonomy.
36. A. M. Buttar, N. Arshad, and M. A. Akbar, "Innovative solutions for sustainability: quantum and blockchain technologies," In: R. Buyya, M. A. Akbar, and S. K. Garg (Eds.), *Quantum and Blockchain-based Next Generation Sustainable Computing* (pp. 47–74). Springer, 2024.

4 Future of Quantum Computing
Emerging Trends, Challenges, and Applications

Krishan Arora

4.1 INTRODUCTION

Quantum computing is a revolutionary change in computing technology that introduces a computational paradigm not possible with traditional digital computing. An important distinction is that classical computing uses bits that adhere to binary limits of either on or off; it is either 0 or 1. Quantum computing utilizes quantum bits (qubits) that exist as a superposition of both states at the same time. Quantum processors can leverage superposition and quantum entanglement to compute certain computations more efficiently than classical machines [1].

As computing keeps needing to take greater and greater sizes into measures and calculations, the limitations of conventional computing are manifest. Quantum computing offers a strong response to those limitations that classical computing will never be able to handle and will do so across all domains—including cybersecurity (with quantum cryptography), drug discovery, and material science [2].

Recognized as a disruptive technology, quantum computing has the potential to reimagine how scientists, engineers, and industries solve complex problems. This chapter introduces some of the basics of the underlying quantum mechanics principles, examines the opportunities for quantum computing, identifies the technology challenges, and highlights the ongoing research and future pathway to practical quantum systems.

4.2 BASICS OF QUANTUM COMPUTING

Quantum computing approaches data in a way that contrasts sharply with classical systems. Rather than representing information with binary units restricted to definite values, quantum systems employ qubits, which can hold several possibilities simultaneously. This is due to a quantum trait where a qubit's state is not fixed until it is observed, allowing computations to occur across many potential paths at once.

One of the more intriguing behaviors in quantum systems is a kind of deep linkage between particles, where the condition of one influences another, no matter the distance. This relationship, known in physics as entanglement, allows distributed qubits to act in coordinated ways, essential for both speed and encryption tasks in quantum computing.

Additionally, the mechanism of interference is used to direct these probabilities, reinforcing favorable computational paths while reducing less useful ones. This makes it possible for a quantum algorithm to narrow down the right answer more efficiently than trial-and-error techniques used in classical computing.

Despite their promise, quantum systems face several technical hurdles. These include maintaining coherence in unstable environments and preventing the accumulation of minor errors that disrupt accuracy. Researchers continue to work on building scalable systems with error-correcting protocols to ensure stable and functional quantum operations.

4.3 OBJECTIVES

The primary goals of this work are to:

- Describe foundational concepts for quantum computing: qubits, superposition, entanglement, and key quantum algorithms.
- Discuss current challenges facing quantum computers: Decoherence, hardware limitations, error correction techniques, and software limitations [3].
- Discuss the future of quantum computing: Rising hardware manufacturers, importance of a multidisciplinary approach, effects on society, and international standards.

4.4 QUBITS

Quantum computing relies on a fundamental unit known as the qubit, which differs significantly from the classical binary bit. Unlike conventional bits that can represent only one of two fixed values, qubits possess the capacity to exist in multiple states at once, a behavior rooted in quantum superposition. This characteristic enables quantum processors to explore a broader solution space during computation [4].

The ability of a qubit to encode overlapping probabilities enhances the system's capacity for parallel processing. As a result, certain computational problems may be solved more efficiently compared to traditional digital systems.

DOI: 10.1201/9781003530800-4

4.4.1 Representation of Qubits in Quantum Systems

Qubits can be physically implemented using a range of quantum systems. Common approaches include encoding information in the spin state of an electron, the polarization of a photon, or specific energy levels within superconducting circuits. For instance, when using electron spin as the physical medium, the spin aligned upward may correspond to the $|0\rangle$ basis state, while a downward orientation can represent the $|1\rangle$ basis state.

These physical representations serve as practical platforms for constructing and manipulating qubits, each with its own advantages in terms of coherence time, scalability, and ease of control. The choice of system often depends on the specific requirements of the quantum algorithm and the underlying hardware architecture.

4.4.2 Mathematical Formalism of Qubits

In quantum mechanics notation, qubit states can be expressed using Dirac notation like $|0\rangle$ and $|1\rangle$, the two basis states. A general qubit state is a linear combination (or superposition) of the two basis states and is written as $|\psi\rangle=\alpha|0\rangle+\beta|1\rangle$. The coefficients α and β are complex numbers, known as probability amplitudes, that express the probability of measuring the qubit in either of the basis states if measured [5].

4.5 SUPERPOSITION

Superposition is an important aspect of quantum systems because it allows a system to exist in multiple states at the same time. This means that qubits are able to store and process information in both the $|0\rangle$ and $|1\rangle$ states simultaneously, enabling computations that are fundamentally infeasible classically [6].

4.5.1 Explanation of Superposition

A qubit in superposition is similar to a probabilistic mix of the $|0\rangle$ and $|1\rangle$ states. We can write a qubit state as $|\psi\rangle=\alpha|0\rangle+\beta|1\rangle$; where the probability amplitudes α and β follow the normalization condition $|\alpha|^2+|\beta|^2=1$ [7].

4.6 ENTANGLEMENT

Entanglement occurs when the quantum state of a composite system cannot be expressed as the product of the quantum state of its constituent/core units. This means that one particle's qualities are intrinsically associated with another particle's qualities despite their differences [8]. Entanglement is illustrated in Figure 4.1, and it is recognized for quantum computing as a means to obtain strong quantum algorithms and protocols.

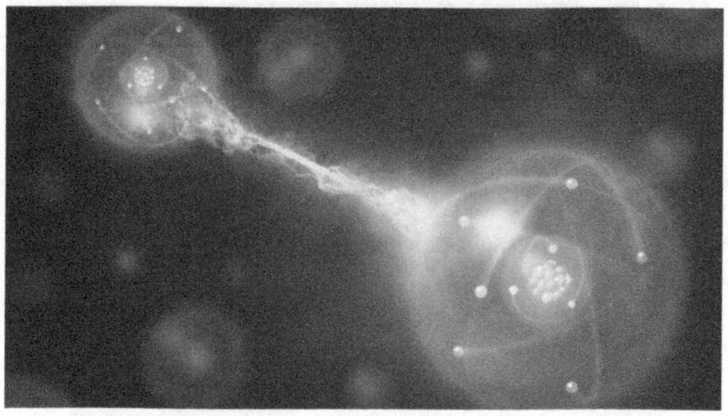

FIGURE 4.1 Entanglement computing.

4.6.1 EPR Paradox and Bell's Theorem

The Einstein–Podolsky–Rosen (EPR) paradox and Bell's theorem jointly provide the theoretical framework to understand entanglement and its implications. The EPR paradox suggests that quantum mechanics may exhibit nonlocal correlations between entangled particles, whereas Bell's theorem excludes only the possibility of eliminating hidden variables that explain such correlations.

4.6.2 Applications of Entanglement

Entanglement is utilized in numerous quantum protocols and technologies with quantum error rectification, quantum cryptography, and quantum teleportation.

4.7 QUANTUM CIRCUITS

Quantum circuits are the essential element of quantum algorithms, which consist of interconnected quantum gates that manipulate qubits to perform computational tasks.

4.7.1 Introduction to Quantum Circuits

Quantum circuits complete the counterparts of classical circuits but function like qubits in place of traditional bits. They consist of a series of quantum gates applied to qubits to perform computations.

4.7.2 Circuit Examples

Quantum circuits are often represented diagrammatically, with qubits represented as lines and quantum gates represented as symbols acting on these lines. In this circuit, Qubit Q_0 undergoes Hadamard Gate operations, shown in Figure 4.2, along with CNOT Gate operations (unchecked) as control operations, followed by measurement with qubit q_0 [8]. For instance, a simple quantum circuit with Hadamard Gate could be followed by measurements as follows.

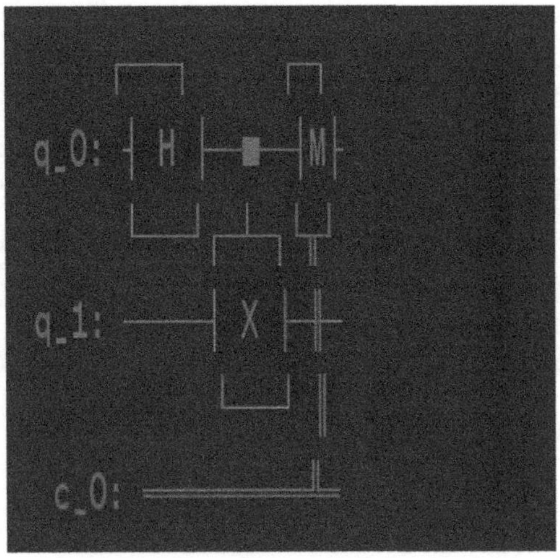

FIGURE 4.2 Quantum circuits.

4.8 QUANTUM ALGORITHMS

Quantum algorithms are computational implementations that are designed exclusively for a quantum system and are related to the essential quantum properties of a system (i.e., superposition, entanglement, and interference), as they provide speed-ups in solving particular problems compared to their traditional counterparts.

4.8.1 Overview of Notable Quantum Algorithms

There are a number of well-known quantum algorithms that exemplify the capabilities of quantum processing. The most commonly discussed and often referred to algorithm is Shor's algorithm, which can demonstrate an efficient integer decomposition of very large integers (more than a thousand digits), and consequently challenges the traditional forms of encryption. Another important quantum algorithm is Grover's database search algorithm, which essentially speeds up database search by reducing the number of operations it takes to search through the database by a factor of two (i.e., quadratic speed up) [8].

4.8.2 Explanation of Quantum Parallelism

Quantum parallelism is the term used to describe a quantum computer's ability to perform multiple calculations simultaneously. A quantum computer can evaluate many inputs in parallel because of superposition, which can make the algorithm run significantly faster and, therefore, have a greater computational reach. This is one of the primary reasons why some quantum algorithms vastly outperform classical algorithms when dealing with complex and problem-constrained spaces.

4.9 CURRENT APPLICATIONS OF QUANTUM COMPUTING

Even though quantum computers are still being developed and improved, both researchers and industries are looking to understand how quantum computing will be able to apply and solve real-world problems more efficiently than classical systems. Current applications include cryptography, optimization, and intelligent data processing, among others.

4.9.1 Cryptographic Applications

- **Quantum-Resistant Cryptography**: As quantum computers threaten classical encryption methods such as Rivest–Shamir–Adleman (RSA) and Elliptic Curve Cryptography (ECC), new cryptographic schemes are being developed to withstand such attacks. These post-quantum algorithms rely on problems believed to be difficult even for quantum systems, such as lattice-based constructions, hash-based signatures, and multivariate polynomial equations. Their goal is to provide long-term security in a future where quantum computing is practical.
- **Quantum Key Distribution**: It is a secure technique for sharing encryption keys using quantum mechanics. Protocols such as BB84 and E91 use properties such as entanglement and the uncertainty principle to detect any attempt at interception.

4.9.2 Quantum Approaches in Optimization

- **Quantum Annealing:** Quantum annealing, developed by organizations like D-Wave, harnesses quantum mechanics to find a best or near-best solution of somewhat complex optimization problems. Quantum annealing is useful in logistics, resource allocation, and financial modeling, where identifying global minima within complex landscapes is vital.
- **Quantum-Inspired Optimization:** Some optimization techniques operate on principles of quantum theory in the limit prior to complete classical quantum hardware being available. The Quantum Approximate Optimization Algorithm and quantum-inspired genetic algorithms are some examples of algorithms that utilize bits of quantum behavior integrated into classical algorithms, improving efficiency and converging on difficult problems [9].

4.9.3 Machine Learning and Artificial Intelligence

- **Quantum Machine Learning (QML)**: QML aims to leverage quantum computing with machine learning workflows efficiently to improve the speed and performance of machine learning processes, especially when working on data-driven tasks [10]. Figure 4.3 shows the logic behind QML process.
- **Quantum Generative Models:** Quantum algorithms are also being developed for generative AI tasks. Examples include quantum generative adversarial networks and quantum variational

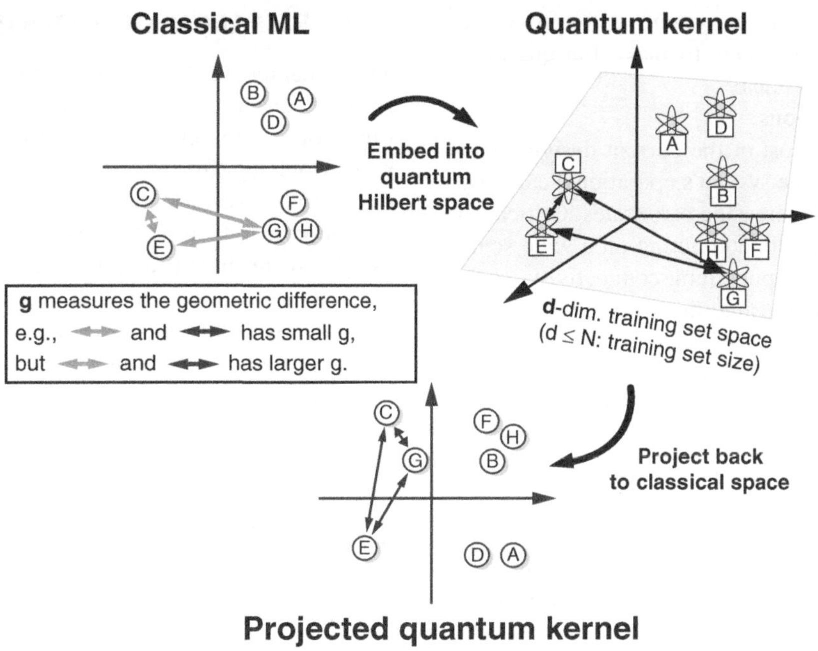

FIGURE 4.3 Quantum machine learning.

autoencoders, which could enhance applications in anomaly detection, data synthesis, and probabilistic inference [11,12].

4.9.4 Chemistry and Materials Science

- **Quantum Simulation:** Quantum computers are uniquely suited for simulating molecular interactions and quantum phenomena, as shown in Figure 4.4. This makes them valuable in studying chemical reactions, electronic structures, and material properties. Algorithms such as quantum phase estimation are used for tasks such as determining molecular energy levels.
- **Materials Discovery and Design:** Quantum computing can facilitate rapid screening of new materials with prescribed properties. The combination of quantum simulation, machine learning, and optimization allows scientists to explore large chemical spaces affordably, while producing candidates for catalysis, superconducting, and pharmaceutical applications [8].

4.9.5 Finance and Portfolio Optimization

- **Portfolio Optimization:** In finance, quantum algorithms are being evaluated for portfolio management. These techniques can evaluate large pools of assets and provide investment strategies in real time [13].
- **Option Pricing and Risk Management:** Quantum computers could increase accuracy in computing prices on complex derivatives and managing risk for more quickly changing markets.

FIGURE 4.4 Quantum simulation.

These algorithms are aiming to improve speed and accuracy in computational finance [14].

4.10 CHALLENGES AND RESTRICTIONS

In spite of the possibilities of quantum computing, there remain many technical challenges to be solved for it to be a practical force.

Major challenges include preserving quantum coherence, scaling hardware, avoiding faults, and utilizing useful codes and software tools.

a. Decoherence
    - Quantum systems are extremely sensitive to the environment, which will cause qubits to lose their quantum state, or decoherence, which will limit the time available to complete the computation before errors begin to appear.
    - **Ways to Mitigate**: Researchers are developing various techniques using quantum error correction codes of various forms and active

suppression of noise systems to improve the decoherence of qubits to make the quantum computation reliable.

b. Hardware Limitations
   - **Scalability**: Most of the current designs only add qubits to the system's operational capacity at the cost of increasing error rates. Critical to practical quantum computing on a wide scale is further developing qubit connectivity while not increasing the amount of noise.
   - **Quality of Qubits**: All gate operations, especially qubit connects, are not done perfectly yet. Improving gate fidelity to eliminate errors and increasing correlation connectivity for all protocols are key directions for future hardware generations.

c. Error correction and fault tolerance
   - **Quantum Error Correcting**: Quantum systems are highly susceptible to a variety of errors, and it's not trivial to eliminate them. Often, specialized codes incur a large overhead in qubit resources and processing time to rectify the errors.
   - **Threshold Theorem**: Quantum computation only becomes possible if the maximum rate of error is below a certain threshold. The challenge of keeping error rates below a threshold is a major obstacle that current technology faces.

d. Gate and measurement errors
   - **Gate Errors**: Quantum logic gate flaws can cause substantial computational errors. Enhancing the accuracy and dependability of these gates is paramount.
   - **Measurement Errors**: Accurate measurement of the quantum state is vital for the algorithm output. Any deviation in the process will result in incorrect outputs, so precise calibration of measurement tools remains an ongoing priority.

e. Software and algorithmic challenges
   - **Algorithm Design**: Developing quantum — algorithms that actually leverage quantum benefits—utilizing as few qubits and operations as possible—is a hard problem to solve [15].

     Software Platforms: There is no need for specialized languages such as Q# or Cirq to program quantum devices just yet, and each platform has its own compilation, debugging, and hardware abstraction issues [16].

Tackling these challenges would require collaborative research across disciplines such as quantum physics, materials science, computer science, and engineering. Successfully addressing these issues could pave the way for building practical quantum computers capable of solving real-world problems.

4.11 RESEARCH METHODOLOGY

This chapter relies on an amalgamation of literature review, conceptual analysis, and findings from the literature. Sources involve peer-reviewed journal articles, white papers, and legitimate conference proceedings with the aim of creating a well-rounded perspective about the field.

The research aimed at extracting and compiling key insights regarding the quantum computing's underlying theories, its applications, its technical constraints, and its way forward. By systematically doing so, the research hopes to bring clarity to the present state of quantum computing and its direction for the future. It seeks not just to compile what is already known but also to generate interest and further research into this revolutionary technology.

4.12 FUTURE PROSPECTS

Quantum computing is poised to revolutionize computation, offering unprecedented computational power, and unlocking new frontiers in science, technology, and industry. This section will examine quantum computing's prospects for the future and possible social effects. Quantum computing holds immense promise as a transformative technology that will reshape computation and unlock new possibilities across various domains. With continued research, innovation, and collaboration, quantum computing is expected to revolutionize science, technology, and society in the decades to come [17].

a. Advancements in quantum hardware
   - **Scaling Up the Number of Qubits**: Improvements in the production of qubits are enabling more efficient processors with more qubits and increased coherence times. Improved materials and stronger error correction techniques will have quantum machines increasingly able to tackle real-world problems.
   - **Novel Qubit Architectures**: Researchers are exploring alternative qubit architectures, such as topological qubits, Majorana fermions, and trapped ions, which offer enhanced coherence and error resilience. These novel qubit platforms hold the potential to overcome existing limitations and enable fault-tolerant quantum computation [18].

b. Quantum supremacy and beyond
   - **Quantum Supremacy Landmarks**: Quantum supremacy is a milestone where quantum supremacy over the best classical systems in a given task is attained. Not only does this landmark justify quantum competence but it also makes the field available for broader usage.
   - **Beyond Quantum Supremacy**: Beyond demonstrating quantum supremacy, researchers aim to leverage quantum computers to solve practical problems with societal and scientific impact. Applications in drug discovery,

climate modeling, cryptography, and optimization represent areas where quantum computing could bring transformative changes [19].

c. Interdisciplinary collaborations
  - **Bridging Disciplines**: Quantum computing requires interdisciplinary collaborations between physicists, computer scientists, engineers, and domain experts. Collaborative efforts across academia, manufacturing, and government organizations will hasten the enlargement and adoption of quantum tools.
  - **Education and Workforce Development**: Training the next generation of quantum scientists and engineers is essential for building a skilled workforce capable of advancing quantum computing research and development. Educational programs, workshops, and training initiatives will play a vital part in nurturing talent in the quantum computing ecosystem.

d. Ethical and societal implications
  - **Ethical Considerations**: As developments progress, issues of privacy, equity, and ethical use will increase in urgency. Use of quantum resources must be guaranteed as secure and equitable as possible.
  - **Societal Implications**: Quantum computing can convert various trades, create new economic opportunities, and address global challenges in healthcare, energy, and the environment. Understanding the broader societal implications of quantum technologies and fostering public engagement will shape the accountable growth and positioning of quantum computing [20–24].

e. International collaboration and standards
  - **Global Cooperation**: Quantum computing is a universal endeavor. Countries and organizations around the world are investing in research and development in this new field. Global partnerships will drive development faster, end duplication, and foster best practices across the discipline.
  - **Standardization Efforts**: Establishing standards for quantum computing hardware, software, and algorithms will enable compatibility, interoperability, and benchmarking across different platforms and implementations. Institute of Electrical and Electronics Engineers (IEEE) and International Organization for Standardization (ISO) are already taking the lead on this effort [25,26].

4.13 CONCLUSION

The study of quantum computing has been growing rapidly and has the potential to fundamentally alter how we think about and perform computation. The basic ideas that set quantum systems of qubits, superposition, and entanglement apart have been addressed throughout this chapter, along with the ways that these ideas underpin a novel paradigm in processing power. This chapter has examined key areas where quantum computing is already showing promise: Cryptography, optimization, artificial intelligence, materials science, and financial modeling. At the same time, substantial challenges ranging from hardware limitations and decoherence to algorithm design and error correction continue to slow its journey toward full-scale, fault-tolerant systems.

The advancement is unquestionable in spite of all of these obstacles. A robust foundation for the upcoming wave of innovation is being established through hardware advancements, the expansion of interdisciplinary research, increased understanding of ethical and societal consequences, and international standardization initiatives. Nowadays, quantum computing is a real scientific and engineering project rather than just a theoretical interest. For those who are interested in its intricacies, it symbolizes not just a subject of study but also a quest for knowledge and devotion. As research advances, quantum computing has the potential to redefine what is conceivable in science and technology and provide answers to issues that were previously believed to be intractable.

REFERENCES

1. Nielsen, M. A., & Chuang, I. L. (2010). *Quantum Computation and Quantum Information*. Cambridge University Press.
2. Preskill, J. (2018). Quantum computing in the NISQ era and beyond. *Quantum*, 2, 79.
3. Ladd, T. D., Jelezko, F., Laflamme, R., Nakamura, Y., Monroe, C., & O'Brien, J. L. (2010). Quantum computers. *Nature*, 464(7285), 45–53.
4. Farhi, E., Goldstone, J., & Gutmann, S. (2014). A quantum approximate optimization algorithm. arXiv preprint arXiv:1411.4028.
5. Arute, F., Arya, K., Babbush, R., Bacon, D., Bardin, J. C., Barends, R., ... & Cincio, L. (2019). Quantum supremacy using a programmable superconducting processor. *Nature*, 574(7779), 505–510.
6. Hidary, J. D. (2019). *Quantum Computing: An Applied Approach*. Springer.
7. Aharonov, D., & Vazirani, U. (2018). Quantum computation and hidden variables. arXiv preprint arXiv:1805.05086.
8. Cao, Y., Romero, J., Olson, J. P., Degroote, M., Johnson, P. D., Kieferová, M., ... & Aspuru-Guzik, A. (2019). Quantum chemistry in the age of quantum computing. *Chemical Reviews*, 119(19), 10856–10915.
9. Georgescu, I. M., Ashhab, S., & Nori, F. (2014). Quantum simulation. *Reviews of Modern Physics*, 86(1), 153.
10. Lloyd, S. (1996). Universal quantum simulators. *Science*, 273(5278), 1073–1078.
11. Biamonte, J., Wittek, P., Pancotti, N., Rebentrost, P., Wiebe, N., & Lloyd, S. (2017). Quantum machine learning. *Nature*, 549(7671), 195–202.
12. Perez-Delgado, C. A., Kokail, C., & Hauke, P. (2019). Quantum simulation and machine learning. *Quantum*, 3, 128.

13. Boixo, S., Isakov, S. V., Smelyanskiy, V. N., Babbush, R., Ding, N., Jiang, Z., ... & Neven, H. (2018). Characterizing quantum supremacy in near-term devices. *Nature Physics*, 14(6), 595–600.
14. Katam, N. K., Mukhanov, O. A., & Pedram, M. (2018). Superconducting magnetic field programmable gate array. *IEEE Transactions on Applied Superconductivity*, 28(2), 1–12.
15. Shor, P. W. (1994). Algorithms for quantum computation: discrete logarithms and factoring. In: *Proceedings 35th Annual Symposium on Foundations of Computer Science*, Santa Fe, New Mexico (pp. 124–134).
16. Grover, L. K. (1996). A fast quantum mechanical algorithm for database search. In: *Proceedings 28th Annual ACM Symposium on Theory of Computing*, Philadelphia, Pennsylvania (pp. 212–219).
17. Mohseni, M., Read, P., Neven, H., & Boixo, S. (2017). Commercialize quantum technologies in five years. *Nature News*, 543(7644), 171.
18. Pednault, E., Gunnels, J., Nannicini, G., Horesh, L., Magerlein, K., Solomon, E., ... & King, J. (2017). Breaking the 49-qubit barrier in the simulation of quantum circuits. arXiv preprint arXiv:1710.05867.
19. Martinis, J. M., & Kendall, M. A. (2019). Quantum supremacy using a programmable superconducting processor. *Nature*, 574(7779), 500–506.
20. Singh, P., Arora, K., Rathore, U. C., Joshi, G. P., & Cho, W. (2024). Comparative study of controllers in battery energy storage system integrated with doubly fed induction generator-based wind energy conversion system for power quality improvement. *Energy Reports*, 11, 4587–4600.
21. Sandhu, R., Channi, H. K., Ghai, D., Cheema, G. S., & Kaur, M. (2024). An introduction to generative AI tools for education 2030. In: R. Doshi, M. Dadhich, S. Poddar and K. K. Hiran (Eds.), *Integrating Generative AI in Education to Achieve Sustainable Development Goals* (pp. 1–28). IGI Global.
22. Ghai, D., Tripathi, S. L., Saxena, S., Chanda, M., & Alazab, M. (Eds.). (2022). *Machine Learning Algorithms for Signal and Image Processing*. John Wiley & Sons.
23. Ghai, D., Rawal, K., Dhir, K., Tripathi, S. L., (Eds.). (2024) *Artificial Intelligence Techniques for Sustainable Development*. CRC Press.
24. Ghai, D., Saxena, S., Dhingra, G., & Tripathi, S. L. (2024). A comprehensive review on performance-based comparative analysis, categorization, classification and mapping of text extraction system techniques for images. *Multimedia Tools and Applications*, 83, 1–158.
25. Sandhu, R., Channi, H. K., Ghai, D., Prabha, C., & Kaur, H. (2024). From stress to success: optimizing brain performance with resilience. In: S. Saluja, J. Kukreja and S. Sharma (Eds.), *Building Organizational Resilience With Neuroleadership* (pp. 194–214). IGI Global.
26. Arora, C., Sandhu, R. (2025). Adoption of quantum NLP for improved healthcare system. In: A. K. Bairwa, V. Tiwari, S. K. Vishwakarma, M. Tuba and T. Ganokratanaa (Eds.), *Computation of Artificial Intelligence and Machine Learning. ICCAIML 2024. Communications in Computer and Information Science* (vol. 2185). Springer. https://doi.org/10.1007/978-3-031-71484-9_5.

5 Quantum Encryption Techniques for Quantum Computers

Gopal Usha and Kumar Gautaum

5.1 INTRODUCTION TO QUANTUM ENCRYPTION TECHNIQUES WITH QUANTUM AI

Classification of quantum encryption techniques with quantum artificial intelligence (AI) is shown in Figure 5.1. This diagram depicts single-key encryption algorithms. Various algorithms that use the same key for encryption and decryption are also used traditionally [1–5]. This algorithm works with strong security techniques with various keys. The weakness of this algorithm includes complex key distribution and management, making them vulnerable to brute-force attacks. The strength of this algorithm lies in its simple implementation. These algorithms rely on strong security techniques involving different keys.

Rivest–Shamir–Adleman (RSA) algorithm uses the key pairs based on the mathematical difficulty, which makes it difficult to factor large integers. The strength of this algorithm lies in secure key exchange, where the digital signatures and certificates can be generated efficiently. The weakness of RSA is that it is slower than symmetric algorithms, and is also suffers from more vulnerable quantum attacks.

The next asymmetric algorithm is elliptic curve cryptography, where the security concepts are similar to the RSA algorithm. The strength of the algorithm is that it is very efficient, which uses smaller keys and faster performance. The weakness of the algorithm is that it is very complex in implementation. The next classical technique includes the secure hash algorithm (SHA), where the various versions—such as SHA2 and SHA3—produce fixed-size hash values for the input data. This hash algorithm uses integrity verification methods [6–10]. Figure 5.2 explains the overview of the classical encryption algorithm.

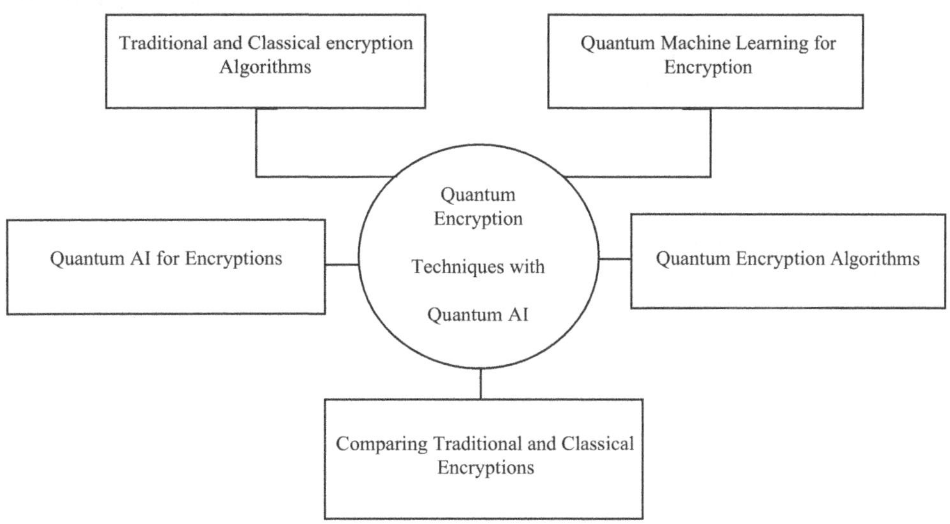

FIGURE 5.1 Classification of quantum encryption techniques with quantum AI.

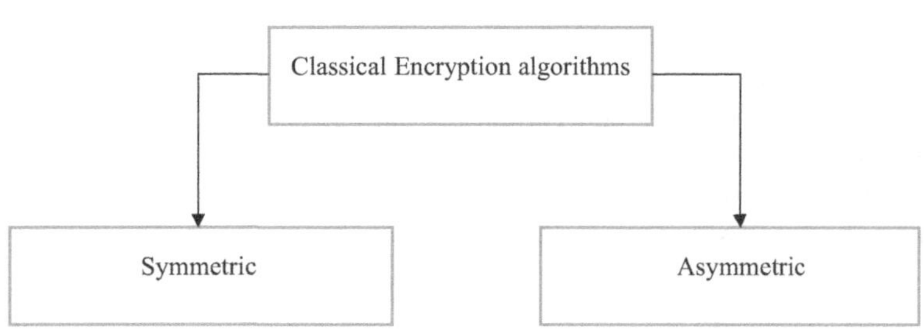

FIGURE 5.2 Overview of classical encryption algorithm.

DOI: 10.1201/9781003530800-5

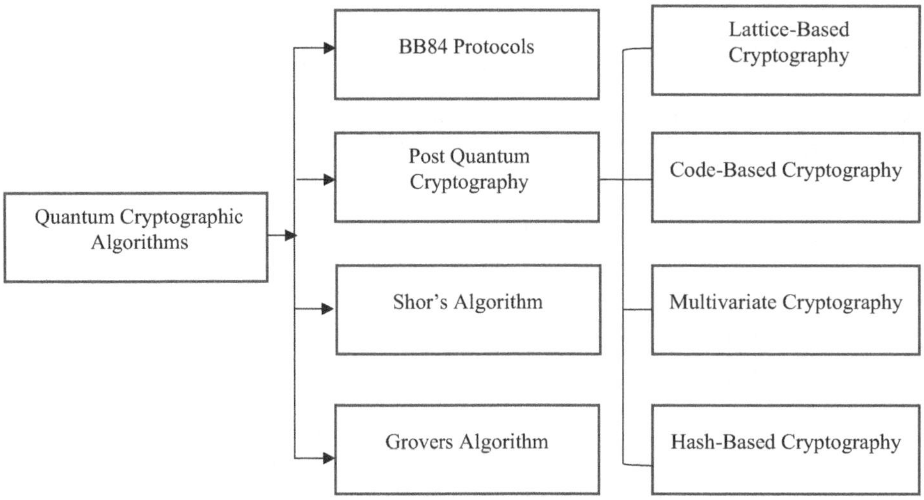

FIGURE 5.3 Types of quantum encryption algorithms.

5.2 QUANTUM ENCRYPTION ALGORITHMS

5.2.1 BB84 Protocol

Polarization states are used to represent the qubits in BB84; this is done by using the polarization states of photons and particles of light. This uses four possible states: Horizontal (0°) and vertical (90°), which form the "rectilinear" or "standard" basis. Diagonal (+45°) and anti-diagonal (–45°), which together form a base that may be called the "diagonal" or "Hadamard" basis.

The key exchange concept of the BB84 protocol includes transmitting qubits in different states, measuring the receiver, detecting the eavesdropping through error rate with shared secret key for secure communication. There are four possible polarisation states for each photon: 0°, 90°, +45°, and –45°. He picks one at random for each photon. The bases that Alice and Bob used to measure each photon are then made public, but not the exact value that was measured. Finally, both only use the bits whose bases are lined up and throw away the rest. Figure 5.3 depicts various types of quantum encryption algorithms.

Bob checks errors by properly implementing necessary error corrections. If the error rate is low, they assume no eavesdropping occurred and proceed; otherwise, they abort the protocol. The privacy Amplification is done to further shield the key against the partial information of Eve, Alice and Bob perform privacy amplification techniques in such a way that the length of the key will be reduced, reducing Eve's knowledge about this key. The key utilization [11–15] done by the shared key is used for symmetric encryption, such as with the one-time pad or some other encryption algorithm for secure communication. If Eve listens in on the conversation [16–18] while measuring the photons, she has to make mistakes that can be seen, which is why Alice and Bob know she is there. The BB84 application is the first and most well-known system for sharing quantum keys, and it is also the one that has been used the most so far. A lot of experimental and commercial quantum communication systems have tried and used it. It's the basis for safe communication in the age of quantum computing.

5.2.1.1 BB84 Encryption in Artificial Intelligence

Figure 5.4 explains the process of quantum encryption algorithms, that is, the BB84 protocol [19–23]. The following steps make an application of the BB84 protocol [24–27] in AI encryption.

5.2.1.2 Advantages of Using BB84 Protocol in AI

a. **Quantum Security**: The quantum nature of BB84 ensures that any attempted interception or eavesdropping during key distribution [24,28–30] since that interception will introduce errors in the key generation process—this makes the encryption more secure against potential quantum computing attacks.

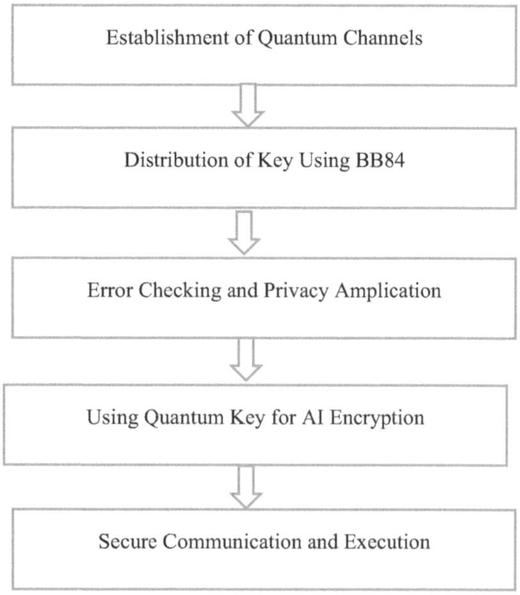

FIGURE 5.4 Process of quantum encryption algorithms (BB84 protocol).

b. **Future Proof Security:** Standard encryption built on RSA or error correcting codes would not work on quantum computers. Using the BB84 method to distribute keys makes AI systems ready for quantum computing and ensures security for a very long time.
c. **Sharing AI Models Securely:** AI systems usually share models or work on tasks collaboratively. BB84 can ensure secure exchanges that protect proprietary models and sensitive data confidentiality.

5.2.1.3 Challenges of Using BB84 Protocol in AI

a. **Quantum Infrastructure:** An implementation of BB84 assumes a quantum communication infrastructure underneath. This quantum communication infrastructure comprises quantum channels—for instance, fiber optic or free-space channels—and quantum hardware, as, for example, detectors of single photons. All these are costly in terms of complexity and expense.
b. **Error Rates and Practicality:** Quantum communication might be noisy, due to noisy environmental conditions. However, the BB84 scheme relies on low error rates. If the scheme should be practically applied, this would require error correction codes, further complicating it.
c. **Scalability:** Successful scaling of the BB84 protocol for securing communications between multiple AI [31–33] systems or across large networks will need a well-thought-out consideration concerning the architecture and key management of a quantum network.

5.2.1.4 Potential Applications of Using BB84 Protocol in AI

a. **Secure AI Training:** AI systems training on sensitive data sets can take advantage of BB84 to guarantee that the training data remains confidential, no matter if it is across nodes.
b. **Quantum-Safe AI Cloud Services:** AI cloud services will be able to incorporate BB84-based technique for quantum-safe encryption schemes in inter-AI communications and, therefore, even provide their data and model protection against future quantum attacks.
c. **Inter-AI Communication:** A network containing several AI agents, such as autonomous cars or IoT devices, can use the BB84 scheme to distribute secret keys among them in such a manner that their communication cannot be tampered with or eavesdropped.

5.2.2 Post-Quantum Cryptography

Post-quantum cryptography is a very fast-developing field that lies at the intersection of cryptography and quantum computing [34–39]. The goal is to save data from the unprecedented computational powers that quantum computers are likely to endow. Quantum computers harness principles of superposition and entanglement, promising a new generation of computational speed in the solution of a few problems, especially those on which classical computers take years to compute. The looming threat has catalyzed the development of post-quantum cryptographic algorithms designed to remain secure once quantum computers are viable for real use.

5.2.2.1 Lattice-based Cryptography

In this technique, some quite promising approaches have emerged recently, which consist of different strengths and trade-offs [40,41]. Lattice-based cryptography has established a lead, where Learning With Errors (LWE) and Ring-LWE. The lattice-based cryptography is versatile; it enables key exchange, encryption, and digital signatures, thus making it a complete solution to provide quantum-resistant cryptographic protocols.

5.2.2.2 Code-Based Cryptography

Another core approach in the area is code-based cryptography, based on the McEliece cryptosystem, whose security is founded on problems related to the hardness of general linear code decoding [4,11]. Although it came along with large key sizes, McEliece has weathered very well as one of the oldest and best-studied quantum-resistant cryptographic schemes. This robustness has risen to make it seriously considered for use in applications where key size is less of an issue, such as key sizes for securing long-term storage of sensitive data.

5.2.2.3 Multivariate Cryptography

Multivariate cryptography addresses the hardness problem of computing a solution for quantum computers. In particular, these systems allow for digital signatures. Schemes such as Unbalanced Oil and Vinegar (UOV) [14,42] can provide a possible way for obtaining quantum-resistant signatures. However, this area of cryptography is still under active research, and some schemes have proven more secure and efficient than others.

5.2.2.4 Hash-based Cryptography

The hash-based techniques are used to offer simple design which maintains strong performance. The main drawback is that these signatures can be large and one-time-use, but they provide an easy way to achieve quantum resistance [43–46]. Although in the early stage, the potential for isogeny-based cryptography remains very high in terms of both efficiency and security.

5.2.3 Shor's Algorithm

The potential applications [47,48] of this algorithm extend far beyond cryptography. In the area related to AI validation, disclosure of model components and encrypted data seems to be an important problem. This does not hold for sensitive information, and this fact may shatter the existing security strategies once Shor's algorithm is established.

5.2.3.1 Quantum Mechanics and the Foundations of Shor's Algorithm

To understand Shor's algorithm, it is essential to grasp the basic principles of quantum mechanics that it leverages:

a. **Superposition:** A qubit can represent both 0 and 1 simultaneously, described by a linear combination of these states in equation (Eq. 5.1).

$$|\Psi_1\rangle = \alpha|0\rangle + \beta|1\rangle \tag{5.1}$$

Complex numbers α and β are probability amplitudes for the corresponding states.

As a direct implication of this property, quantum computers perform parallel computations on an exponentially large number of states, therefore offering a gigantic advantage in computational power compared to classical systems.

b. **Entanglement:** Quantum entanglement is a process where the state of one qubit becomes intrinsically linked with that of another, regardless of the distance separating them.

c. **Quantum Interference:** Quantum interference can combine quantum states in such a way that some results amplify, and others cancel each other. In algorithms like Shor's, interference is used to enhance the correct solutions and diminish the probability of incorrect ones, hence making a computation more efficient. Now we discuss on shore's algorithm with its impact on classical encryption. We take the classical encryption algorithm RSA. RSA algorithm relies on factoring large prime numbers, which is infeasible within a particular time for large prime numbers. Shor's algorithm enables the identification of the factoring to find the period of a function using an equation (Eq. 5.2).

$$f(x) = a^x \bmod N \tag{5.2}$$

Quantum computers are used to solve period-finding problems, which allow to solve factoring large numbers quickly. In Shor's algorithm, quantum Fourier transforms enable the identification of the transfer of a quantum state into a form where the measurement reveals the period with high probability. Shor's algorithms are against various classical encryption algorithms that are secure against quantum attacks. Shor's algorithm has a complexity with polynomials where it solves the problems in an exponentially longer time than classical computers. For example, Shor's algorithm only uses $O((\log N)3)$, where N is the number that is used to be factored. The Shor's algorithm improves the classical algorithm by providing sub-exponential time complexity. To be more clear 2048 bit numbers are required for 4000 qubits where a few hundred qubits are not enough to run Shor's algorithm in large numbers.

5.2.4 Grover's Algorithm

This algorithm finds a specific item in an unsorted database [49,50]. The quantum state is used to represent the database with a quantum query to search the database. The algorithm uses the following steps to search the database. Hadamard gate can be implemented to all qubits where the superposition of all possible values is implemented. Then quantum query is superposition to find the items that are used for searching the values. Then the Grover iteration is used to amplify the amplitude which is used for searching.

5.3 Quantum Machine Learning Techniques for Quantum Encryption

Figure 5.5 explains the diagram of quantum machine learning technique which are intersection of Quantum computing and machine learning algorithms.

The optimization of QKD protocols includes quantum key distribution techniques with huge datasets which are used for providing security vulnerabilities and optimizes the key exchange process. Using AI models, various patterns in quantum noise are detected and analyzed. The quantum key distribution protocols improve security with the help of machine learning techniques. With the help of anomaly detection, quantum machine learnings are used to identify the irregular behaviors of unauthorized access when the key distribution process. Quantum-resistant cryptographic algorithms are used to resist quantum attacks whereas Shor's and Grover's algorithms are resistant to quantum attacks. The large datasets are subjected to various quantum attacks demonstrating strong resistance to quantum machine learning algorithms. With the help of quantum machine learning algorithms testing and verification can be done with post-quantum cryptographic algorithms which are used to secure under various attacks which are included that includes quantum computing. With the help of quantum algorithms, the security of the dynamic network is maintained by various encryption protocols and various key management practices. The implementation of these algorithms in real time faces various challenges

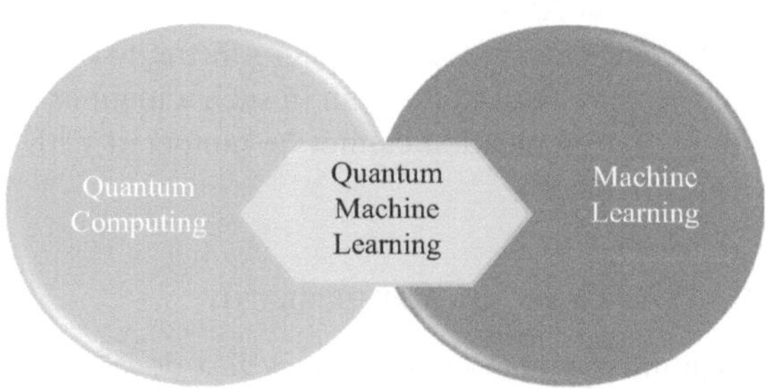

FIGURE 5.5 Quantum machine learning.

which includes limitations in quantum hardware, issues with quantum state stability, high error rates, and difficulties in scaling the systems [51–59].

5.3.1 Comparison between Traditional and Quantum Encryption Algorithms

Comparing traditional and classical encryption algorithms deals with two different ways of protecting data. Usually, traditional encryption involves symmetric methods, where only one key is used for both encoding and decoding. Classic encryption, on the other hand, encompasses both symmetric and asymmetric methods; in the former, only one key is employed, but in the latter, a pair of keys is used—a private and a public key for these very tasks. Traditional symmetric algorithms, such as the Advanced Encryption Standard, are very fast and efficient for large volumes of data because they are built on rather simple mathematical operations. On the other hand, they suffer from problems with key management, since the same key must be distributed extremely securely to all parties using it. The classic encryption algorithms, such as RSA [51], introduced the world to asymmetric encryption systems for solving issues related to key distribution by using a public key for encryption and a private key for decryption to communicate securely with each other, without either ever exchanging common secretive keys with the other. In comparison to symmetric encryption, asymmetric one is usually slower and more resource-intensive, because the operations are implemented mathematically. Therefore, it is less appropriate for large-scale data encryption, but quite useful when it comes to secure key exchange, digital signatures, and authentication. In addition, both types of encryptions are currently exposed to challenges in the face of quantum computing, which would break with the traditional cryptographic methods through algorithms like Shor's and Grover's, dictating the evolution of quantum-proof algorithms. Symmetric encryption remains dependable and fast when it is necessary to protect large information flows, especially where speed is a critical concern and key management is properly implementable, while classical encryption is a bit slower—it applies in cases requiring safe key exchange and digital signature, so even in complex, scalable systems, data security is confirmed for a long time.

5.4 CONCLUSION

With the advent of quantum computing and AI, strong methods of quantum encryption become more and more critical. Quantum computing will be able to wind off a great number of problems that are intractable by classical computers; it is this same power that has the potential to undermine traditional encryption methods. By introducing new dimensions of challenges and, similarly, opportunities, quantum AI employed the computing power of quantum to further machine learning and AI, thus enabling quantum encryption techniques in the said scope. This conclusion thus looks into the need for these techniques in protecting data, making sure that communication is secure, and given the future threats arising from quantum. Quantum encryption, particularly quantum key distribution, is the vanguard frontier of quantum information security. QKD employs the principles of quantum mechanics, such as superposition and entanglement principles, in setting up secure platforms of communication that cannot be eavesdropped upon. Classical encryption schemes, on the other hand, are based on hardness assumptions against computation, and quantum encryption is done based on physical laws. This makes it an essential element of classified information protection against classical and quantum attacks. Shor's algorithm is a quantum algorithm that can efficiently solve these problems and thus realizes most of the traditional cryptographic techniques. In this regard, quantum encryption methods, such as QKD, explicitly define the process for a highly secure key distribution scheme, such that, even in the era of powerful quantum computers, data integrity and confidentiality are maintained. Quantum AI represents the intersection of quantum computing and AI in such a way as to bring the strengths of the two fields together to give better solutions to complex problems. This integration also gives rise to unique security challenges. That is, any quantum AI system that makes it advisable to process sensitive information will have to have encryption methods resistant to quantum attacks. The fact that a quantum AI could break classical encryption schemes makes the development of quantum-resistant encryption methods mandatory to safeguard data from both classical and quantum threats. Quantum resistance is the forefront requirement given the approaching quantum era. These algorithms are based on mathematical issues that are suspected to be hard for a quantum computer to understand, for example, lattice-based cryptography, hash-based cryptography, and multivariate polynomial cryptography. In the development of quantum-resistant algorithms, they need to be integrated into quantum AI systems for end-to-end security. The security promised here further extends to the data being handled or manipulated in quantum AI and the communication interlinked between quantum AI systems. As such systems interconnect and become indispensable to the decision-making processes of many important aspects of life, including finance, health, and so on, it becomes of utmost importance to keep them secure from quantum threats. Quantum machine learning, as a subset of quantum AI, allows for applications that may turn out to be far more promising for the development of encryption methods. Quantum Machine Learning (QML) might be used in the optimization of encryption protocols, detection of anomalies in encrypted communications, and development of adaptive encryption methods to answer emerging threats. For example, QML models could be trained to identify patterns in quantum noise or eavesdropping attempts, enhancing the security of Quantum Key Distribution (QKD) protocols. Additionally, QML could be applied to simulations and tests on the security of post-quantum cryptographic algorithms that ensure their robustness against quantum attacks. QML, being powered by quantum computation, will be capable of an enhanced exploration of datasets and exploration in cryptographic structures, which cannot be done by classical methods, and hence pave the way for the development of more secure encryption techniques.

5.5 CHALLENGES AND FUTURE DIRECTIONS

The integration of quantum encryption techniques into quantum AI systems won't be easy. Even though quantum hardware is advancing quickly today, it still suffers from problems related to qubit stability, error rate, and scalability, which in turn affect the practical implementation of quantum encryption and quantum AI. Moreover, upgrading existing systems to quantum-resistant encryption will be very labor- and coordination-intensive across industries. Some of the key steps toward a quantum future include deploying new cryptographic standards, upgrading the necessary infrastructure, and providing professionals with education in quantum-safe good practice. Looking beyond, the development of hybrid encryption systems combining both classical and quantum techniques may provide a transitional solution that offers enhanced security while quantum technology continues to mature. Modularity allows hybrid systems to combine the power of classical and quantum encryption in securing data through the impending shifts in computational capability. More than this, international collaboration and standardization will be key to the successful adoption of quantum encryption techniques. Because quantum technologies respect no national borders, standards on quantum encryption and quantum AI security at the global level will be equally critical in ensuring trust and interoperability within a quantum-powered world. Quantum encryption techniques are important in securing quantum AI systems, ensuring data handled or received by these systems is confidential, integral, and authentic in the quantum information age. As quantum computers develop in scale and power, traditional encryption will have increased vulnerabilities and quantum-resistant algorithms, and embedding quantum encryption into AI systems will be needed. Indeed, the challenges derived from this technology, like the quantum-enhanced cryptanalysis and quantum optimization of ciphering protocols, uniquely illuminate the need for continuous research and development in quantum security. The future of encryption lies at the intersection of quantum computing, quantum AI, and quantum encryption—each field lifting and reinforcing the others. The most essential things, however, as humankind moves forward into this future, are security in quantum encryption methods, strength in quantum AI systems, and prepping for an assuredly quantum-safe shift in our digital environment of today. It is under the aegis of such safeguards that the vast potential unleashed by quantum technologies may transform our world, ensuring the privacy and security of information in our hyper-connected, quantum-driven age.

REFERENCES

1. Shor, P. W. (1997). "Polynomial-Time Algorithms for Prime Factorization and Discrete Logarithms on a Quantum Computer." *SIAM Journal on Computing*, 26(5), 1484–1509.
2. Bennett, C. H., & Brassard, G. (1984). "Quantum Cryptography: Public Key Distribution and Coin Tossing." In: *Proceedings of IEEE International Conference on Computers, Systems, and Signal Processing,* Bangalore, India, pp. 175–179
3. Grover, L. K. (1996). "A Fast Quantum Mechanical Algorithm for Database Search." In: *Proceedings of the 28th Annual ACM Symposium on Theory of Computing,* Philadelphia, Pennsylvania, USA, pp. 212–219.
4. Nielsen, M. A., & Chuang, I. L. (2000). *Quantum Computation and Quantum Information.* Cambridge University Press.
5. Gisin, N., Ribordy, G., Tittel, W., & Zbinden, H. (2002). "Quantum Cryptography." *Reviews of Modern Physics*, 74(1), 145–195.
6. Rivest, R. L., Shamir, A., & Adleman, L. (1978). "A Method for Obtaining Digital Signatures and Public-Key Cryptosystems." *Communications of the ACM*, 21(2), 120–126.
7. Ekert, A. K. (1991). "Quantum Cryptography Based on Bell's Theorem." *Physical Review Letters*, 67(6), 661–663.
8. Chen, L., Jordan, S., Liu, Y. K., Moody, D., Peralta, R., Perlner, R., & Smith-Tone, D. (2016). *Report on Post-Quantum Cryptography.* NIST Interagency/Internal Report (NISTIR) 8105, National Institute of Standards and Technology, Gaithersburg, MD.
9. Childs, A. M., & van Dam, W. (2008). "Quantum Algorithms for Algebraic Problems." *Reviews of Modern Physics*, 82(1), 1–52.
10. Scarani, V., Bechmann-Pasquinucci, H., Cerf, N. J., Dušek, M., Lütkenhaus, N., & Peev, M. (2009). "The Security of Practical Quantum Key Distribution." *Reviews of Modern Physics*, 81(3), 1301–1350.
11. Lloyd, S. (1996). "Universal Quantum Simulators." *Science*, 273(5278), 1073–1078.
12. Wiesner, S. (1983). "Conjugate Observables and the Secure Transmission of Information." *ACM SIGACT News*, 15(1), 78–88.
13. Mosca, M. (2018). "Cybersecurity in an Era with Quantum Computers: Will We Be Ready?" *IEEE Security & Privacy*, 16(5), 38–41.
14. Arute, F., Arya, K., Babbush, R., Bacon, D., Bardin, J. C., Barends, R., ... & Neven, H. (2019). "Quantum Supremacy Using a Programmable Superconducting Processor." *Nature*, 574(7779), 505–510.
15. Rieffel, E. G., & Polak, W. H. (2011). *Quantum Computing: A Gentle Introduction.* MIT Press.
16. Preskill, J. (2018). "Quantum Computing in the NISQ Era and Beyond." *Quantum*, 2, 79.
17. Dam, W. van, & Hallgren, S. (2002). "Efficient Quantum Algorithms for Shifted Quadratic Character Problems." In: *Proceedings of the 14th Annual ACM-SIAM Symposium on Discrete Algorithms,* San Francisco, California, USA, pp. 489–498.
18. Brassard, G., & Fuchs, C. A. (1999). "A Quantum Analog of Nonlocality: Bell's Theorem." *Fortschritte der Physik*, 48(9–11), 769–774.

19. Pirandola, S., Braunstein, S. L., & Lloyd, S. (2008). "Characterization of Collective Gaussian Attacks and Security of Coherent-State Quantum Cryptography." *Physical Review Letters*, 101(20), 200504.
20. Giovannetti, V., Lloyd, S., & Maccone, L. (2004). "Quantum-Enhanced Measurements: Beating the Standard Quantum Limit." *Science*, 306(5700), 1330–1336.
21. Yao, A. C. (1982). "Protocols for Secure Computations." In: *Proceedings of the 23rd Annual Symposium on Foundations of Computer Science,* Chicago, Illinois, USA, pp. 160–164.
22. McEliece, R. J. (1978). "A Public-Key Cryptosystem Based on Algebraic Coding Theory." *Deep Space Network Progress Report*, 42–44, 114–116.
23. Boneh, D., & Franklin, M. (2001). "Identity-Based Encryption from the Weil Pairing." *SIAM Journal on Computing*, 32(3), 586–615.
24. Grover, L. K. (1997). "Quantum Mechanics Helps in Searching for a Needle in a Haystack." *Physical Review Letters*, 79(2), 325–328.
25. Hogg, T., & Huberman, B. A. (2000). "Quantum Search Heuristics." *Physical Review Letters*, 88(1), 017901.
26. Ambainis, A. (2004). "Quantum Walks and their Algorithmic Applications." *International Journal of Quantum Information*, 1(4), 507–518.
27. Lloyd, S., & Weedbrook, C. (2018). "Quantum Generative Adversarial Learning." *Physical Review Letters*, 121(4), 040502.
28. Buhrman, H., Cleve, R., Watrous, J., & de Wolf, R. (2001). "Quantum Fingerprinting." *Physical Review Letters*, 87(16), 167902.
29. Bennett, C. H., Bessette, F., Brassard, G., Salvail, L., & Smolin, J. (1992). "Experimental Quantum Cryptography." *Journal of Cryptology*, 5(1), 3–28.
30. Hohenberger, S., & Waters, B. (2014). "Online/Offline Attribute-based Encryption." In: *Proceedings of the 21st ACM Conference on Computer and Communications Security,* Scottsdale, Arizona, USA, pp. 121–130.
31. Farhi, E., Goldstone, J., & Gutmann, S. (2000). "A Quantum Approximate Optimization Algorithm." arXiv preprint arXiv:1411.4028.
32. Calude, C. S., & Paun, G. (2001). "Bio-Steps beyond Turing." *Biosystems*, 62(3), 185–194.
33. Ryu, H., & Lee, S. (2020). "Quantum Random Number Generation Using Quantum Computer." *Entropy*, 22(5), 513.
34. Renner, R., & Gisin, N. (2008). "Quantum Cryptography based on Secret Keys." *Nature Physics*, 4(4), 315–319.
35. Mermin, N. D. (1985). "Is the Moon There When Nobody Looks? Reality and the Quantum Theory." *Physics Today*, 38(4), 38–47.
36. Lidar, D. A., & Brun, T. A. (Eds.). (2013). *Quantum Error Correction*. Cambridge University Press.
37. Ambainis, A. (2007). "Quantum Walks and Quantum Algorithms." In: *Proceedings of the 17th International Congress of Mathematical Physics, Rio de Janeiro, Brazil,* pp. 156–176.
38. Aaronson, S. (2013). *Quantum Computing since Democritus*. Cambridge University Press.
39. Cirac, J. I., & Zoller, P. (1995). "Quantum Computations with Cold Trapped Ions." *Physical Review Letters*, 74(20), 4091–4094.
40. Bennett, C. H., DiVincenzo, D. P., Smolin, J. A., & Wootters, W. K. (1996). "Mixed-State Entanglement and Quantum Error Correction." *Physical Review A*, 54(5), 3824–3851.
41. Calderbank, A. R., & Shor, P. W. (1996). "Good Quantum Error-Correcting Codes Exist." *Physical Review A*, 54(2), 1098–1105. doi: 10.1103/PhysRevA.54.1098.
42. Okey, O. D., Maidin, S. S., Lopes Rosa, R., Toor, W. T., Carrillo Melgarejo, D., Wuttisittikulkij, L., Saadi, M., & Zegarra Rodríguez, D. (2022). "Quantum Key Distribution Protocol Selector Based on Machine Learning for Next-Generation Networks." *Sustainability*, 14(19), 15901. doi: 10.3390/su142315901.
43. Chakraborty, A., Kouali, M., Shaqadan, A. (2025). Post Quantum Cryptography: Preparing for the Quantum Era. In: Musleh Al-Sartawi, A.M.A., Nour, A.I., Abdeljawad, I. (eds) *Business Resilience and Business Innovation for Sustainability. Studies in Systems, Decision and Control*, vol 587. Springer, Cham. doi: 10.1007/978-3-031-87584-7_210.
44. Smith, D., & Samuel, A. J. (2024). "Post-Quantum Cryptography: Securing AI Systems against Quantum Threats." *Journal of Science, Technology and Engineering Research*, 2(2), 1–17. doi: 10.64206/snz0jq38.
45. Alshaer, N. A., & Ismail, T. I. (2024). AI-driven Quantum Technology for Enhanced 6G Networks: Opportunities, Challenges, and Future Directions." *Journal of Laser Science and Applications*, 1(1), 26–29. doi: 10.21608/jlsa.2024.290093.1004.
46. Radanliev, P. (2024). "Artificial Intelligence and Quantum Cryptography." *Journal of Analytical Science and Technology*, 15(1), 4. doi: 10.1186/s40543-024-00416-6.
47. Imran, M., Altamimi, A. B., Khan, W., Hussain, S., & Alsaffar, M. (2024). "Quantum Cryptography for Future Networks Security: A Systematic Review." *IEEE Access*, 12, 180048–180078. doi: 10.1109/ACCESS.2024.3504815.
48. Kuznetsov, O., Dmytro Z., & Emanuele, F. (2024). "Deep Learning-based Biometric Cryptographic Key Generation with Post-Quantum Security." *Multimedia Tools and Applications* 83(24), 56909–56938. doi: 10.1007/s11042-023-17714-7.
49. Chhetri, G., Somvanshi, S., Hebli, P., Brotee, S., & Das, S. (2025). Post-quantum cryptography and quantum-safe security: A comprehensive survey. arXiv preprint arXiv:2510.10436.
50. Dibie, E. U. (2024). "Enhancing Cybersecurity for Renewable Energy with Quantum Algorithms and Cloud-Based AI." Journal of Advances in *Mathematics and Computer Science*, 38(11), 10–9734. doi: 10.9734/jamcs/2024/v39i111944.
51. Tyagi, A. K., Mishra, A. K., Aswathy, S. U., & Kumari, S. (2024). "Quantum Computing, Qubits with Artificial Intelligence, and Blockchain Technologies: A Roadmap for the Future." *Automated Secure Computing for Next-Generation Systems*, 367–384. doi: 10.1002/9781394213948.ch18.
52. Ghai, D., Tripathi, S. L., Saxena, S., Chanda, M., & Alazab, M. (Eds.). (2022). *Machine Learning Algorithms for Signal and Image Processing.* John Wiley & Sons.
53. Ghai, D., Rawal, K., Dhir, K., & Tripathi, S. L. (Eds.). (2024). *Artificial Intelligence Techniques for Sustainable Development.* CRC Press.
54. Ghai, D., Saxena, S., Dhingra, G., & Tripathi, S. L. (2024). "A Comprehensive Review on Performance-based Comparative Analysis, Categorization, Classification and Mapping of Text Extraction System Techniques for Images." *Multimedia Tools and Applications*, 84(5), 2327–2484.
55. Sandhu, R., Channi, H. K., Ghai, D., Cheema, G. S., & Kaur, M. (2024). "An Introduction to Generative AI Tools for Education 2030." In: R. Doshi, M. Dadhich, S. Poddar, &

K. K. Hiran (Eds.), *Integrating Generative AI in Education to Achieve Sustainable Development Goals* (pp. 1–28). IGI Global.

56. Arora, C., Sandhu, R. (2025). Adoption of Quantum NLP for Improved Healthcare System. In: A. K. Bairwa, V. Tiwari, S. K. Vishwakarma, M. Tuba, & T. Ganokratanaa (Eds.), *Computation of Artificial Intelligence and Machine Learning. ICCAIML 2024. Communications in Computer and Information Science* (vol. 2185, pp. 51–59). Springer. https://doi.org/10.1007/978-3-031-71484-9_5.
57. Sandhu, R., Kumar, P., Bhasin, C., Fatima, N., & Pal, A. (2023). "Resnet-34 Model for Human Activity Recognition on Smartphone Sensor Data." *International Journal of Intelligent systems and applications in Engineering*, 11(9s), 644–652.
58. Faiz, M., Sandhu, R., Akbar, M., Shaikh, A. A., Bhasin, C., & Fatima, N. (2023). "Machine Learning Techniques in Wireless Sensor Networks: Algorithms, Strategies, and Applications." *International Journal of Intelligent Systems and Applications in Engineering*, 11(9s), 685–694.
59. Soewu, T., Kaur, H., Sandhu, R., Sandhu, P., Ghai, D., Dhir, K., & Tripathi, S. L. (2025). "Machine learning models for text and image processing." In: S. L. Tripathi, V. E. Balas, M. Mahmud, & S. Banerjee (Eds.), *Machine Learning Models and Architectures for Biomedical Signal Processing* (pp. 153–177). Academic Press.

6 Quantum Artificial Intelligence and Its Benefits for Businesses

Abhishek Bhattacharjee, Ajay Kumar Badhan, Raman Kumar, and Rita Roy

6.1 INTRODUCTION

At the frontline of contemporary scientific advancement, quantum computing (QC) has the potential to revolutionize computational capacity and problem-solving skills. QC practices the ideas of quantum physics for handling quantum bits, otherwise called qubits, compared to classical computing, which uses bits to encode information as 0s or 1s. Because of these qubits' special superposition and entanglement qualities, which permit them to occur in multiple states at once and show interconnection, quantum computers can do computations at a pace and scale never before possible. QC has several potential uses, including medicine development, material research, cybersecurity, encryption, logistics, and financial optimization. It means that quantum computers have the potential to transform a variety of sectors completely.

6.1.1 Quantum Mechanics Fundamentals

Theoretically, quantum mechanics provides the framework to comprehend particular behavior at the quantum level, which forms the basis for QC. It utilizes three essential features of quantum physics [1]. They are:

a. **Superposition**: Superposition is the capacity of a quantum system to exist in several states concurrently. In a technical sense, unlike bits that are classical and present in one of the two states: 0 and 1. In traditional computers, qubits are the basic building block in quantum computers capable of simultaneously existing in both superposition modes. This allows the systems to investigate the solutions to various complex problems at once and carry out concurrent calculations.
b. **Interferences**: It allows for biasing of quantum systems toward the desired state through the use of quantum interference. The primary target is to produce an interference pattern in which the pathways that lead to the wrong answer get terminated, while the paths that lead to the right answer reinforce one another.
c. **Entanglement**: It is a fascinating phenomenon in quantum physics, where the states of two or more particles exhibit correlation, regardless of their distance from one another, so that the condition of one particle instantly affects the state of another. The entangled qubits can carry out some computations more quickly than traditional computers. This phenomenon has significant ramifications for QC.

6.1.2 Classical vs. Quantum Computing

Within computational technology, there are two radically different methods of information processing in computer technology. One among them is classical computing, and another is QC. In classical computing, bits serve as the fundamental unit of information. The states of the bits have two possible states: 0 and 1. Logic gates are designed for handling these bits by applying the sequence of logical operations that allows classical computers to perform various tasks. Even though classical computers' processing capacity and efficiency have greatly increased, they still have constraints in handling massive data and solving complex problems that can take an unfeasibly long time [2].

Conversely, QC introduces a paradigm shift by exploiting the ideas of quantum physics. The qubits that represent the fundamental building block of quantum information exist in a superposition of states concurrently in place of 0 and 1. A huge number of possible solutions can be generated by quantum computers exploiting the superposition, and extremely effective parallel processing can be obtained through entanglement that establishes a correlation between qubits. Problems like NP-hard are challenging for classical computers to solve in polynomial time and are handled by quantum computers very effectively. Similarly, contrasting the efficiency and speed of execution of conventional and quantum models can accentuate the transition to a quantum-ready world [3].

The computational models of quantum and traditional computing constitute their respective variations outstandingly. In classical computing, responsibilities are accomplished in a predetermined, sequential order through the use of a deterministic version. Then again, QC makes use of a probabilistic version wherein the superposed states of the qubits dictate the results. This enables quantum computers to explore multiple solutions simultaneously, potentially leading to exponential speed-ups.

6.1.3 Quantum Bits (Qubits)

Qubits, known as quantum bits, are the essential unit of quantum information. They leverage the aspects of quantum mechanics to exist in a superposition state. This property

DOI: 10.1201/9781003530800-6

allows the qubits to symbolize 0 and 1 concurrently, forming the foundation for QC's capabilities in parallel processing and intricate problem-solving.

Superposition and entanglement are the essential quantum phenomena that cause cubic strength development. A superposed qubit can exist in more than one state at once. The general representation of a qubit (Eq. 6.1) is as follows:

$$\alpha \mid 0\rangle + \beta \mid 1\rangle \tag{6.1}$$

where

α and $\beta \implies$ represent a multifaceted number whose squares add up to one.

Because of this, quantum computers can process a huge number of problems and provide a possible number of solutions at once, greatly boosting computing efficiency for some jobs.

Entanglement, the other phenomenon, means two qubits are entangled with each other regardless of the distance between them. The state of one qubit instantly affects the state of the other. Because of this entanglement, the systems can operate on qubits in a coordinated manner, resulting in tremendously strong computational capabilities that are not imaginable with conventional systems.

Many technologies exist for the physical realization of qubits, each of them having advantages and disadvantages. Some of the prominent approaches are:

a. **Superconducting Qubits**: The superconducting qubits (Figure 6.1) are operated utilizing microwave pulses. The pulses are essential for manipulating and controlling the state of qubits. They are used for different purposes such as qubits initialization, quantum gates, and qubit readouts. The simplified diagram for a superconducting quantum processor with three qubits, each linked to a superconducting loop, as shown in Figure 6.1.

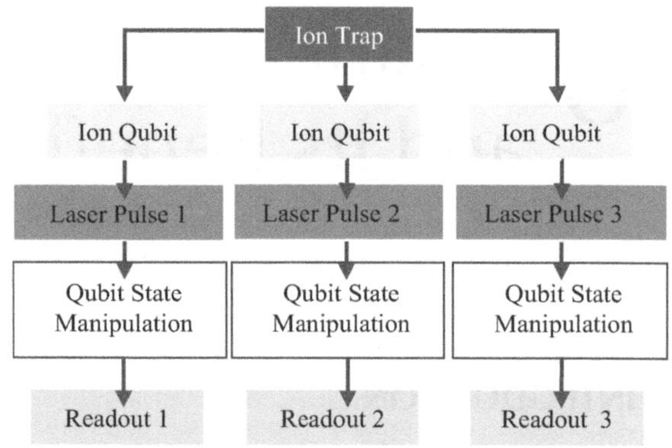

FIGURE 6.2 Essential components and operations in a trapped-ion quantum computing system.

b. **Trapped Ions**: It is one of the methods for generating a scalable and useful quantum computer. Qubits are the rudimentary building blocks for quantum information. Individual ions are constrained and manipulated by electromagnetic fields in this approach. Because of their extended coherence durations and well-known accuracy, these systems are excellent choices for QC. Even the authors, Haffner et al., in the paper [4], discussed the possibilities of quantum computers outperforming conventional computers. They have mainly focused on the latest experimental developments using trapped ions to create quantum computers. The overview includes the important experiments in the area and various implementations of qubits and quantum gates, followed by unrelated algorithmic implementations such as error correction techniques and deterministic quantum information teleportation. The simple structural view of trapped ions is shown in Figure 6.2.

As shown in Figure 6.2, the first and foremost layer is the ion trap, which confines and holds the

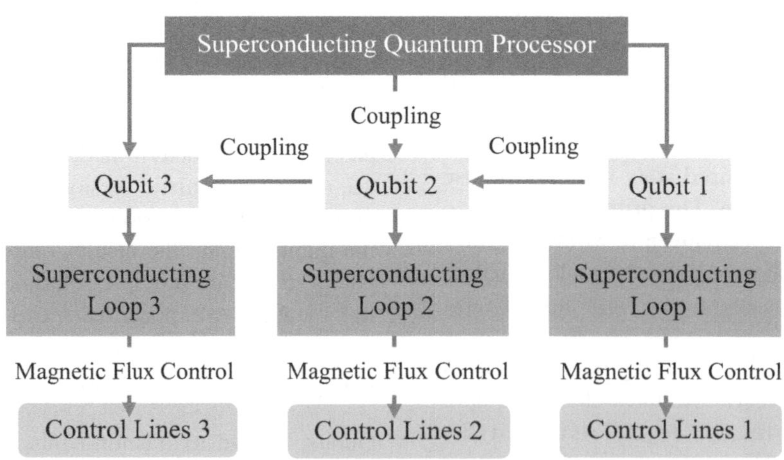

FIGURE 6.1 Superconducting quantum processor using three qubits linked to a superconducting loop.

ion qubits in place using electromagnetic fields. The second layer is the ion qubits, which can be manipulated and studied. The third layer, the laser pulse, is used to manipulate the internal ion qubits' states. These pulses can induce a transition between different energy levels of the ions. The next layer is the qubit state manipulation, and the last is the readout layer. It is the measurement method deployed to ascertain the ion qubits' ultimate state upon modification.

c. **Topological Qubits**: It is a novel method in QC that holds promises in addressing some of the longest-standing issues, including decoherence and error rates. These qubits utilize the global features of topological states of matter, which offer resilience against mistakes and local disruptions. Several researchers have utilized topological qubits to enhance quantum technologies. In [5], the resilience of a few-particle states with two topological protections, according to the author, has the potential to improve quantum technology. This work mainly focuses on the topological characteristics of a 1-D array of qubits connected to their closest neighbors through alternating inductances. The diagrammatic representation of topological qubits is shown in Figure 6.3.

As shown in Figure 6.3, the first layer is called the "Topological quantum processor", the main unit for managing the topological qubits. The second layer in the diagram represents the individual topological qubits in the processor. The third layer is called the braiding. The braiding operations are performed on the anyons that encode and manipulate the qubits' states. The last layer is the measurement layer, which reads out the state of the topological qubits after braiding.

d. **Photonic Qubits**: A potential and adaptable method of QC is represented by photonic qubits. It encodes and processes quantum information using light particles or photons. Due to its intrinsic qualities—such as limited contact with the environment—and fast transmission, photons are very beneficial and are perfect for quantum networking

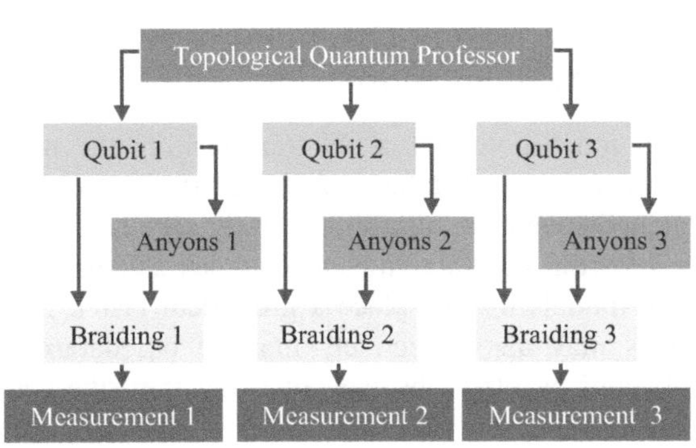

FIGURE 6.3 Topological quantum computing system.

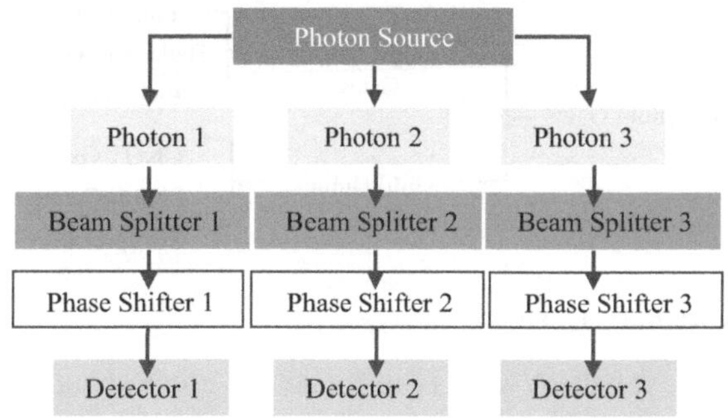

FIGURE 6.4 Basic structure of quantum computing system using photonic qubits.

and communication. Even P. Kok et al. [6] discussed a protocol for effective, scalable QC using single photons, linear optical components, and projective measurement. It highlights the important advances in theory and practice that have happened since the protocol's inception. The basic source diagram for photonic qubits is presented in Figure 6.4.

In Figure 6.4, the photon source is the source of the single photons that the photonic QC systems use as qubits. The next layer—the photon layer—is the individual photons emitted from the photon source, each photon acting as a qubit. The immediate next layer, called the beam splitters, is responsible for the edifice of superpositions and entanglements between photonic qubits by splitting the photon paths. The next layer is the phase shifters, which is responsible for adjusting the phases of the photons. These phases are used for manipulating the quantum states of the photonic qubits. The last layer is the detectors. It is used for measuring the state of the photonic qubits after passing through the layers that consist of beam splitters and phase shifters.

e. **Quantum Gates and Circuits**: These are vital components that trigger quantum computers to perform sophisticated computations by manipulating qubits. Quantum gates are the quantum equivalents of traditional logic gates operating on the tenets of quantum physics. They retain the overall probability since they are reversible and can process qubits through unitary transformations. In [7], the author introduces the idea of quantum gates and compares them with classical gates that are logically reversible and irreversible. Three bits are mandatory for the smallest universal classical reversible gates, whereas only 2 bits are required for the lowest universal quantum gates. In general, the quantum gates are classified into two types, as presented in Figure 6.5.

- **Pauli Gates (U, V, W)**: These are the basic gates for a single qubit. In this, the qubit state is flipped by the U-gate—NOT gate. The role

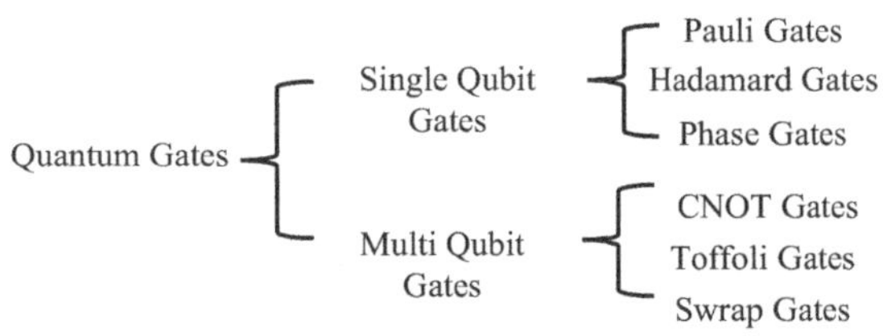

FIGURE 6.5 Quantum gate types.

of the V-gate is to rotate the qubit about the y-axis of the Bloch sphere, and the W-gate will rotate the qubit around the z-axis.

- **Hadamard Gates (H)**: The Hadamard gates are responsible for superposition states, transforming the qubit from a basis state to an equal superposition of both basis states.
- **Phase Gates (S, T)**: These gates apply a phase shift to the qubit's state. A 90-degree phase shift is applied by the S gate, while a 45-degree phase shift is applied by the T gate.
- **CNOT Gates (Controlled-Not)**: In CNOT gates, there will be two-qubit gates, where one qubit gate's state serves as the controller, and the other qubit gate acts as a target. The controller gate determines if the target gate is flipped. It acts as a fundamental gate for creating entanglement.
- **Toffoli Gates (CCNOT)**: The Toffoli gate represents a three-qubit gate in which the target qubit state is switched only if both control qubits are in the state of 1. It is called the universal gate for classical reversible computations.
- **SWAP Gate**: It exchanges the state of two qubits.

6.2 QUANTUM ARTIFICIAL INTELLIGENCE (QAI)

A growing multidisciplinary topic is quantum AI (QAI), which uses the idea of QC to improve the algorithms and applications of AI. The fundamental property behind this quantum AI is quantum mechanics, which is used for solving complicated problems faster than traditional AI techniques. It might revolutionize the fields of data analysis, machine learning, and optimization.

6.2.1 Definition and Scope of QAI

The combination of AI learning capabilities and QC processing capabilities leads to the emergence of quantum AI. The fundamental reason for using quantum algorithms in quantum AI is to perform tasks that are either impossible or extremely inefficient for conventional computers. The following is the range of quantum AI:

- **Quantum Machine Learning**: The primary goal of quantum machine learning is to improve the performance of machine learning models and train them using quantum algorithms. Support vector machines, neural networks, and clustering approaches are examples of classical algorithms with quantum counterparts.
- **Quantum Optimization**: Utilizing QC to improve the speed and accuracy of optimization problem-solving. This is helpful in industries such as material science, banking, and logistics.
- **Quantum Data Analysis**: Enhancing data processing capabilities by leveraging quantum algorithms for data classification, regression analysis, and pattern recognition.
- **Quantum Computing, AI Relationship**: AI and quantum computing have a mutually beneficial connection, with each discipline providing special advantages to the other. Many potential works have been carried out in QC and AI. In one of the papers, the author delivers an overview of the state of machine learning (a subset of AI [8]) applications on quantum computers [9]. They highlighted the boundaries of classical computers for handling huge, multidimensional data due to significant time and computational resource requirements. In addition, quantum computers consisting of qubits capable of superposition and entanglement can process large tensors making them the most suitable for machine learning algorithms. However, the major benefits of the two are provided below:
- **Enhanced Computational Power**: With the exponential speed-ups that QC offers to some algorithms, AI can now have the ability to handle huge datasets and more byzantine models.
- **Improved Algorithms**: AI approaches have become more effective and efficient due to the ability of quantum algorithms like the Fourier transform, which process information in a way that conventional algorithms cannot.
- **Scalable Solutions**: QC can be used by AI to provide scalable solutions for real-world problems. Using quantum computers, massively parallel processing power can significantly reduce the amount of time required to train the AI models and solve optimization problems.

6.2.2 Advantages of Quantum Computing in Artificial Intelligence

There is much potential of AI transforming the world in various fronts with the help of QC. More importantly, its unmatched speed can also significantly accelerate AI software, allowing such activities as complex calculations and training models to take place a great deal faster. [10]. AI packages may also effectively manage big datasets and complicated problems by way of using the inherent parallelism of quantum structures. This is especially fine for optimization duties like aid allocation and route optimization. Moreover, quantum algorithms are especially true to

TABLE 6.1
Advantages of Quantum Artificial Intelligence

Advantages	Explanation
Supercharged speed	Complicated issues can be solved via quantum computer systems far more quickly than by way of traditional computer systems, which makes tasks like training AI models or analyzing large datasets distinctly short.
Multitasking mastery	Multitasking is possible with quantum computers, corresponding to juggling many balls in the air. This implies that they can manage several tasks at once, accelerating AI strategies.
Tackling big data	Handle and comprehend enormous volumes of data more easily because quantum computers are adept at processing enormous amounts of data.
Solving tough problems	For complex optimization problems like determining the optimum route for delivery trucks or making financial investments, quantum computers excel at solving problems.
Smarter AI	By processing information more effectively, quantum computers can aid AI systems in learning more quickly and making more intelligent decisions.
Spotting patterns quickly	The ability of quantum computers to detect patterns in data is crucial for jobs like anticipating customer behavior or identifying trends in financial markets.
Fortified security	By enhancing cybersecurity protocols, quantum computers can better safeguard sensitive data and artificial intelligence systems from cyber attacks.
Faster simulations	Clinical research is aided by use of quantum computer systems, which could simulate complicated structures, including chemical reactions or climatic patterns, some distance faster than conventional computer systems.
Error resilience	Because quantum computers are more error-resistant, AI computations are more precise and dependable.
Sharper predictions	AI systems can predict future events more accurately due to the ability of quantum computers to generate more accurate predictions.
Scaling up	Greater AI tasks can be handled by quantum computers with ease, opening the door to the creation of more potent and complex AI applications.
Taming unstructured data	Unstructured statistics, such as textual content or snapshots, may be processed greater correctly via quantum computers, which enables AI structures to derive valuable insights from a variety of resources.
Understanding language	Natural language processing can be enhanced by quantum computing, which will facilitate AI systems' comprehension and response to spoken language.
Fine-tuning models	AI models can be optimized more successfully by quantum computers, improving both efficiency and effectiveness.
Efficient resource allocation	AI systems can function more effectively when resources are allocated optimally, as demonstrated by quantum computers' ability to manage supply chains and assign jobs to employees.
Speeding up discoveries	Because quantum computers can simulate complex processes more quickly, they can speed up scientific discoveries, including the discovery of novel medications or substances.
Tailored recommendations	Content recommendation systems can be improved by quantum computers, giving users more precise and tailored suggestions.
Protecting privacy	By strengthening data privacy safeguards, quantum computers can guarantee that AI systems handle personal data sensibly and safely.
Fuelling innovation	Innovation and multidisciplinary research are made possible by quantum computing, which propels advances in AI and other domains.
Transformative potential	AI and technology as we know it could be completely transformed by quantum computing, opening the door for future breakthrough discoveries and advancements.

dealing with unstructured information, including multimedia and natural language textual content, and hence hold awesome promise for trends in the AI domains such as content recommendation and natural language processing. Advanced capability for sample identity and version optimization is provided by quantum device mastering algorithms, which may bring about greater specific forecasts and higher overall performance [11]. Table 6.1 shows the advantages of QAI.

A number of the superior benefits are as follows:

- **Exponential Speedup in Computation**: In comparison to standard machines, QC offers the interesting opportunity of exponential speed-ups in computation. The utilization of quantum phenomena includes superposition and entanglement, which allow quantum algorithms to investigate numerous computing routes simultaneously, causes this high-quality acceleration. Consequently, with quantum computer systems, certain calculations that could need an unfeasible quantity of time on classical computer systems may be finished tenfold faster [12].
- **Solving Complex Optimization Problems**: The potential of QC to efficiently solve tricky optimization problems is astonishing. Quantum algorithms are capable of concurrently exploring wide areas and fast finding accurate or almost top-quality answers by making use of the standards of quantum physics. This feature may be very helpful for

optimization troubles with lots of variables and complex constraints, that are typical in lots of special industries like engineering, finance, and logistics [12].

- **Enhanced Parallelism and Simultaneous Processing**: The possibilities for improved parallelism and simultaneous processing that QC offers are unmatched, appreciably changing the character of computation. Quantum computer systems use the concepts of both entanglement and superposition to technique numerous computational tasks concurrently, in contrast to classical computer systems, which work sequentially. Because of its intrinsic parallelism, quantum algorithms may also have a look at huge solution spaces immediately, allowing for the quick observation of complex problems and large data sets. QC, which uses this simultaneous processing capability to accelerate tasks such as pattern recognition, optimization, and data analysis. This has revolutionary implications for an extensive range of fields, which include medical research, AI, and cryptography [13].
- **Handling Big Data with Quantum Speed**: A fascinating option for handling massive records at a never-before-seen speed and efficiency is provided through QC. Due to their intrinsic limits in terms of processing power and memory capability, conventional computing structures often find it difficult to technique huge amounts of information quickly. But QC can cope with large datasets in parallel because of its ability to take advantage of superposition and entanglement, which speeds up operations like data evaluation, sample preparation, and optimization. At extraordinary speed, quantum algorithms created in particular for massive data jobs may effectively type through massive amounts of data, extract insightful data, and locate significant patterns [14].

6.2.3 Quantum Computing Applications in Business

Considering its capacity to address data at a notably faster fee, QC has the capability to completely remodel numerous industries, which include business. Because of this simple distinction, quantum computers might also perform a little computations far more quickly than traditional computers. As a result, they are especially useful for handling hard statistics processing, cryptography, and optimization-demanding situations. Because of its potential to open up new avenues for commercial enterprise packages, the nexus of AI and QC or QAI, has attracted plenty of interest these days. Via the usage of quantum algorithms and device learning methodologies, QAI provides firms with the chance to enhance decision-making procedures, streamline operations, and stimulate innovation in various fields.

6.2.4 Quantum AI in Financial Modeling and Risk Analysis

Because QC offers formerly unheard-of computational capacity to cope with complicated issues, it has the capability to transform numerous industries, including finance. QAI suggests promise in financial modeling and threat evaluation in numerous areas:

a. **Portfolio Optimization**: The intention of portfolio optimization, a crucial aspect of investment control, is to bring together an asset portfolio that minimizes risk and optimizes returns. Although they are significantly applied, conventional portfolio optimization strategies—like Harry Markowitz's modern portfolio theory (MPT) aren't very good at dealing with tricky and big-scale funding situations [15]. Due to its ability to address significant volumes of facts and efficiently solve hard optimization issues, QC provides a probable way to recover from those restrictions and remodel portfolio optimization. For portfolio optimization demanding situations, quantum algorithms which include quantum variational algorithms and quantum annealing are being investigated. These algorithms scan through the full-size area of capability funding combos and discover the high-quality portfolios in terms of risk-return alternatives by utilizing the ideas of quantum mechanics.
b. **Option Pricing**: A key concept within the monetary markets, particularly in trading derivatives, is option pricing. Underneath an option contract, the container has the authority to purchase or sell the underlying asset at a predetermined price within a predetermined window of time. For buyers, traders, and economic institutions to make wise picks and correctly control danger, options pricing accuracy is vital. The usage of its processing functionality to tackle the complexity concerned in pricing uncommon alternatives or in markets with excessive volatility and non-linear charge dynamics, QC offers a feasible method to improve alternative pricing. Simulating the quantum states of underlying assets, quantum algorithms, like Quantum Monte Carlo techniques or Quantum Variational Algorithms, can extra precisely replicate their behaviour. This makes it viable to estimate choice fees more precisely [16].
c. **Risk Assessment**: A vital part of making economic selections is risk assessment, which facilitates people and businesses understand, quantify, and control specific styles of dangers that could affect their operations, investments, or normal financial fitness. With its computational functionality, QC can examine large volumes of statistics and more efficaciously and efficiently version

complex chance situations, which can improve threat evaluation approaches. QAI can help with hazard assessment inside the monetary industry in numerous approaches, including marketplace, credit score, practical, systemic, statistics safety, and lots extra.

d. **Algorithmic Trading**: The use of algorithms to quickly and properly execute trade orders is called algorithmic trading. With its unrivaled processing strength to evaluate tremendous volumes of monetary statistics, spot trading possibilities, and carry out offers greater quickly, QAI has the ability to absolutely trade algorithmic buying and selling. QAI can have an effect on algorithmic buying and selling in numerous approaches, together with handling risks, market making, quantitative modeling, market evaluation, and high-frequency trading and selling (HFT), and so forth [17].
e. **Fraud Detection**: For monetary establishments, organizations, and online platforms, fraud detection is a critical aspect of risk management. Its aim is to apprehend and forestall fraudulent behaviors like theft of identities, cash laundering, and hijacking of accounts. By means of the use of its processing capability to analyze huge volumes of transactional facts, spot tendencies, and abnormalities, and apprehend suspicious interest more exactly and speedy, QAI has the capability to revolutionize the sector of fraud detection. QAI has the potential to affect fraud detection in several ways, including recognition of patterns, anomaly detection, identity verification, transaction monitoring, fraud forecasting, and many others [18]. Figure 6.6 shows QAI in financial modeling and risk analysis.

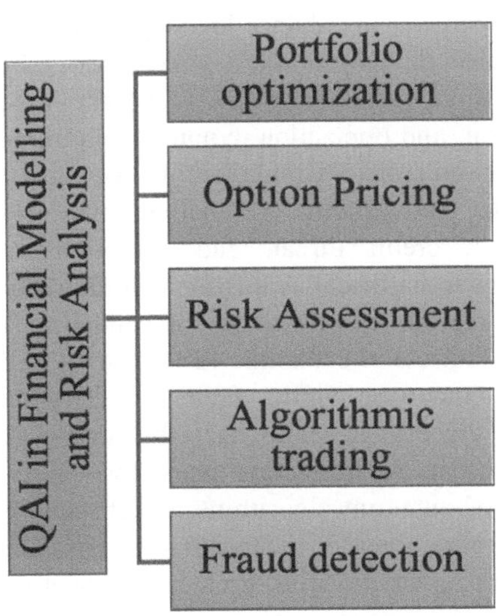

FIGURE 6.6 Consolidated diagram for quantum AI in financial modelling & risk analysis.

6.2.5 Quantum Optimization in Supply Chain Management

The use of quantum optimization in supply chain management has the potential to completely transform how businesses run their operations, distribution networks, and logistics. Utilizing the power of QC to tackle intricate optimization issues with efficiency enables companies to improve a range of supply chain functions, including predicting demand, production planning, managing stocks, and transit routing [19]. Quantum optimization can have the following effects on supply chain management:

a. **Inventory Management**: Organizations can manage their stock ranges by means of the usage of quantum optimization techniques, which take lead instances, supply chain restrictions, and variations in demand into consideration. Quantum algorithms can determine the excellent stock guidelines that strike the balance between stockouts and stock maintenance fees, enhancing stock turnover and reducing carrying charges. Those algorithms examine huge datasets of historical sales data and inventory levels.
b. **Production Scheduling**: By allocating employees, machinery, and substances correctly as feasible to lessen expenses and increase productivity, quantum optimization can improve scheduling for production. Complex manufacturing tactics may be modeled the use of quantum algorithms, which can then be used to locate the exceptional manufacturing schedules that decrease downtime, decrease changeover prices, and more effectively satisfy purchaser demands.
c. **Transportation Routing**: To reduce transportation fees and transport times, delivery chain networks can use quantum optimization algorithms to improve automobile assignment and direction choice. Quantum algorithms can determine the excellent routing plans that reduce electricity use, decrease car idle time, and improve the rate of delivery by considering variables like path distances, car capacities, and delivery time limits [20].
d. **Demand Forecasting**: By using examining substantial databases of beyond income data, enterprise tendencies, and outdoor variables like climate patterns and economic signs that could have an effect on demand, quantum optimization can improve the accuracy of demand forecasting. To estimate destiny demand more accurately, agencies can use quantum algorithms to find patterns and correlations in the facts. This allows them to adjust production and stock stages accurately, stopping stockouts or surplus inventory [21].
e. **Supply Chain Resilience**: Via the identification of feasible hazards and vulnerabilities in deliver chain networks and the development of mitigation

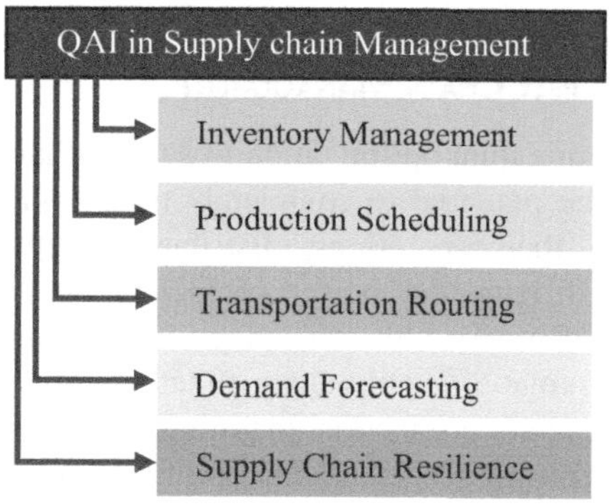

FIGURE 6.7 Quantum AI in supply chain management.

techniques, quantum optimization can improve deliver chain resilience. To lessen delays at the same time as maintaining the continuity of commercial enterprise, quantum algorithms may determine replacement procurement alternatives, means of shipping, or buying techniques. These algorithms can also analyze the impact of disruptions, along with herbal screw ups, geopolitical events, or supplier failures, on deliver chain operations. Figure 6.7 shows QAI in supply chain management.

6.2.6 Quantum Enhanced Data Analysis for Market Insights

Groups' capacity to glean vital records from big datasets and use them to make deft judgments in dynamic and complicated market situations could be absolutely converted by quantum-improved facts evaluation for marketplace insights. The potential of QC to handle state-of-the-art probabilistic models and methods huge amounts of information in parallel opens up new opportunities for deriving beneficial insights from market records. This is how marketplace insights can be impacted via quantum-better facts analysis:

a. **Pattern Recognition**: Large databases of marketplace statistics, together with beyond fee moves, trading volumes, and sentiment inside the information, may be analyzed by quantum algorithms to locate styles and correlations that could factor to abnormalities or trends in the market. Agencies can expect market movements and make well-timed investment decisions by using utilizing quantum-greater records evaluation, which uses QC's parallel processing capabilities to discover tiny styles and linkages within the records that may not be visible the usage of traditional processes [22].
b. **Predictive Analytics**: With the aid of inspecting beyond marketplace statistics and applying quantum system getting to know algorithms to predict future market patterns and practices, quantum-more advantageous information analysis might boost predictive analytics models. Due to the fact quantum algorithms are more powerful at dealing with complicated probabilistic models, it's miles possible to expect marketplace developments, customer conduct, and product call for with extra accuracy. Quantum-improved predictive analytics additionally lets in organizations to dynamically modify their plans to maximize possibilities and reduce risks due to the fact it may adjust to changing market conditions and contain new data in real-time.
c. **Market Segmentation**: Market segmentation may be improved using quantum-better records analysis, which groups purchasers or market segments in keeping with their developments, behavior, and tendencies. Big databases of demographic statistics, online conversations, and statistics approximately patron transactions may be analyzed the usage of quantum algorithms to pick out discrete market segments and better customize product services and advertising techniques to every segment's needs. Furthermore, specific possibilities and developing market tendencies that may not be visible via traditional segmentation strategies may be determined via quantum-stronger market segmentation.
d. **Sentiment Analysis**: Through analyzing massive amounts of unstructured text statistics, which includes information memories, customer opinions, and social media posts, quantum-greater records analysis can improve sentiment evaluation techniques through determining the sentiment of the general public and the market [23]. Due to the fact that quantum algorithms are extra efficient at extracting semantics that means and context from text facts, companies are better equipped to music public opinion, spot new tendencies, and recognize opportunities or threats in real-time. Moreover, companies can enhance logo loyalty and optimize advertising and marketing techniques by gaining more insights into client possibilities, brand notion, and opposition dynamics via the usage of quantum more desirable sentiment evaluation [24].
e. **Risk Assessment**: To better analyze market threat, credit threat, and operational hazard, stronger statistical evaluation can improve hazard evaluation methods by way of evaluating substantial datasets of economic facts, market indicators, and macroeconomic elements. Organizations can discover feasible hazard sources and create proactive mitigation plans by means of the use of quantum algorithms, which may simulate elaborate interdependencies and correlations in records. Additionally, greater chance assessment can offer groups real-time insights into changing market conditions and growing risks, letting them dynamically alter their threat control plans

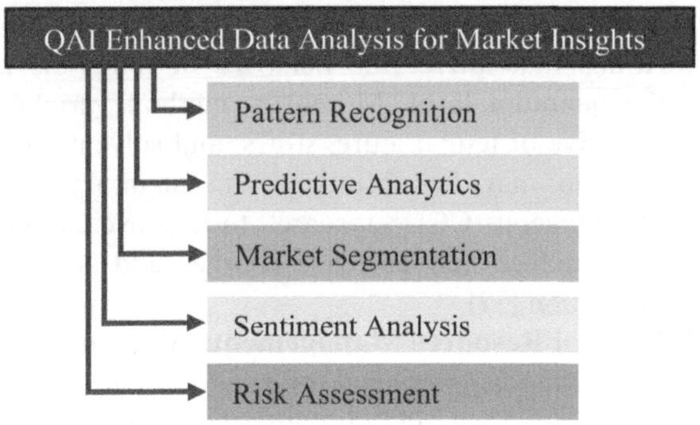

FIGURE 6.8 Quantum AI in enhanced data analysis for market insights.

to guard against financial losses and troubles with regulatory compliance. Figure 6.8 shows QAI in enhanced data analysis for market insights.

6.2.7 Quantum AI for Drug Discovery in Healthcare

There's excellent capacity for drug development in healthcare with QAI. The extensive combinatorial space of possible drug candidates and their interactions with organic structures make conventional drug discovery strategies time-consuming and pricey. This method may be revolutionized via QC, which may perform complicated calculations speedy and look at several options without delay.

a. **Molecular Simulation**: With the aid of exactly simulating atom and molecular pastime at the quantum level, QAI can improve molecular simulation techniques. With the use of quantum algorithms, researchers can also greater exactly version the interactions among medicinal molecules and biological targets, together with proteins or enzymes, improving their capacity to forecast the safety and efficacy of novel therapeutic applications. Furthermore, the identity of lead compounds and the optimization in their chemical systems for accelerated medicinal potency and selectivity can be elevated via quantum-more desirable molecular modeling [25].
b. **Virtual Screening**: By comparing full-size databases of chemicals and forecasting their binding affinities to specific therapeutic objectives, QAI enhance digital screening techniques. By means of extra effective searching throughout the huge chemical area, quantum algorithms can find viable drug candidates with the needed pharmacological features, saving money and time on experimental testing. Moreover, lead compounds with higher possibilities of fulfillment can be prioritized the use of quantum-stronger virtual screening, raising the possibility of finding novel treatments [26].
c. **Drug Repurposing**: By using inspecting organic pathways and molecules, QAI can assist in drug repurposing by way of figuring out prescribed drugs which are already available on the market and may be effective for novel symptoms. Researchers can find undetected hyperlinks among medicines and problems and repurpose current drugs for new treatments by using quantum algorithms to evaluate complicated relationships between capsules and organic objectives. Moreover, regular drug discovery methods won't be as realistic for uncommon or not-noted sicknesses; in those cases, quantum-stronger drug repurposing can accelerate the identification of feasible treatment applicants [27].
d. **Precision Medicine**: By means of evaluating affected person facts, consisting of genomic statistics, medical information, and treatment results, QAI can help precision medicine missions by determining individualized treatments for sufferers relying on their wonderful genetic profiles and contamination functions. Large affected person statistics sets may be analyzed by quantum algorithms to find biomarkers, genetic variants, and disorder subtypes that can have an effect on how well an affected person responds to remedy. This lets scientific professionals to customise care for person sufferers. Quantum-improved precision medication can also make it less complicated to build associated diagnostics and targeted drugs that maximize therapeutic efficacy and reduce side effects [28].
e. **Biological Data Analysis**: To study more about ailment mechanisms and capability remedy targets, QAI can improve the processing of biological data, together with proteomics, metabolomics, and genomics records. Massive omics datasets may be analyzed with the aid of quantum algorithms to find drug targets, signaling pathways, and contamination biomarkers that might be critical for healing intervention. Additionally, multidimensional statistics from various omics structures may be included using quantum-more advantageous organic facts processing, which enables researchers to locate elaborate networks and connections that underlie disease pathophysiology and medication response [29]. Figure 6.9 shows QAI for drug discovery in healthcare.

6.2.8 Quantum AI for Climate Change and Sustainability

via combining the analytical capabilities of AI with the processing potential of QC, QAI for climate trade and sustainability offers a unique way to deal with urgent environmental troubles. Researchers desire to create innovative methods to better recognize and mitigate climate trade, sell sustainability, and control Earth's resources by way of making use of quantum algorithms and methodologies [30].

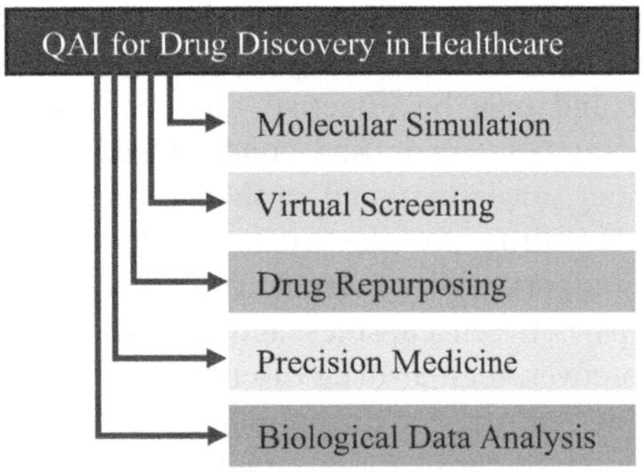

FIGURE 6.9 Quantum AI for drug discovery in healthcare.

Here's how attempts to fight climate change and sell sustainability can be impacted via QAI:

a. **Climate Modelling**: By way of extra, as it should be and thoroughly replicating complex Earth system dynamics, including air movement, ocean currents, and carbon cycle processes, QAI can enhance weather modeling methodologies. Researchers are higher equipped to forecast future weather scenarios and evaluate the feasible outcomes of weather exchange on ecological systems, financial increase, and civilizations due to the extra accurate modeling of the relationships between the physical, chemical, and organic components of the climate system that quantum algorithms provide. Moreover, through enhancing our comprehension of the comments approaches and thresholds that might both exacerbate or reduce weather exchange, quantum-weather modeling can assist increase mitigation and response plans [31].
b. **Renewable Energy Optimization**: To enhance efficiency, dependability, and sustainability, QAI can optimize the combination and operation of renewable power assets, together with hydroelectric, solar, and wind power, along with internal power structures. Massive databases of electricity production, intake, and climate patterns can be analyzed the use of quantum algorithms to improve infrastructure for the development, garage, and distribution of renewable energy. Moreover, quantum-based electricity optimization can help with the introduction of microgrids, clever grids, and electricity management systems which could decrease greenhouse gasoline emissions, balance deliver and demand in real-time, and inspire the uptake of easy strength era.
c. **Carbon Capture and Storage**: The improvement of substances and techniques for Carbon capture, utilization, and storage (CCUS) technology—which reduce greenhouse gasoline emissions from commercial operations and the production of energy—can be sped up by the usage of QAI. Promising candidates for the seize and sequestration of CO_2 from flue gases and business emissions may be recognized by the use of quantum algorithms that mirror the behavior of materials at the quantum level. Moreover, method variables inclusive of temperature, stress, and solvent composition may be optimized via quantum-more advantageous CCUS research to improve capture performance and decrease charges and strength utilization [32].
d. **Natural Resource Management**: With the aid of comparing geographical information, satellite TV for PC imaging, and climate sensor facts to tune land use, biodiversity, and surroundings fitness, QAI can help sustainable agricultural control. Big-scale environmental datasets may be analyzed using quantum algorithms to decide regions of biological cost, evaluate the quality of habitats, and set priorities for conservation efforts. Moreover, using land strategy and allocation of assets can be optimized with quantum-more suitable natural aid control to reduce environmental impacts, maintain ecological services, and improve sustainable growth [33].
e. **Climate Risk Assessment**: By evaluating weather-related risks, along with intense storms, rising sea levels, and ecological difficulties, in addition to their potential results on infrastructure, humans, and economies, quantum synthetic intelligence (AI) can improve weather threat assessment and resilience planning. Through simulating the probabilistic nature of weather dangers and modeling cascade consequences throughout interconnected structures, quantum algorithms can assist groups, corporations, and policymakers in identifying vulnerabilities, ranking the significance of mitigation techniques, and growth resilience to the results of weather alternate. Figure 6.10 shows QAI for climate change and sustainability.

6.2.9 Quantum AI for Cyber Security

A state-of-the-art method for handling the constantly changing risks and difficulties in the digital sphere is QAI for cybersecurity. Through the utilization of QC's

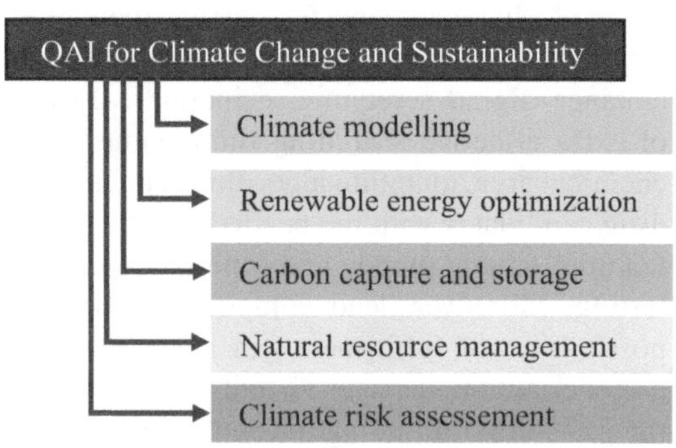

FIGURE 6.10 Quantum AI for climate change and sustainability.

computational power and cryptographic capabilities, researchers want to create sophisticated cybersecurity solutions that improve the safety of communication networks, safeguard confidential data, and fight off cyber attacks [34]. This is how cybersecurity may be impacted by QAI:

a. **Quantum Cryptography**: By the usage of the thoughts of quantum mechanics to create secure communication protocols and encryption algorithms that might be impervious to quantum assaults, AI can enhance cryptography systems. For instance, Quantum Key Distribution (QKD) techniques produce and distribute cryptographic keys securely using quantum features like entangled and superposition, providing complete protection from eavesdropping attempts. moreover, touchy statistics can be protected from decryption by destiny quantum computer systems by using the usage of quantum-resistant encryption techniques, inclusive of hash-based signatures and lattice-based cryptography.
b. **Post-Quantum Cryptography**: To protect modern-day virtual infrastructure in opposition to quantum attacks, post-quantum cryptography standards and protocols may be developed and applied greater speedy due to quantum synthetic intelligence. It's miles viable to create encryption systems that might be resistant to quantum adversaries by means of the usage of quantum algorithms to evaluate the security of cryptographic primitives and examine their resilience against such assaults. For secure conversation in a post-quantum environment, quantum more suitable key exchange protocols like the FrodoKEM and New Hope algorithms can offer a comfortable key setup [35,36].
c. **Threat Detection and Prevention**: By analyzing vast quantities of network visitors, gadget logs, and protection alerts, QAI can improve threat detection and prevention abilities by speedy identifying unusual interest and potential cyber threats. Safety analysts may additionally react quickly and decrease risks earlier than they worsen with the aid of using quantum algorithms to find patterns and correlations in data that would point to dangerous activity, which includes malware infections, data breaches, or insider threats. Furthermore, with the aid of adjusting to changing threats along with assault techniques, quantum-more advantageous chance detection structures can improve cybersecurity defenses [37].
d. **Vulnerability Assessment**: By analyzing software code, system configurations, and network topologies to find vulnerabilities and viable access sites for cyber attacks, QAI can enhance vulnerability assessment techniques. Code vulnerabilities, including buffer overflows and injection holes, may be analyzed the use of quantum algorithms, which can also compare their impact on device safety and exploitability [38]. Quantum-stronger vulnerability evaluation technology additionally permits companies to greater successfully allocate resources to address massive vulnerabilities by prioritizing protection updates and remediation efforts consistent with risk severity and feasible impact.

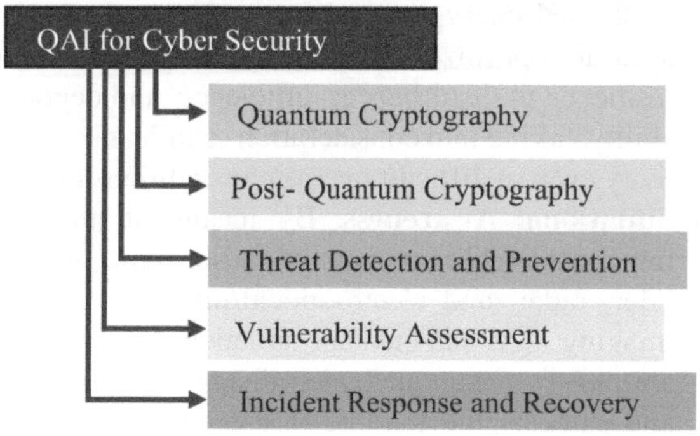

FIGURE 6.11 Quantum AI for cyber security.

e. **Incident Response and Recovery**: By investigating cyber attacks, forensically examining security breaches, and restoring compromised information and systems, QAI can improve incident response and recovery ability. Digital data, such as log files and memory dumps, can be analyzed using quantum algorithms to reconstruct attack scenarios and pinpoint the underlying causes of security breaches. Quantum-enhanced incident response frameworks can also automate cleanup and containment processes to rapidly return to normal operations and lessen the effect of cyber attacks [39]. Figure 6.11 shows QAI for cybersecurity.

6.2.10 Quantum AI in Military Equipment

A revolutionary development in military technological devices, QAI in military gear offers novel features and tactical advantages in a range of military operations. QAI allows for the development of future-oriented military systems with improved communication, sensing, intelligence analysis, and decision-making capabilities by combining QC, AI, and advanced sensing technologies [40]. This is how military gear may be affected by QAI:

a. **Secure Communication**: With the aid of utilizing quantum cryptography strategies like QKD to provide unbreakable encryption keys and shield critical navy communications from surveillance and eavesdropping, QAI can improve secure communication structures. The confidentiality and integrity of verbal exchange channels are guaranteed via quantum encryption, even if quite skilled attackers own quantum computers that can crack traditional encryption schemes. QAI can also be used to optimize communication networks for resilience to disturbances, efficiency, and dependability, taking into consideration seamless connectivity even in difficult operating conditions [41].

b. **Situational Awareness**: By means of processing considerable amounts of sensor data, such as lidar, radar, and electrooptical/infrared (EO/IR) imaging, QAI can enhance situational recognition abilities by using quick identification, monitoring, and categorizing feasible threats. More effective processing of sensor statistics and the extraction of beneficial records by means of quantum algorithms can assist army operators and commanders in making choices. Furthermore, target detection and identity abilities can be improved by means of QAI, taking into account greater accuracy and successful engagement of adversary forces and property [42].

c. **Intelligence Analysis**: By way of evaluating diverse statistical sources, consisting of open-source intelligence, signals intelligence, and human intelligence, QAI may enhance intelligence analytic abilities by seeing patterns, traits, and anomalies that would be signs of adversary activity. To expose hidden hyperlinks and networks, quantum algorithms can perform state-of-the-art record fusion and correlation. This functionality allows intelligence analysts to supply speedy and particular critiques of opportunities and risks. QAI can also assist in chance prediction and statistical analysis to foresee enemy conduct and manual proactive reaction plans [43].

d. **Autonomous Systems**: The improvement of autonomous navy systems, including autonomous underwater vehicles, autonomous ground vehicles, and unmanned aerial vehicles, which can feature both independently and cooperatively in hard and complicated situations, is made viable by way of quantum synthetic intelligence. Quantum algorithms have the potential to improve independent structures' sensing, planning, and decision-making capacities, permitting them to adapt to changing and unpredictable occasions without the need for human involvement [44]. Moreover, swarming behaviors and cooperative autonomy among several independent structures may be facilitated by means of QAI, taking into consideration coordinated activities and the accomplishment of missions.

e. **Cyber Defence**: Via reading device logs, network visitors, and safety warnings, QAI can enhance cyber protection talents by quickly identifying and addressing cyber dangers and assaults. Cyber defenders can lessen dangers and safeguard essential navy networks and structures by using quantum algorithms to come across styles and abnormalities that indicate malicious interest, which include malware infections, information breaches, and insider threats. QAI can also improve attribution and cyber threat intelligence, making it feasible to quickly and appropriately pick out and neutralize cyber enemies [45]. Figure 6.12 shows QAI in military equipment.

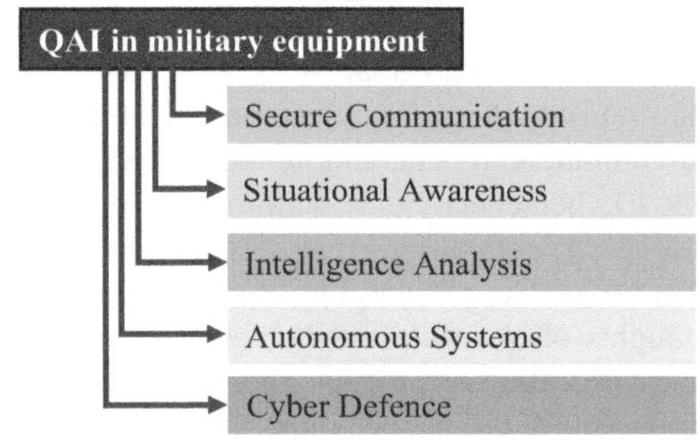

FIGURE 6.12 Quantum AI in military equipment.

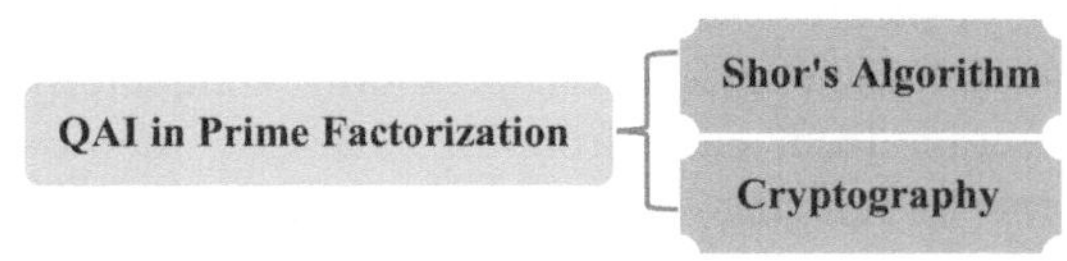

FIGURE 6.13 Quantum AI in prime factorization.

6.2.11 Quantum AI in Prime Factorization

Prime factorization is a novel use of QC that could upend contemporary encryption and computational security (Figure 6.13). This is known as QAI. For many cryptographic techniques, such as Rivest–Shamir–Adleman algorithm, which depend on the challenge of factoring big numbers to guarantee the integrity of encrypted data, prime factorization—the process of breaking down a composite number into its prime factors—is essential. This is how QAI may impact prime factorization [46].

6.2.11.1 Shor's Algorithm

QAI can factorize large integers exponentially quicker using Shor's algorithm, a quantum method created by mathematician Peter Shor. Shor's algorithm searches through a large number of possible factors at once by using quantum entanglement and parallelism to perform arithmetic operations on a superposition of states. Therefore, Shor's technique, as opposed to the exponential difficulty of classical algorithms like the general number field Sieve, may factorize huge integers with a complexity that is polynomial in the number of bits [47].

6.2.11.2 Cryptography

Classical cryptography schemes like Rivest–Shamir–Adleman and Diffie–Hellman key exchange, which rely on the difficulty of prime factorization for security, are seriously threatened by QAI's capacity to factor big numbers quickly. These cryptographic techniques would become open to discussion if Shor's algorithm could factor large numbers rapidly on a quantum computer. This could jeopardize the security and secrecy of sensitive data sent across unsecured networks. Because of this, the development of feasible quantum computers that can execute Shor's algorithm presents a serious cybersecurity threat, necessitating the development of quantum-resistant cryptographic techniques.

6.2.12 Optimized Space Exploration Using Quantum AI

QAI-enabled optimized space exploration is a paradigm shift for space agencies and commercial enterprises operating missions beyond Earth's atmosphere. Through the utilization of QC's computational power and algorithmic capabilities in conjunction with sophisticated AI methodologies, QAI has the potential to improve multiple facets of space exploration, such as mission preparation, spacecraft architecture, controlling resources, trajectory optimization, and data analysis [48]. Here's how optimal space exploration may be impacted by QAI:

a. **Mission Planning**: Through examining problematic challenge parameters, barriers, and dreams, QAI can optimize undertaking making plans and create the pleasant possible trajectories and assignment architectures. Compared to standard algorithms, quantum algorithms are better in exploring large seek spaces of ability venture configurations. This makes it feasible to become aware of price-powerful routes, release home windows, and orbital maneuvers that lessen undertaking time and gasoline consumption. Furthermore, to plot missions that maximize overall venture fulfillment and clinical output, QAI can remember an expansion of targets, including medical return, assignment protection, and utilization of resources [49].
b. **Trajectory Optimization**: To accomplish correct navigation and encounters with favored locations, including planets, moons, asteroids, and comets, QAI can optimize spacecraft trajectories and orbital maneuvers. Complicated trajectory optimization troubles, such as multi-body dynamics and gravitational perturbations, can be resolved by quantum algorithms, which can then be used to calculate the high-quality routes that lessen gasoline use and travel time. Furthermore, spacecraft may additionally navigate through complicated and dynamic environments more efficiently to QAI's capacity to adaptively modify trajectories in real-time based on assignment wishes and dynamic environmental variables [50].
c. **Resource Management**: Throughout missions in space, QAI can optimize the use and distribution of assets, along with fuel, strength, and onboard materials. To maximize challenge operations, reduce waste, and lengthen undertaking period, quantum algorithms can help in restrictions and consumption prices. Furthermore, in space environments with variable solar radiation and electricity requirements, QAI can improve strength era and distribution systems, together with solar panels and batteries, to enhance energy efficiency and reliability [50].
d. **Autonomous Exploration**: Robotic spacecraft and rovers with QAI can be prepared with self-sustaining exploration talents, permitting them to make judgments in real-time and adapt to changing environmental conditions without the need for human intervention. To discover scientifically exciting targets, including geological formations, atmospheric conditions, and feasible proof of extraterrestrial life, quantum algorithms can interpret sensor records and verify environmental clues. Moreover, self-sufficient navigation and hazard avoidance can be made viable by means of QAI, ensuring the safety and independence of robot explorers in dangerous and remote regions [51].
e. **Data Analysis and Scientific Discovery**: Large quantities of scientific records, which include photographs, spectra, and telemetry, which might be gathered throughout area missions, can be highly analyzed with the assistance of QAI. Scientists can distinguish novel events, describe planetary bodies, and clear up cosmic mysteries by the use of quantum algorithms to extract enormous insights and patterns from massive, complicated datasets. Additionally, QAI can assist with anomaly identification and real-time information processing to help prioritize medical observations and react to unanticipated findings made at some stage in area missions. Figure 6.14 indicates QAI for optimized area exploration.

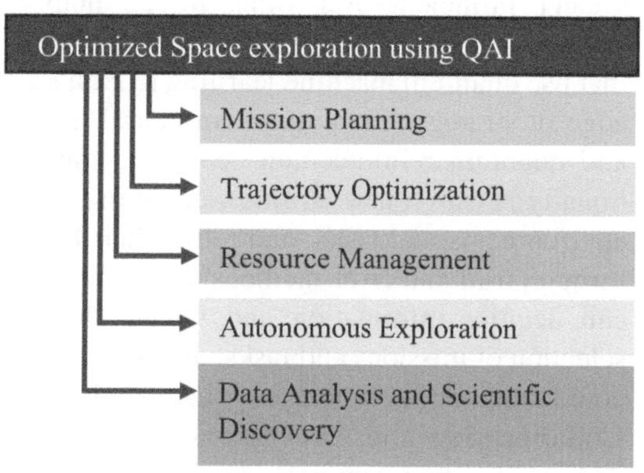

FIGURE 6.14 Quantum AI for optimized space exploration.

6.2.13 Autonomous Robotics Using Quantum AI

A promising area of robotics examine is autonomous robotics, the use of QAI. This technique holds the promise of making more clever, flexible, and self-sustaining robot structures that can perform well in demanding and dynamic settings. Robots can now see, think, and act beyond the mixing of QC, AI, and sensor technologies. This allows robots to make choices in real-time and regulate to convert environmental situations without the need for human intervention [52]. The capacity impact of QAI is primarily based on independent robotics on robot systems.

a. **Perception and Sensing**: Robots' perception and sensing capacity will be stepped forward by QAI through more effective processing of sensor records and the extraction of precious facts from ambiguous or noisy signals. Using sensor records from cameras, lidar scans, and inertial measurements, quantum algorithms can apprehend gadgets, barriers, as well as surroundings with drastically improved precision and readability. Furthermore, sensor fusion methods may be made possible with the aid of QAI, permitting records to be combined from diverse sensors and modalities. These robots need to become more accurate with thorough representations in their environment [10].
b. **Planning and Decision-Making**: Due to the fact that QAI is better at navigating ambiguity and tackling complicated optimization issues, it can help independent robots emerge as extra capable of making plans and making selections. Route planning, work distribution, and useful resource optimization can also be executed in real-time by way of quantum algorithms, while taking dreams and converting environmental restrictions into consideration. Furthermore, in unpredictable contexts, proactive decision-making and chance control are made feasible by way of robots' potential to forecast destiny states and consequences way to QAI.
c. **Learning and Adaptation**: Because QAI lets robots study from experience and come to be greater proficient over time, it can help self-sustaining robots understand and trade. Robots that use quantum machine learning to gain knowledge of strategies, like quantum neural networks and quantum reinforcement learning, may additionally research new abilities, adapt to changing environments and tasks, and refine their behavior through trial and error methods. Moreover, robots can acquire information and talents through a selection of missions and tasks due to QAI, which could facilitate lifetime mastering techniques [53].
d. **Collaboration and Coordination**: Coordination and cooperation amongst numerous self-reliant robots running in the same space may be made viable via QAI. Robots can work more efficiently to perform duties by way of speaking, negotiating, and coordinating through the use of quantum algorithms. Moreover, robots might be capable of dealing with their moves and adjusting to new troubles without centralized control, due to QAI's capability to enable swarm intelligence and self-organization behaviors.
e. **Fault Tolerance and Resilience**: By allowing autonomous robots to get better from setbacks and adjust to unforeseen disturbances, QAI can enhance their error endurance and robustness. Robots may be designed to independently diagnose, isolate, and recover from faults using quantum algorithms, permitting them to perform their missions and remain safe in difficult or perilous situations. Furthermore, QAI can facilitate self-recuperation and self-repair structures, permitting robots to adjust and trade their configuration in response to damage or malfunction. Figure 6.15 shows QAI for autonomous robotics.

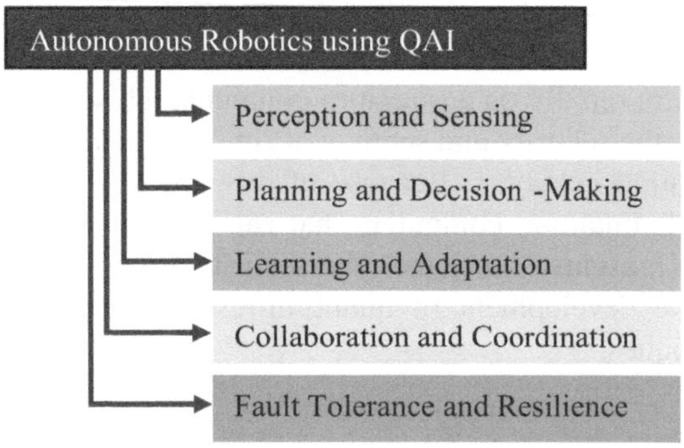

FIGURE 6.15 Quantum AI for autonomous robotics.

6.2.14 Large Language Model Using Quantum AI

An exciting new course in natural language processing (NLP) is the development of big language models using QAI. This approach combines the potential of QC with AI strategies to supply language models that are extremely complex and effective. Generative pre-trained transformer or models [54], that are massive language models, have shown extremely good overall performance in a number of NLP responsibilities, which include query-answering, summarizing, textual content generation, and translation. The following are a few methods that NLP may be impacted with the aid of growing a large language model (LLM) with QAI:

a. **Training Efficiency**: LLM training can be enhanced using QAI, with the help of taking advantage of QC's parallel processing powers. Compared to classical methods, quantum algorithms can expedite convergence and shorten training times by means of effectively navigating the huge space of version parameters. The advent of bigger, more potent language models that could take care of even greater tough linguistic troubles may be made viable with the aid of this progressed training efficiency.

b. **Model Scaling**: LLMs can be scaled up with the assistance of QAI to handle additional information sets, as well as diverse linguistic settings. Big-scale optimization troubles may be handled with the aid of QC, which makes it feasible to create language models with extra parameters and extract contextual knowledge and higher semantics using textual data. Furthermore, model architectures can be advanced by means of QAI to deal with longer enter sequences and more correctly constitute the subtleties of human language.
c. **Semantic Understanding**: The ability of massive language models for semantic information could be improved with the aid of QAI through the application of quantum algorithms to handle and interpret textual content facts quickly. To encode and adjust semantic facts in increasingly more complex and diffuse techniques, quantum algorithms can take advantage of quantum parallelism and superposition. This can result in efficient and contextually applicable language production and interpretation. Massive language models can be capable of producing responses which can be extra logical and human-like in a range of scenarios and activities because of this progressed semantic knowledge [55].
d. **Contextual Adaptation**: LLM may be enabled to hastily adapt to many linguistic contexts and domain names way to quantum synthetic intelligence. Large language models may also now produce more contextually relevant and customized responses due to quantum algorithms' capacity to evaluate contextual elements and adjust model conduct in real-time based on incoming textual content inputs and alert remarks. Language models feature higher in a selection of applications, such as sentiment evaluation, content material advent, and conversational bots, because of these contextual adaptation abilities.
e. **Privacy and Security**: Security and privacy of LLMs can be improved by way of QAI by permitting encrypted, privacy-keeping computations on sensitive text statistics. Textual content facts can be safeguarded through inference and schooling techniques using quantum encryption techniques such as homomorphic encryption and QKD [56]. This guarantees confidentiality and integrity while preserving the statistics' usefulness for subsequent NLP obligations. Furthermore, even as safeguarding sensitive data, QC can allow safe multi-birthday celebration computation and federated getting to know techniques for cooperative version schooling and expertise exchange [57–62]. Figure 6.16 shows QAI for developing LLMs.

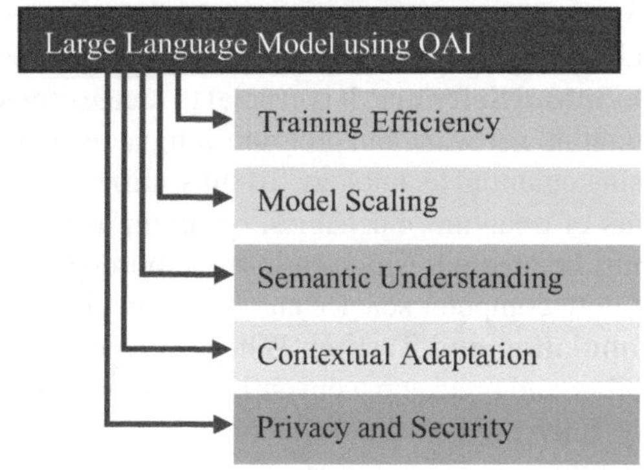

FIGURE 6.16 QAI for developing large language models.

6.3 OVERCOMING CHALLENGES IN QUANTUM AI ADOPTION

To reach its full potential, QAI adoption faces numerous obstacles that ought to be conquered. These difficulties includes skills acquisition, hardware and software program improvement, interaction with present enterprise systems, and current limitations of QC.

6.3.1 Current Limitations of Quantum Computing

Apart from its predicted potential, QC is still in its early stage and has numerous limitations that can affect the adoption of quantum synthetic intelligence.

a. **Error Rates and Decoherence**: Computations using quantum structures are liable to errors and have a lack of coherence, posing various issues. Important issues include maintaining qubit integrity and balance over time.
b. **Scalability**: The complexity of issues that may be solved by modern quantum computer systems is restricted by way of the amount of qubits to be had to them. For realistic packages, scaling up the qubit count at the same time as retaining mistake corrections is critical.
c. **Algorithm Development**: AI quantum algorithms are still inside the manner of being created and stepping forward. Due to the lack of direct quantum opposite numbers for many traditional AI techniques, novel techniques are needed to utilize quantum advantages.

6.3.2 Hardware and Software Challenges

Progress is needed in both the hardware and software program domains of quantum computing to facilitate QAI.

a. **Hardware Development**: Overcoming boundaries about qubit pleasant, connection, and error correction is important to assemble reliable and scalable quantum architectures. Technologies with unique demanding situations include photonic qubits, trapped ions, and superconducting qubits.

b. **Quantum Software**: It is crucial to create efficient quantum software and programming languages by using quantum technology. To fully utilize the benefits of quantum mechanics, quantum algorithms must be created, which calls for a thorough grasp of both computer science and quantum physics.
c. **Simulation and Testing**: When it comes to scalability and precision, conventional simulations are typically used in the development and testing of quantum algorithms because quantum technology is still in its early stages of development.

6.3.3 Training and Talent Acquisition

A highly specialized skill set combining knowledge of computer science, AI, and quantum physics is needed in the subject of QAI.

a. **Educational Programs**: Training programs and educational initiatives that concentrate on QC and its uses in AI are becoming increasingly necessary. Universities and other entities are offering specialized degrees and certificates [59].
b. **Interdisciplinary Talent**: It's difficult to find talent with the requisite multidisciplinary understanding. Since there are few experts available in both AI and quantum physics, businesses must provide ongoing training and growth opportunities for their current professionals.
c. **Collaborative Research**: Fostering partnerships among academics, businesses, and government can aid in the skill gaps and prompting innovations in QAI.

6.3.4 Integration with Existing Business Systems

To make QAI widely used, contemporary corporate strategies and structures should be implemented.

a. **Compatibility**: It's far critical to make certain quantum answers paintings with the prevailing IT architecture. This involves developing middleware, and interfaces that allow quantum algorithms speak with classical structures.
b. **Cost and Investment**: Many companies can also find it difficult to overcome high cost of quantum technology, and the significant integration effortrequired. Corporations should not ignore the possible benefits of adopting QAI, nor should they hesitate to invest in it.
c. **Scalability and Flexibility**: Solutions that are adaptable and scalable to meet changing demands of corporate demands are crucial. Among these are cloud-based QC services, which offer access to quantum resources without requiring a large upfront investments.

6.3.5 Future Trends and Implications for Business

QAI has the capacity to revolutionize industrial practices and deliver long-term advantages in the future. It's anticipated that as the QC generation continue to advance, its integration with AI will reshape several sectors by providing unprecedented processing power and innovative solutions.

6.3.5.1 Impact of Quantum AI on Business Strategies

QAI is poised to extensively transform business techniques in several approaches:

a. **Enhanced Decision-Making**: Compared to standard systems, QAI can process and analyze considerable volumes of information far more quickly, giving corporations better insights and more precise forecasts. This improved decision-making capacity may additionally result in stronger competitiveadvantages and more effective planning strategies.
b. **Optimization and Efficiency**: Quantum-enhanced optimization algorithms can support aid allocation, logistics, supply chain management, and various industrial strategies. By quickly identifying quality solutions, QAI may additionally save costs and increase operational effectiveness.
c. **Innovation and Production Development**: Through the simulation of tricky chemical interactions and other phenomena, QAI enables the investigation of novel substances, medicinal drugs, and product designs. This has the capacity to shorten invention cycles and expedite the release of recent items.
d. **Risk Management**: By identifying patterns and anomalies more accurately, QAI can enhance risk modeling and fraud detection in the insurance and financial industries. This leads to more effective mitigation and control strategies.

6.3.5.2 Long-term Benefits and Opportunities

The long-time period advantages and opportunities of QAI are enormous. A number of them are:

a. **Sustainable Competitive Advantage**: Early QAI adopters have a large competitive gain. Agencies that have integrated the QC methodologies into their operations will be better positioned to harnessits full potential before it becomes broadly available.
b. **New Business Models**: QAI helps in the development of new business models and services that were previously unimaginable. For example,

organizations can offer systems that enable other corporations to apply QC and resources for their specific needs.

c. **Breakthrough in Research and Developments**: Breakthroughs in chemistry, material science, genetics, and other domains may emerge from the ability of QAI to tackle complex problems that are, in my opinion, unsolvable. This capability could drive major advancements in fields such as biotechnology, energy, and pharmaceuticals.
d. **Global Collaboration**: The development of QAI will inspire extra cooperation among authorities, business, and academia. This cooperative setting may additionally quicken the price of innovation and assure that QAI's benefits are substantially dispersed during various industries and geographical areas.
e. **Ethical and Responsible AI**: Because the QAI advances, there may be a threat to include ethical ideas and conscientious conduct into its shape. In packages that exercise AI, groups can set novel requirements for duty, justice, and transparency.

6.4 CONCLUSION

QAI represents a transformative bounce for organizations, imparting extraordinary skills in records analysis, device getting to know, and complicated problem-solving. by way of leveraging the principles of quantum mechanics, QAI allows agencies to address challenges previously beyond the attain of traditional AI, driving innovation in sectors like pharmaceutical research, financial modeling, and logistics. Apart from cutting-edge obstacles, along with hardware complexity and error correction, ongoing improvements promise to enhance the reliability and scalability of QAI. Businesses must stay informed about these developments and discover QAI's potential to gain a competitive edge in an increasingly more data-driven world. The integration of QAI could redefine operational performance and decision-making, heralding a brand new era of commercial enterprise innovation.

REFERENCES

1. F. Zickert, *Hands-On Quantum Machine Learning With Python Volume 1: Get Started*. Amazon Digital Services LLC, 2021.
2. M. Belkhir, H. Benkaouha, and E. Benkhelifa, "Quantum Vs Classical Computing: A Comparative Analysis," In: *Proceedings of the 7th International Conference on Fog and Mobile Edge Computing (FMEC 2022)*, Paris, France, pp. 1–8, 2022. doi:10.1109/FMEC57183.2022.10062753.
3. S. S. Tripathy, N. Koul, and H. Patel, "Comparative Study between Quantum and Classical Methods: Few Observations from Portfolio Optimization Problem," In: *Proceedings of the 2022 International Conference on Trends in Quantum Computing and Emerging Business Technologies (TQCEBT 2022)*, Mumbai, India, pp. 1–5, 2022. doi:10.1109/TQCEBT54229.2022.10041475.
4. H. Häffner, C. F. Roos, and R. Blatt, "Quantum Computing with Trapped Ions," *Phys. Rep.*, vol. 469, no. 4, pp. 155–203, 2008. doi:10.1016/j.physrep.2008.09.003.
5. A. Stepanenko, M. Lyubarov, and M. Gorlach, "Quantum Circuits with Topological Two-Photon Phases Induced by Interactions," In: *Proceedings of the 16th International Congress on Artificial Materials for New Wave Phenomena (Metamaterials 2022)*, Siena, Italy, pp. X428–X430, 2022. doi:10.1109/Metamaterials54993.2022.9920800.
6. P. Kok, W. J. Munro, K. Nemoto, T. C. Ralph, J. P. Dowling, and G. J. Milburn, "Linear Optical Quantum Computing with Photonic Qubits," *Rev. Mod. Phys.*, vol. 79, no. 1, pp. 135–174, 2007. doi:10.1103/RevModPhys.79.135.
7. P. Roe, "Explorations in Quantum Computing," *AIAA J.*, vol. 36, no. 11, 1998. doi:10.2514/2.321.
8. A. K. Badhan and R. Gill, "Explainable machine learning model for Industrial 4.0," In: S. Kumar and P. Sharma (Eds.), *Machine Learning for Sustainable Manufacturing in Industry 4.0*. CRC Press, 2024, pp. 184–200.
9. S. B. Ramezani, A. Sommers, H. K. Manchukonda, S. Rahimi, and A. Amirlatifi, "Machine Learning Algorithms in Quantum Computing: A Survey," *Proc. Int. Jt. Conf. Neural Netw.*, 2020. doi:10.1109/IJCNN48605.2020.9207714.
10. V. Dunjko and H. J. Briegel, "Machine Learning & Artificial Intelligence in the Quantum Domain: A Review of Recent Progress," *Reports Prog. Phys.*, vol. 81, no. 7, 2018. doi:10.1088/1361-6633/aab406.
11. M. Schuld and N. Killoran, "Is Quantum Advantage the Right Goal for Quantum Machine Learning?," *PRX Quant.*, vol. 3, no. 3, p. 1, 2022. doi:10.1103/PRXQuantum.3.030101.
12. Y. Liu, S. Arunachalam, and K. Temme, "A Rigorous and Robust Quantum Speed-Up in Supervised Machine Learning," *Nat. Phys.*, vol. 17, no. 9, pp. 1013–1017, 2021. doi:10.1038/s41567-021-01287-z.
13. A. Ahmadi, "Quantum Computing and AI: The Synergy of Two Revolutionary Technologies," *Asian J. Electr. Sci.*, vol. 12, no. 2, pp. 15–27, 2023. doi:10.51983/ajes-2023.12.2.4118.
14. T. A. Shaikh and R. Ali, "Quantum Computing in Big Data Analytics: A Survey," In: *2016 IEEE International Conference on Computer and Information Technology (CIT)*, Nadiad, India, 2016, pp. 112–115. doi:10.1109/CIT.2016.79.
15. C. Arora and R. Sandhu, "Adoption of Quantum NLP for Improved Healthcare System," In: A. K. Bairwa, V. Tiwari, S. K. Vishwakarma, M. Tuba and T. Ganokratanaa (Eds.), *Computation of Artificial Intelligence and Machine Learning. ICCAIML 2024: Communications in Computer and Information Science*. Springer, vol. 2185, 2025. doi:10.1007/978-3-031-71484-9_5.
16. C. P. Gonçalves, "Financial Market Modeling with Quantum Neural Networks," vol. 3, no. 4, pp. 44–63, 2015. https://arxiv.org/abs/1508.06586.
17. R. D. Taylor, E. D. Palmer, and L. Emeritus, *Quantum Technology Development, Policy and Governance in the U.S.* Technical Report, Pennsylvania State University, November 2021.
18. N. Innan, M. A. Z. Khan, and M. Bennai, "Financial Fraud Detection: A Comparative Study of Quantum Machine Learning Models," *Int. J. Quantum Inf.*, vol. 22, no. 2, pp. 1–30, 2024. doi:10.1142/S0219749923500442.
19. S. Souza and S. D. Souza, *Intelligent Supply Chain Management Using Quantum*. 2022, https://hal.archives-ouvertes.fr/hal-03740772.

20. S. Wang, Z. Pei, C. Wang, and J. Wu, "Shaping the Future of the Application of Quantum Computing in Intelligent Transportation System," *Intell. Converg. Netw.*, vol. 2, no. 4, pp. 259–276, 2021. doi:10.23919/ICN.2021.0019.
21. A. Bhattacharjee and R. Kumar, "Environmental Impact of Operations and Supply Chain from Fourth Industrial Revolution and Machine Learning Approaches," In: S. Kumar and P. Sharma (Eds.), *Machine Learning for Sustainable Manufacturing in Industry 4.0*. CRC Press, 2024, pp. 76–104.
22. S. Das, J. Zhang, S. Martina, D. Suter, and F. Caruso, "Quantum Pattern Recognition on Real Quantum Processing Units," *Quant. Mach. Intell.*, vol. 5, no. 1, 2023. doi:10.1007/s42484-022-00093-x.
23. Y. Liu, Q. Li, B. Wang, Y. Zhang, and D. Song, "A Survey of Quantum-cognitively Inspired Sentiment Analysis Models," *ACM Comput. Surv.*, vol. 56, no. 1, 2023. doi:10.1145/3604550.
24. Y. Zhang, D. Song, P. Zhang, X. Li, and P. Wang, "A Quantum-Inspired Sentiment Representation Model for Twitter Sentiment Analysis," *Appl. Intell.*, vol. 49, no. 8, pp. 3093–3108, 2019. doi:10.1007/s10489-019-01441-4.
25. E. O. Pyzer-Knapp and A. Curioni, "Advancing Biomolecular Simulation through Exascale HPC, AI and Quantum Computing," *Curr. Opin. Struct. Biol.*, vol. 87, p. 102826, 2024. :doi:10.1016/j.sbi.2024.102826.
26. M. S. Jeyalakshmi et al., "Quantum Computing and Healthcare: Drug Discovery and Molecular Simulation with Machine Learning," *Int. J. Intell. Syst. Appl. Eng.*, vol. 12, no. 14s, pp. 557–564, 2024.
27. R. E. D. Popa, "Drug Discovery in the 21st Century: Exploring the Promises and Potential of Quantum Machine Learning." *J. Contemp. Healthc. Analytics,* vol. 7, pp. 1–13, 2023.
28. A. Lele, "Global Investments," In: S. Raj and P. Mehta (Eds.), *Quantum Technologies and Military Strategy*. Springer, 2021, pp. 75–114. doi:10.1007/978-3-030-72721-5_7.
29. A. Pyrkov, A. Aliper, D. Bezrukov, D. Podolskiy, F. Ren, and A. Zhavoronkov, "Complexity of Life Sciences in Quantum and AI Era," *Wiley Interdiscip. Rev. Comput. Mol. Sci.*, vol. 14, no. 1, pp. 1–21, 2024. doi:10.1002/wcms.1701.
30. A. Nammouchi, A. Kassler, and A. Theocharis, "Quantum Machine Learning in Climate Change and Sustainability: A Short Review," *Proc. AAAI Symp. Ser.,* vol. 2, no. 1, pp. 107–114, 2024. doi:10.1609/aaaiss.v2i1.27657.
31. M. Singh, C. Dhara, A. Kumar, S. S. Gill, and S. Uhlig, "Quantum Artificial Intelligence for the Science of Climate Change," *Artif. Intell. Mach. Learn. Blockchain Quant. Satell. Drone Netw.*, pp. 199–207, 2022. doi:10.1201/9781003250357-13.
32. M. A. Metawei, H. Eldeeb, S. M. Nassar, and M. Taher, "Quantum Computing Meets Artificial Intelligence: Innovations and Challenges," In: M. Virvou, G. A. Tsihrintzis, N. G. Bourbakis, and L. C. Jain (Eds.), *Handbook on Artificial Intelligence-Empowered Applied Software Engineering: Novel Methodologies to Engineering Smart Software Systems*. Springer, 2022, vol. 1, pp. 303–338. doi: 10.1007/978-3-031-08202-3_12.
33. A. Efe, "Assessment of the Artificial Intelligence and Quantum Computing in the Smart Management Information Systems," *Bilişim Teknol. Derg.*, vol. 16, no. 3, pp. 177–188, 2023. doi:10.17671/gazibtd.1190670.
34. H. Kim et al., Quantum Artificial Intelligence on Cryptanalysis. IACR Cryptol, 2023, https://eprint.iacr.org/2023/004.pdf.
35. R. Bavdekar, E. J. Chopde, A. Bhatia, K. Tiwari, S. J. Daniel, and Atul, "Post Quantum Cryptography: Techniques, Challenges, Standardization, and Directions for Future Research," *arXiv preprint* arXiv:2202.02826. https://arxiv.org/abs/2202.02826.
36. V. B. Dang, F. Farahmand, M. Andrzejczak, and K. Gaj, "Implementing and Benchmarking Three Lattice-Based Post-Quantum Cryptography Algorithms Using Software/Hardware Codesign," In: *Proceedings of the 2019 International Conference on Field-Programmable Technology (ICFPT 2019)*, Melbourne, Australia, vol. 2019, pp. 206–214, 2019. doi:10.1109/ICFPT47387.2019.00032.
37. A. R. P. Reddy, "The Role of Artificial Intelligence in Proactive Cyber Threat Detection In Cloud Environments," *NeuroQuant.*, vol. 19, no. 12, pp. 764–773, 2021.
38. J. Shuford, "Quantum Computing and Artificial Intelligence: Synergies and Challenges," *J. Artif. Intell. Gen. Sci.* vol. 1, no. 1, 2024. doi:10.60087/jaigs.v1i1.35.
39. C. Blanco, A. Santos-Olmo, and L. E. Sánchez, "QISS: Quantum-Enhanced Sustainable Security Incident Handling in the IoT," *Information*, vol. 15, no. 4, p. 181, 2024. doi:10.3390/info15040181.
40. M. Krelina, "Quantum Technology for Military Applications," *EPJ Quant. Technol.*, vol. 8, no. 1, 2021. doi:10.1140/epjqt/s40507-021-00113-y.
41. E. Science, "Quantum Secure Communication and 6G Critical Infrastructure Miloslav Hoschek Tetiana Bukoros," *Eur. Sci.*, vol. 2, pp. 149–157, 2020.
42. C. A. Wargo, G. C. Church, J. Glaneueski, and M. Strout, "Unmanned Aircraft Systems (UAS) Research and Future Analysis," *IEEE Aerosp. Conf. Proc.*, pp. 1–16, 2014. doi:10.1109/AERO.2014.6836448.
43. Kallioras, A., Pliakas, F., Diamantis, I., & Kallergis, G, SWOT analysis in groundwater resources management of coastal aquifers: a case study from Greece. Wat. Int., vol. 35, no. 4, pp. 425–441, 2010.
44. M. A. J. René and G. Berendsen, *The Weaponization of Quantum Mechanics: Quantum Technology in Future Warfare*. Technical Report, School of Advanced Military Studies, U.S. Army, 2019.
45. M. Barbeau and J. Garcia-Alfaro, "Cyber-Physical Defense in the Quantum Era," *Sci. Rep.*, vol. 12, no. 1, pp. 1–11, 2022. doi:10.1038/s41598-022-05690-1.
46. D. Zhang, H. Wang, S. Li, and B. Wang, "Progress in the Prime Factorization of Large Numbers," *J. Supercomput.*, vol. 80, no. 8, pp. 11382–11400, 2024. doi:10.1007/s11227-023-05876-y.
47. M. Mosca, "Quantum Algorithms," In: J. van Leeuwen (Ed.), *Computational Complexity: Theory, Techniques, and Applications*. Springer, 2012, pp. 2303–2333. doi:10.1007/978-1-4614-1800-9_144.
48. I. P. Idoko, O. M. Ijiga, L. A. Enyejo, S. I. Ugbane, O. Akoh, and M. O. Odeyemi, "Exploring the Potential of Elon Musk's Proposed Quantum AI: A Comprehensive Analysis and Implications," *Glob. J. Eng. Technol. Adv.*, vol. 18, no. 3, pp. 48–65, 2024. doi:10.30574/gjeta.2024.18.3.0037.
49. M. Cutugno, A. Giani, P. M. Alsing, L. Wessing, and A. Schnore, "Quantum Computing Approaches for Mission Covering Optimization," *Algorithms*, vol. 15, no. 7, pp. 1–21, 2022. doi:10.3390/a15070224.
50. H. T. Nguyen, M. Usman, and R. Buyya, "QSimPy : A Learning-centric Simulation Framework for Quantum Cloud Resource Management," *arXiv preprint* 2405.01021, 2024.

51. V. Stanev, K. Choudhary, A. G. Kusne, J. Paglione, and I. Takeuchi, "Artificial Intelligence for Search and Discovery of Quantum Materials," *Commun. Mater.*, vol. 2, no. 1, pp. 1–11, 2021. doi:10.1038/s43246-021-00209-z.
52. H. Hohenfeld, D. Heimann, F. Wiebe, and F. Kirchner, "*Quantum Deep Reinforcement Learning for Robot Navigation Tasks*," *IEEE Access*, vol. 12, pp. 87217–8723, 2022.
53. G. K. Arora, R. Mutha, M. S. Sangari, U. Aswal, A. Bhattacherjee, and A. Agarwal, "An Analysis of the Effects and Interaction of Hyper Parameters in Convolutional Neural Networks," In: *Proceedings of the 2023 Second International Conference on Electronics and Renewable Systems (ICEARS 2023)*, Jaipur, India, 2023, pp. 1057–1063.
54. F. Amanov and A. Pradeep, "The Significance of Artificial Intelligence in the Second Scientific Revolution: A Review," In: *2023 15th International Conference on Electronics, Computers and Artificial Intelligence (ECAI)*, Bucharest, Romania, 2023, pp. 1–5. doi:10.1109/ECAI58194.2023.10194056.
55. M. Ying, "Quantum Computation, Quantum Theory and AI," *Artif. Intell.*, vol. 174, no. 2, pp. 162–176, 2010. doi:10.1016/j.artint.2009.11.009.
56. W. Wang and H. K. Lo, "Machine Learning for Optimal Parameter Prediction in Quantum Key Distribution," *Phys. Rev. A*, vol. 100, no. 6, 2019. doi:10.1103/PhysRevA.100.062334.
57. D. Ghai, S. L. Tripathi, S. Saxena, M. Chanda, and M. Alazab (Eds.), *Machine Learning Algorithms for Signal and Image Processing*. Wiley, 2022.
58. D. Ghai, S. Saxena, G. Dhingra, and S. L. Tripathi, "A Comprehensive Review on Performance-based Comparative Analysis, Categorization, Classification and Mapping of Text Extraction System Techniques for Images," *Multim. Tools Appl.*, vol. 84, 2327–2484, 2024.
59. R. Sandhu, H. K. Channi, D. Ghai, G. S. Cheema, and M. Kaur, "An Introduction to Generative AI Tools for Education 2030," In: P. Sharma and A. Verma (Eds.), *Integrating Generative AI in Education to Achieve Sustainable Development Goals*. Springer, 2024, pp. 1–28.
60. T. Soewu, H. Kaur, R. Sandhu, P. Sandhu, D. Ghai, K. Dhir, and S. L. Tripathi, "Machine Learning Models for Text and Image Processing," In: R. Patel and S. Gupta (Eds.), *Machine Learning Models and Architectures for Biomedical Signal Processing*. Academic Press, 2025, pp. 153–177.
61. M. Faiz, R. Sandhu, M. Akbar, A. A. Shaikh, C. Bhasin, and N. Fatima, "Machine Learning Techniques in Wireless Sensor Networks: Algorithms, Strategies, and Applications," *Int. J. Intell. Syst. Appl. Eng.*, vol. 11, no. 9s, pp. 685–694, 2023.
62. R. Sandhu, P. Kumar, C. Bhasin, N. Fatima and A. Pal, "Resnet-34 Model for Human Activity Recognition on Smartphone Sensor Data," *Int. J. Intell. Syst. Appl. Eng.*, vol. 11, no. 9s, pp. 644–652, 2023.

7 E-Business Using Quantum Computing and Quantum Artificial Intelligence Methodologies

Harpreet Kaur Channi, Surinder Kaur, Ramandeep Sandhu, and Nimisha Singh

7.1 INTRODUCTION

In view of today's rapid evolution in the field of digital technology, quantum computing (QC), and quantum artificial intelligence (QAI), the transformation of corporate analytics and optimization simply adapts these principles of quantum mechanics to process information at rates far exceeding even the most advanced classical computers. This, in simple terms, means delivering an unparalleled capacity in solving complex problems and simulating real-world scenarios. These capabilities combine with QAI to implement quantum algorithms, yielding better data analytics, pattern recognition, and decision-making. Some of these technologies are going to prove fundamentally promising for changing e-business strategies [1].

The work aims to explore the transformational potential of QC and QAI in e-business. Advanced computational power allow businesses to gain deeper insights from customer behavior, devise optimized marketing strategies, and improve overall operational efficiency. Conventional computation methods cannot handle scale and complexity issues arising in modern large datasets; QC provides the essential computational power required to process such volumes of data in near real-time [2].

E-businesses, striving to become more efficient, secure, and competitive, find their place in digitalization by seeking innovative solutions. Traditional computational methods are gradually reaching the ceiling when trying to resolve a variety of modern business challenges. QC and QAI methodologies introduce completely new opportunities in computational power and problem-solving capabilities. This chapter discusses how QC and QAI might shape the e-business world. Quantum computers can manipulate vast amounts of information simultaneously, due to quantum superposition and entanglement. This enables exponential speedup over classical computers in solving optimization, simulation, and cryptographic problems that are pervasive in e-business applications. Quantum algorithms-embedded intelligence, such as Grover's and Shor's algorithms, will disrupt data analysis, encryption, and decryption processes in their flows; hence, the security of e-business will be strengthened against emergent threats. Quantum AI methodologies will also introduce new data analytics methods, customer behavior prediction, personalized marketing, and supply chain optimization by leveraging quantum machine learning (QML), neural networks, and reinforcement learning. For QAI, leveraging principles of quantum parallelism and quantum entanglement will enable e-businesses to derive actionable insights from large unstructured datasets for informed decision-making, leading to improved customer experiences. However, serious challenges lie ahead in the adoption of business-specific quantum technologies. For instance, there is a severe shortage of quantum-ready infrastructure, high demand for highly specialized talent, and complicated integration processes of quantum solutions within the existing architecture of business. These issues need serious collaboration between academia, industry, and policymakers for significant advances in quantum research, scalable quantum algorithms, and robust QC architecture that could be used for e-business applications. In summary, a fusion of QC and QAI techniques offers unparalleled opportunities to all e-businesses to break themselves free from the shackles of classical computing, reap novel sources of revenues, and surge ahead of their rivals in the digital market space. Quantum technologies may rewrite the current landscape of e-business. It is expected to open new frontiers of innovation, efficiency, and sustainability [3–5].

This paper sets out to describe how QC and QAI will drive innovation with a competitive advantage in e-business. When unleashed into new computations and arrangements of intelligence, the organizations are poised to advance not only the frontiers of decision-making capabilities but also of development in digital commerce and customer engagement strategies.

7.1.1 Overview of Quantum Computing and Quantum Artificial Intelligence

QC brings in a new way of performing computation, primarily inspired by the fundamentals of quantum mechanics, to work with information in ways that are fundamentally different from classical computers. At the core of all this are quantum bits—qubits—that, by using superposition and entanglement, can hold a combination of states

DOI: 10.1201/9781003530800-7

simultaneously. This feature allows quantum computers to solve complex problems much faster than their classical counterparts. Quantum algorithms are examples of quantum computation that include Shor's algorithm for factorizing large integers and Grover's algorithm for searching an unsorted database—not to mention the extensive list of applications, including cryptography, optimization, and simulation of quantum systems [1]. This, in turn, enables the capability to advance into the realms of artificial intelligence (AI) by applying QC principles for the betterment of AI (Artificial Intelligence) algorithms and techniques. QAI targets the essential enhancement of efficiency and accuracy of AI models while processing Big Data, optimization of algorithms, and solving complex optimization problems. The applications are QML, quantum neural networks (QNNs), and quantum-inspired optimization, promising major advances in highly diverse domains, ranging from finance and healthcare to logistics and e-commerce. The convergence of QC with QAI holds the promise to transform industries by unlocking unparalleled computing power and intelligence. Thus, a set of these technologies makes decision processes and customer experiences more personalized and secures an e-business by bringing innovation and competitiveness to the firm in a digital economy [2].

7.1.2 Significance of Quantum Artificial Intelligence in E-Business

QAI will be highly influential in e-businesses, as it opens new sets of possibilities for the redefinition of how organizations could operate, compete, and innovate in the digital economy. Specifically, integrating principles of QC into AI techniques increases data processing and analysis efficiency, speed, and scalability, enabling e-businesses to unlock new opportunities and solve complex challenges [6]. The following are the key aspects that signify the importance of QAI to e-business:

- **Improved Data Analysis**: QAI enables e-businesses to analyze vast amounts of data in ways that classical AI cannot. Some quantum algorithms include QML and quantum optimization, which are highly beneficial in deducing insights from large datasets much faster. It helps in real-time decision-making and predictive analytics.
- **Optimized Decision-Making**: QAI will let an e-business firm optimize decision-making processes in many domains, such as price strategy, inventory management, or customizing customer experiences. Quantum algorithms work out various scenarios simultaneously to come up with the ultimate solution that works most effectively.
- **Advanced Customer Personalization**: QAI-enhanced customer relationship management would enable personalized recommendations, dynamic pricing models, and tailored marketing strategies. Quantum-inspired algorithms mine the nuances in customer behavior for better engagement and loyalty.
- **Cybersecurity and Data Privacy**: QC's cryptographic capabilities further strengthen cybersecurity measures for e-commerce websites. QAI algorithms enhance encryption processes that protect customers' sensitive data and transactions from emerging cyber threats.
- **Innovation and Competitive Advantage**: Integrating QAI keeps an e-business at the frontier of technological innovation. Through QC, an organization can lead in generating new products, services, and business models that make unique differences in competitive markets.

In other words, QAI enables e-businesses to take full advantage of QC for operational optimization, enhanced customer experience, and innovations that were impossible to imagine with traditional computing approaches. In such a context, embracing QAI is a strategic imperative for organizations that want to lead in the digital economy by using quantum power to drive sustainable growth and competitive advantage [5,7].

7.1.3 Scope of the Study

The presented research is focused on the adoption of QAI in e-business. It will analyze the feasibility and expected impact of integrating QAI with data analytics, decision processes, Customer Relationship Management (CRM), and cybersecurity applications within e-business. This chapter shall cover the technological advances of QC, case studies for practical demonstrations of QAI applications, challenges, and opportunities for adoption. It will show how QAI can help online businesses maintain operational efficiency, innovation capability, and competitive advantage in this continuously changing digital environment [8,9].

7.1.4 Objectives of the Study

- Daily sales and website visitation data are to be collated to further enhance operational planning, inventory management, and resource allocation. The peak periods of sales and high-traffic days are to be determined to enhance efficiency in meeting such demand and assure revenue opportunities.
- Utilize customer satisfaction scores to enhance customer experience strategies. Analyze satisfaction trends to identify areas for enhancement in product quality, service responsiveness, and overall customer support, aiming to increase customer retention and loyalty.
- Evaluate marketing campaign effectiveness metrics to refine promotional strategies. Use insights from campaign performance to optimize marketing spend, messaging, and channel allocation, thereby improving customer acquisition and conversion rates.

7.2 RELATED WORK

Jahin et al. [9] developed a supply chain backorder prediction system for big data sets. This work allowed quantum-inspired machine learning models to interact with QC on supply chain optimization. In contrast, Rajendran et al. [10], 2023, proposed such a piece of hardware-software co-design research that brings physical insights into designing the computational substrate, neuroscientific principles enabling information processing efficiently, the information-theoretic results for optimal quantification of uncertainty, and the communication theoretic guidelines of distributed processing for efficient and trustworthy AI. Dada et al. [11], 2024, provided new design methods for accuracy and uncertainty quantification using in-memory, neuromorphic, and QC hardware architectures. Internet of Things (IoT) and AI in smart water management transform water sustainability, and explore these technologies' pros, disadvantages, regulations, and future developments. Future water data security will include enhanced sensors, decentralized systems, QC, and blockchain. Weinberg and Faccia [12], 2024, studied quantum algorithms for financial fraud prevention. Financial crimes are becoming more complex and need creative solutions. QC is compared to conventional and Machine Learning (ML) approaches to demonstrate its merits. These two branches merge with QNNs and parameterized quantum circuits. Gohel and Joshi [13], 2024, forecast time series data using QLSTM neural networks. Fraud detection must become nimble, accurate, and predictive. Shoetan and Familoni [14], 2024, conducted a detailed investigation on how AI algorithms can improve fintech fraud detection. Computational architectures in deep neural network models are being developed, along with AI accelerators and quantum processing units. According to Schmidt and Hildebrandt [15], in 2024, the three acceleration waves for bioinformatics were Graphics Processing Units (GPU) computing, AI, and next-generation quantum computers. Qubit, noise, and non-stationary noise parameter distributions are the hindrances to QC. Dasgupta [16], 2024, identified the issue of noise-parameter non-stationarity in transmon processors used for QC. Neural Metaheuristics (NMH) emulates neural network dynamics, while QC simplifies optimization. Diaz-Pier and Carloni [17], 2024, presented quantum and neuromorphic computing on biomolecular simulations: current and future. Machine learning and AI applied to NMH and QC can accelerate data analysis and investigation.

7.2.1 Evolution and Development of Quantum Computing

The development and evolution of QC is a fascinating journey through the breakthroughs in science, theory advancements, and eventual transition into practice, shaping the very perception of computation and information processing. Conceived in the early 1980s by physicists like Richard Feynman and David Deutsch, QC draws on the power of quantum mechanics to deliver results that can be processed exponentially when compared with classical computers.

- **Theoretical Grounds**: The theoretical grounds for QC are based on quantum mechanics, the branch of physics through which scientists explain how particles act at subatomic levels. Key concepts include superposition—wherein quantum bits or qubits can exist in various states at the same time—and entanglement, wherein qubits become connected in such a way that changing one instantly affects another, regardless of the distance between them.
- **Milestones and Progress**: From the perspective of the field, significant milestones ranged from early theoretical frameworks to experimental realizations. In 1994, Peter Shor developed a quantum algorithm for efficiently factoring large integers. This result opened up new questions about QC and further research areas in quantum algorithms.
- **Technological Advances**: QC has become difficult to realize practically owing to the sensitive nature of qubits and the fact that it often requires an extremely specific environment, including extremely low temperatures to sustain a quantum state. Various qubit platforms have been explored by researchers, namely superconducting circuits, trapped ions, and topological qubits with unique advantages and challenges.
- **Current Landscape**: Today, major technology companies, leading research institutions, and governments all over the world invest intensively in research and development concerning QC. Companies like IBM, Google, and Rigetti Computing have built quantum processors that, via cloud platforms, can be reached by researchers and developers who would like to tinker with quantum algorithms and applications.
- **Future Directions**: QC holds immense promise for solving complex computational problems far beyond the realm of classical computers. Applications are numerous, from cryptography and optimization to material science and drug discovery. Development in qubit technologies, error correction, and algorithms will further drive QC to practical scalability and mainstream adoption over the coming decades.

The path from the creation of theoretical concepts to experimental realizations is one of transformation, carrying immense implications not only for computing but also for science and society. As QC research evolves and technologies mature, it is likely that industries across the globe will be revolutionized and, in the process, solve some of the major challenges humanity faces today [18].

7.2.2 Applications of Quantum Computing in Business and Technology

QC can exponentially accelerate computation and should continue to take a more significant role in revolutionizing both business and technology. The following are a few applications of major significance in the industry, where QC has huge potential to perform better:

- **Optimization Problems**: QC can handle particularly well some of the very complex optimization problems that are extremely difficult to perform on classical computers. Practical applications of this might be effectively solving optimization issues in areas such as supply chain logistics, task scheduling, and route planning. Quantum algorithms like Quantum Approximate Optimization Algorithm (QAOA) may provide gains in efficiency by simultaneously exploiting massive solution areas.
- **Cryptography and Security**: Quantum computers can break traditional cryptographic techniques like Rivest-Shamir-Adleman (RSA) and Elliptic Curve Cryptography (ECC), which are essentially based on the hardness of factoring large numbers. In contrast, quantum cryptography promises ultra-secure channels through the application of principles like quantum key distribution, meaning messages cannot be intercepted without being detected.
- **Machine Learning and AI**: The effective processing of Big Data can make machine learning algorithms better and help optimize QML and its efficiency in pattern recognition. QML algorithms aim to improve processes in model training, accelerate feature selection, and improve the precision of prediction for applications such as financial modeling or drug discovery.
- **Materials Science and Chemistry**: Quantum simulation enables the accurate modeling of molecular structures and chemical reactions that are extremely computationally intensive for traditional classical-level methods. It allows new capacities to design materials with bespoke properties and to optimize catalysts; the simulation of complex quantum systems helps in pharmaceutical development and renewable energy research.
- **Financial Modeling and Risk Analysis**: QC offers promise to improve areas of financial modeling, portfolio optimization, and risk analysis by rapidly investigating multi-scenario investment plans and optimizing investment strategies. Quantum algorithms can make fast, accurate, and more precise calculations of complex financial derivatives from the available market trends.
- **Artificial Intelligence and Natural Language Processing**: Through QC, acceleration of certain AI applications, including natural language processing, sentiment analysis, and speech recognition, will further be enabled. QNNs and quantum algorithms seek to make AI models more efficient and enable them to work on data-intensive tasks on a very large scale.
- **Analysis of Big Data**: Quantum computers could do much more than regular ones for analysis of databases or large-scale datasets, for instance, huge pattern searches, recognition, and real-time analytics. Quantum algorithms such as Grover's algorithm promise a quadratic acceleration in the unsorted database search, where fast data-driven decision-making has a critical significance in various industries.

These applications are expected to be transformative in QC, across various industries, and to reach critical limits of computational efficiency, security, and innovation. As quantum technologies advance, companies and researchers are finding more innovative ways to leverage QC power in the solution of complex problems for driving technological advancements into the future [19].

7.2.3 Role of QAI in Enhancing Business Intelligence and Decision-Making

QAI is bound to bring a sea change in business intelligence (BI) and the decision-making process by applying the power of QC integrated with rich artificial intelligence algorithms. QAI thus enables organizations to process large volumes of data at speed and find complex patterns and correlations that might be difficult or impossible for traditional computing methods to reach. This would further empower BI with deeper insights into customer behaviors, market trends, and operational efficiencies, as shown in Figure 7.1. In addition, QAI enhances decision-making by simulating complex scenarios and multiple variable assessments simultaneously. This capability is of special value in strategic planning, risk management, and resource allocation, in which the precision and timeliness of the insight have the potential

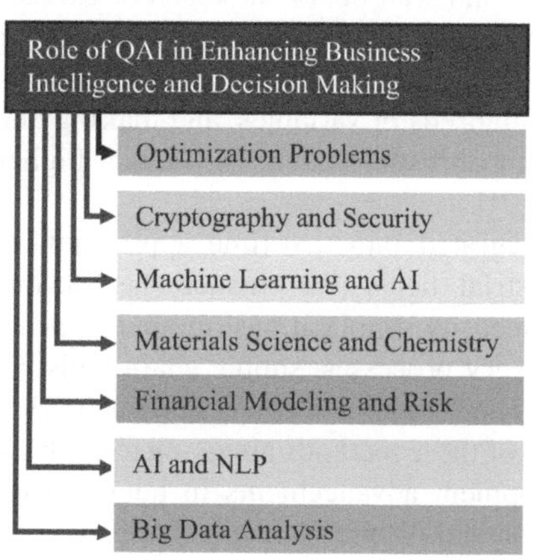

FIGURE 7.1 Role of QAI in enhancing business intelligence and decision-making.

to create a competitive advantage. QA-powered predictive analytics makes forecasts more accurate, which can help businesses predict market change and proactively change their strategies. Besides, QAI may speed up the training of an AI model, improving the capability of machine learning algorithms to process and analyze data even faster, providing for more responsive AI systems that make real-time decisions. QAI also enhances data security through quantum cryptography, thus offering solid security to protect vital information and transactions. All in all, QAI positions organizations to innovate, optimize operations, and unlock actionable insights to inform decision-making. As QC continues to evolve, the integration of QAI in BI frameworks certainly promises to redefine how businesses leverage data toward the fulfillment of strategic objectives and the maintenance of competitive relevance in a rapidly changing digital landscape [20].

7.3 QUANTUM ARTIFICIAL INTELLIGENCE METHODOLOGIES

QAI methods are an innovation in the field of the intersection between QC and artificial intelligence. They promise very radical changes in computational capabilities and problem-solving facilities. Whereas classical computing is based on 0s and 1s, the binary bits, QC uses quantum bits or qubits, which can exist in many states simultaneously because of superposition and entanglement. Consequently, QAI offers massive computational power that has enabled calculations that are exponentially faster than classical methods. QAI takes advantage of the parallelism of QC to enhance tasks involving machine learning algorithms, optimization problems, and data analysis in the field of artificial intelligence. For example, QML explores the fact that quantum algorithms may have a speedup in pattern recognition, predictive modeling, and data classification based on the use of quantum operations on quantum states and quantum interference for computation. Moreover, QAI methodologies also go beyond regular machine learning approaches and tackle problems that are computationally burdensome and well out of the reach of classical computers. This encompasses the most appropriate organization of Big Data, solving the most complex optimization problems involving hundreds of variables, and making queries about complex probabilistic models with much higher accuracy and speed [21].

QAI integrated into real-time applications will transform industrial fields like finance, healthcare, logistics, and cybersecurity. Implications abound in acceleration in drug discovery processes, supply chain logistics, financial forecasting, and the enhancement of data-encryption protocols. Many of these methods are going to evolve as research and development advancements in quantum technologies become practical. While there are challenges in scalability, error correction, and special hardware required for running quantum computations, active innovations and continuous collaborations within academia, industry, and government sectors should provide a blueprint toward realizing the full potential of QAI in moving future technological frontiers in their domain and solving real-world complex problems.

7.3.1 Quantum Neural Networks

QNNs are a new concept of machine learning in which QC principles are seen together with the principles of artificial neural networks. Where the classical neural network comprises classical bits, the QNN will use qubits for capturing and manipulating information. Important components of the QNN are:

- **Quantum Gates**: Much like classical layers in a neural network, quantum gates operate on qubits to extend and manipulate the same set of operations, referred to as superposition and entanglement. Some practice quantum mechanics functionalities are Hadamard gates, Pauli gates, and controlled gates.
- **Quantum Circuits**: QNNs are architected as quantum circuits in which qubits undergo initialization, manipulation via gates, and measurement at the output. The structure and arrangement of these circuits determine the abilities of the network to learn and generalize from data.
- **Training Algorithms**: QNN training, fundamentally, is an optimization method that optimizes the change of parameters to decrease the difference between estimated and real results. Quantum gradient descent and variational algorithms adjust the QNN parameters in quantum-classic hybrid manners.

Applications of QNNs span at least from pattern recognition to quantum chemistry simulations and optimization problems. Major urgent research challenges include qubit noise, error correction, and scalability in an attempt to improve QNN performance and applicability [22].

7.3.2 Quantum Machine Learning (QML) Algorithms

QML algorithms leverage the powers of QC to amplify the possibility of classical machine learning tasks by exploiting quantum properties such as superposition and interference. Such algorithms can efficiently perform tasks that might take a very long time on a classical computer, perhaps even exponentially longer. Key QML algorithms include quantum support vector machine (QSVM), which uses quantum kernels/feature maps in classifying data points in high-dimensional spaces. Quantum clustering, like quantum k-means, makes use of the quantum speedup in computing distances for the study of data partitions. Quantum principal component analysis is yet another area of research where quantum states are used to perform principal component analysis on data matrices, which allows better data compression and feature extraction. Considering all these promising capabilities, in practice, QML often boils down to hybrid quantum-classical approaches owing to limitations in current hardware and due to error mitigation strategies. These QML developments are to help overcome problems in Big Data analytics, optimization, and pattern recognition.

7.3.3 Quantum Reinforcement Learning

Quantum reinforcement learning (QRL) represents the junction of reinforcement learning and QC techniques into one framework to enhance decision-making in dynamic environments. QRL provides quantum agents acting in quantum environments with quantum states and measurements that optimize decision-making via exploration-exploitation trade-offs and policy optimization. Basic components include quantum Markov decision processes, which model state transitions and rewards as quantum states to enable efficient policy evaluation and selection. QRL has enormous potential for effective speedups in tasks related to robotics control, financial portfolio management, and game-theory simulations. The main difficulties are represented by quantum memory constraints, coherence times, and algorithmic complexity. Research in QRL focuses on the development of scalable quantum algorithms and hybrid architectures that can confront these challenges and enable practical applications in autonomous systems and adaptive control scenarios. Combined with the new development of QNNs and QML algorithms, QRL represents a new cutting-edge area related to quantum computation. Undoubtedly, it promises breakthrough applications spanning everything from artificial intelligence to computational chemistry [23].

7.4 METHODOLOGY

The research design consists of both quantitative and qualitative methodologies. This should provide a structured approach to leveraging advanced quantum technologies in digital commerce environments. This is the methodology by which e-business applications will be explored using QC and QAI methodologies. The process involves evaluating the computational efficiencies and performance benchmarks of quantum algorithms in simulated e-business scenarios, as depicted in Figure 7.2. It qualitatively involves an understanding of user perceptions and organizational impacts through interviews and case studies with stakeholders who have businesses at the forefront of QC and QAI adoption. Primary data will be gathered through experimentation, while secondary data will come from existing literature and industry reports.

These insights will contribute to formulating and testing quantum algorithms that are necessary in e-business, for example, for secure transactions via quantum cryptography, including QML while analyzing customers' behavior for offering personalized recommendations. The implementation phase will be core to testing and prototyping of these algorithms in controlled e-business environments, feasibility analysis, scalability, operational efficiencies, and customer experience. Quantitative techniques will analyze the data to measure the performance metrics, and qualitative methods will be used to interpret user feedback and organizational readiness for quantum technology adoption. Ethical considerations will include data privacy concerns, discussion of security risks associated with QC, and regulatory issues in digital commerce. In addition, the findings will be validated through peer review, expert consultation, and comparative analysis against existing research in the QC, QAI, and e-business domains. Finally, the paper concludes with a discussion of the limitations of quantum hardware capability, resources, and the development of quantum technologies within commercial areas to further explain both the potential and challenges associated with the integration of QC and QAI in e-business contexts [24].

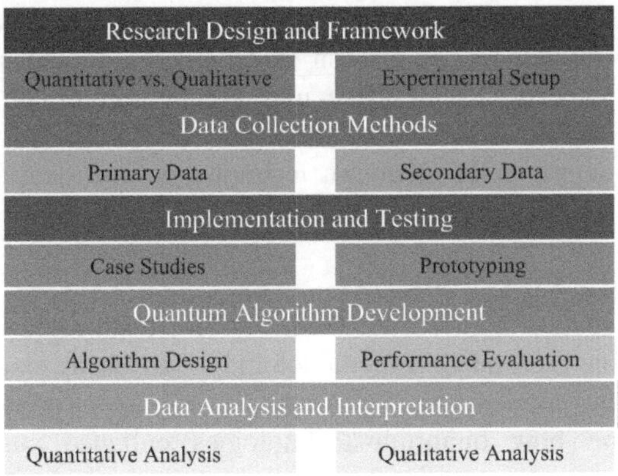

FIGURE 7.2 Methodology for performance benchmarks of quantum algorithms in simulated e-business scenarios.

7.4.1 Data Analysis and Results

The data analysis below showcases the performance and effectiveness of QC and QAI methodologies in e-business. Further, this section is a structured review of quantitative metrics and qualitative insights that were derived during research.

- **Quantitative Analysis**: Quantitative analysis deals with the measurement of a set of performance indicators influenced by the integration of QC and QAI in e-business. The main measures are computational efficiency of processing, resource utilization, and financial metrics. For example, execution times of quantum algorithms are compared with classical executions, showing possible speedups. Financial metrics include economic savings or revenue gains due to QAI applications, which are quantified.
- **Qualitative Analysis**: Qualitative analysis shall delve into user experiences, organizational impacts, and strategic implications of adopting QC and QAI in e-business. This analysis shall be done by

drawing insight from interviews, surveys, and case studies carried out on stakeholders and industry experts. Themes like user acceptance, organizational readiness, and challenges faced while implementing the quantum technologies are identified and discussed.

7.4.1.1 Case Study

This section explores case studies of e-businesses implementing QC and QAI methodologies. Each study examines specific applications, challenges, and outcomes, demonstrating how quantum technologies enhance customer engagement, optimize operations, and drive innovation in digital commerce. Findings are discussed in relation to the study's objectives and existing literature, highlighting implications for e-business strategy, technological adoption, and competitive advantage. The strengths and limitations of QC and QAI in real-world contexts are critically assessed. Google Colaboratory (Colab) is a web-based platform for creating, executing, and publishing Python code. Similar to Jupyter Notebooks, it enables users to run experiments and display results interactively. Supporting popular Python libraries, Colab provides access to powerful computing resources like GPUs and Tensor Processing Units (TPUs) without requiring local installations. Its integration with Google Drive and GitHub facilitates data storage, version control, and collaboration, making it an ideal tool for research, development, and education. Online retail has emerged as a competitive global industry, with retaining customers being a critical challenge. Retention is more cost-effective than acquiring new customers, as retained customers typically spend more over time. A case study examines how an online retailer uses data-driven insights to understand key drivers of customer engagement, such as time spent on the mobile app, website, and membership duration. The study prescribes strategies to enhance customer loyalty and increase yearly spending through personalized retention approaches [25,26].

7.4.1.2 Data Analysis and Insights

To address the challenge, customer data was analyzed with a focus on key metrics such as average session length, time spent on an app and website, membership length, and yearly spending. A scatter plot revealed a positive correlation between membership length and yearly spending, emphasizing the value of fostering long-term customer relationships to boost revenue. A histogram of annual spending highlighted distinct customer segments, including high-spending outliers—an invaluable group that could be nurtured through targeted marketing and personalized offers. A correlation heatmap further confirmed strong positive relationships between membership length, time spent on the app, and yearly spending. These insights suggest that enhancing customer engagement, particularly through the mobile app, could significantly increase revenue, aligning with the rising trend of mobile commerce. Additionally, a pair plot provided a comprehensive view of how various features interact with each other. This analysis revealed that customers who spend more time on the app and website are likely to have higher yearly spending, reinforcing the importance of digital engagement in customer retention strategies. Finally, a box plot analysis segmented customers based on their membership duration, revealing that those with longer memberships not only have higher median spending but also exhibit a wider range of spending behaviors. This variability suggests that while many long-term customers are high spenders, there is still potential to increase spending among those who are currently spending less [27,28]. The graphs created from the dataset provide insights into the relationships and distributions of various features. Figure 7.3 shows the scatter plot of the length of membership versus the yearly amount spent, revealing how customer loyalty (measured by membership length) correlates with their spending. The plot likely shows a positive relationship, indicating that customers who have been members longer tend to spend more annually, suggesting that loyalty may lead to higher spending.

The histogram of the Yearly Amount Spent visualizes the distribution of customer spending, as shown in Figure 7.4. This graph helps identify patterns, such as whether most customers spend within a certain range or if there are any significant outliers. The inclusion of a Kernel Density Estimate (KDE) curve provides a smooth approximation of the distribution, highlighting where the data is concentrated. Figure 7.5 shows the heatmap that displays the correlation between all features in the dataset. It shows how strongly each feature is related to the others on a scale from -1 to 1. A higher correlation between the Length of Membership and the Yearly Amount Spent would suggest that increasing membership duration is associated with higher spending, while low or negative correlations between other variables could indicate weaker or inverse relationships. The box plot

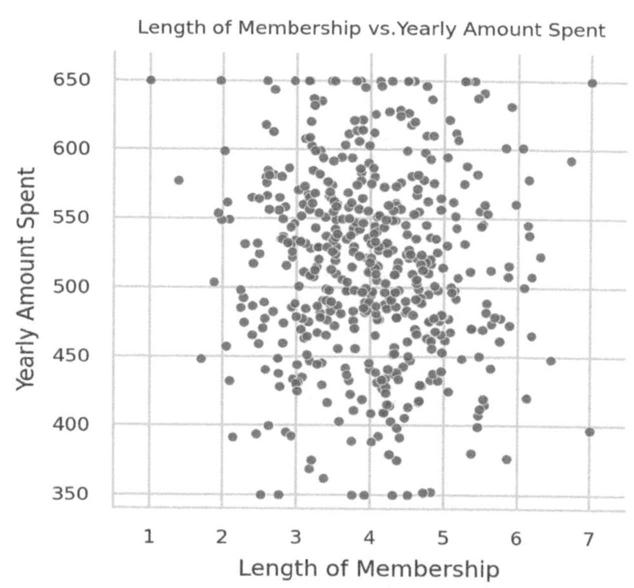

FIGURE 7.3 Scatter plot of the length of membership versus the yearly amount spent.

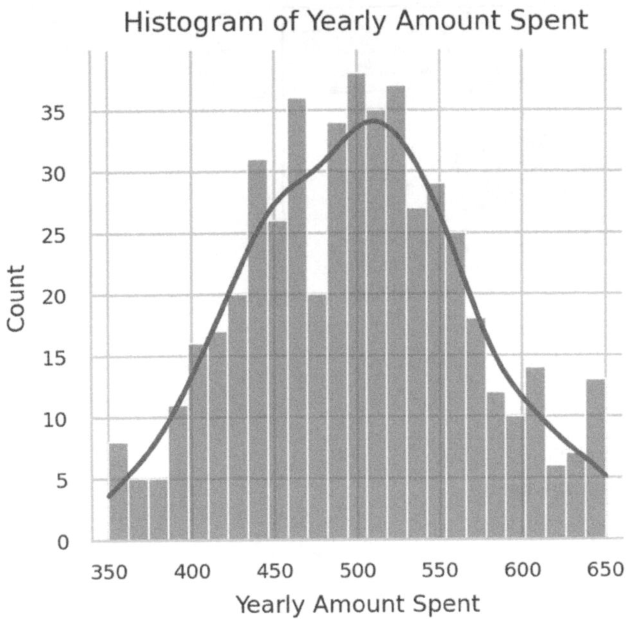

FIGURE 7.4 Histogram of yearly amount spent.

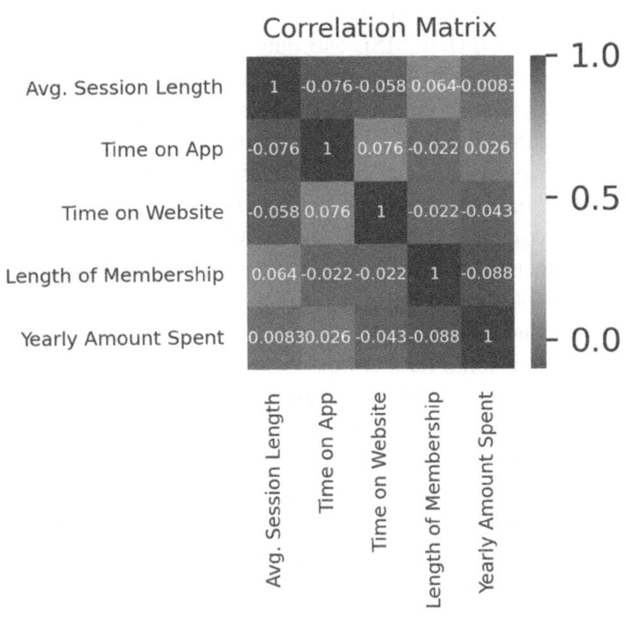

FIGURE 7.5 Correlation heatmap.

compares the distribution of Yearly amounts spent across different quartiles of Length of Membership, as shown in Figure 7.6. It highlights the central tendency, spread, and potential outliers within each group. This graph might show that customers with longer memberships (classified into quartiles such as 'Low', 'Medium', 'High', and 'Very High') have higher median spending, with some variability and outliers indicating diverse spending habits within each group.

The scatter plot that visualizes the performance of a linear regression model is shown in Figure 7.7. Each point represents a customer's actual yearly spending (on the x-axis)

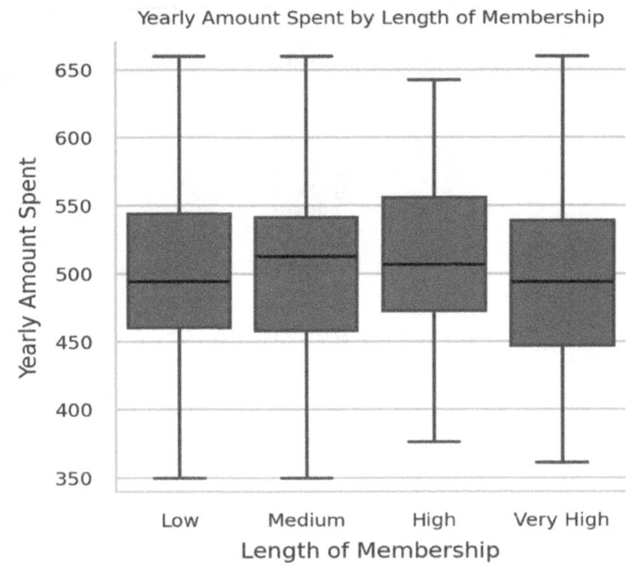

FIGURE 7.6 Box plot.

compared to the predicted spending (on the y-axis). Ideally, points should align closely with the 45° diagonal line, indicating that the model's predictions are accurate. The chart below shows that if the points are grouped closer to this diagonal line, the better the model performs in determining an individual's yearly amount spent. Those that fall off this line are discrepancies in overestimation or underestimation by the model. It is relevant to discuss here the mean squared error (MSE), which refers to the average of squares of the errors of prediction, and also the value of R-squared, which defines how much variance in spending a certain model explains. The higher the value of R^2 and the lower the value of MSE, the better the performance and accuracy of predictions in the model [29–32].

7.4.1.3 Strategic Recommendations

Armed with these valuable insights, this would enable the retailer to formulate a few focused strategies that will not only improve customer retention and increase spending but also enhance profitability. Firstly, by enhancing the experience of the mobile app, the company can facilitate more sessions and longer sessions, which are highly correlated with increased monetary value. Secondly, the company may introduce a loyalty program or improve the existing scheme further by offering deeper and richer rewards that will encourage long-standing loyalty from customers. Finally, by identifying and targeting high-value customers with personalized offers, the retailer can milk this critical segment for maximum revenue. The case study, in the end, underlines how data-driven insights can elaborate an effective strategy for customer retention in the online retail segment. It helps the retailer understand what drives key customer engagement and spending, so appropriate strategies can be put into place that enhance loyalty and revenues, respectively, to ensure competitiveness within a crowded market [33–35].

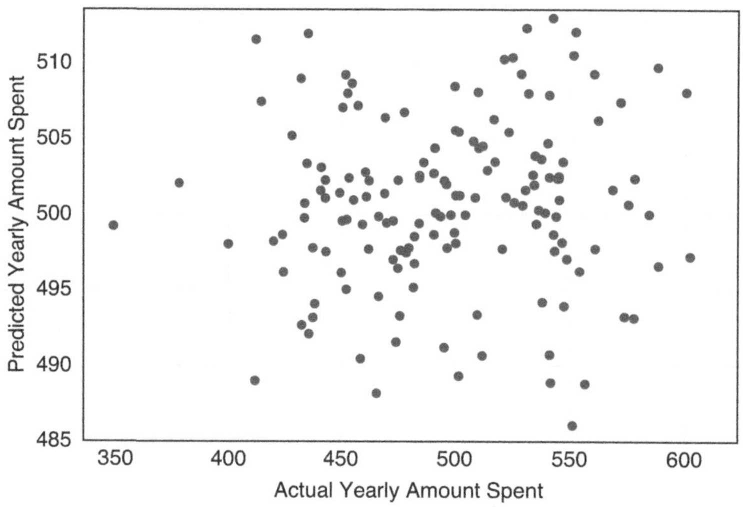

FIGURE 7.7 Actual vs. predicted yearly amount spent graph.

7.5 RESULTS AND DISCUSSION

QC and QAI approaches were sought for the analysis of improvements in the prediction of customer spending in this chapter about e-business. A classical model of linear regression for predicting annual spending by customers was determined using a set of metrics describing customer engagement, including session length, time on the app, website activity, and membership length. The performance of the classical model is characterized by its MSE and R-squared. The MSE was the average of the squared difference between the actual and predicted yearly spending. The higher the value of R^2, the larger the proportion of variance in yearly spending explained by the model, and the better this is. The actual by-prediction scatter graph showed that, although the predictions were closer to the actual values generally, large deviations were a pointer to QC in refining the model. QC and QAI methodologies promise a leading edge over classical models. QC on large and cumbersome datasets would reduce prediction errors since high-quality model development would be greatly enhanced. Quantum algorithms, such as QSVM or QNNs, hold the promise of better accuracy and enhanced handling of high-dimensional data. Therefore, the integration of quantum-enhanced models into the current scenario allows much more accurate predictions and far greater insight into customer behavior. This kind of positioning would eventually optimize resource utilization and greatly enhance customer engagement strategies, hence leading to higher revenues. A new era of quantum technologies is expected to dramatically improve the practice of e-business analytics with much-enhanced customer spending forecasts.

7.6 CONCLUSION

The integration of QC and QAI methodologies might, in the future, present an opportunity for new-generation improvements in predictive accuracy and efficiency in business analytics. However, the models had some limitations, as obtained in our case study for analyzing customer behavior and spending patterns in an online retail industry. The performance of the classical model was checked using MSE and R-squared (R^2). MSE estimated the average prediction error, while the R^2 value showed the share of variance in yearly spending explained by this model. Even though the actual versus predicted values scatter plot seemed to show that the predictions matched relatively actual spending, these deviations did show areas where the model should be improved. QC and QAI methodologies offer this place in advanced data processing and better accuracy in predictions of the limitations. Quantum algorithms, such as QSVM and QNNs, hold a greater advantage in handling high-dimensional data compared to other classical models. This could lead to more accurate predictions in customer spending, efficient resource allocation, and fine-tuning of engagement strategies. With continuous improvements in quantum technologies, the potential integration into e-business analytics would unleash profound value. Quantum's full capability will undoubtedly enable enterprises to enhance performance in forecasting customer behavior for increased revenues through more effective operations. In the future, e-business will be increasingly dependent upon quantum methodologies as a way to gain insights that will keep a company competitive within the dynamic market.

REFERENCES

1. Paramesha, M., Rane, N., & Rane, J. (2024). Big Data Analytics, Artificial Intelligence, Machine Learning, Internet of Things, and Blockchain for Enhanced Business Intelligence. Available at SSRN 4855856. doi:10.2139/ssrn.4855856.
2. Tellez, F., & Ortíz, J. (2024). Comparing AI Algorithms for Optimizing Elliptic Curve Cryptography Parameters in e-Commerce Integrations: A Pre-Quantum Analysis. *International Journal of Advanced Computer Science & Applications*, 15(6), 1539–1553.

3. Tellez, F., & Ortiz, J. (2023). Comparing AI Algorithms for Optimizing Elliptic Curve Cryptography Parameters in Third-Party E-Commerce Integrations: A Pre-Quantum Era Analysis. arXiv preprint arXiv:2310.06752.
4. Baldassarre, M. T., De Vincentiis, M., Pal, A., & Scalera, M. (2023). Quantum Artificial Intelligence for Cyber Security Education in Software Engineering. In: *Proceedings of the 1st International Workshop on Cyber Security Education for Industry and Academia (CSE4IA), co-located with IS-EUD 2023, CEUR Workshop Proceeding*, Cagliari, Italy.
5. Kasula, B. Y., Whig, P., Vegesna, V. V., & Yathiraju, N. (2024). Unleashing Exponential Intelligence: Transforming Businesses through Advanced Technologies. *International Journal of Sustainable Development Through AI, ML and IoT*, 3(1), 1–18.
6. How, M. L., & Cheah, S. M. (2024). Forging the Future: Strategic Approaches to Quantum AI Integration for Industry Transformation. *AI*, 5(1), 290–323.
7. Bahiyah, S. D., Budi, P. T., & Freitas, B. L. (2024). Community Challenges Facing IM-POIN (Impact of Artificial Intelligence) as a Development Effort Sustainability in the Electronic Market. *Elegant: Journal of Arts, Media, and Technology*, 1(1), 1–11.
8. Ghai, D., Saxena, S., Dhingra, G., & Tripathi, S. L. (2024). A Comprehensive Review on Performance-based Comparative Analysis, Categorization, Classification and Mapping of Text Extraction System Techniques for Images. *Multimedia Tools and Applications*, 84(5), 2327–2484.
9. Jahin, M. A., Shovon, M. S. H., Islam, M. S., Shin, J., Mridha, M. F., & Okuyama, Y. (2023). QAmplifyNet: Pushing the Boundaries of Supply Chain Backorder Prediction Using Interpretable Hybrid Quantum-Classical Neural Network. *Scientific Reports*, 13(1), 18246.
10. Rajendran, B., Simeone, O., & Al-Hashimi, B. M. (2023). Towards Efficient and Trustworthy AI Through Hardware-Algorithm-Communication Co-Design. arXiv preprint arXiv:2309.15942.
11. Dada, M. A., Majemite, M. T., Obaigbena, A., Daraojimba, O. H., Oliha, J. S., & Nwokediegwu, Z. Q. S. (2024). Review of Smart Water Management: IoT and AI in Water and Wastewater Treatment. *World Journal of Advanced Research and Reviews*, 21(1), 1373–1382.
12. Weinberg, A. I., & Faccia, A. (2024). Quantum Algorithms: A New Frontier in Financial Crime Prevention. arXiv preprint arXiv:2403.18322.
13. Gohel, P., & Joshi, M. (2024, April). Quantum Time Series Forecasting. In: *Sixteenth International Conference on Machine Vision (ICMV 2023)*, Yerevan, Armenia, vol. 13072, pp. 390–398. SPIE.
14. Shoetan, P. O., & Familoni, B. T. (2024). Transforming Fintech Fraud Detection with Advanced Artificial Intelligence Algorithms. *Finance & Accounting Research Journal*, 6(4), 602–625.
15. Schmidt, B., & Hildebrandt, A. (2024). From GPUs to AI and Quantum: Three Waves of Acceleration in Bioinformatics. *Drug Discovery Today*, 29, 103990.
16. Dasgupta, S. (2024). Stability of Quantum Computers. arXiv preprint arXiv:2404.19082.
17. Diaz-Pier, S., & Carloni, P. (2024). Impact of Quantum and Neuromorphic Computing on Biomolecular Simulations: Current Status and Perspectives. *Current Opinion in Structural Biology*, 87, 102817.
18. Vishwakarma, S., Harkins, F., Golecha, S., Bajpe, V. S., Dupuis, N., Buratti, L., ... & Cruz-Benito, J. (2024). Qiskit HumanEval: An Evaluation Benchmark For Quantum Code Generative Models. arXiv preprint arXiv:2406.14712.
19. Rane, N., Paramesha, M., Choudhary, S., & Rane, J. (2024). Business Intelligence through Artificial Intelligence: A Review. Available at SSRN 4831916.
20. Chen, C. M., Tso, G. K. F., & He, K. (2024). Quantum Optimized Cost Based Feature Selection and Credit Scoring for Mobile Micro-Financing. *Computational Economics*, 63(2), 919–950.
21. Olaiya, O. P., Adesoga, T. O., Adebayo, A. A., Sotomi, F. M., Adigun, O. A., & Ezeliora, P. M. (2024). Encryption Techniques for Financial Data Security in Fintech Applications. *International Journal of Science and Research Archive*, 12(1), 2942–2949.
22. Singh, N., Singh, S. K., Kumar, S., Rawat, Y., Arya, V., Bansal, R., & Chui, K. T. (2024). Next-Gen Security With Quantum-Safe Cryptography. In: B. B. Gupta, D. Kalra, and A. Almomani (Eds.), *Innovations in Modern Cryptography* (pp. 131–164). IGI Global.
23. Ogunleye, O. S. (Ed.). (2024). *Machine Learning and Data Science Techniques for Effective Government Service Delivery*. IGI Global.
24. Gupta, P. (2024). Synergizing Success: Harnessing AI-Infused Business Intelligence to Propel Exponential Business Growth. In: P. Keikhosrokiani (Ed.), *Data-Driven Business Intelligence Systems for Socio-Technical Organizations* (pp. 105–127). IGI Global.
25. Kumar, S., & Aithal, P. S. (2024). Tech-Business Analytics in GIG Economy–A Futuristic Technology Supported Online Business Model. *Poornaprajna International Journal of Teaching & Research Case Studies (PIJTRCS)*, 1(1), 28–59.
26. Varshney, A. K., Garg, A., Pandey, T. R., Singhal, R. K., Singhal, R., & Sharma, H. (2024). The Development of Manufacturing Industry Revolutions from 1.0 to 5.0. *Journal of Informatics Education and Research*, 4(1), 1230–1242.
27. Asaithambi, S., Ravi, L., Devarajan, M., Almazyad, A. S., Xiong, G., & Mohamed, A. W. (2024). Enhancing Enterprise's Trust Mechanism through Integrating Blockchain Technology into E-Commerce Platforms for SMEs. *Egyptian Informatics Journal*, 25, 100444.
28. Sandhu, R., Kumar, P., Bhasin, C., Fatima, N., & Pal, A. (2023). Resnet-34 Model for Human Activity Recognition on Smartphone Sensor Data. *International Journal of Intelligent systems and applications in Engineering*, 11(9s), 644–652.
29. Arora, C., & Sandhu, R. (2024, January). Adoption of Quantum NLP for Improved Healthcare System. In: A. K. Bairwa, V. Tiwari, S. K. Vishwakarma, M. Tuba, and T. Ganokratanaa (Eds.), *International Conference on Computation of Artificial Intelligence & Machine Learning* (pp. 51–59). Springer Nature Switzerland.
30. Ghai, D., Tripathi, S. L., Saxena, S., Chanda, M., & Alazab, M. (Eds.). (2022). *Machine Learning Algorithms for Signal and Image Processing*. John Wiley & Sons.
31. Sandhu, R., Channi, H. K., Ghai, D., Cheema, G. S., & Kaur, M. (2024). An Introduction to Generative AI Tools for Education 2030. In: R. Doshi; M. Dadhich; S. Poddar; K. K. Hiran (Eds.), *Integrating Generative AI in Education to Achieve Sustainable Development Goals* (pp. 1–28). IGI Global.
32. Channi, H. K., Sandhu, R., Cheema, G. S., Kumar, P., Singh, P., & Ghai, D. (2025). Classification Techniques for Renewable Energy: Identifying Renewable Energy Sources and Features. In: J. Muktha, V. Jain, S. B. Tsai (Eds.), *Digital Innovations for Renewable Energy and Conservation* (pp. 21–46). IGI Global.

33. Channi, H. K., Giri, N. C., Sandhu, R., El-Sebah, M. I. A., & Syam, F. A. (2024). Potential and Economic Feasibility Analysis of Solar-Biomass-based Hybrid System for Rural Electrification. *Bulletin of Electrical Engineering and Informatics*, 13(6), 3833–3840.
34. Channi, H. K., & Sandhu, R. (2024). 3 Big Data Tools for. Data-Driven Modelling and Predictive Analytics in Business and Finance: Concepts. *Designs, Technologies, and Applications*, 35–51.
35. Channi, H. K., Kumar, P., Sandhu, R., & Syam, F. A. (2025). Energy Storage Using Computer Vision: Control and Optimization of Energy Storage. In: A. K. Dubey, A. Kumar, U. C. Pati, F. P. García Marquez, V. García-Díaz, & A. L. Srivastav (Eds.), *Computer Vision and Machine Intelligence for Renewable Energy Systems* (pp. 223–239). Elsevier.

8 A Comprehensive Analysis of the Integration of Quantum Artificial Intelligence with the Internet of Things

Manorama Patnaik and Sakshi Gupta

8.1 INTRODUCTION

Artificial intelligence (AI) and quantum computing (QC) are two trending technologies that have changed the way to compute and solve problems. This chapter gives a detailed overview of the integration of AI with QC [1]. We also try to show how this integration is useful in many applications such as security, healthcare, aviation, manufacturing, and drug discovery [2,3].

With quantum physics, complex computations can be carried out through QC. On the other hand, AI aims to develop systems that can analyze data, learn, and make decisions on their own [4]. Through the proliferation of QC and AI, researchers hope to tackle challenging problems in various fields [5]. The convergence of quantum AI (QAI) could lead to groundbreaking advancements in various fields. Here are a few potential areas of converging Internet of Things (IoT) with QAI, as shown in Figure 8.1.

These are just a few examples of how combining the IoT and QAI could revolutionize various industries [6]. QAI can also work with a wireless sensor network to provide more accurate values and decision-making. QAI algorithms can be used for energy optimization and energy conservation [7]. IoT devices collect data in a region of interest, which can be analyzed by QAI. IoT data collected from various applications such as smart healthcare, smart city, smart environment can be analyzed and provide more efficient drug discovery, optimized traffic flow, improved supply chain, and mitigate environmental disasters, respectively [8–10]. Figure 8.2 shows the integration of IoT with QAI.

Algorithms for QAI use the concepts of QC to tackle difficult problems faster than classical algorithms [11]. Some key algorithms used in QAI are explained in Figure 8.3.

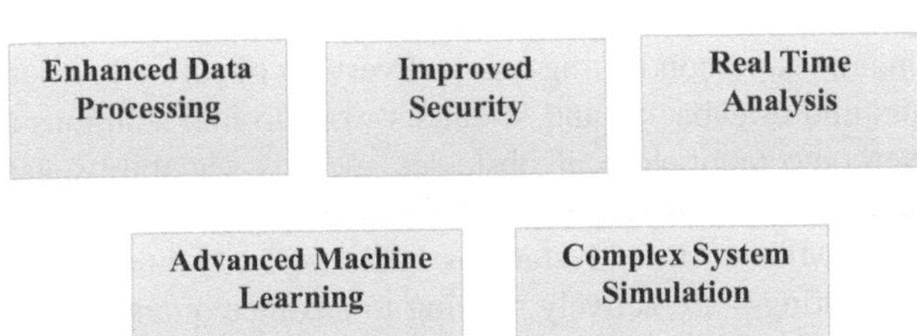

FIGURE 8.1 Benefits of converging IoT with QAI.

DOI: 10.1201/9781003530800-8

- **Quantum Annealing**: This algorithm finds the minimum energy state of a system by slowly cooling it down, which is useful for problems associated with optimization [12].
- **Quantum Variational Algorithms**: These algorithms are a mixture of quantum and classical algorithms to provide approximate solutions to various issues. The examples of variational algorithms are Quantum Approximate Optimization Algorithm, variational quantum eigensolver, and variational quantum linear solver [13].
- **Grover's Algorithm**: This algorithm provides a Grover's approach similar to a quadratic speedup technique over conventional algorithms, and is employed for unstructured search issues [14].
- **Quantum Phase Estimation**: It evaluates the unitary operators that estimate the eigenvalues of unitary operators, which is useful in many quantum-based algorithms, including Shor's algorithm [14].
- **Shor's Algorithm**: This quantum integer factoring technique is ten times faster than the other popular classical methods. Cryptography will be significantly impacted by this algorithm [14].
- **Quantum Machine Learning (QML) Algorithms**: These algorithms are the integration of the concept of quantum and the logic of machine learning algorithms to solve the complex problems [14].

The practical implementations of these algorithms are still in the early stages due to the challenges of building reliable and scalable quantum computers. This chapter is going to provide insight into all possible areas of QAI with IoT [15].

This article investigates the relationship between AI and QC and how it may result in revolutionary technological breakthroughs. Through case studies and analyses, we will examine the uses, difficulties, and potential future applications of using QC for AI-driven tasks, finally underlining the revolutionary potential of this synergy [16]. This chapter is structured in the following way: Section 8.1 depicts the Introduction part; Section 8.2 deals with Principles of Quantum mechanics, Quantum Bits, and Quantum gates in AI. Its one of the subparts (Section 8.2.3.1) covered the

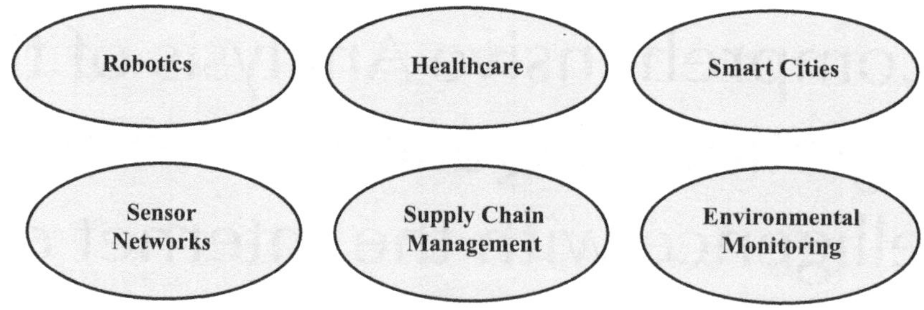

FIGURE 8.2 Proliferation of IoT with QAI.

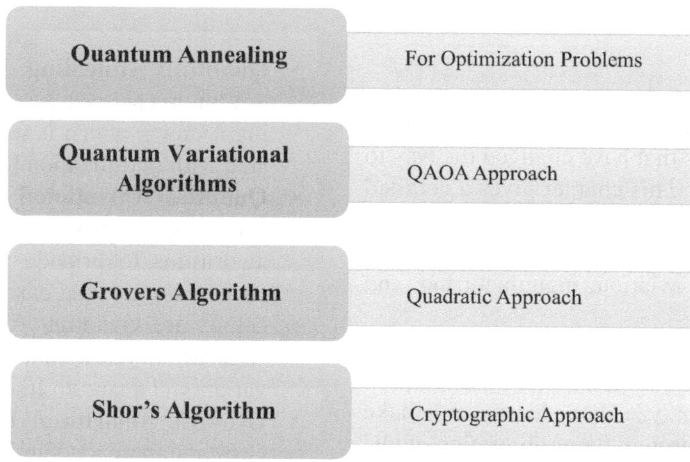

FIGURE 8.3 Various algorithms used in quantum-based AI applications.

discussion over Shor's algorithms; Section 8.3 discusses the foundations of AI for QC; Section 8.4 discusses the convergence of QC and AI; Section 8.5 discusses case studies based on QAI applications; Section 8.6 provides the conclusions and future directions.

8.2 PRINCIPLES OF QUANTUM MECHANICS, QUANTUM BITS (QUBITS), AND QUANTUM GATES IN ARTIFICIAL INTELLIGENCE

Quantum computing is based on the fundamental ideas of quantum physics, which control subatomic particle behavior, are the basis of QC. Quantum computers work on quantum bits, or qubits, which use bits to represent information as either 0 or 1. Superposition is a process of allowing qubits to be present in different states concurrently, allowing quantum computers to do operations in parallel [17].

Compared to classical bits, qubits are the fundamental building blocks of quantum information. Qubits exist in a superposition of two states: 0 or 1. Because of this feature, the computational capability of quantum computers can be increased exponentially by processing a large number of possibilities at once [18]. The fundamental components of quantum circuits are quantum gates such as logic gates. By manipulating qubits to carry out tasks such as phase shifts, entanglement, and superposition, they make it possible for quantum algorithms to quickly process complex calculations [19].

8.2.1 Quantum Supremacy and Quantum Advantages

Quantum computers solve problems quickly and conveniently as compared to classical computers, and can be called quantum supremacy. The accomplishment of quantum supremacy shows how QC is used to tackle problems that traditional computers are unable to handle [20]. On the contrary, quantum advantage describes the point at which a quantum computer can outperform a classical computer for most jobs, if not all of them, in practical applications. Although quantum supremacy has been proven in experimental environments, achieving quantum advantage in practical applications is still somewhat difficult [21].

8.2.2 Major Quantum Computing Architectures in AI

The creation of quantum computers is pursuing several strategies, including the use of photonic, topological, trapped ion, and superconducting qubits. Every architecture has benefits and drawbacks, and scientists work to find solutions to overcome technological obstacles such as scalability, gate faults, and decoherence. The field's major players—Google, IBM, Microsoft, and startups such as IonQ and Rigetti Computing—are actively striving to advance quantum software and hardware [22,23]. Figure 8.4 shows the architecture for quantum architecture computing with AI.

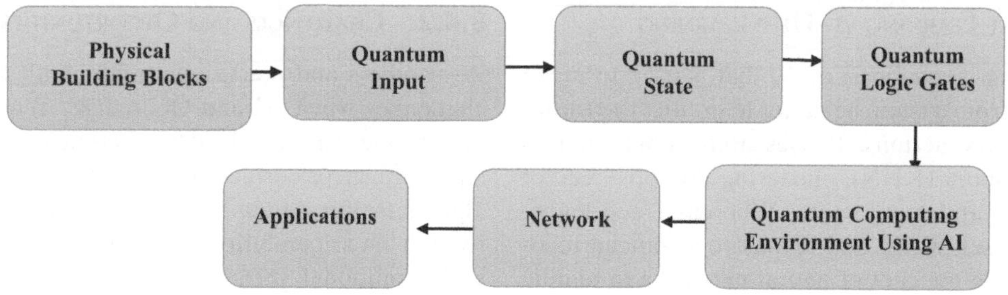

FIGURE 8.4 Architecture for quantum architecture computing with AI.

8.2.3 Quantum Algorithms

Compared to classical algorithms, quantum algorithms solve problems with the advantage of the special characteristics of quantum physics. Classical cryptography faces danger from Shor's algorithm, which allows quantum computers to factor huge integers exponentially faster than the most well-known classical algorithms. In contrast, Grover's approach provides a quadratic speedup for unstructured search issues, which has consequences for jobs related to database search and optimization. These techniques are but a handful of the ways that QC can transform computation across a wide range of fields [24].

8.2.3.1 Shor's Algorithm

Shor developed the factoring algorithm to demonstrate the power of QC to the world. Using this algorithm requires a good knowledge of quantum computation [25,26]. Choosing a random integer less than the number to be factored is the first step in factoring numbers using Shor's algorithm. The target number is then divided by the random number using the greatest common divisor, which is computed classically, to see if the target number has already unintentionally been factored. This entire process may appear rather straightforward on the surface. That is a possibility for lesser numbers. It could be necessary to use a supercomputer for higher numbers. Furthermore, a quantum computer will be required for numbers that are thought to be cryptographically secure [27]. The period of the number that needs to be factored in is what the quantum computer is supposed to figure out. The computation results establish if the desired factors have been found or if a fresh random integer needs to be checked [28].

a. **Applications of Shor's Algorithm**: Shor's algorithm is structured around three main components: an initial classical stage, a quantum stage, and a final classical stage. As previously mentioned, the algorithm consists of six major phases in total. The quantum stage of Shor's factoring algorithm is further divided into four subcomponents, each of which might stand alone as a whole article of explanation. Furthermore, of these four subcomponents, two are particularly important—they form the core quantum subroutines that enable the algorithm's exponential speed-up—while the remaining two are conceptually simple to understand [29].

   Quantum phase estimation is one of the essential quantum subcomponents. The key point to remember from this is that it executes the modular arithmetic required to determine the number. The inverse quantum Fourier transform is the name of the other important quantum subcomponent. In other words, measurement is the method by which the inverse quantum Fourier transform converts the quantum result of the modular arithmetic that comes right before it into classical information that can be extracted from the quantum circuit [30].

b. **Required Number of Qubits for Shor's Algorithm**: To solve this topic, it is first necessary to distinguish between logical and physical qubits. Physical qubits are what all qubits are now. They are prone to errors because they are very "noisy." Any meaningful quantum computation produces findings that make it hard to discriminate between right and wrong responses [31]. The likelihood that any given solution will be correct is the same for all potential solutions, meaning that there are no wrong responses. This is the application of logical qubits. To be deemed "fault-tolerant," physical qubits must be arranged and coupled in a way that allows them to give sufficient error correction to one another. These qubit collectives are thus referred to as "logical qubits," or occasionally "perfect qubits" [32].

8.3 FOUNDATIONS OF ARTIFICIAL INTELLIGENCE FOR QUANTUM COMPUTING

8.3.1 History and Evolution of Artificial Intelligence

The creation of intelligent systems that can perceive, reason, learn, and act on their own is the broad topic of AI. The phrase "artificial intelligence" was first used at the Dartmouth Conference in 1956, from where the origins of AI may be found. Since then, machine learning, neural networks, and computing power advancements have fueled the rapid progress of AI [33].

8.3.2 Machine Learning vs. Deep Learning

Machine learning is a subpart of AI that is used to make models to learn from system behavior to predict the future and take necessary actions. It uses algorithms such as K-Nearest Neighbors (KNN), clustering, Support Vector Machine (SVM), and many more. Whereas Deep learning (DL) is a subset of ML and is a more advanced technique that uses the concept of neural networks to handle and simplify complex tasks such as image and speech recognition [34,35].

8.3.3 Reinforcement Learning and Generative Models Applied in QAI

In reinforcement learning, an agent learns by interacting with the environment, making decisions, and receiving rewards to improve future actions. The agent discovers the best methods for making decisions in challenging situations by making mistakes and trying again. In contrast, generative models seek to produce fresh data samples that bear similarities to those seen in the training dataset. Popular generative models for picture production, data analysis, and anomaly detection include variational autoencoders and generative adversarial networks [36].

Numerous industries, including healthcare, banking, retail, automotive, and entertainment, have found uses for AI. AI-powered healthcare systems can help with medication discovery, disease diagnostics, and individualized treatment planning. Algorithmic trading, risk assessment, fraud detection, and customer service automation are among the financial applications of AI algorithms [37].

8.4 Convergence of Quantum Computing and Artificial Intelligence

8.4.1 Quantum Machine Learning (QML) and Quantum Neural Networks (QNNs)

An emerging multidisciplinary field called QML is the junction between QC and ML. With the help of quantum concepts and algorithms, QML can develop advanced machine-learning models [38].

Neural network designs called QNNs are developed to imitate quantum dynamics with neural networks. This field focuses on developing new QNN models, training methods, and expanding their applications in areas such as quantum chemistry, optimization, and pattern recognition [39–41].

These methods use quantum computers as accelerators in traditional machine learning pipelines or for subroutines. For instance, variational quantum eigensolver algorithms guide quantum circuits [42] to solve molecular energy issues using classical optimization techniques. Comparably, for data synthesis tasks, quantum-enhanced sampling methods can outperform classical generative models.

8.4.2 Challenges and Opportunities

Researchers and practitioners face both opportunities and challenges when AI and QC merge. Technical difficulties of this merger include the creation of scalable quantum hardware, error correction methods, and effective quantum algorithms for AI applications [43]. Moreover, compatibility and interoperability issues arise when combining QC with traditional infrastructure and algorithms. However, the potential uses of QAI are broad and involve a variety of fields [44], including climate modeling, drug discovery [45], materials research, finance, and cybersecurity. Interdisciplinary cooperation, creative thinking, and consistent investment in R&D will be necessary to meet these obstacles and realize the full promise of QAI [46].

8.5 Case Studies Based on QAI Applications

8.5.1 Drug Discovery

Because chemical space is so large and biological systems are so complex, the pharmaceutical industry has a difficult time finding new medications. AI and QC present viable ways to accelerate the drug discovery process and create more efficient treatments. Case studies show how drug-protein interactions, molecular property optimization, and molecular structure simulation are all possible with quantum algorithms. For instance, Google researchers have paved the way for more precise creation of pharmaceuticals by simulating the electrical structure of tiny molecules using quantum algorithms [47].

8.5.2 Optimization in Logistics

Complex optimization issues like resource allocation, inventory control, and route planning are part of supply chain management and logistics. Logistics operations can be made more efficient by using quantum-inspired optimization algorithms, which uncover optimal solutions more quickly than traditional methods. The use of quantum-inspired algorithms for demand forecasting, warehouse optimization, and vehicle routing is demonstrated through case studies. For example, Volkswagen optimized the logistics of shipping cars from factories to dealerships by using quantum-inspired algorithms, which help in reducing costs and carbon emissions [48].

8.5.3 Financial Modeling and Risk Analysis

Because of the uncertainty, volatility, and complexity of the financial markets, precise forecasting and risk management are difficult undertakings. AI and QC provide sophisticated modeling methods for evaluating portfolio risk, forecasting asset values, and analyzing market patterns. Case studies demonstrate how trading techniques can be improved, fraud can be detected, and investment portfolios can be optimized by QML algorithms. For instance, JPMorgan Chase used optimization algorithms with quantum inspiration to effectively rebalance its multi-asset portfolio, increasing returns and lowering risk [49–54].

8.5.4 Cryptography and Data Security

Cryptography is essential for private, secure, and confidential digital communications and transactions. Traditional encryption techniques such as Rivest–Shamir–Adleman and elliptic curve cryptography have been susceptible to attacks based on quantum algorithms since the introduction of quantum computers. The significance of post-quantum cryptography methods and quantum-resistant encryption is illustrated through case studies [55–68].

8.5.5 Natural Language Processing and Sentiment Analysis

Natural language processing tasks can be improved by quantum-based computing and AI through faster text processing, better language modeling, and the ability to extract semantic meaning from enormous datasets [61–68]. Case studies demonstrate how QML algorithms can perform better in document categorization, sentiment analysis, and text summarization than traditional methods [49–54].

8.6 CONCLUSION AND FUTURE DIRECTIONS

The integration of AI and QC has a profound and positive impact on society, business, and research. These new developments can shape the future of modern computing and enable rapid solutions to complex problems that are beyond the capabilities of classical computers. This article explored the possibility of merging AI and QC with IoT applications and established its applicability for future work. These technologies can also be very useful in cryptography, drug discovery, and manufacturing. Indeed, a great, deep knowledge and practical implementations are required in this context. We have a very strong opportunity and clear future directions to work in this area, as the literature shows that only limited work has been done so far. Advancing this field requires more practical experimentation with qubits and deeper engagement with quantum physics.

REFERENCES

1. Herbal, S., Zier, A., Hebbal, S., Louai, L., & Annan, B., Security in Internet of things: a review of approaches based on blockchain, machine learning, cryptography, and quantum computing. *Journal of Supercomputing*, 80(3) (2024) 3738–3816.
2. Dong, S., & Chen, H., Artificial intelligence and IoT based optical quantum computing application legal implications in privacy and regulatory analysis. *Optical and Quantum Electronics*, 56(4) (2024) 556.
3. Cai, J., Lu, J., Ming, Z., & Wu, J., Quantum computing for real-time big data analysis: opportunities and challenges. *Journal of Network and Computer Applications,* 120 (2018) 129–142. https://doi.org/10.1016/j.jnca.2018.05.015.
4. Farid, A., Shabani, A., Song, Y., Nishimura, H., Awais, M., Amin, M. B., & Kim, S. W., Quantum-enhanced artificial intelligence (2021). arXiv preprint arXiv:2108.05580.
5. Leymann, F., Barzen, J., Falkenthal, M., Vietz, D., Weder, B., & Wild, K. (2020). Quantum in the cloud: application potentials and research opportunities. arXiv preprint arXiv:2003.06256.
6. Jain, S., Ziauddin, J., Leonchyk, P., Yenkanchi, S., & Geraci, J. Quantum and classical machine learning for the classification of non-small-cell lung cancer patients. *SN Applied Sciences*, 2(6) (2020) 1088. https://doi.org/10.1007/s42452-020-2847-4.
7. Prateek, K., Ojha, N. K., Altaf, F., & Maity, S. Quantum secured 6G technology-based applications in internet of everything. *Telecommunication Systems*, 82(2) (2023) 315–344.
8. Bonab, A. B., Fedele, M., Formisano, V., & Rudko, I. Urban quantum leap: a comprehensive review and analysis of quantum technologies for smart cities. *Cities*, 140 (2023) 104459.
9. Hassija, V., Chamola, V., Goyal, A., Kanhere, S. S., & Guizani, N., Forthcoming applications of quantum computing: peeking into the future. *IET Quantum Communication*, 1 (2020) 35–41. https://doi.org/10.1049/iet-qtc.2020.0026.
10. Krithika, S., & Kesavmurthy, T., Securing IOT network through quantum key distribution. *International Journal of Innovative Technology and Exploring Engineering,* (2019) 693–696. https://doi.org/10.35940/ijitee.F1141.0486S419.
11. Ahmed, J., Garg, A. K., Singh, M., Bansal, S., & Amir, M., *Quantum Cryptography Implementation in Wireless Networks*, 3 (2014) 129–133.
12. Cheng, S. T., Wang, C. Y., & Tao, M. H., Quantum communication for wireless wide-area networks. *IEEE Journal on Selected Areas in Communications,* 23 (2005) 1424–1432. https://doi.org/10.1109/JSAC.2005.851157.
13. Broadbent, A., & Schaffner, C., *Quantum Cryptography beyond Quantum Key Distribution*. Springer, 2016. https://doi.org/10.1007/s10623-015-0157-4.
14. Moulick, S. R., & Panigrahi, P. K., Quantum cheques. *Quantum Information Processing*, 15 (2016) 2475–2486. https://doi.org/10.1007/s11128-016-1273-4.
15. Mitchell, C. J., The impact of quantum computing on real-world security: a 5G case study. *Computers & Security*, 93 (2020) 1–11. https://doi.org/10.1016/j.cose.2020.101825.
16. Ralegankar, V. K., Bagul, J., Thakkar, B., Gupta, R., Tanwar, S., Sharma, G., & Davidson, I. E., Quantum cryptography-as-a-service for secure UAV communication: applications, challenges, and case study. IEEE Access, 10 (2022) 1475–1492.
17. Kang, M. S., Hong, C. H., Heo, J., Lim, J. I., & Yang, H. J., Controlled mutual quantum entity authentication using entanglement swapping. *Chinese Physics B,* 24 (2015). https://doi.org/10.1088/1674-1056/24/9/090306.
18. Jian, L., Na, L., Yu, Z., Shuang, W., & Wei, D., Wenping, A survey on quantum cryptography. *Chinese Journal of Electronics,* 27 (2018) 223–228. https://doi.org/10.1049/cje.2018.01.017.
19. Behera, B. K., Banerjee, A., & Panigrahi, P. K., Experimental realization of quantum cheque using a five-qubit quantum computer. *Quantum Information Processing*, 16 (2017) 1–12. https://doi.org/10.1007/s11128-017-1762-0.
20. Teja, V., Banerjee, P., Sharma, N. N., & Mittal, R. K., Quantum cryptography: state-of-art, challenges and future perspectives. In: *2007 7th IEEE International Conference on Nanotechnology (IEEE NANO 2007)*, Hong Kong, China, 2007, pp. 1296–1301. https://doi.org/10.1109/NANO.2007.4601420.

21. Nurhadi, A. I., & Syambas, N. R., Quantum key distribution (QKD) protocols: a survey. In: *Proceedings of the 2018 4th International Conference on Wireless and Telematics (ICWT 2018),* Nusa Dua, Bali, Indonesia, 2018, pp. 1–5. https://doi.org/10.1109/ICWT.2018.8527822.
22. Niederhagen, R., & Waidner, M. *Practical Post-Quantum Cryptography.* Fraunhofer SIT, 2017.
23. Routray, S. K., Jha, M. K., Sharma, L., Nyamangoudar, R., Javali, A., & Sarkar, S., Quantum cryptography for IoT: a perspective. In: *Proceedings of the 2017 IEEE International Conference on IoT and Its Applications (ICIOT 2017),* Nagapattinam, India, 2017. https://doi.org/10.1109/ICIOTA.2017.8073638.
24. Chawla, D., & Mehra, P. S. A survey on quantum computing for Internet of Things Security. *Procedia Computer Science*, 218 (2023) 2191–2200.
25. Mohapatro, M., & Snigdh, I., An experimental study of distributed denial of service and sinkhole attacks on IoT based healthcare applications. *Wireless Personal Communications,* 121(1) (2021) 707–724.
26. Mohapatro, M., & Snigdh, I., Security in IoT healthcare. In: S. K. Sharma, B. Bhushan and N. C. Debnath (Eds.), *IoT Security Paradigms and Applications.* CRC Press, 2020, pp. 237–259.
27. Mohapatro, M., & Snigdh, I., Principal component analysis in body sensor networks for secure data transmission. In: *Trends in Wireless Communication and Information Security: Proceedings of EWCIS 2020,* Amity University Jharkhand, Ranchi, India, 2021, pp. 237–245.
28. Shor, P. W. Introduction to quantum algorithms. *Proceedings of Symposia in Applied Mathematics*, 58 (2002) 143–160.
29. Ugwuishiwu, C. H., Orji, U. E., Ugwu, C. I., & Asogwa, C. N., An overview of quantum cryptography and Shor's algorithm. *International Journal of Advanced Trends in Computer Science and Engineering,* 9(5) (2020) 7487–7495.
30. Hayward, M., *Quantum Computing and Shor's Algorithm.* Technical Report, Macquarie University Mathematics Department, Sydney, 2008.
31. Ekert, A., & Jozsa, R., Quantum computation and Shor's factoring algorithm. *Reviews of Modern Physics*, 68(3) (1996) 733.
32. Strubell, E., An introduction to quantum algorithms. *COS498 Chawathe Spring*, 13 (2011) 19.
33. Bhatia, V., & Ramkumar, K. R., An efficient quantum computing technique for cracking RSA using Shor's algorithm. In: *2020 IEEE 5th International Conference on Computing Communication and Automation (ICCCA)*, Greater Noida, Uttar Pradesh, India, 2020, October, pp. 89–94. IEEE.
34. Raj, C. V., Phaneendra, H. D., & Shivakumar, M. S., Quantum algorithms and hard problems. In: *2006 5th IEEE International Conference on Cognitive Informatics*, Beijing, China, 2006, Vol. 2, pp. 783–787. IEEE.
35. Rahmi, M., Shamanta, D., & Tasnim, A., Basic quantum algorithms and applications. *International Journal of Computer Applications*, 56(4) (2012) 26–31.
36. Portugal, R. Basic quantum algorithms (2022). arXiv preprint arXiv:2201.10574.
37. Ying, M., Quantum computation, quantum theory and AI. *Artificial Intelligence*, 174(2) (2010) 162–176.
38. Dunjko, V., & Briegel, H. J., Machine learning\& artificial intelligence in the quantum domain. (2017) arXiv preprint arXiv:1709.02779.
39. Bhatia, A., Bibhu, V., Lohani, B. P., & Kushwaha, P. K., An application framework for quantum computing using Artificial intelligence techniques. In: *2020 Research, Innovation, Knowledge Management and Technology Application for Business Sustainability (INBUSH)*, Greater Noida, India, 2020 February, pp. 264–269. IEEE.
40. Robson, B., & St Clair, J., Principles of quantum mechanics for artificial intelligence in medicine: discussion with reference to the quantum universal exchange language (Q-UEL). *Computers in Biology and Medicine,* 143 (2022) 105323.
41. Vernuccio, F., Bresci, A., Cimini, V., Giuseppi, A., Cerullo, G., Polli, D., & Valensise, C. M., Artificial intelligence in classical and quantum photonics. *Laser & Photonics Reviews*, 16(5) (2022) 2100399.
42. Gupta, S., Mohanta, S., Chakraborty, M., & Ghosh, S., Quantum machine learning-using quantum computation in artificial intelligence and deep neural networks: quantum computation and machine learning in artificial intelligence. In: *2017 8th Annual Industrial Automation and Electromechanical Engineering Conference (IEMECON)*, Bangkok, Thailand, 2017 August, pp. 268–274. IEEE.
43. Mangini, S., Tacchino, F., Gerace, D., Bajoni, D., & Macchiavello, C., Quantum computing models for artificial neural networks. *Europhysics Letters*, 134(1) (2021) 10002.
44. Narayanan, A., & Menneer, T., Quantum artificial neural network architectures and components. *Information Sciences*, 128(3–4) (2000) 231–255.
45. Krenn, M., & Zeilinger, A., Predicting research trends with semantic and neural networks with an application in quantum physics. *Proceedings of the National Academy of Sciences*, 117(4) (2020) 1910–1916.
46. Ayoade, O., Rivas, P., & Orduz, J., Artificial intelligence computing at the quantum level. *Data*, 7(3) (2022) 28.
47. Li, W., Lu, Z. D., & Deng, D. L. Quantum neural network classifiers: a tutorial. *SciPost Physics Lecture Notes* (2022) 061. https://doi.org/10.21468/SciPostPhysLectNotes.61.
48. Krenn, M., Landgraf, J., Foesel, T., & Marquardt, F. (2023). Artificial intelligence and machine learning for quantum technologies. *Physical Review A*, 107(1), 010101.
49. Raparthi, M. Real-time AI decision making in IoT with quantum computing: investigating & exploring the development and implementation of quantum-supported AI inference systems for IoT applications. *Internet of Things and Edge Computing Journal*, 1(1) (2021) 18–27.
50. Zeguendry, A., Jarir, Z., & Quafafou, M., Quantum machine learning: a review and case studies. *Entropy*, 25(2) (2023) 287.
51. Khan, M. M., Bari, I., Khan, O. U., Akbar, A., Jeehan, S., & Ullah, N., Quantum AI: uniting the future of smart technologies. In: I. Ullah Khan, M. Ouaissa, M. Ouaissa, M. Fayaz, R. Ullah (Eds.), *Artificial Intelligence for Intelligent Systems.* CRC Press, 2024, pp. 86–102.
52. Sanchez, M., Everly, C., & Postigo, P. A. (2024). Advances in machine learning optimization for classical and quantum photonics. *Journal of the Optical Society of America B*, 41(2), A177–A190.
53. Chauhan, V., Negi, S., Jain, D., Singh, P., Sagar, A. K., & Sharma, A. K. Quantum computers: a review on how quantum computing can boom AI. In: *2022 2nd International Conference on Advance Computing and Innovative Technologies in Engineering (ICACITE)*, Greater Noida, India, 2022 April, pp. 559–563. IEEE.
54. Ghai, D., Saxena, S., Dhingra, G., & Tripathi, S. L. (2024). A comprehensive review on performance-based comparative analysis, categorization, classification and mapping of text extraction system techniques for images. *Multimedia Tools and Applications*, 84(5), 2327–2484. https://doi.org/10.1007/s11042-024-20257-0.

55. Somayajula, V. K. A., Ghai, D., & Kumar, S. Land use/land cover change analysis using NDVI, PCA. In: *2021 5th International Conference on Computing Methodologies and Communication (ICCMC)*, Erode, Tamil Nadu, 2021 April, pp. 849–855. IEEE.
56. MahiDar, P. R., & Ghai, D. Bio-inspired optimization algorithms for machine learning in agriculture applications. *Smart Agriculture* (2021) 53–60. https://doi.org/10.1201/b22627-4.
57. Sandhu, R., Channi, H. K., Ghai, D., Cheema, G. S., & Kaur, M. An introduction to generative AI tools for education 2030. In: R. Doshi; M. Dadhich; S. Poddar; K. Kant Hiran (Eds.), *Integrating Generative AI in Education to Achieve Sustainable Development Goals.* IGI Global, 2024, pp. 1–28.
58. Arora, C., & Sandhu, R. Adoption of Quantum NLP for Improved Healthcare System. In: *International Conference on Computation of Artificial Intelligence & Machine Learning*, Jaipur, India, 2024 January, pp. 51–59. Springer Nature.
59. Faiz, M., Sandhu, R., Akbar, M., Shaikh, A. A., Bhasin, C., & Fatima, N. (2023). Machine learning techniques in wireless sensor networks: algorithms, strategies, and applications. *International Journal of Intelligent Systems and Applications in Engineering*, 11(9s), 685–694.
60. Gupta, S., & Snigdh, I., Leveraging data aggregation algorithm in LoRa networks. *Journal of Supercomputing*, 78(15) (2022) 16861–16875.
61. Musa, U. I., Gupta, S., & Mensah, Q. E. *AI-Driven Intelligent Transportation Systems in the Age of 5G/6G Networks.* Research Square Platform LLC, 2023.
62. Gupta, S., Manorama, & Snigdh, I. An energy conserving MANET-LoRa architecture for wireless body area network. In: A. Swaroop, Z. Polkowski, S. Duarte Correia, and B. Virdee (Eds.), *International Conference on Data Analytics & Management*, 2023, pp. 603–615. Springer Nature.
63. Gkotsiopoulos, P., Zorbas, D., & Douligeris, C. (2021). Performance determinants in LoRa networks: A literature review. *IEEE Communications Surveys & Tutorials*, 23(3), 1721–1758. 64. Gupta, S., & Snigdh, I. A review on parameters that impact IOT application: an experimental evaluation. In: V. Nath and J. K. Mandal (Eds.), *Microelectronics, Communication Systems, Machine Learning and Internet of Things: Select Proceedings of MCMI 2020.* Springer, 2022, pp. 203–213.
65. Gupta, S., Snigdh, I., & Sahana, S. K. A fuzzy logic approach for predicting efficient LoRa communication. *International Journal of Fuzzy Systems*, 24(5) (2022) 2591–2599.
66. Gupta, S., & Snigdh, I. Applying Bayesian belief in LoRa: smart parking case study. *Journal of Ambient Intelligence and Humanized Computing*, 14(6) (2023) 7857–7870.
67. Gupta, S., Gupta, U., Sharma, M., & Malik, K. (Eds.). *Generative Intelligence in Healthcare: Transforming Patient Care with AI Creativity.* CRC Press, 2025.
68. Gupta, S., & Snigdh, I. Multi-sensor fusion in autonomous heavy vehicles. In: R. Krishnamurthi, F. Xhafa, A. Kumar, and S. S. Gill (Eds.), *Autonomous and Connected Heavy Vehicle Technology.* Academic Press, 2022, pp. 375–389.

9 Quantum Adaptive Key Management and Optimization Network (QAKM-ON)

Blockchain Integration to Enhance the Efficiency and Privacy in Quantum Networks

J. Viji Gripsy, N. A. Sheela Selvakumari, John T. Mesia Dhas, and S. Sahul Hameed

9.1 INTRODUCTION

In recent years, many sectors have adopted digital transformation, which integrates new technologies to improve transaction security and data processing efficiency [1]. Quantum networks provide a decentralized, tamper-resistant, and traceable architecture for safe data flow without depending on centralized control [2]. It emerges as an optimistic solution to address the thrust challenges across multiple sectors. The applications of quantum networks already extend to many domains, which include financial systems, healthcare, social networks, and digital currencies [3]. The public quantum networks provide transparency for secure auditing, and they also reduce privacy breaches and offer robust mechanisms [4]. While the anonymity inherent in the quantum networks can hide the identities of those initiating transactions, it also creates challenges in handling the malicious content, which cannot be changed once it is recorded [5]. These privacy auditing issues create significant barriers for further innovation and the extensive adaptation of quantum network applications [6].

To protect user privacy, quantum networks frequently use encryption techniques to provide data security, ensuring that the authorized parties, which include auditors only, can access it [7]. Mostly, a session key is shared between the transaction participant and the auditors to encrypt the sensitive information [8]. To prevent malicious activities, the auditing process can be done in the consortium quantum networks for the quick detection of accounts that spread harmful content [9]. To prevent centralized control, single points of failure, and any other specific vulnerability, the audits in the consortium quantum networks are distributed across multiple nodes [10]. The auditors depend on the transaction originators to encrypt the keys with each auditor's public key, which helps to decrypt the session key [11]. This approach may be inappropriate because the transaction initiator has to be available to respond to each auditor for the session key [12].

Like wireless sensor networks (WSNs), quantum networks can have tens of thousands or even millions of nodes. A decentralized network architecture is required due to the unpredictable placement and distribution of nodes to provide reliable communication even in challenging environments [13]. Even though the possible node failures or connectivity losses are frequently caused by noisy channels or shadow zones, WSNs must retain the functionality [14]. In WSNs, it is important to reduce energy consumption during data transmission and processing, which relies on battery-powered sensors [15].

In WSNs, secure communication is enabled through a trusted key distribution center on a base station or through a peer-to-peer system in which nodes independently exchange keys. It is important to develop a key distribution method that enables secure and efficient communication between sensor nodes within a decentralized network without restricting their mobility [16]. The literature describes several resource constraints affecting many similar nodes and highlights the need for efficient key management due to the lack of general asymmetric encryption features [17].

The most important contribution of this work is the introduction of the concept of the Quantum Adaptive Key Management and Optimization Network (QAKM-ON). This is a new approach to solving integration problems between quantum networks and blockchain technologies, mainly in collaborative environments that require privacy and auditing. QAKM-ON uses an adaptive key management system that generates and handles quantum keys dynamically, thereby ensuring safety and efficiency in data processing. The suggested framework integrates enhanced quantum consensus and collaborative quantum encryption for supporting private and anonymous data audits, thereby avoiding the requirement of continuous online presence for such transaction initiators. Figure 9.1 depicts the interaction of quantum nodes and sensor nodes through a base station with quantum channels and key distribution so that it has secure communications. It also shows a decentralized

DOI: 10.1201/9781003530800-9

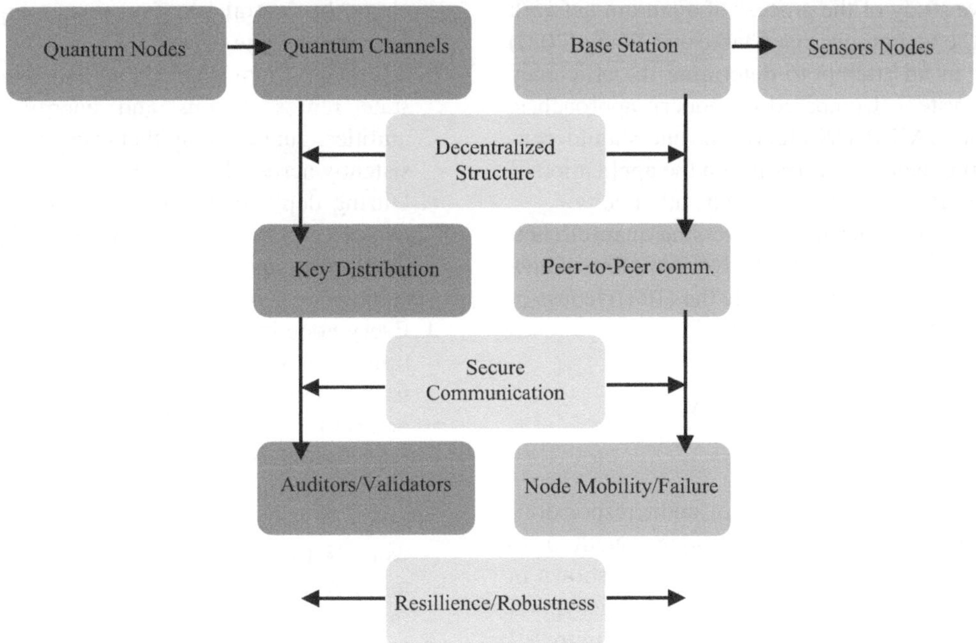

FIGURE 9.1 Components of the quantum networks and WSN framework.

structure with peer-to-peer communications against node mobility or failure resistance. Auditors/validators and robust mechanisms improve the security and efficiency of networks.

The structure of this paper is as follows: Section 9.9.2 reviews related research on security in quantum networks. Section 9.9.3 describes the proposed model to improve the security and privacy in quantum network design. Section 9.9.4 presents the comparison results and discussion. Finally, Section 9.9.5 concludes with results and future work.

9.2 RELATED WORK

The quantum network is integrated with blockchain technology and has been discovered to address the security and privacy issues in decentralized systems. Due to their quantum properties, quantum networks that use quantum entanglement and superposition offer a high level of security [18]. In consortium environments, integrating these networks with blockchain technology involves resolving the complexities that maintain privacy and ensure effective data control [19]. The need for advanced cryptography and dynamic key management methods to address these challenges is highlighted in recent studies [20].

For a secure connection, quantum cryptography has established itself as a robust method. The concept of quantum key distribution (QKD) introduced by Bennett, Brassard, and Ekert offers a theory for secure key exchange based on quantum mechanics [21]. This method makes sure that any eavesdropping strives can be detected, making it the fundamental principle of secure quantum communication systems. Current quantum network research focuses on optimizing the efficiency of QKD systems and integrating them into practical applications [22]. When executed, the QAKM-ON algorithm must be constructed to comply with the requirements of adaptive key management schemes.

Various alternate methods are being investigated in quantum computing by employing artificial intelligence (AI). According to the researchers, machine learning algorithms could enhance the performance of the quantum processes and the entire system. Hsu and Li (2022) [23] examine the application of AI in quantum systems and explore the methods' potential. The results of his research present the potential for optimization using AI to optimize the general performance of quantum networks according to the needs of the QAKM-ON architecture. Besides, research has also been investigating the application of quantum-inspired evolutionary algorithms during the network optimization process. The results of this research have created greater awareness of the benefits of utilizing AI alongside quantum computing [24]. For the sake of fulfilling the requirement of effective consensus procedures in quantum networks, a complex quantum consensus algorithm has been designed. To enhance the efficacy and security of quantum communications, such algorithms are intended to bypass the limitations inherent in traditional methods [25]. Besides, several cooperative quantum cryptography protocols have been proposed to protect humans' privacy and promote the proper handling of data in quantum networks [26].

These designs are fundamental elements within the QAKM-ON strategy, which utilizes a quantum consensus of better quality to address issues related to control and privacy. Studies are being carried out in quantum network simulation and performance measurement to authenticate new algorithms and methods to authenticate new algorithms and methods. This is done for authenticating new algorithms.

A comprehensive study of the process of quantum network simulation and the techniques that Clarke and Wang (2021) [27] formulated in an attempt to determine the efficiency of the network system. Compared to modern approaches, in evaluating the QAKM-ON algorithm, one should consider the following factors: constraints on the application of resources, processing time intervals, and authenticity.

Several performance metrics for assessing quantum networks, Adams and Thompson (2020) give an outline of how these metrics might be used to evaluate the effectiveness of the proposed QAKM-ON framework [28].

9.3 PROPOSED METHODOLOGY

9.3.1 Network Model

Figure 9.2 illustrates the assignment of audit responsibility between nodes and auditors. Five nodes, Node 1 to Node 5, which comprise a quantum network, are shown in Figure 9.2. Auditor 1 is shown to handle the Encryption Keys. Auditor 2 handles the session keys. Hence, Figure 9.2 captures the sharing of auditing responsibilities by the participating auditors. There exist different auditors responsible for different aspects of the network to ensure security and handle the keys. The arrows indicate the responsibility flows from the nodes in the direction of the auditors, therefore reflecting decentralized auditing within the network.

Before the quantum network was developed, several assumptions were made:

a. The set of all quantum nodes in the network is represented by N. Every quantum node q_i keeps track of its quantum neighbors using a quantum neighbor list and monitors its quantum location position about the central quantum processing unit (QPU) or quantum gate driver.
b. All quantum nodes in the network have the same state representations and energy consumption abilities, guaranteeing that every node works consistently across the network.
c. During deployment, the quantum nodes are distributed randomly within the network. It maintains fixed positions during its operation. It became static once deployed.
d. Every node in the network is provided with quantum state sensing, which allows it to access and track quantum state information from all other nodes in the network.
e. Each quantum node calculates its distance to the nearest central QPU. Moreover, the transmission range of each node is determined within the network N to ensure efficient quantum state transmission and accurate distribution of quantum information.
f. Conversely, calculations are performed to determine the distance between each quantum node and the closest central QPU or quantum gate driver. Furthermore, the range of transmission for each node is calculated in N to ensure the effective transfer of quantum states and the exact distribution of entanglement throughout the entire network.

The central unit, the QPU in Figure 9.3, connects the five quantum nodes labeled q1 through q5. It allows the design to operate as a network system. Two-way communication between the central QPU and the quantum nodes is depicted using arrows. Establishing this connection enables

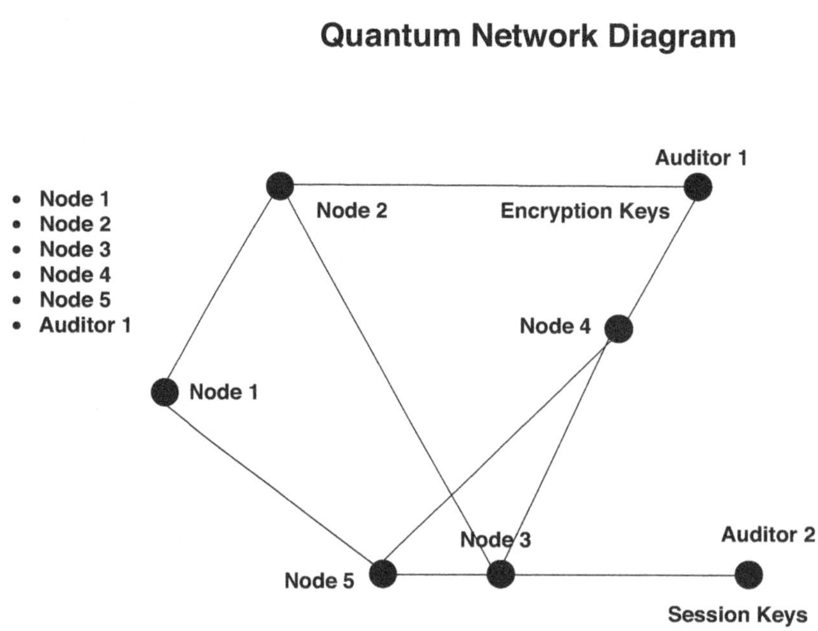

FIGURE 9.2 Distribution of audit responsibilities among various auditors.

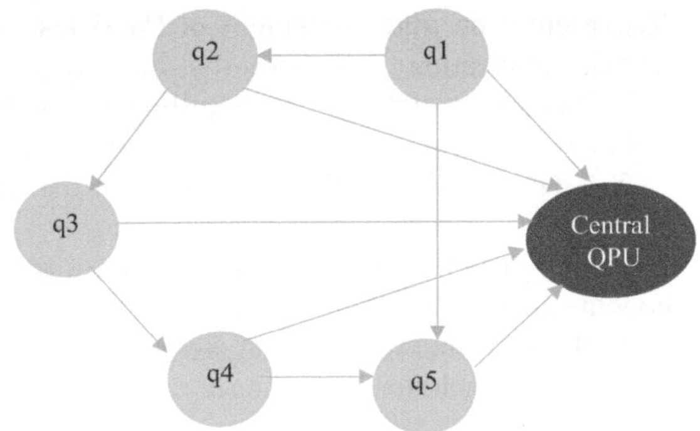

FIGURE 9.3 Architecture diagram of a quantum network.

the creation of a highly interconnected quantum network that facilitates effective data processing and exchange.

9.4 THE PROTECTION OF PERSONAL INFORMATION IN QUANTUM NETWORKS THROUGH THE GENERATION OF ADAPTIVE KEYS

This discussion explains advanced quantum cryptography algorithms to secure the safety and efficacy of data processing on quantum networks. Extensive privacy protection is strictly required to protect sensitive operations and quantum states from unauthorized access and interference.

The system generates secure quantum keys dynamically to encrypt and decrypt data. It is achieved by implementing adaptive key generation protocols that exploit the features peculiar to quantum physics. Such keys, generated in real-time from the constantly varying quantum states of the network, offer a strong level of security and resistance to any form of manipulation or eavesdropping that occurs. Regarding the methodology, the two most critical aspects are the safety and dependability of quantum processing and communications. Technology could play a secure role in managing resources and decision-making through AI.

This technology significantly improves quantum networks in a way that doesn't depend on conventional blockchain procedures. An analysis and forecasting of the optimal path for QKD and state transfer is performed using AI technologies such as machine learning and quantum neural networks. AI-driven systems can dynamically adapt to the network topology changes to ensure a secure and efficient operation [29–34]. Furthermore, quantum mechanics-inspired genetic algorithms optimize the quantum network architecture and position the quantum gates strategically. Due to this optimization technique, the system can handle applications requiring reduced energy utilization and increased computing efficacy.

These applications are instances of Quantum Internet of Things (QIoT) applications. Upgrading quantum systems with AI can increase the number of connected devices within a QIoT, enabling secure data processing and efficient communication within a quantum network. The flow diagram in Figure 9.4 presents the operational structure of the envisioned

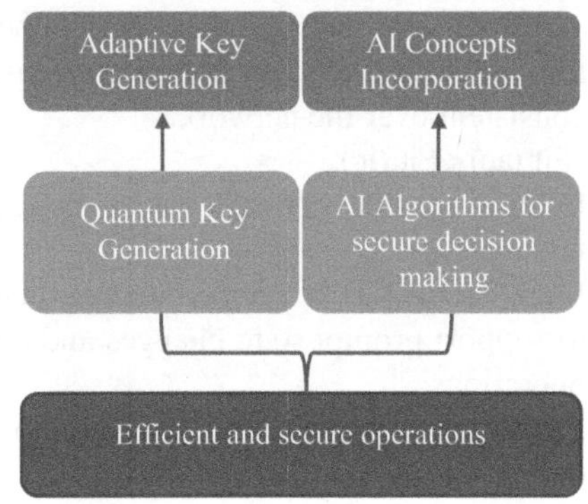

FIGURE 9.4 Operational framework of the proposed quantum network.

quantum network. Under this setup, AI elements have a pivotal role in enabling decentralized and secure decision processes, which fundamentally do away with the need to depend on a central authority. With this decentralized setup, the preservation of the entanglement state and the sharing of the quantum key are done promptly and transparently, leading to a system marked with reliability and tamper-proof.

The final aim of the quantum network is to optimize the utilization of computer resources with high security and privacy. Low energy consumption and AI optimization methods render this system the best fit for applications concerning the Internet of Things. The biggest challenge of modern quantum technology is to preserve user security and confidentiality while at the same time yielding information that is acceptable and adequate for a wide range of quantum nodes. The method that has been introduced increases the overall efficiency of quantum networks while simultaneously increasing the level of security and privacy in quantum activities. This achievement creates ground for further communication and quantum computing technology developments.

9.5 ADAPTIVE KEY MANAGEMENT ALGORITHM IN QUANTUM NETWORK

Algorithm 9.1: Proposed Methodology-QAM AI

1. Get started
2. Initialize all the nodes within the network's quantum states.
3. Test the reliability and performance of each node separately.
4. Test the average quantum fidelity or coherence of all the nodes in the network and evaluate the preservation of their quantum states.
5. If the Fidelity Fit(ac) of the existing quantum state is greater than the set threshold Fit(ic), the network continues with the following steps
   - Accumulate nodes with high dependability and low decoherence rates to create enduring clusters.
   - Upgrade node states to reduce decoherence and stay stable.

Make sure that the structure of the quantum network is a stable node arrangement and consistent over the network.

6. Else Fit (ac) < Fit (ic):
   - Reorganize the network to create dynamic node groups.
   - Increase the rate of interaction between nodes to support prompt state changes and optimize operations.
   - Each network configuration comprises a dynamic configuration of transitioning nodes that adapt until reaching the target state.
7. Stop

9.6 THE ENHANCED PARTICLE SWARM OPTIMIZATION (EPSO) METHOD FOR THE GENERATION OF QUANTUM NETWORKS

This part presents an enhanced particle swarm optimization (EPSO) strategy for creating quantum network topologies by integrating swarm intelligence and adaptive attraction concepts. This approach, which uses a modular design approach, attempts to optimize the organization and behavior of quantum networks. Here, every "particle" is a feasible solution present within the quantum network's parameter space.

9.6.1 Optimization of the EPSO Process as a Whole

Two phases are covered by the EPSO method:

a. **Optimization of the Parameters**: This phase involves optimizing the quantum network design parameters, along with the nodes' configurations and quantum points' interconnections. Preliminary estimations of control parameters are set forth to decide how to proceed with the initial exploration of the solution space.
b. **Control Parameter Refinement**: Once the design parameters are optimized, the second step is to optimize the control parameters. This is the subsequent step following the optimization of the design parameters. Refining is the process of adjusting the control settings recursively to completely search the solution space in an attempt to reach optimum performance. After optimizing the design parameters, the next step focuses on improving the control parameters. This involves factors like the synchronization of quantum opera, the coordination of quantum processes, and error correction protocols. The refining process involves repetitive changes of control parameters to allow extensive probing of the solution space to achieve optimum performance.
c **Representation and Movement of Particles**: In EPSO, the location of particles that indicate possible solutions is defined in a coordinate system. Below is a description of each particle's position:

   $X_{I,j}$: The position of the jth particle in the ith iteration

   p: the particle population size, which affects how far the search will go overall

   n: the maximum number of iterations, which acts as a threshold for convergence

Based on the objective functions, the algorithm iteratively adjusts particle positions that measure the quality of the solution. The primary goals of the function used in this optimization are:

i. **Quantum Network Fidelity**: This feature guarantees the fidelity of quantum operations and ensures accurate and reliable quantum calculations. High fidelity is vital for the practical implementation of quantum networks because it minimizes errors in deploying the quantum state.
ii. **Quantum Resource Efficiency**: Enhancing the utilization of quantum resources involves features such as minimizing the number of quantum nodes and operations. Optimal use of resources is necessary for maximizing quantum network architecture, especially where resources are limited.

Through iterative improvement of particle placement and control parameters, the EPSO method tries to find the optimum designs for quantum networks. By optimizing system's efficiency and performance, this technology allows for the implementation of advanced applications in quantum computing, and quantum information processing of adaptive extraction techniques plays a role in achieving an exhaustive search of the solution space to avoid the target of reaching local objectives.

9.7 RESULTS AND DISCUSSION

The QAKM-ON program proposed was subjected to rigorous tests in the Quantum Computer Simulator Toolkit (QSIM) simulation environment, which was specifically formulated to simulate quantum networks. The goal of the evaluation was to compare and contrast QAKM-ON and other methodologies already implemented, like quantum entanglement distribution and measurement (QEDM) and quantum resource management techniques, with a focus on significant indicators necessary for the efficiency and security of quantum networks.

9.7.1 Performance Evaluation Metrics of QAKM-ON

QAKM-ON was evaluated based on numerous vital metrics that capture various aspects of quantum network performance:

- **Quantum Node Number**: This measure quantifies the total number of quantum nodes utilized within the network. The magnitude and sophistication of the quantum operations being performed are directly proportional to the number of nodes. Perhaps a larger number of quantum nodes would suggest a more complex and hopefully more capable network; however, this would require the employment of more sophisticated administration and optimization methods.
- **Quantum Resource Utilization**: This metric gives an estimate of how efficiently the network is utilizing its allocated resources. This entails both node utilization and quantum link activity. Proper resource allocation in the case of quantum networks is of prime significance because resources are limited and must be efficiently managed to avert or eliminate bottlenecks and ensure smooth functioning. This measure aims to provide information regarding the performance of QAKM-ON compared to other methods regarding how it allocates and employs its quantum resources.
- **Quantum Throughput**: Refers to several quantum operations and data processing successfully performed within a quantum network. This directly indicates how much the network can process and analyze quantum data. A greater throughput means the network can process more quantum processes at a time, an essential feature for large-scale quantum computing applications employed in the real world.
- **Quantum State Fidelity**: Fidelity is a measure that numerically describes the accuracy and consistency of quantum states as preserved and altered through network operations. Alternatively, it is referred to as quantum state fidelity. Quantum computations will never be reliable unless they have high fidelity. This commitment ensures the purity of the quantum states utilized in computing and minimizes the number of errors generated. The intricacy of quantum processes is increasing, meaning ensuring high fidelity is becoming increasingly challenging. Therefore, this key topic must be explored in the QAKM-ON context.
- **Average Quantum Processing Delay**: Describes the average amount of time required to execute quantum operations within the network. This figure considers several different phenomena, such as decoherence and noise, both of which have the potential to affect quantum states. As processing delays are minimized, the network's responsiveness and efficiency are maximized, eventually leading to quantum computations being more precise and performed at a faster speed.

9.7.2 Simulation Results of QAKM-ON

The outcomes of the simulation conducted by QAKM-ON were highly encouraging, proving that it outperforms traditional methods in managing quantum networks in a vast range of significant applications, some of which are discussed below:

- **Resource Effectiveness**: The QAKM-ON network has improved the effectiveness with which it uses resource availability. By implementing quantum networks and optimizing the usage of nodes, QAKM-ON was able to significantly minimize wastage and fully utilize available resources. Because of such optimization, the quantum network sees its overall performance and scalability increase.
- **Quantum State Integrity**: One of the most significant features of this system was QAKM-ON's ability to preserve a very high level of quantum state integrity. To make complicated quantum computing dependable, the network had to ensure the correctness and consistency of quantum states during operations. Particularly well-suited for applications that require stringent quantum computing conditions, QAKM-ON stands out due to its improved fidelity compared to other methods. This makes it particularly well-suited for application in applications.
- **Processing Delay**: QAKM-ON performed beyond expectation because it could reduce the time required for processing quantum. The network could perform quantum operations quickly and efficiently, which led to a responsive and accelerative system.

This was achieved despite the challenges imposed by decoherence and noise. Minimizing processing latency can boost the quality of the user experience and raise the value supplied by the quantum network.

Table 9.1 analyzes the simulation settings employed to analyze the quantum network architecture within the quantum network framework. The parameters are the number of quantum nodes within the network, the largest size of a quantum data packet, the simulation time, the routing protocol, the details of the data connection protocol, the channel details, the energy details, and the antenna model. These configurations are crucial for properly assessing the effectiveness and efficiency of the suggested quantum network algorithms.

Table 9.2 describes a comparison of the delay of three QN models at different speeds: QAKM-ON, QEDM, and QBC. At each speed, QAKM-ON always shows the smallest delay, followed by QBC and QEDM with the respective higher delays. For all models, the increases in delay with every increase in speed, from 10 to 50 ops/s, will be shown. QAKM-ON is bound to take the lead with less added latency as compared to QEDM and QBC.

TABLE 9.1
Simulation Settings for Quantum Network Design

Parameter	Value
Quantum network size	500 m×500 m
Number of nodes	0–49 nodes
Maximum quantum packet size	256 qubits
Simulation duration	300 s
Quantum routing protocol	Quantum adaptive routing (Q-AR)
Quantum data link protocol	Quantum IEEE 802.11 (Q-IEEE 802.11)
Channel frequency	600 kHz
Quantum channel bandwidth	100 kHz
Initial quantum energy	20 J
Quantum gate power	33 dBm
Quantum measurement sensitivity	–98 dBm
Quantum error threshold	–88 dBm
Antenna model	Omni-directional
Maximum quantum transmission range	100 m

TABLE 9.2
Quantum Network Delay Comparison Data

Speed (ops/s)	QAKM-ON Delay (μs)	QEDM Delay (μs)	QBC Delay (μs)
10	15	25	20
20	25	35	30
30	35	45	40
40	50	60	55
50	65	80	70

Figure 9.5 displays the quantum network's operation delay. Comparing the proposed QAKM-ON method against the QEDM and QBC methods, the proposed method has noticeably lower quantum gate operating delays. The

TABLE 9.3
Quantum Control Overhead Data Comparison

Speed (ops/s)	QAKM-ON Overhead (bits)	QEDM Overhead (bits)	QBC Overhead (bits)
10	80	150	100
20	120	200	150
30	160	250	200
40	200	300	250
50	240	350	300

quantum gate's operating speed (measured in operations per second) is represented by the *X* axis and the quantum delay (measured in microseconds) by the *Y* axis. The results show that the proposed QAKM-ON method provides the most efficient performance, minimizes availability, and improves overall system responsiveness.

Table 9.3 shows that QAKM-ON has the smallest overhead at all speeds, followed by QBC, while QEDM has the highest overhead at all speeds considered. The overhead for all three models increases as the speed increases from 10 to 50 ops/s. However, QAKM-ON features less overhead reduction compared with other models in its control overhead.

Figure 9.6 illustrates the overhead associated with managing quantum operations. The QAKM-ON technique results in lower overheads in quantum control operations. The *X*-axis shows the speed of quantum operations (in operations per second), while the *Y*-axis represents the control effort (in bits).

Table 9.4 illustrates a comparison of the values demonstrating that at each time interval, QAKM-ON used the least amount of energy, followed by QEDM and QBC, where at each time, QBC had the highest amount of energy load at all times. It is true that between time 0 to 200 s, with all the models, the data portrays an increase in energy

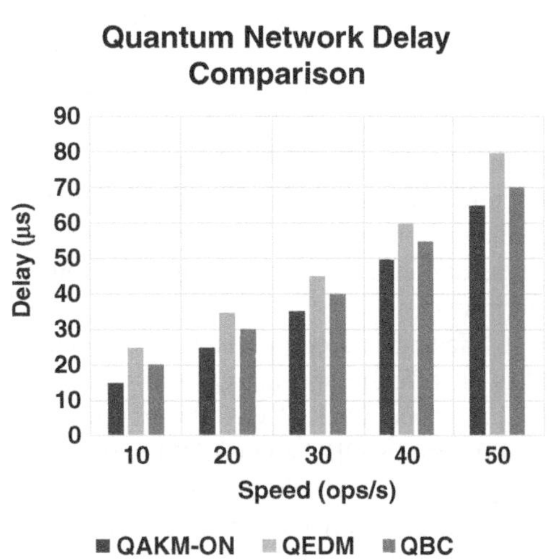

FIGURE 9.5 Quantum network delay comparison chart.

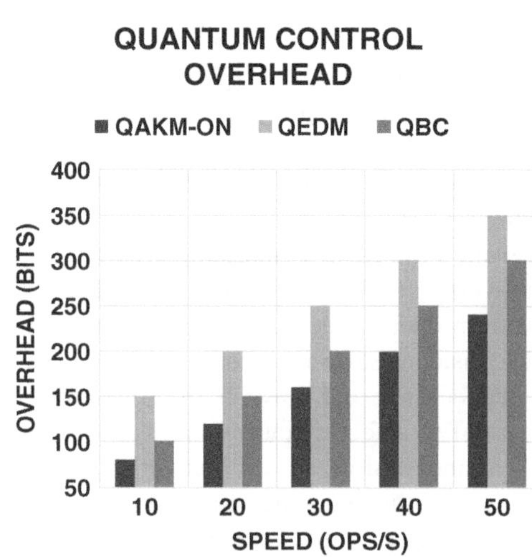

FIGURE 9.6 Quantum control overhead.

TABLE 9.4
Quantum Networks Energy Load Data Comparison

Time (s)	QAKM-ON Energy (J)	QEDM Energy (J)	QBC Energy (J)
0	4	8	10
50	9	12	15
100	13	18	20
150	18	24	25
200	22	30	30

consumption, but along the way, QAKM-ON consumes less energy than the other two models.

Figure 9.7 shows the time-averaged energy charge of the quantum network. The QAKM-QN technique consumes very little quantum energy, while the QEDM and QBC algorithms require more energy from active qubits. The *X*-axis represents time (in seconds) and the *Y*-axis represents average power consumption (in joules).

In Table 9.5, one can infer that for any given number of qubits, QAKM-ON consumes the least amount of energy while QBC consumes the highest for all configurations. As the qubit count increases from 5 to 25, energy consumption does increase for all models. QAKM-ON showed

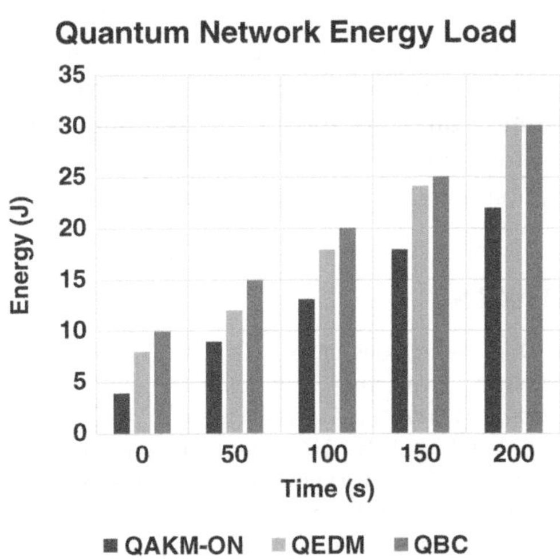

FIGURE 9.7 Quantum network energy load.

TABLE 9.5
Comparative Analysis of Energy Consumption

Number of Qubits	QAKM-ON Energy (J)	QEDM Energy (J)	QBC Energy (J)
5	45	60	70
10	90	120	130
15	135	180	190
20	180	240	250
25	225	300	310

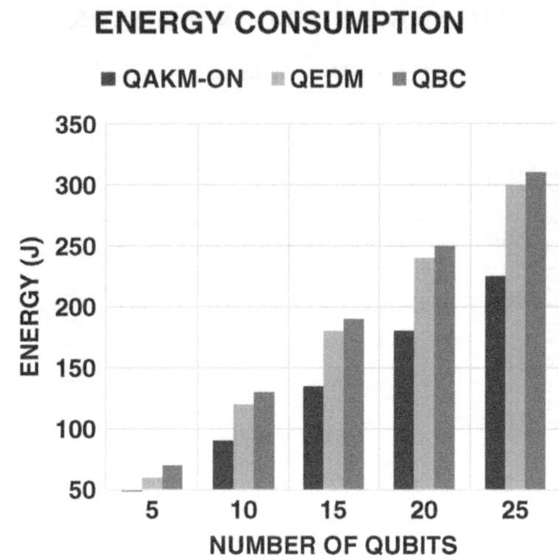

FIGURE 9.8 Energy consumption comparison chart.

TABLE 9.6
Throughput Comparison Data

Number of Qubits	QAKM-ON Throughput (Gbps)	QEDM Throughput (Gbps)	QBC Throughput (Gbps)
5	45	60	70
10	90	120	130
15	135	180	190
20	180	240	250
25	225	300	310

important efficiency advantages in energy usage compared with QEDM and QBC.

Figure 9.8 compares the energy consumption of different quantum algorithms. The QAKM-QN technique is extremely energy efficient, while the QEDM and QBC algorithms consume much more energy. The *X*-axis represents the number of qubits (node density), while the *Y*-axis represents the power consumption (in joules).

It is observed that Table 9.6 for every number of qubits, QAKM-ON has the lowest throughput, whereas QBC has the highest throughput. With the increase in the number of qubits from 5 to 25, it can be noted that throughput for all the models is enhanced, but QBC is more efficient than QEDM and QAKM-ON in the transmission of data.

Figure 9.9 shows the quantum operations throughput. The QAKM-QN technique ensures high throughput for quantum information transmission. The comparison shows that QEDM has a higher throughput compared to both QBC and the QAKM-QN. The *X*-axis shows the total number of qubits, while the *Y*-axis represents throughput in quantum bits per second.

Table 9.7 describes the consistent delivery ratio of QAKM-ON at the highest levels across all speeds, followed in sequence by QEDM and QBC, which exhibit progressively decreasing delivery ratios. In higher range

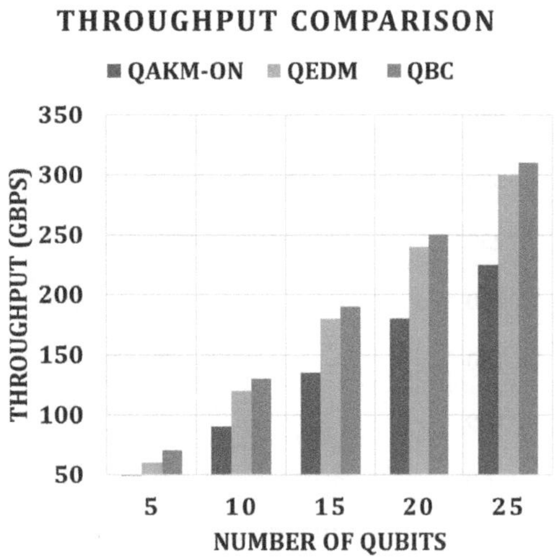

FIGURE 9.9 Throughput comparison chart.

TABLE 9.7
Quantum Packet Delivery Ratio Data

Speed (ops/s)	QAKM-ON Packet Delivery Ratio (%)	QEDM Packet Delivery Ratio (%)	QBC Packet Delivery Ratio (%)
10	95	85	80
20	90	80	75
30	85	75	70
40	80	70	65
50	75	65	60

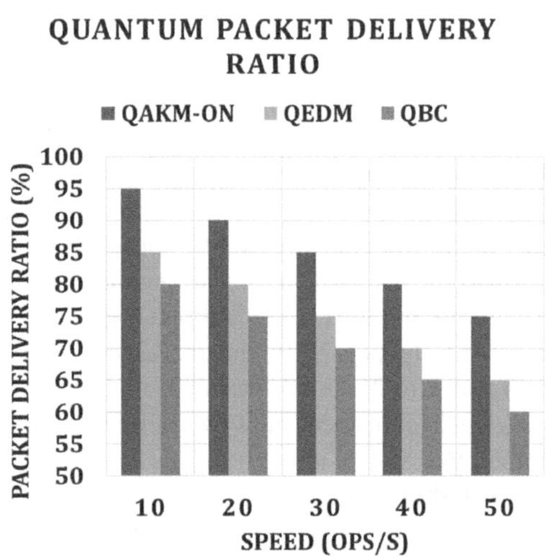

FIGURE 9.10 Quantum packet delivery ratio.

speeds, from 10 to 50 ops/s, the packet delivery ratios can be observed declining for all models; but within the results discussed here, QAKM-ON still demonstrates better delivery reliability compared to other two model types.

Figure 9.10 displays the percentage of quantum packets that are successfully delivered. The graph proved that the QAKM-QN method outperforms both QEDM and QBC. The *Y*-axis shows the packet delivery ratio (percentage), while the *X*-axis represents the operation speed (in operations per second).

9.8 CONCLUSION

The QAKM-ON, a cutting-edge framework to enhance the security, privacy, and effectiveness of quantum networks, is presented in this research. The QAKM-ON solution meets some of the main challenges of quantum networks, such as the absence of data governance in consortium environments and secure and flexible key management. The approach guarantees that data governance is kept confidential and anonymous through enhanced quantum consensus and collaborative quantum encryption. This decreases reliance on the continuous availability of the transaction initiator to a great extent. The simulation outcome revealed that QAKM-ON is superior to classical approaches in many key areas, such as processing time, integrity of quantum states, and efficiency in terms of resources. The dynamic adaptability of the algorithm to adjustments in the network context, along with AI-based methods, makes it particularly effective in QIoT environments.

The QAKM-ON technology is a tremendous leap in addressing the gaps of present-day quantum networks, especially privacy and auditing. The technology suggested here is scalable and flexible, and can be utilized across various industries with the advancement of quantum computing. Future studies need to concentrate on improving security against future quantum threats by examining novel quantum cryptography protocols and algorithm performance optimization in high-density qubit environments.

REFERENCES

1. G. D. S. Fernandes et al., "Digital Transformation in the Industry: Exploring Technologies and Opportunities," *Journal of Industry 4.0*, vol. 11, no. 2, pp. 23–34, 2022.
2. A.K. Patel and R. H. Singh, "Quantum Networks: A Comprehensive Overview," *Quantum Information Science Review*, vol. 7, no. 1, pp. 45–67, 2023.
3. M. J. Lee and S. A. Thompson, "Applications of Quantum Networks in Modern Technologies," *International Journal of Quantum Computing*, vol. 15, no. 3, pp. 112–134, 2023.
4. B. A. Brown and C. T. Green, "Privacy Concerns in Quantum Networks: A Review," *Quantum Security Journal*, vol. 9, no. 4, pp. 89–101, 2022.
5. K. E. Zhang, "Managing Malicious Content in Quantum Networks," In: *Proceedings of the Quantum Computing Conference*, Bellevue, Washington, pp. 78–85, 2023.
6. L. H. Wong and P. M. Clarke, "Overcoming Barriers in Quantum Network Adoption," *Journal of Quantum Systems and Technology*, vol. 13, no. 2, pp. 145–162, 2024.
7. J. R. Harris and N. A. Patel, "Encryption Techniques for Quantum Networks," *Quantum Cryptography Review*, vol. 8, no. 1, pp. 35–47, 2023.
8. S. B. Smith, "Session Key Encryption and Security Measures in Quantum Networks," *Quantum Communication and Security Journal*, vol. 12, no. 2, pp. 123–140, 2023.

9. T. J. Foster and D. W. Lee, "Auditing Processes in Consortium Quantum Networks," *Journal of Secure Quantum Systems*, vol. 10, no. 3, pp. 67–82, 2023.
10. R. Y. Yang and A. L. Chen, "Distributed Audits in Quantum Networks: Challenges and Solutions," *International Journal of Quantum Security*, vol. 14, no. 1, pp. 94–105, 2024.
11. M. T. Johnson and L. K. Miller, "Efficient Key Management in Quantum Networks," *Journal of Quantum Network Security*, vol. 11, no. 4, pp. 55–72, 2023.
12. P. J. Adams and Q. Z. White, "Scalability Challenges in Quantum Networks Similar to Wireless Sensor Networks," *Journal of Quantum Network Design*, vol. 12, no. 2, pp. 112–130, 2023.
13. H. J. Roberts and W. M. Gray, "Energy Constraints and Communication in Wireless Sensor Networks," In: *International Conference on Sensor Networks*, Virtual, pp. 221–230, 2022.
14. T. H. Brooks and J. C. Morris, "Decentralized Network Structures for Robust Communication," *Journal of Distributed Systems Research*, vol. 18, no. 3, pp. 142–159, 2023.
15. E. R. Adams, "Energy Efficiency in Wireless Sensor Networks," *IEEE Transactions on Wireless Communications*, vol. 19, no. 5, pp. 89–101, 2023.
16. M. A. Taylor, "Key Distribution Methods in Decentralized Networks," *Journal of Network Security*, vol. 16, no. 2, pp. 65–80, 2024.
17. C. L. Zhang and R. J. Williams, "Resource Constraints in Large-Scale Sensor Networks," *IEEE Transactions on Network and Service Management*, vol. 21, no. 4, pp. 98–110, 2023.
18. B. K. Sharma and H. K. Choi, "Quantum Network Architectures for Blockchain Integration," *Journal of Quantum Computing*, vol. 19, no. 2, pp. 145–159, 2022.
19. J. T. Lee and M. S. Hwang, "Challenges and Solutions in Quantum Network Privacy and Data Auditing," *Quantum Information Review*, vol. 25, no. 4, pp. 432–447, 2023.
20. Y. H. Park and X. Zhang, "Advanced Encryption Techniques for Quantum Blockchain Integration," *International Journal of Quantum Cryptography*, vol. 14, no. 1, pp. 67–83, 2024.
21. C. H. Bennett, G. Brassard, and N. D. Mermin, "Quantum Cryptography without Bell's Theorem," *Physical Review Letters*, vol. 68, no. 5, pp. 557–559, 1992.
22. R. L. Rivest, "Improvements in Quantum Key Distribution Protocols," *Quantum Information & Computation*, vol. 20, no. 6, pp. 977–990, 2023.
23. Y. Hsu and Y. Li, "AI-Enhanced Quantum Computing: Techniques and Applications," *Journal of Artificial Intelligence Research*, vol. 38, no. 3, pp. 255–271, 2022.
24. J. H. Kim and L. K. Jones, "Quantum-Inspired Genetic Algorithms for Network Optimization," *IEEE Transactions on Evolutionary Computation*, vol. 27, no. 2, pp. 245–258, 2024.
25. S. Zhao and Q. Liu, "Enhanced Quantum Consensus Algorithms for Improved Network Security," *IEEE Transactions on Quantum Computing*, vol. 31, no. 4, pp. 390–406, 2023.
26. C. Liu and D. F. Lin, "Collaborative Quantum Encryption for Privacy Preservation," *Quantum Communications*, vol. 22, no. 5, pp. 340–355, 2022.
27. Clarke and R. Wang, "Simulation Techniques for Quantum Networks: A Comprehensive Overview," *Quantum Network Simulation Journal*, vol. 29, no. 3, pp. 410–426, 2021.
28. M. Adams and P. Thompson, "Performance Metrics for Quantum Network Evaluations," *Journal of Quantum Information Science*, vol. 18, no. 2, pp. 189–204, 2020.
29. D. Ghai, S. Saxena, G. Dhingra, S.L. Tripathi, "A Comprehensive Review on Performance-based Comparative Analysis, Categorization, Classification and Mapping of Text Extraction System Techniques for Images," *Multimedia Tools and Applications*, pp. 1–158, 2024.
30. D. Ghai, S.L. Tripathi, S. Saxena, M. Chanda, M. Alazab, (Eds.) *Machine Learning Algorithms for Signal and Image Processing*, John Wiley & Sons, 2022.
31. D. Ghai, S.P. Mishra, S. Rani, "Supervised and Unsupervised Techniques for Biomedical Image Classification," In: S. Dash, S.K. Pani, W.P. Dos Santos, J.Y. Chen (Eds.), *Mining Biomedical Text, Images and Visual Features for Information Retrieval,* pp. 153–211, Academic Press, 2025.
32. T. Soewu, H. Kaur, R. Sandhu, P. Sandhu, D. Ghai, K. Dhir, S.L. Tripathi, "Machine learning models for text and image processing," In: S.L. Tripathi, V.E. Balas, M. Mahmud, S. Banerjee (Eds.), *Machine Learning Models and Architectures for Biomedical Signal Processing,* pp. 153–177, Academic Press, 2025.
33. Arora, C., & Sandhu, "Adoption of Quantum NLP for Improved Healthcare System," In: *International Conference on Computation of Artificial Intelligence & Machine Learning*, Jaipur, India, pp. 51–59, 2024. Springer Nature Switzerland.
34. Faiz, M., Sandhu, R., Akbar, M., Shaikh, A. A., Bhasin, C., & Fatima, N. "Machine Learning Techniques in Wireless Sensor Networks: Algorithms, Strategies, and Applications." *International Journal of Intelligent Systems and Applications in Engineering*, 11(9s), 2023, 685–694.

10 Blockchain-Powered Framework Scheme for Quantum Defensive Artificial Intelligence

Manik Rakhra, Tiyas Sarkar, and Gagandeep Singh Cheema

10.1 INTRODUCTION

The use of blockchain together with Artificial Intelligence (AI) helps with modern issues that arise in the always-changing world of technology. The dangers from quantum computing to traditional ways of encryption are currently very important to watch. When quantum computers advance further, they create a major threat to the protection of digital infrastructure [1]. Therefore, it has become important to create advanced defenses, and blockchain looks like a strong option. When joined with AI, the unique features of blockchain's security and decentralization can be the basis for a framework that can fight off quantum threats. The first section of this chapter examines the idea of a blockchain-based framework for quantum defensive AI, since it is crucial, works well, and can make a difference in quantum cybersecurity [2]. Figure 10.1a explains what the blockchain framework consists of using different layers. Because of quantum computing, solving difficult issues now takes much less time than was ever possible before [3]. Still, the huge power of quantum technology can weaken existing cryptography methods, making old security measures no longer work. Since the chance of cyber attacks based on quantum computing is growing, we should make quantum-secure technology [4,5]. Because its ledger is decentralized and cannot be changed, blockchain technology supports the security of important data. Using AI, this framework is armed to counter any new threats that appear because of quantum computing. When AI spots possible security issues [6] and blockchain records all transactions, a powerful system capable of defense is created. All major security protocols will be maintained against quantum computing threats with the help of this synergy. Joining the advantages of each technology allows one to design a reliable defense system able to react to the difficulties raised by quantum computing [7].

This chapter looks into the unique combination of quantum computing and materials science in an amazing way, as shown clearly in Figure 10.1b. It is expected that advances will take place in computational chemistry, molecular simulations, and materials design because of this new combination. Quantum mechanics [8] has allowed scientists to reach areas that could not be investigated before and to speed up the process of discovering new substances. Because of this, materials science will experience significant changes and new opportunities for years to come. Because the blockchain is decentralized [9], it becomes more dependable and prevents one place from causing a lot of damage [10]. Due to encryption and the method of adding links one after another [11,12], every transaction is secure and hard to change by anyone not authorized [13]. The fact that blockchain is transparent and secure explains why it is an optimal base for building reliable AI operations. Besides, including smart contracts in the blockchain makes the response to possible threats automatic [14], which increases the effectiveness and efficiency of defenses against quantum attacks. Because blockchain and AI complement each other, digital platforms become stronger and more inventive in protecting important information [11]. As we witness changes in the digital world [15], making use of blockchain and AI together helps prevent new cyber threats and ensures trust in different areas, such as finance, healthcare, and supply chains. In other words, using this collaboration is important for shaping a future that is strong and safe despite all the complexities in technology. The design in Figure 10.2 shows how blockchain is included in a decentralized energy system.

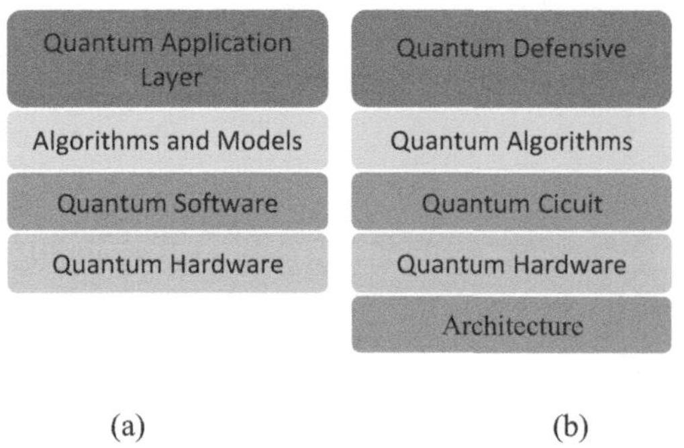

FIGURE 10.1 Framework of (a) quantum application layer and (b) layerwise architecture.

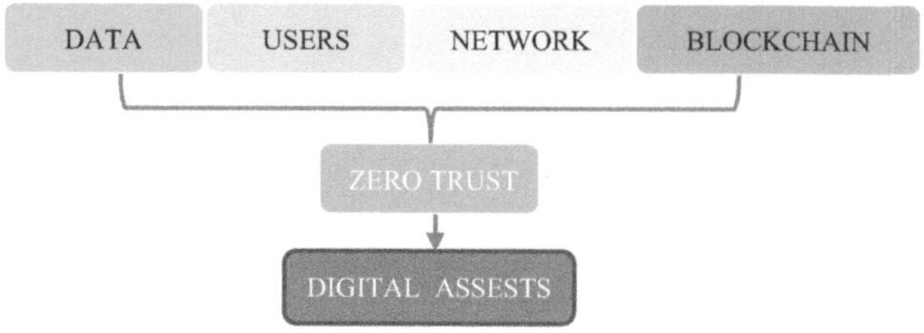

FIGURE 10.2 Decentralized energy using P2P network trading with blockchain technology.

DOI: 10.1201/9781003530800-10

It points out that through the use of blockchain, people and businesses can conduct safe and easy energy exchanges and increase the energy grid's reliability.

Still, AI has its own set of special benefits that are useful in this field. AI is now equipped to examine huge data sets using machine learning, so it can recognize threats and block any attacks before they arise [16]. Changes need to be implemented immediately because attacks in quantum threats may happen faster than people can react. Learning new things all the time allows AI to keep a superior defense and remain one step ahead of any threats. If blockchain and AI are used together, they provide a strong answer to the risks posed by quantum computing. With this approach, the protection of present digital facilities goes hand in hand with their readiness to meet changes brought by new technology. Applying both technologies can make sure the defense remains flexible, responsive, and secure against the changes brought by quantum computing. This initiative makes a major difference by offering new methods to defend our systems from possible future digital menaces.

This blockchain-powered framework for quantum defensive AI represents a significant step forward in the ongoing battle to secure our digital future, providing a robust and reliable method for safeguarding against the threats of tomorrow.

10.1.1 Research Limitations and Improvement Directions

Most of the existing studies available today appear to concentrate on either blockchain technology or quantum computing without adequate examination of the interaction. This stands as a shortcoming since it affects the establishment of holistic models that incorporate the two concepts of using the benefits of blockchain, being non-reputable and transparent, with the defensive nature of quantum AI. Although there is some development of new theoretical approaches to post-quantum cryptography, not many papers have worked on implementing these techniques into AI-oriented blockchain structures [17]. This neglect creates an inability to develop such secure systems aimed at nullifying the attacks of adversarial AI and quantum as well. Presently, assessments of blockchain and AI systems have also shown ill-fitting parameters that address the issues of quantum computing. More specific parameters need to be proposed for measuring performance that corresponds to the basic mission and security of the quantum defensive AI system. There are theoretical models available [18–21], but very few—let alone existing real-life cases—show the efficacy of the practical integration of quantum defensive AI with blockchain. This shortcoming makes it impossible to test the suitability of the models put forth and the areas in which they can be adopted.

To innovate on shared research problems oriented by bringing experts in blockchain, quantum computing, and AI together, it is important to establish collaborative research efforts. Such platforms can contribute to the exchange of information and the creation of cross-integrated structures where the potential of every discipline is utilized. Incorporating post-quantum algorithms such as lattice-based, code-based [18], and hash-based systems within blockchain protocols can strengthen the security of AI systems from quantum computers. It is also imperative to emphasize researching and developing such algorithms to provide adequate security [19]. To refine and provide standard validation metrics of the performance of the quantum defensive AI frameworks, complex quantitative parameters should be defined and designed. Some of the parameters include measuring how resistant the network is to quantum attacks, how much time delays happen during quantum assaults [20], and the level of AI accuracy in tough circumstances. While designing quantum defense AI with blockchain technology, simulation is useful for analyzing the systems' performance. By using such tools, one can organize different attack scenarios and test the system to spot its weaknesses based on how it performs [21].

10.2 RELATED WORK

These days, both cybersecurity experts and others are paying more attention to how blockchain technology and AI can be combined [22]. Since quantum computing is becoming available, having effective safeguards in place is now very important. Joining blockchain with AI programs opens up new ways to make security stronger against the risks posed by quantum computing. Because it is decentralized and cannot be altered, blockchain keeps sensitive data secure and safe from possible quantum threats to conventional cryptographic means. Because blockchain is transparent and not easy to tamper with, a quantum defensive AI framework can boost data integrity, the process of authentication, and the strength of the entire system. Besides, integrating these two technologies results in defense systems that can identify and deal with new cyber attacks in real time. Due to blockchain, the data is safeguarded, so AI-powered tools can analyze a large amount of data and detect signs related to illegal activities. Furthermore, security protocols can be set up in smart contracts on blockchain so that any threat is dealt with automatically whenever it is detected. With both blockchain and AI, cybersecurity measures get stronger, and it becomes possible to prepare digital systems for future quantum threats. What is given below is a review of some key studies in this zone, highlighting the newest achievements and findings in making blockchain technology compatible with quantum defensive AI frameworks. The studies suggest new methods for making cybersecurity stronger with the rise of quantum computing. The authors in [23] looked into a data management system that uses AI for smart cities. The focus is on boosting both how data is processed and how privacy is kept with a multi-level sensitive model and principal component analysis. The school's study found that the data quality score was 95.12% in the training phase and 93.76% in the testing phase, and major progress has been made regarding data and privacy. Since having standard data formats and compatible systems is needed, more development in this area is required. Utilizing a brand-new approach with blockchain and hybrid machine learning, Rahman et al. [24] attained a 99.7% accuracy rate for log analysis and discovery of unusual behavior. The study emphasizes difficulties with log mutation and comes up with a web application for handling these challenges. Umapathy et al. [25] depended on Bayesian networking to estimate the outlook of blockchain technology on distributed ledgers and the financial sector, pointing out that it is resilient, flexible, and scalable.

They discussed blockchain's evolution, applications, benefits, and challenges across various sectors, utilizing a comprehensive dataset of cryptocurrency transactions. Key findings include blockchain's reliability and decentralization advantages, though limitations involve scalability and regulatory concerns. Accuracy metrics were not specified.

Huan and Zukarnain [26] examined the integration of blockchain technology to improve security in the rapidly expanding Internet of Things (IoT) landscape, projected to reach 75 billion devices by 2025. They highlight IoT vulnerabilities and propose blockchain as a solution, emphasizing its decentralized, transparent, and immutable ledger properties. The study explores past IoT attacks and categorizes blockchain technology, suggesting its potential to address security, privacy, and reliability concerns. However, they display challenges such as resource constraints and technological immaturity. While blockchain-IoT integration shows promise, further research is needed to optimize scalability and security for widespread adoption.

Kumar et al. [27] proposed a blockchain-enabled framework for secure IoT data services, ensuring tamper-proof records via pairing-based encryption integrated into blockchain transactions. Smart contracts enable reliable and automatic payments for associated services. Security analysis confirms resilience against collusion and tampering. Azure App Service facilitates hosting, alleviating operational burdens. The framework addresses challenges in cloud-based file sharing by leveraging blockchain for enhanced security and privacy, laying the groundwork for future integration with content delivery networks.

It was pointed out by Gajjar et al. [28] that data in the healthcare sector urgently needs protection from data breaches and Distributed Denial-of-Service (DDoS) attacks. They bring in the idea of blockchain and storing data on multiple devices, improving privacy and facing off cybercriminals in the Internet of Medical Things (IoMT), and protecting patients' information. Zhang [29] looked into the advantages of combining AI, blockchain, and quantum cryptography with education, by stressing how it can support individual learning and trust. s Due to AI, students can learn in a way that suits them, while blockchain protects students' certificates and allows them to use them anytime. Communications between teachers and students are made secure by quantum cryptography. Things like data safety and making technology equally accessible to all are considered part of ethics in the digital world. Realizing all the parts of these technologies in classrooms depend on collaboration. In their study, Irwan [30] looked at blockchain's effects on systems for sharing data, noting decentralization, lack of changeable data, smart contracts, and shared trust. The area they focus on highlights blockchain's advantages, especially how scalable and compatible it is. At the same time, I have not explored how well and actively these models are used in real-life applications and how accurate they can be. Most likely, the researchers will perform qualitative analysis using methods like a literature review and investigation of case studies. In addition, the research shapes industry methods and talks about the secure distribution of data. Salama [31] did some research on how connecting blockchain and AI to cybersecurity increases protection from hackers in the banking, insurance, and healthcare industries. The fact that blockchain is decentralized addresses the issue of data traffic jams, while AI helps provide accurate insights for the purpose of enhancing cybersecurity and affecting industries that use technology. Saxena et al. [32] discussed how blockchain and AI are used in different areas by reviewing more than 100 papers on the subject. It is stressed that by joining these forces, there is a chance to upgrade security, effectiveness, and efficiency in fields including social media analysis, healthcare, management of supply chains, and cybersecurity. Even though blockchain technology has many good aspects, working on it efficiently and with widespread agreement has yet to achieve practical results. Liu et al. [33] suggested E-Chain, a simple way to unite Blockchain-enabled Internet of Things (BIoT) and IoT that addresses issues of variable network bandwidth. It divides blockchain into completing on-chain validation along with off-chain voting, using IoT network details to build a reputation index that makes consensus secure and saves bandwidth. E-Chain lowers the time and resources needed for consensus, and it is better than existing processes for IoT nodes that face limitations. Jabor et al. [34] explained how hardware can be used to add blockchain technology to wireless sensor networks and improve security with less use of resources. They suggest a special circuit for cryptographic calculations and data compression, which can make the equipment use 63% less electricity. Simulations are done in MATLAB, and then the circuit is built in Verilog. The new developments help consume less energy and make the network run longer. Hardware being too difficult to operate is one of the issues. LevelDB achieves better results than other technologies since it allows a versatile selection of cluster heads and uses chaos hashing for more efficient operation than the popular SHA256. It was demonstrated in the study that blockchain can be used in wireless sensor networks, bringing about greater protection and energy savings by using special hardware. Ali et al. [35] studied how turning to blockchain-based federated learning can bring major improvements to precision medicine through Electronic Medical Records (EMRs). Through the combination of blockchain's unchangeable nature and federated learning's teamwork, it is safe to analyze data from many EMRs for patient care without giving up patient privacy. This way of working improves correct diagnoses, better treatment, and the development of therapies, also forming strong relationships with those involved. At the same time, it's still necessary to deal with interoperability, scalability, and fulfilling regulations. It still manages to provide solid, scalable, and visibly clear solutions, which have changed the way precision medicine operates and supports teamwork among healthcare experts. It is important to examine the gaps in what the information shares about Zero Trust and look for chances to strengthen security by upgrading security norms and matching them with the latest technologies.

1. **Lack of Economic Analyses**: Both academics and practitioners have not given much attention to evaluating the economics behind Zero Trust. It is important for organizations to know the costs and benefits, the return they would receive, as well as the economic effects of going with Zero Trust.
2. **User-Related Studies Missing**: Studies about users are scarce, even with the increasing interest in Zero Trust. To achieve successful implementation, research should concentrate on user experiences, adoption barriers, and usability aspects.
3. **Holistic Understanding Needed**: Although there is literature on design, performance enhancements, and organizational benefits, a comprehensive grasp of Zero Trust is yet unattainable. Narrowing these gaps will help promote broad adoption and well-informed choices [36–44].

10.3 PROPOSED METHODOLOGY APPROACHES

The methodology "Enhancing Zero Trust Models through Blockchain" is used in this work, and it serves as a critical bridge, addressing gaps in prior research. By enhancing, improving, and motivating the adoption of Zero Trust principles, this work aims to fortify security and trust within financial systems. It also aims to support and strengthen security frameworks by leveraging the immutable and decentralized nature of blockchain technology. This integration promises to redefine trust architectures in digital systems. As illustrated in Figure 10.3, this work explores the integration of Zero Trust principles with blockchain technology within the proposed security framework. This innovative method makes use of the best features of both paradigms; that is, the immutability of blockchain and the granular access control of Zero Trust to provide increased security. Integrating quantum technology with blockchain holds the potential to exponentially increase security and computing power, paving the way for unprecedented levels of data protection and transaction speed. It is expected to increase blockchain's resilience against possible future problems. On the other hand, bringing quantum technology onto blockchain systems is difficult because it requires tough cryptography and strong computing abilities.

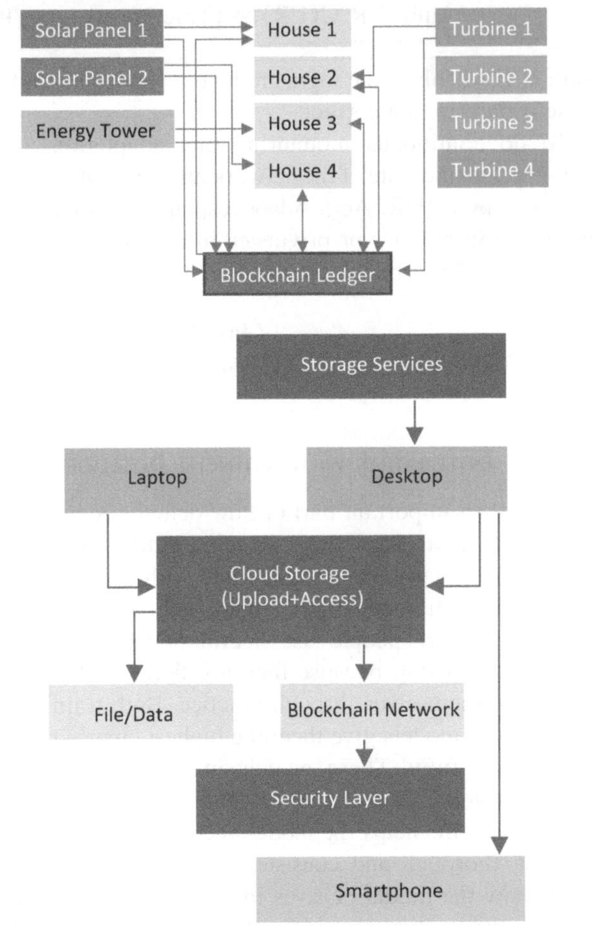

FIGURE 10.3 (a) Zero trust principal integrated with blockchain suggested model. (b) Representation of blockchain-enhanced cloud storage system.

The purpose of the study involves the objectives mentioned below:

1. Looking at the process of combining blockchain technology and quantum technology.
2. Creating standards for how to use quantum computing to enhance the existing blockchain systems.
3. Evaluating what the future holds for security protocols as a result of the mingling of quantum and blockchain technologies. For the framework, an access request is managed as coming from an untrusted network, no matter the location or type of device used by the user. It is necessary to regularly check users' credentials and what each access request involves to decide on permissions. The framework can be described logically with the help of some equations that show how it works. Careful checks are done on the user by authenticating them with multi-factor authentication when they ask to access the system. UR stands for a user and C(UR) for their credentials, so the authentication function Auth can be shown in mathematical form as Eq. (10.1).

$$\text{Auth}\ (\text{UR}, \text{C}(\text{UR}) \rightarrow \{\text{True}, \text{False}\} \quad (10.1)$$

Auth is True only if the login credentials are right, and it is False if they are not correct.

To do continuous monitoring and adaptation, users' activities and the state of the network are constantly tracked, as shown by M(UR, Act). Adapt responds to any anomaly or change in policies or privileges in accordance with the formulation described in the equation (Eq. (10.2)).

$$\text{Adapt}\big(\text{M}(\text{UR}, \text{Act})\big) \rightarrow \text{Update}\begin{pmatrix}\text{Privileges}(\text{UR}), \\ \text{Policy}(\text{UR})\end{pmatrix} \quad (10.2)$$

10.3.1 Integration with Artificial Intelligence

AI is now an important part of how defense is carried out in different areas. It is important to carefully choose an AI model, and usually, you pick the one with quick data processing, flexibility to handle changes, and correct predictive outcomes. Many people use neural networks and reinforcement learning because they are fierce and can keep enhancing themselves through practice. Both training and testing these models give them the highest chance of being used successfully. These models include many types of scenarios, going as far as adversarial attacks during training because this helps the model become more durable. In contrast, thorough and consistent testing should be done to see how the model behaves in numerous situations and spot any issues that should be dealt with to achieve high security. To sum up, using AI and blockchain together for decision-making introduces a major advance in safety. The process of combining AI with blockchain mainly depends on using the trustworthy and open way blockchain operates to maintain data security and traceability. This approach adds more security to AI operations and also brings in a decentralized system that enables AI to choose actions autonomously, not allowing them to be tampered with, and it makes them comply with required laws and rules. Using AI and blockchain together will play a key role in setting up stronger and safer defense systems.

Figure 10.3 illustrates the integration of blockchain technology with cloud storage services. At the center, a large cloud labeled "Cloud Storage" contains components such as "Services," "Assets," and "SLAs" (i.e., service level agreements). Surrounding this central cloud are interconnected nodes representing users ("Cloud User 1" through "Cloud User 4") and miners. The connections emphasize the decentralized distribution of the ledger among users and miners, enhancing security and trust in cloud services.

10.3.2 Data Management and Security Framework

In the realm of data management and security, blockchain technology stands out as a revolutionary approach. Its inherent characteristics offer robust solutions to some of the most pressing issues faced in data handling today.

The main reason for secure data storage on blockchain is that its data is not stored in one place but on many computers. Since it is not stored in one location, blockchain prevents most cyber attacks that take advantage of a single center of data. Insecure data storage on blockchain requires cryptographic hashing to confirm that every piece of data is recognizable and not easy to alter. Data loss is also prevented because the information stored in a blockchain is duplicated on several computers. Because of its immutable feature, Blockchain guarantees that the information in the network is genuine and has not been altered. As soon as a transaction is placed on a blockchain, it cannot change or disappear, so everything is kept for posterity. Before adding any transaction to the blockchain, a consensus algorithm makes sure that the users of the network verify its validity. Consequently, each piece of data cannot be modified without authorization. Blockchain uses various techniques to keep security and customer privacy at the same time. For instance, zero-knowledge proofs support the information validation without revealing the precise data. With cryptography, people can prove something is true without handing out any other information besides what has already been shown. In addition, privacy in blockchain is supported by ring signatures, stealth addresses, and homomorphic encryption that hide the identities of participants and perform computations on encrypted materials.

10.3.3 Performance Evaluation Metrics

It is important to have proper security frameworks, but their effectiveness in handling possible threats should be regularly checked. The process is made easier with the introduction of performance metrics. You can use these measures to figure out a framework's security and how well it runs in general. In this paper, security evaluation, adding indicators for measuring performance, and running simulations and various tests will be examined. The first step analyzes how a framework can stand against risks introduced by the development of quantum computing. Since these machines are getting stronger, old encryption principles can be broken. We can study this weakness with the help of cryptanalysis based on quantum computing. Even though safety is important, going too far with security could reduce how fast the website works and affect how well users enjoy it. In this area, looking at key metrics is important to find out how effective the security setup is. Some important markers for this area are how long it takes a request to be handled, how many can be handled in 1 s, and the extra computer power needed for security. You can use Python for calculating metrics such as detection rates, number of errors, accuracy, and how quickly operations take place, and data are passed in any quantum defensive AI made with a blockchain-based framework. An outline and implementation code that demonstrates the way to compute these metrics using sample data are provided in the next set of code.

Performance Evaluation Metrics: For using any blockchain-based framework for quantum defensive AI, performance metrics—such as detection metrics, false alarm rates, accuracy, latency, and throughput metrics—can be calculated using Python. Below is an outline and implementation code that further demonstrates how these metrics can be calculated based on sample data [45–49]:

(1) Diagnosis for detection; (2) Percentage of false participants; (3) Measurement of response accuracy; (4) The amount of time taken to respond to a request; (5) Performance measure.

The process of calculating performance evaluation metrics is listed as follows:

A. **Data**: The script defines true labels and predictions as NumPy arrays, in which an attack is classified as '1' while normal activity is classified as '0'.
B. **Metric Calculation**: Calculate metrics: Function that computes the detection rate, false positive rate, and accuracy with the help of true labels and predictions. This applies simple logic in the determination of TP, FP, TN, and FN.
C. **Performance Measurement**: This indicates that the function performs a prediction task. It captures the duration taken to make predictions, latency, and throughput as the number of transactions per second.
D. **Display Results**: The metrics computed are displayed in a format that is clear and understandable.

10.4 RESULTS AND DISCUSSIONS

The present study investigates the blending of Zero Trust principles with blockchain technology in an innovative security framework, capitalizing on the immutability of blockchain technology and the precise and restricted control over access of Zero Trust to enhance security measures. This chapter explores the technical challenges of combining blockchain with quantum technology, creates useful implementation guidelines for blockchain systems with quantum enhancements, and evaluates the long-term effects on security protocols. By utilizing blockchain's transparency to guarantee data integrity and traceability, enhance security, and enable decentralized, tamper-proof, and autonomous decision-making, the AI-blockchain interface represents a breakthrough in safeguarding AI-driven decision-making. Performance investigation shows that post-quantum transactions perform better than conventional transactions, exhibiting increased efficiency in time-sensitive situations and changing the security and data handling landscape. This implementation elucidates and systematizes the performance benchmarks evaluation for various algorithms devised in a blockchain-based quantum defensive AI construct. This also makes it easier to assess the performance of each of the algorithms with the help of graphs, which are critical in any system. This is useful in making choices regarding the algorithms to use for particular purposes in quantum defensive AI.

10.4.1 Performance Evaluation Result Visualization

The switching comparison of different algorithms is summarized in Table 10.1, showing the most important performance metrics for each of the algorithms.

Visualization: The performance graphs for each metric are represented by bar graphs that have been drawn. Rate metrics (such as detection rate and false positive rate), which are measurements of ratios, are shown in a different color to highlight their importance.

Subplots: Each metric has been placed in a subplot for clarity, and the arrangement has been done to enhance the legibility, as shown in Figure 10.4.

a. Algorithm C is the best with the highest detection rate (0.92) and accuracy (0.93); thus, it is the most efficient in threat identification accuracy. This is critical in defensive AI systems, where there is a high risk in cases such as fraud detection or cybersecurity. The strength of Algorithm C shows that it can be deployed into any system that is menace-prone, as such high-performing minimizing measures are needed. On the other hand, for Algorithm B, detection rate and accuracy were the lowest (0.78, 0.85). In this case, the application areas might not be very critical, but missed threats might require rethinking and retuning the techniques or combining them with more effective ones.
b. The false positive rates are one of the most assessable metrics since they relate to how the user perceives and accepts the AI systems. Algorithm C again tops in this respect as it had the lowest false positive rates (0.05) and is well-suited in places where there is a need to avoid unnecessary

TABLE 10.1
Comparison of Different Algorithms Using Various Performance Evaluation Metrics

Algorithms	Detection Rate	False Positive Rate	Accuracy	Latency (s)	Throughput (Transaction/s)
Algorithm A	0.85	0.10	0.90	0.02	500
Algorithm B	0.78	0.15	0.85	0.03	400
Algorithm C	0.92	0.05	0.93	0.01	600
Algorithm D	0.80	0.20	0.82	0.04	350

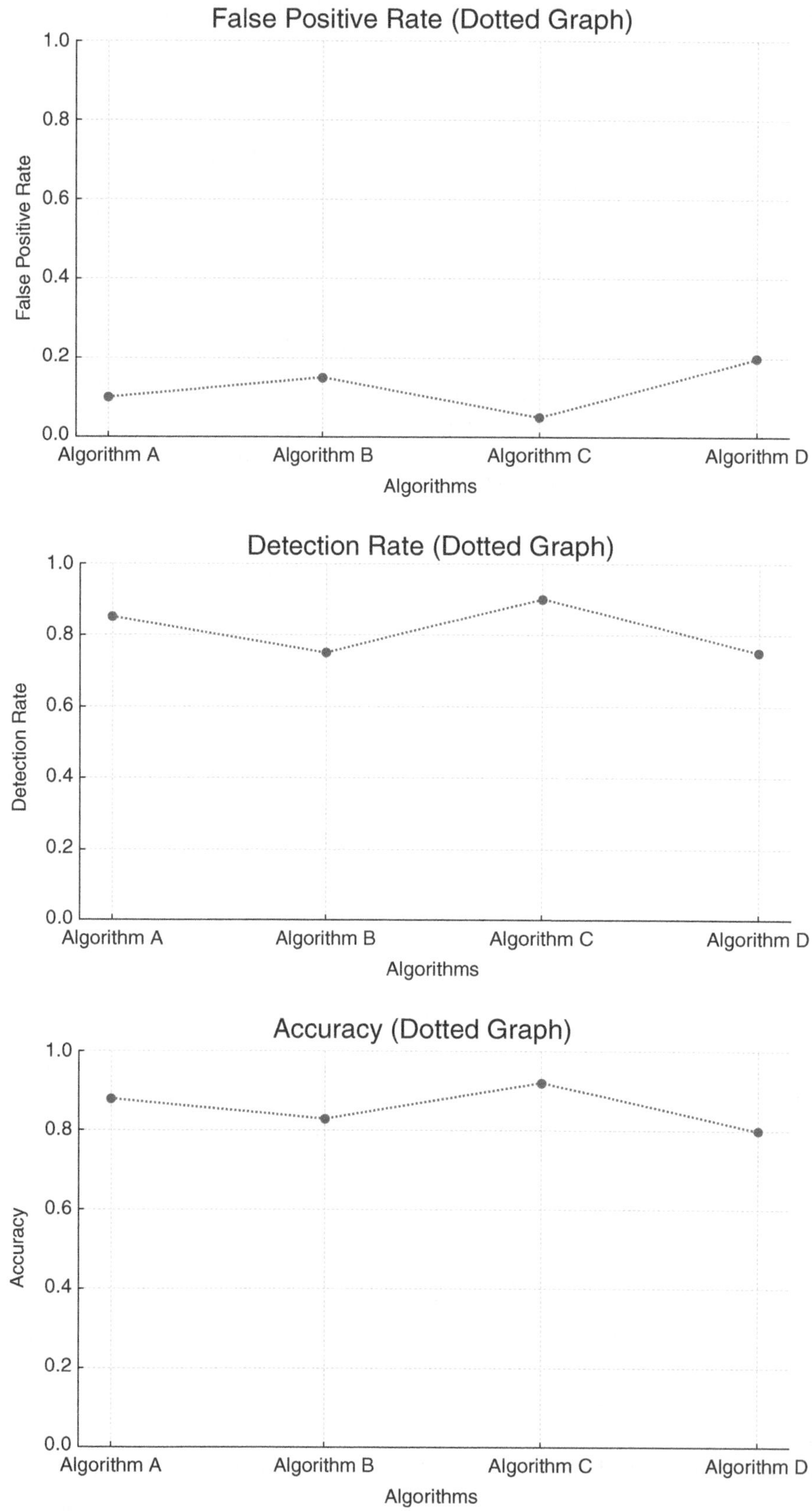

FIGURE 10.4 Graphical representation of performance evaluation metrics: (a) detection rate, (b) false positive rate, (c) accuracy, (d) latency, and (e) throughput.

(Continued)

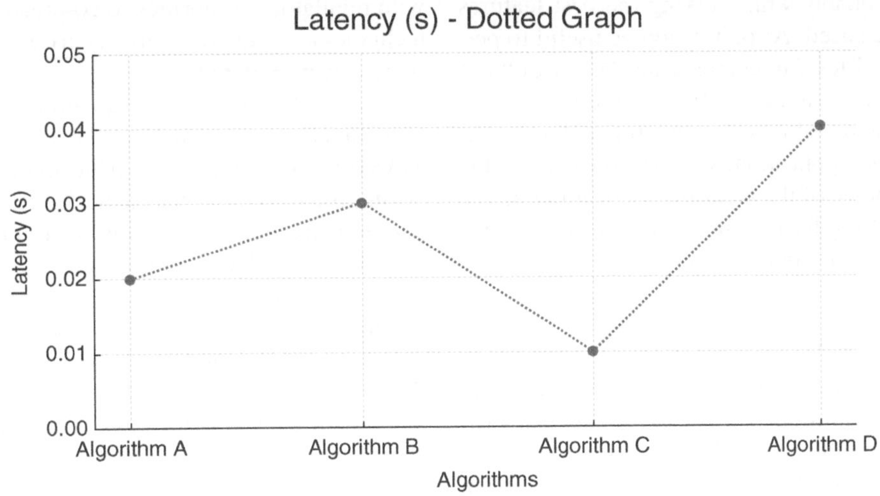

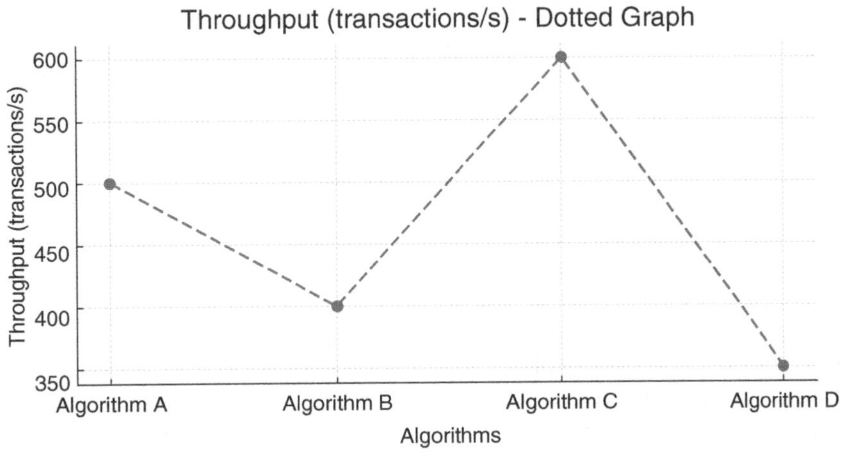

FIGURE 10.4 ***(Continued)*** Graphical representation of performance evaluation metrics: (a) detection rate, (b) false positive rate, (c) accuracy, (d) latency, and (e) throughput.

notifications. On the contrary, however, Algorithm D also had the highest false positive rates (0.20), which would cause a loss of vigilance from the security teams due to over-alerting. In a more general picture, algorithms with lower false alarms are preferred in sensitive situations; hence, while Algorithm D performs satisfactorily on detection rates, its performance will be undermined by the high false alarms.

c. Latency and throughput metrics are very important in real-time applications. Algorithm C's performance also exceeds expectations with the low latency of (0.01 s) and the greatest throughput of (600 transactions/s). This performance indicates that it will perform well with a high transaction load as it will not lose its quickness hence making it useful in applications where speed is critical such as financial transactions or real-time threat detection. Algorithm A comes second with a latency of 0.02 s and a throughput of 500 transactions/s. The other two algorithms, B and D however have higher latencies (0.03 and 0.04 s) and lower throughputs which may be unsuitable in situations where immediate action is needed.

d. The result also shows that Algorithm C occupies the least compromise in the performance of all algorithms under consideration. For enhanced quantum defensive AI applications, especially those with stringent accuracy and latency requirements, it would be prudent to make use of Algorithm C within the blockchain structure. In most situations, however, the selection of an algorithm must also consider the environment in which it is to be deployed. For less demanding applications, if there are limitations on available resources, such as time, computation, or money burden, Algorithm B will perform satisfactorily.

Table 10.1 illustrates the comparative analysis of different algorithms based on crucial performance metrics such as accuracy, detection rate, false positive rate, latency, and throughput, and how effective the algorithms are when used in applications for blockchain security. Attention in possible future work might be directed toward improving these algorithms, probably while mixing the best features of several approaches used. Also, it would be useful to perform cumulative field tests to corroborate these results in practice under various conditions. To sum up, the evaluation demonstrates the possibilities of quantum defensive AI in a blockchain-based application, stressing the care that is to be taken in the choice of the algorithm depending on the use. As a result, looking for new improvements could lead to higher levels of security in this area.

10.5 CONCLUSION

All things considered, combining blockchain with quantum AI results in strong and future-proof strategies against various attacks in today's digital life. By using the unchangeable and transparent blockchain, the enhanced computation of quantum, and the adaptive intelligence of AI, this system greatly improves the standards of data confidentiality, security, and traceability. Due to the nature of blockchain, both non-centralized control and strict compliance with rules are ensured, since data protection is now more important than ever. Studies have proven that this strategy works better than others, mainly when traditional security systems would not function well in a post-quantum situation. Defense strategies and protecting data may be transformed by using blockchain technology along with quantum computing and AI. As a result, there will be improved security in the digital infrastructure that can last even against the dangers of the future. With this approach in place, new data security standards are developed and used as the base for future protocols and processes. More studies may be conducted to make the integration of blockchain, quantum tech, and AI more efficient and increase the system's scalability. It will be important to study actual uses of AI and create common frameworks for putting them into practice. Looking into how quantum algorithms could affect the system might help us gain more understanding of what it could do. With this step, the way for future security solutions in different fields, including finance and healthcare, is opened.

10.6 FUTURE DIRECTIONS AND SCOPE

Design and assess hybrid algorithms based on quantum computing and classical machine learning to improve defense against AI threats. Investigate the applicability of non-centralized approaches like blockchain to AI model management that demonstrate the reliability of the algorithms used and eliminate the possibility of bias. Explore new possibilities of quantum encryption on AI, especially in blockchains, where different network nodes require secure communication. Build dynamically evolving models that can detect and respond to threats in real-time by harnessing the processing power of quantum systems to sift through enormous datasets in search of anomalies. Develop ethical considerations and governance frameworks to ensure the safety of quantum defensive AI technologies to prevent abuses and negative consequences. Collaborate with regulatory authorities to co-create guidelines on these technologies, ensuring all security, privacy, and ethical issues are considered.

Explore the potential of quantum defensive AI in multiple domains such as finance, healthcare, national security, as well as cold machinery, detailing the problem and proposing the resolution for each case. Examine the potential consequences for society's future arising from the introduction of advanced technologies such as artificial intelligence, along with the integration of blockchain and quantum technologies, including their impact on job displacement, privacy control, and the reduction of the digital divide. Propose the lack of a need to prepare society in advance that will be educated in areas of quantum computing, blockchain technology, and AI so that any ideas become reality. Investigate the survivability of quantum defensive AI systems in power, movement, ecology and waste, and lifecycle of management. Build up the international capability to understand and exchange knowledge and the abilities for the development of the quantum defensive AI solutions with the aim at safety and well-being.

REFERENCES

1. Kumar, A. et al. *Sustainable Security Practices Using Blockchain, Quantum and Post-quantum Technologies for Real Time Applications*. Springer, 2024.
2. Ahakonye, L. A. C., Nwakanma, C. I., and Kim, D.-S. "Tides of Blockchain in IoT Cybersecurity." *Sensors* 24.10 (2024): 3111.
3. Rahman, A. et al. "Blockchain-based AI Methods for Managing Industrial IoT: Recent Developments, Integration Challenges and Opportunities." arXiv preprint arXiv:2405.12550 (2024).
4. Nita, S. L., and Mihailescu, M. I. "A Novel Authentication Scheme Based on Verifiable Credentials Using Digital Identity in the Context of Web 3.0." *Electronics* 13.6 (2024): 1137.
5. Mahajan, H., and Reddy, K. T. V. "Secure Gene Profile Data Processing Using Lightweight Cryptography and Blockchain." *Cluster Computing* 27 (2023): 1–19.
6. Xu, M. et al. "Unleashing the Power of Edge-Cloud Generative AI in Mobile Networks: A Survey of Aigc Services." *IEEE Communications Surveys & Tutorials* 26 (2024): 1127–1170.
7. Zhu, J., Li, F., and Chen, J. "A Survey of Blockchain, Artificial Intelligence, and Edge Computing for Web 3.0." arXiv preprint arXiv:2311.13731 (2023).
8. Chen, H. et al. "The Role of Blockchain in Finance Beyond Cryptocurrency: Trust, Data Management, and Automation." *IEEE Access* 12 (2024). doi:10.1109/ACCESS.2024.3395918.
9. Gupta, S. et al. "Blockchain-based Voting System Powered by Post-Quantum Cryptography (BBVSP-pqc)." In: *2022 Second International Conference on Power, Control and Computing Technologies (ICPC2T)*, Raipur, India. IEEE, 2022.
10. Tsoniotis, N. "Smart Cities as Identities." In: P. M. Pardalos, S. Th. Rassia and A. Tsokas (Eds.), *Artificial Intelligence, Machine Learning, and Optimization Tools for Smart Cities: Designing for Sustainability*. Springer, 2022, pp. 51–62.

11. Tychola, K. A., Voulgaridis, K., and Lagkas, T. "Beyond Flight: Enhancing the Internet of Drones with Blockchain Technologies." *Drones* 8.6 (2024): 219.
12. Garg, S. et al. "Guest Editorial Introduction to the Special Section on AI-Driven Cybersecurity for Healthcare Cyber Physical Systems." *IEEE Transactions on Network Science and Engineering* 10.5 (2023): 2396–2401.
13. Geng, J. "Taking Computation to Data: Integrating Privacy-preserving AI techniques and Blockchain Allowing Secure Analysis of Sensitive Data on Premise." PhD Thesis, University of Stavanger, Norway (2023).
14. Andrew, J. et al. "Blockchain for Healthcare Systems: Architecture, Security Challenges, Trends and Future Directions." *Journal of Network and Computer Applications* 25 (2023): 103633.
15. Mao, B. et al. "Security and Privacy on 6g Network Edge: A Survey." *IEEE Communications Surveys & Tutorials* 25 (2023): 1095–1127.
16. Yi, H. "Improving Cloud Storage and Privacy Security for Digital Twin based Medical Records." *Journal of Cloud Computing* 12.1 (2023): 151.
17. Ghai, D., Tripathi, S. L., Saxena, S., Chanda, M., and Alazab, M. (Eds.). *Machine Learning Algorithms for Signal and Image Processing*. John Wiley & Sons, 2022.
18. Kumar, S., Ghai, D., Jain, A., Tripathi, S. L., and Rani, S. (Eds.). *Multimodal Biometric and Machine Learning Technologies: Applications for Computer Vision*. John Wiley & Sons, 2023.
19. Ghai, D., Saxena, S., Dhingra, G., and Tripathi, S. L. "A Comprehensive Review on Performance-based Comparative Analysis, Categorization, Classification and Mapping Of Text Extraction System Techniques for Images." *Multimedia Tools and Applications* 5 (2024): 2327–2484.
20. Sandhu, R., Channi, H. K., Ghai, D., Cheema, G. S., and Kaur, M. "An Introduction to Generative AI Tools for Education 2030." In: R. Doshi, M. Dadhich, S. Poddar and K. Kant Hiran (Eds.), *Integrating Generative AI in Education to Achieve Sustainable Development Goals*. IGI Global, 2024, pp. 1–28.
21. Ghai, D., Mishra, S. P., and Rani, S. "Supervised and Unsupervised Techniques for Biomedical Image Classification." In: S. Dash, S. Kumar Pani, W. Pinheiro Dos Santos and J. Y. Chen. (Eds.), *Mining Biomedical Text, Images and Visual Features for Information Retrieval*. Academic Press, 2025, pp. 153–211.
22. Valencia-Arias, A. et al. "Machine Learning and Blockchain: A Bibliometric Study on Security and Privacy." *Information* 15.1 (2024): 65.
23. Jyothi, V. et al. "A Data Management System for Smart Cities Leveraging Artificial Intelligence Modeling Techniques to Enhance Privacy and Security." *Journal of Internet Services and Information Security* **14.**1 (2024): 37–51.
24. Rahman, R. et al. "Advanced Techniques for Digital Evidence Preservation: The Power of Blockchain and Machine Learning." In: A. Kumar, N. J. Ahuja, K. Kaushik, D. S. Tomar and S. B. Khan (Eds.), *Sustainable Security Practices Using Blockchain, Quantum and Post-Quantum Technologies for Real Time Applications*. Springer, 2024, pp. 99–124.
25. Umapathy, K. et al. "Theories of Blockchain and Distributed Systems." In: R. Sharma, R. P. Mahapatra and G. Jeon (Eds.), *Artificial Intelligence and Blockchain in Industry 4.0*. CRC Press, 2024, pp. 52–68.
26. Huan, N. T. Y., and Zukarnain, Z. A. "A Survey on Addressing IoT Security Issues by Embedding Blockchain Technology Solutions: Review, Attacks, Current Trends, and Applications." *IEEE Access* 12 (2024): 69765–69782.
27. Kumar, R., Kumar, P., and Sobin, C. C. (Eds.). *Blockchain and Digital Twin Enabled IoT Networks: Privacy and Security Perspectives*. CRC Press, 2024.
28. Gajjar, P. et al. "Security and Privacy Solutions for Healthcare Informatics." In: P. Bhattacharya, A. Verma and S. Tanwar (Eds.), *Federated Learning for Internet of Medical Things*. CRC Press, 2023, pp. 169–189.
29. Zhang, L. "Education Reinvented: AI, Blockchain, and Quantum Cryptography for Trust and Security." (2024).
30. Irawan, D. S. "Blockchain-Powered Fortification: Transformative Security Measures in Data Distribution Systems." *Journal Basic Science and Technology* 12.3 (2023): 75–82.
31. Salama, R. et al. "Blockchain Technology and Artificial Intelligence's Future Applications in Cyber Security." In: *2023 3rd International Conference on Advancement in Electronics & Communication Engineering (AECE)*, Ghaziabad, India, 2023. IEEE.
32. Saxena, R., Gayathri, E., and Kumari, L. S. "Semantic Analysis of Blockchain Intelligence with Proposed Agenda for Future Issues." *International Journal of System Assurance Engineering and Management* 14.Suppl 1 (2023): 34–54.
33. Liu, G. et al. "E-Chain: Lightweight and Secure BIoT Voting Mechanism on Variable Bandwidth Networks." *IEEE Internet of Things Journal* 10 (2023): 13341–13351.
34. Jabor, M. S. et al. "New Approach to Improve Power Consumption Associated with Blockchain in WSNs." *Plos ONE* 18.5 (2023): e0285924.
35. Ali, A. et al. "Empowering Precision Medicine: Unlocking Revolutionary Insights through Blockchain-Enabled Federated Learning and Electronic Medical Records." *Sensors* 23.17 (2023): 7476.
36. Kawalkar, S. A., and Bhoyar, D. B. "Design of an Efficient Cloud Security Model through Federated Learning, Blockchain, AI-Driven Policies, and Zero Trust Frameworks." *International Journal of Intelligent Systems and Applications in Engineering* 12.10s (2024): 378–388.
37. Sarkar, T. et al. "Comparative Analysis of Empirical Research on Agile Software Development Approaches." In: *2024 11th International Conference on Reliability, Infocom Technologies and Optimization (Trends and Future Directions)(ICRITO)*, Noida, India, 2024. IEEE.
38. Sarkar, T. et al. "Comparative Study of Object Recognition Utilizing Machine Learning Techniques." In: *2024 International Conference on Communication, Computer Sciences and Engineering (IC3SE)*, Gautam Buddha Nagar, India, 2024. IEEE.
39. Sarkar, T. et al. "An Empirical Comparison of Machine Learning Techniques for Bank Loan Approval Prediction." In: *2024 International Conference on Communication, Computer Sciences and Engineering (IC3SE)*, Gautam Buddha Nagar, India, 2024. IEEE.
40. Talwani, S., Rakhra, M., and Sarkar, T. "Perspectives on the Future of Agriculture and Recent Developments in Agricultural Technology." In: *2024 11th International Conference on Reliability, Infocom Technologies and Optimization (Trends and Future Directions)(ICRITO)*, Noida, India, 2024. IEEE.
41. Chakrabarty, P. et al. "Enhanced Data Security Framework Using Lightweight Cryptography and Multi-Level

Encryption." In: *2024 International Conference on Communication, Computer Sciences and Engineering (IC3SE),* Gautam Buddha Nagar, India, 2024. IEEE.
42. Singh, D. et al. "Predictions on the Future of Agriculture and Recent Developments in Agricultural Technology." In: *International Conference On Artificial Intelligence Of Things For Smart Societies,* Near East University, Northern Cyprus, 2024. Springer.
43. Sarkar, T. et al. "Review Paper of Performance Analysis in Wireless Sensor Networks." *Kilby* 100 (2023): 7th.
44. Verma, A. K., and Sarkar, T. "Utilizing Imaging Steganographic Improvement using LSB & Image Decoder." In: *2024 International Conference on Communication, Computer Sciences and Engineering (IC3SE),* Gautam Buddha Nagar, India, 2024. IEEE.
45. Arora, C., and Sandhu, R. Adoption of Quantum NLP for Improved Healthcare System. In: A. K. Bairwa, V. Tiwari, S. K. Vishwakarma, M. Tuba and T. Ganokratanaa (Eds.), *International Conference on Computation of Artificial Intelligence & Machine Learning.* Springer, 2024 January, pp. 51–59.
46. Sandhu, R., Kumar, P., Bhasin, C., Fatima, N., and Pal, A. Resnet-34 Model for Human Activity Recognition on Smartphone Sensor Data. *International Journal of Intelligent systems and applications in Engineering* 11.9s (2023): 644–652.
47. Faiz, M., Fatima, N., and Sandhu, R. A Vaccine Slot Tracker Model Using Fuzzy Logic for Providing Quality of Service. In: D. Gupta, R. Chatterjee, A. A. Abd El-Latif and A. K. Sangaiah (Eds.), *Multimodal Biometric and Machine Learning Technologies: Applications for Computer Vision.* CRC Press, 2023, pp. 31–52.
48. Channi, H. K., Sandhu, R., Faiz, M., and Islam, S. M. Multi-Criteria Decision-Making Approach for Laptop Selection: A Case Study. In: *2023 3rd Asian Conference on Innovation in Technology (ASIANCON),* Pune, Maharashtra, India, 2023 August, pp. 1–5. IEEE.
49. Faiz, M., Sandhu, R., Akbar, M., Shaikh, A. A., Bhasin, C., and Fatima, N. Machine Learning Techniques in Wireless Sensor Networks: Algorithms, Strategies, and Applications. *International Journal of Intelligent Systems and Applications in Engineering,* 11.9s (2023): 685–694.

11 Utilizing Quantum Computing for Modern Agriculture

Sakshi Gupta, Archana Singh, and Neetu Singh

11.1 QUANTUM COMPUTING AND AGRICULTURE

Agriculture is a vital and expansive field that requires rapid transformation to improve productivity, sustainability, and adaptability to evolving needs. There are many challenges that exist, such as climate change, crop diseases, limited natural resources, and global food challenges. Modern agriculture has overcome the predefined challenges to a great extent. However, as the population is increasing day by day, there is a need for new and advanced methods to analyze the data and help in modern farming. Various artificial intelligence (AI), machine learning (ML), and deep learning (DL) algorithms have been developed and implemented to provide solutions to the complex problem in modern farming, but there is a need for more accurate, precise, and sustainable solutions [1].

With the integration of quantum computing (QC), various multidisciplinary concepts such as science, mathematics, and quantum physics can help in modern agriculture. QC can be very useful to improve weather forecasting, optimize farming practices, predict rare crop diseases, and crop precision farming [2–6]. By using QC, overall efficiency and decision-making can be improved so that food quality issues can be resolved at the global level [7–12]. Figure 11.1 shows various applications of QC.

The emerging technologies are the integration of Internet of Things (IoT), big data, AI, and robotics into agriculture, addressing the inherent risk aversion prevalent in modern farming practices. Agriculture heavily relies on accurate weather forecasts and optimal resource management to ensure crop yield and quality [13–15].

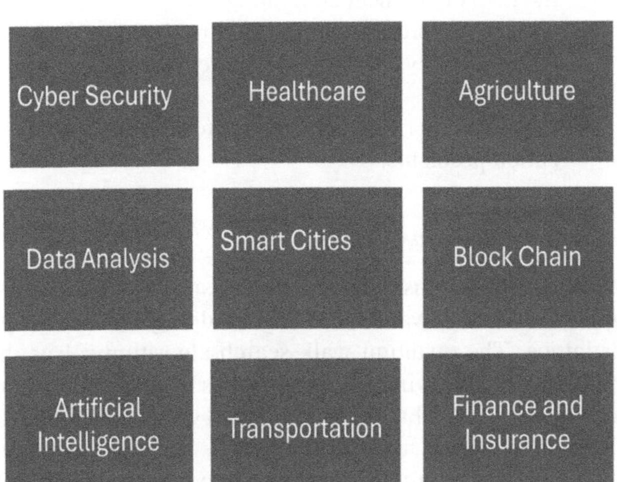

FIGURE 11.1 Applications of quantum computing.

In smart agriculture and irrigation, IoT sensors are used to collect real-time data like weather conditions, soil moisture, and crop health parameters. This data can be processed by AI and ML algorithms to take necessary actions. This proactive approach helps mitigate risks associated with unpredictable weather patterns, ultimately improving productivity and reducing losses [16,17]. In addition, the application of QC and high-performance computing in agriculture is gaining traction. Quantum sensors are used nowadays for deep monitoring of the environmental conditions and plant growth [18–20]. Quantum computers are experts in genetic analysis, which is useful for finding responsible results in plants and crops [21–25]. It holds promise for developing advanced fertilizers, improving field monitoring systems, and providing precise weather forecasts. This chapter focuses on exploring the potential applications of QC in modern agriculture.

11.2 QUANTUM COMPUTING: MODELS AND ALGORITHMS

A quantum computer is a system or computer that leverages the various postulates of quantum mechanics to execute computations with the help of a suitable algorithm [26–28]. Quantum computers differ from traditional digital computers in that they use quantum memory, which consists of particles assigned a value of zero, one, and a state between zero and one, or both. QC has considerably increased in popularity and technology over the last 30 years. The objective of the creation of QC is to tackle different problems that ordinary (classical) computers cannot solve. New technologies, hardware components, and software developments are being developed worldwide to enable this powerful tool's usage.

Quantum systems will have significant processing capacity as compared to traditional computers, which offers a great advantage for tackling massive and complicated issues instantly, whereas a classical computer may take many years to solve the problem. With the above advantages, quantum computers enable them to play a key role in the development of various real-world applications, including healthcare, agriculture, logistics, cybersecurity, finance, and AI.

DOI: 10.1201/9781003530800-11

Quantum computers rely on entirely new information units known as quantum bits, or qubits. These qubits are the primary reason for quantum computers' exponentially rising power. The main advantage of quantum computers is their exponential speed and ability to handle several applications simultaneously. QC, also known as parallel computing, leverages a phenomenon known as quantum tunneling to cut power usage by 100–1000 times when compared to classical computers. QC can sift through vast amounts of data to identify solutions to complex problems by leveraging qubits, which store information in quantum states that combine 0 and 1 simultaneously in a multidimensional form.

11.3 ELEMENTS OF QUANTUM COMPUTING

11.3.1 Bits vs Qubits

Classical computers process data in bits with states of $|0\rangle$ or $|1\rangle$ as this is the smallest unit of information. In quantum computers, data is processed as a series of qubits. The qubit is a superposition of both $|0\rangle$ and $|1\rangle$, whereas the bit is a single value.

11.3.2 Quantum Gates

Building a quantum computer requires a new type of circuit that includes a sequence of quantum gates and a mechanical extension of classical logic gates. Quantum gates have input and output states that are a superposition of $|0\rangle$ and $|1\rangle$. To further comprehend the action of a quantum gate, consider a NOT gate that switches from state $|0\rangle$ to state $|1\rangle$ as shown in the equation (Eq. 11.1) [29–31].

$$\alpha\,|\,0\rangle+\beta\,|\,1\rangle\rightarrow\alpha\,|\,1\rangle+\beta\,|\,0\rangle \tag{11.1}$$

Similar to classical logic gates, a variety of quantum gates are available, including identity gates, global phase gates, and Clifford qubit gates. In addition, there are non-Clifford qubit gates, rotation operator gates, two-qubit interaction gates, and non-Clifford swap gates.

11.4 QUANTUM ALGORITHMS

A quantum algorithm can be defined as an algorithm that solves a computational problem at an exponentially faster rate than conventional algorithms. Quantum algorithms differ from classical algorithms in that they operate on a superposition of all possible inputs simultaneously, rather than executing on a single input at a time, as is the case with classical algorithms. As a result, to tackle actual issues with a quantum computer, we must use a quantum algorithm [32]. Some examples of quantum algorithms are given below.

11.4.1 Shor's Algorithm

Shor's technique, named after mathematician Peter Shor, is a quantum technique used to effectively factor huge composite numbers. It is a well-known and famous algorithm in QC.

The steps involved in Shor's algorithm are using GCD and MOD.

11.4.1.1 Applications of Shor's Algorithm

The applications of Shor's algorithm are listed as follows:

- Shor's technique can factorize incredibly huge numbers on a quantum computer.
- Shor's algorithm could be used to hack the RSA algorithm and other secure data formats.
- Shor's approach can solve the challenge of determining the period of a function.

11.4.2 Grover's Algorithm

This algorithm is used to search an unsorted database. Classical computers use algorithms such as linear search or binary search to locate a specific item in an unsorted or sorted list, respectively. The temporal complexity of these techniques is often related to the size of the dataset, which sometimes results in lengthy computations when working with large volumes of data.

Grover's technique solves this problem by using quantum physics to complete the search much faster than its classical counterparts. The Grover's Algorithm consists of several important steps:

- **Initialization**
- **Grover Iteration**
- **Oracle**
- **Diffusion Operator**

11.4.2.1 Applications of Grover's Algorithm

The applications of Grover's Algorithm are listed as follows:

- Grover's approach can be used to find and visualize patterns in enormous, impossible datasets with the help of classical computing.
- Grover's approach can be used to decipher cryptographic keys to provide more security to the application.
- Grover's algorithm can be used to address optimization problems.

11.4.3 Quantum Walk

A quantum walk is inspired by classical random walks, which involve a walker moving randomly over a graph or lattice. The quantum walk search algorithm solves the problem of identifying marked vertices in a graph by doing a quantum walk. That is, we mark a set of vertices *M*, begin from an arbitrary node in the graph, and proceed along the walk until we reach the marked nodes. This algorithm would theoretically provide a quadratic speed-up over its classical version [33]. The quantum walk is the extension of the classical random walk and predecessor of the "wave walk" depending on the measurement strength of the quantum walker's coin state.

11.4.3.1 Application of Quantum Walk

The applications of quantum walk are listed as follows:

- Quantum walk is used to graph isomorphism techniques.
- Quantum walk is a useful algorithm to detect marked vertices.
- Quantum walk provides the optimal solution for spatial search and detects hidden non-linear structures in graphs.

11.5 CONVENTIONAL COMPUTING AND QUANTUM COMPUTING IN AGRICULTURE

Conventional computing relies on electrical circuits that exist in a single state at any given time, either on or off. In traditional computers, information is stored as bits represented by voltage levels, where low voltage corresponds to 0, and high voltage corresponds to 1. In opposite, QC applies the concept of quantum physics. Quantum computer uses qubits that can have the value 0 and 1 at the same time.

In agriculture, integration of quantum algorithms can solve difficult problems like optimizing crop yields, soil health prediction, weather patterns, and crop health management. Figure 11.2 shows the differences between classical and QC.

Agriculture is an important area for food security. To address modern concerns like climate change and resource sustainability, agriculture requires novel technologies to increase efficiency. Assessing soil fertility is crucial for optimizing fertilizer and resource utilization. Quantum technologies are being used to analyze soil fertility, which is a new method.

Accurate land fertility assessment is crucial for optimizing productivity in modern agriculture. QC offers interesting solutions to complicated data analytics problems in agriculture, addressing the limitations of existing evaluation methods. The authors in [34] investigate the use of a variational quantum classifier (VQC) to accurately measure soil fertility levels. VQC is a quantum learning technique used for classification in QC.VQC received input from quantum feature and ansatz techniques, including ZZFeatureMap and RealAmplitudes.

The authors offer a quantum-inspired decision-making approach for crop cultivation in modern agriculture. The proposed techniques are structured as a graph coloring problem. Using a quantum-inspired metaheuristic technique, the graph coloring issue is transformed into a quadratic unconstrained binary optimization model and solved with a quantum annealer [35].

11.6 QUANTUM COMPUTING APPLICATION IN AGRICULTURE

QC and IoT are innovative applications that are revolutionizing agriculture by enhancing efficiency and precision in farming operations. Quantum computers excel in processing large data, conducting complex simulations, which enables data-driven decisions that significantly boost crop production. QC principles are integrated with robotics to develop quantum robots for crop planting, harvesting, and monitoring soil and plant health based on intricate datasets. For instance, in [36], the authors introduced an IoT-based precision farming system that uses a seed-sowing robot enhanced with QC to achieve high precision in sowing directly seeded crops such as wheat, maize, soybeans, and pigeon peas. IoT can also be integrated with QC applications to perform precise sorting, precision farming, and optimize crop growth. Overall, QC and IoT represent a transformative synergy in precision/smart farming, socioeconomically strengthening farmers by using advanced tools for optimized crop health and soil health management through sustainable agricultural practices.

QC is transforming agricultural production through the concept of digital twins [37], which is a virtual model of a process or product, enhanced by advanced modeling and simulations for accuracy.

Digital twin plays a vital role in modern agriculture as it can mimic the environment suitable for crops and pets. This can be helpful in making the right decisions at the right time to enhance the sustainability of the environment [38,39].

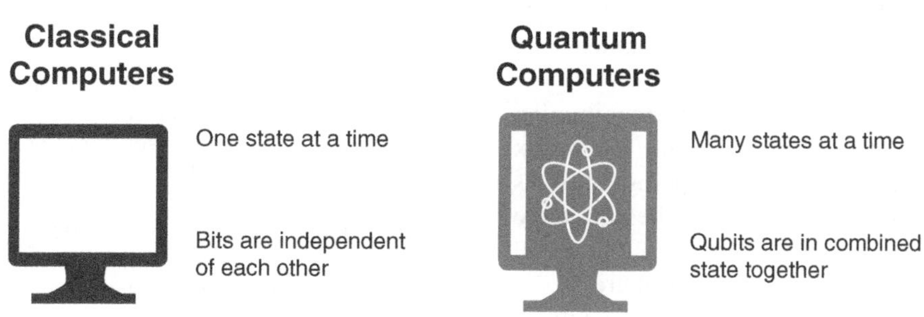

FIGURE 11.2 Classical computing vs quantum computing.

With the help of QC, crop data can be analyzed, and with the integration of ML, new and advanced crop management strategies can be developed.

In [40], the authors used a plant-centroids dataset consisting of 2000 images and analyzed it to make informed decisions about watering, harvesting, improving efficiency, and increasing planting. As per findings in [41], QC algorithms are used to investigate better methods for analyzing multispectral aerial images with the help of unmanned aerial vehicles.

11.7 ENHANCING DATA ANALYSIS WITH QUANTUM COMPUTING

Classical computing systems may take an unacceptable length of time to analyze and interpret huge datasets, delaying decision-making and sometimes resulting in missed opportunities [42]. Classical computer systems have a high latency, which is problematic in circumstances requiring real-time analysis, such as health monitoring systems or fraud detection in financial transactions [43–50].

In classical computer systems, delays are high while sending results to user applications.

In contrast, quantum algorithms provide less delay, more throughput, good reliability, and high efficiency while sending data to the cloud and decisions to the end user applications. In pest and disease management, QC could enable quicker identification of issues in crops, facilitating timely interventions and potentially reducing agricultural losses. By improving the speed and correctness of data processing, quantum algorithms can revolutionize decision-making processes in agriculture, supporting more sustainable farming practices and improving overall crop health and productivity [50–59].

11.8 CHALLENGES AND FUTURE PROSPECTS

QC is increasingly acknowledged as a promising technology in agriculture, with its potential advantages continuing to unfold. However, adopting new technology always brings some challenges with it. Some major challenges are mentioned below:

- To work with QC, expertise is required, which is limited in the agriculture sector, which can also lead to a new job opportunity.
- Hardware and software support is limited for QC as it requires a special type of environment and computers.
- Designing efficient algorithms and programming languages for quantum systems remains a complex challenge, demanding specialized expertise and tools that are still under development. Addressing these obstacles is essential to unlocking the full potential of QC in diverse fields, including agriculture.
- Additionally, quantum computers and specialized software are costly, posing financial barriers that restrict access for many farmers even if the technology is readily available.

11.9 CONCLUSION

QC with the integration of AI can do wonders in modern agriculture. This chapter gives insights into how QC can be merged with the latest ML models to solve the complex problems in agriculture, such as precision farming and the detection of rare crop diseases. This chapter also enlightens the various algorithms that can be used for modern agricultural areas, such as crop monitoring, weather monitoring, and livestock management. According to the literature, very little work has been done till now in this area. In the future, more practical and deep knowledge about quantum mechanics and quantum computing is required to solve these complex problems.

REFERENCES

1. A. Osterloh, L. Amico, G. Falci, R. Fazio (2002). Scaling of entanglement close to a quantum phase transition. *Nature*, 416(6881), 608–610.
2. A. B. Nyamekye, E. Nyadzi, A. Dewulf, S. Werners, E. Van Slobbe, R. G. Biesbroek, C. J. A. M. Termeer, F. Ludwig (2021). Forecast probability, lead time and farmer decision-making in rice farming systems in Northern Ghana. *Climate Risk Management*, 31, 100258. doi:10.1016/j.crm.2020.100258.
3. Maraveas, C., Konar, D., Michopoulos, D. K., Arvanitis, K. G., Peppas, K. P. (2024). Harnessing quantum computing for smart agriculture: Empowering sustainable crop management and yield optimization. *Computers and Electronics in Agriculture*, 218, 108680.
4. C. Maraveas, D. Piromalis, K. G. Arvanitis, T. Bartzanas, D. Loukatos (2022). Applications of IoT for optimized greenhouse environment and resources management. *Computers and Electronics in Agriculture*, 198, 106993. doi:10.1016/j.compag.2022.106993.
5. S. Gupta, I. Snigdh (2023). Applying Bayesian belief in LoRa: Smart parking case study. *Journal of Ambient Intelligence and Humanized Computing*, 14(6), 7857–7870.
6. D. Jones, C. Snider, A. Nassehi, J. Yon, B. Hicks (2020). Characterizing the digital twin: A systematic literature review. *CIRP Journal of Manufacturing Science and Technology*, 29(1755–5817), 36–52. doi:10.1016/j.cirpj.2020.02.002.
7. D. C. Rose, J. Chilvers (2018). Agriculture 4.0: Broadening responsible innovation in an era of smart farming. *Frontiers in Sustainable Food Systems*, 2, 87. doi:10.3389/fsufs.2018.00087.
8. R. F. Da Silva, R. M. Badia, V. Bala, D. Bard, P. T. Bremer, I. Buckley, S. Caino-Lores, K. Chard, C. Goble, S. Jha, D. S. Katz (2023). Workflows community summit 2022: A roadmap revolution. arXiv:2304.00019. doi:10.48550/arXiv.2304.00019.
9. S. Gupta, M. Mohapatro (2023). Healthcare transformation using soft computing approaches and IoT protocols. In: A. Nayyar, M. Abdel-Basset, N. Chilamkurti (Eds.), *Soft Computing Techniques in Connected Healthcare Systems* (pp. 194–217). CRC Press.

10. E. Omia, H. Bae, E. Park, M. S. Kim, I. Baek, I. Kabenge, B. K. Cho (2023). Remote sensing in field crop monitoring: A comprehensive review of sensor systems, data analyses and recent advances. *Remote Sensing*, 15(2), 354. doi:10.3390/rs15020354.
11. G. Fenu, F. M. Malloci (2021). DiaMOS plant: A dataset for diagnosis and monitoring plant disease. *Agronomy*, 11(11), 2107. doi:10.3390/agronomy11112107.
12. H. Li, H. Shi, A. Du, Y. Mao, K. Fan, Y. Wang, Y. Shen, S. Wang, X. Xu, L. Tian, H. Wang, Z. Ding (2022). Symptom recognition of disease and insect damage based on Mask R-CNN, wavelet transform, and F-RNet. *Frontiers in Plant Science*, 13, 922797. doi:10.3389/fpls.2022.922797.
13. U. I. Musa, S. Gupta, Q. E. Mensah (2023). *AI-Driven Intelligent Transportation Systems in the Age of 5G/6G Networks*. Research Square Platform LLC.
14. J. Amin, M. A. Anjum, R. Zahra, M. I. Sharif, S. Kadry, L. Sevcik (2023). Pest localization using yolov5 and classification based on quantum convolutional network. *Agriculture*, 13(3), 662. doi:10.3390/agriculture13030662.
15. K. Kaushik (2023). Smart agriculture applications using cloud and IoT. In: D. B. Rawat, L. K. Awasthi, V. E. Balas, M. K. Mohit, J. K. Samriya (Eds.), *Convergence of Cloud with AI for Big Data Analytics: Foundations and Innovation* (pp. 89–105). Wiley. doi:10.1002/9781119905233.ch5.
16. L. Marchetti, R. Nifosì, P. L. Martelli, E. Da Pozzo, V. Cappello, F. Banterle, M. D'Elia (2022). Quantum computing algorithms: Getting closer to critical problems in computational biology. *Briefings in Bioinformatics*, 23(6). doi:10.1093/bib/bbac437.
17. L. Wright, S. Davidson (2020). How to tell the difference between a model and a digital twin. *Advanced Modeling and Simulation in Engineering Sciences*, 7(1), 1–13. doi:10.1186/s40323-020-00147-4.
18. S. Gupta, I. Snigdh (2022). Multi-sensor fusion in autonomous heavy vehicles. In: R. Krishnamurthi, F. Xhafa, A. Kumar, S. S. Gill (Eds.), *Autonomous and Connected Heavy Vehicle Technology* (pp. 375–389). Academic Press.
19. M. Abdel-Basset, L. A. Shawky, K. Eldrandaly (2020). Grid quorum-based spatial coverage for IoT smart agriculture monitoring using the enhanced multi-verse optimizer. *Neural Computing and Applications*, 32, 607–624. doi:10.1007/s00521-018-3807-4.
20. S. K. X. D. Souza, É. L. Bolfe, M. A. D. A. Leite, M. D. Bambini, M. C. Visoli, A. Luchiari, J. E. D. C. T. Yassitepe (2024). Quantum computing: Current and potential applications in digital agriculture. *Pesquisa Agropecuária Brasileira*, 59, e03753.
21. M. Javaid, A. Haleem, R. P. Singh, R. Suman (2022). Enhancing smart farming through the applications of Agriculture 4.0 technologies. *International Journal of Intelligent Networks*, 3, 150–164. doi:10.1016/j.ijin.2022.09.004.
22. M. Reynolds, M. Kropff, J. Crossa, J. Koo, G. Kruseman, M. A. Milan, J. Rutkoski, U. Schulthess, K. Sonder, H. Tonnang, V. Vadez (2018). Role of modelling in international crop research: Overview and some case studies. *Agronomy*, 8(12), 291. doi:10.3390/agronomy8120291.
23. M. N. Akhtar, A. J. Shaikh, A. Khan, H. Awais, E. A. Bakar, A. R. Othman (2021). Smart sensing with edge computing in precision agriculture for soil assessment and heavy metal monitoring: A review. *Agriculture*, 11(6), 475. doi:10.3390/agriculture11060475.
24. P. Papastefanou, C. S. Zang, T. A. Pugh, D. Liu, T. E. Grams, T. Hickler, A. Rammig (2020). A dynamic model for strategies and dynamics of plant water-potential regulation under drought conditions. *Frontiers in Plant Science*, 11, 373. doi:10.3389/fpls.2020.00373.
25. R. Milla (2020). Crop origins and phylo food: A database and a phylogenetic tree to stimulate comparative analyses on the origins of food crops. *Global Ecology and Biogeography*, 29(4), 606–614. doi:10.1111/geb.13057.
26. R. Rietsche, C. Dremel, S. Bosch, L. Steinacker, M. Meckel, J. M. Leimeister (2022). Quantum computing. *Electronic Markets*, 32(4), 2525–2536. doi:10.1007/s12525-022-00570-y.
27. R. M. Abd El-Aziz, A. I. Taloba, F. A. Alghamdi (2022). Quantum computing optimization technique for IoT platform using the modified deep residual approach. *Alexandria Engineering Journal*, 61(12), 12497–12509. doi:10.1016/j.aej.2022.06.029.
28. R. M. Pujahari, S. P. Yadav, R. Khan (2022). Intelligent farming system through weather forecast support and crop production. In: M. A. Khan, R. Khan, M. A. Ansari (Eds.), *Application of Machine Learning in Agriculture* (pp. 113–130). Academic Press. doi:10.1016/B978-0-323-90550-3.00009-6.
29. C. Arora, R. Sandhu, S. M. Islam (2025, February). Quantum linguistics in patient-clinical trial relations for improved healthcare. In: *2025 International Conference on Pervasive Computational Technologies (ICPCT),* Greater Noida, Uttar Pradesh, India (pp. 186–190). IEEE.
30. R. Li, U. Alvarez-Rodriguez, L. Lamata, E. Solano (2017). Approximate quantum adders with genetic algorithms: An IBM quantum experience. *Quantum Measurements and Quantum Metrology*, 4(1), 1–7.
31. C. Arora, R. Sandhu (2024, January). Adoption of quantum NLP for improved healthcare system. In: *International Conference on Computation of Artificial Intelligence & Machine Learning,* Jaipur, India (pp. 51–59). Springer Nature Switzerland.
32. C. P. Williams (2011). Quantum gates. In: D. Gries, F. B. Schneider (Eds.), *Explorations in Quantum Computing* (pp. 51–122). Springer.
33. K. Kadian, S. Garhwal, A. Kumar (2021). Quantum walk and its application domains: A systematic review. *Computer Science Review*, 41, 100419.
34. D. T. Mukhamedieva (2024). Innovative quantum technologies in agriculture for assessing land fertility. *E3S Web of Conferences*, 494, 04026.
35. C. H. Ou, D. J. Jiang, C. Y. Chen, L. P. Yu, C. R. Chang (2022, September). Smart agriculture decision making scheme using quantum annealing. In: *2022 IEEE International Conference on Quantum Computing and Engineering (QCE),* Broomfield, Colorado, USA (pp. 862–863). IEEE.
36. D. H. Kamatham, A. Prathyusha, K. Kavitha, B. Kumar, K. Manasa, K. Sowmya (2022). IoT based smart and solar operated multi tasking agriculture robot. *RB Journal of Lib & Information Science*, 12(7), 1.
37. W. Purcell, T. Neubauer (2023). Digital twins in agriculture: A state-of-the-art review. *Smart Agricultural Technology*, 3, 100094. doi:10.1016/j.atech.2022.100094.
38. W. Purcell, T. Neubauer, K. Mallinger (2023). Digital twins in agriculture: Challenges and opportunities for environmental sustainability. *Current Opinion in*

Environmental Sustainability, 61, 101252. doi:10.1016/j.cosust.2022.101252.

39. C. Pylianidis, S. Osinga, I. N. Athanasiadis (2021). Introducing digital twins to agriculture. *Computers and Electronics in Agriculture*, 184, 105942.
40. P. R. Rao, R. Sandhu (2024, March). Farmer well-being with metaverse innovations in agriculture. In: *2024 11th International Conference on Reliability, Infocom Technologies and Optimization (Trends and Future Directions) (ICRITO)*, Noida, India (pp. 1–6). IEEE.
41. V. K. Ralegankar, J. Bagul, B. Thakkar, R. Gupta, S. Tanwar, G. Sharma, I. E. Davidson (2021). Quantum cryptography-as-a-service for secure UAV communication: Applications, challenges, and case study. *IEEE Access*, 10, 1475–1492.
42. P. R. Rao, R. Sandhu, S. M. Islam (2025, February). ReIoT-Powered Smart Agriculture in Controlled Environments. In: *2025 International Conference on Pervasive Computational Technologies (ICPCT),* Greater Noida, Uttar Pradesh, India (pp. 6–11). IEEE.
43. J. Wright, H. Kieft, S. von Diest (2017). Quantum-based agriculture: The final frontier. In: *Organic World Congress* 2017, Greater Noida, New Delhi, India (pp. 107–111). Johann Heinrich von Thünen-Institute. doi:10.3220/REP1510907717000.
44. D. Ghai, H. K. Gianey, A. Jain, R. S. Uppal (2020). Quantum and dual-tree complex wavelet transform-based image watermarking. *International Journal of Modern Physics B*, 34(4), 2050009.
45. D. Ghai, S. Tiwari, N. N. Das (2021). Bottom-boosting differential evolution based digital image security analysis. *Journal of Information Security and Applications*, 61, 102811.
46. D. Ghai, S. L. Tripathi, S. Saxena, M. Chanda, M. Alazab (Eds.). (2022). *Machine Learning Algorithms for Signal and Image Processing.* John Wiley & Sons.
47. D. Ghai, S. Saxena, G. Dhingra, S. L. Tripathi (2024). A comprehensive review on performance-based comparative analysis, categorization, classification and mapping of text extraction system techniques for images. *Multimedia Tools and Applications*, 2024, 1–158. **doi:**10.1007/s11042-024-20257-0.
48. S. Kumar, D. Ghai, A. Jain, S. L. Tripathi, S. Rani (2023). *Multimodal Biometric and Machine Learning Technologies: Applications for Computer Vision.* John Wiley & Sons.
49. R. Sandhu, H. K. Channi, D. Ghai, G. S. Cheema, M. Kaur (2024). An Introduction to Generative AI Tools for Education 2030. In: **R. Doshi, M. Dadhich, S. Poddar, K. K. Hiran (Eds.),** *Integrating Generative AI in Education to Achieve Sustainable Development Goals* (pp. 1–28). IGI Global.
50. M. Kaur, R. Aron, R. Tandon, H. Wadhwa, G. Kaur, R. Sandhu, D. Ghai (2024). Impact of artificial intelligence techniques on green applications. In: D. Ghai, K. Rawal, K. Dhir, S. L. Tripathi (Eds.), *Artificial Intelligence Techniques for Sustainable Development* (pp. 64–85). CRC Press.
51. D. Ghai, K. Rawal, K. Dhir, S. L. Tripathi (Eds.). (2024) *Artificial Intelligence Techniques for Sustainable Development.* CRC Press.
52. S. Gupta, I. Snigdh (2022). Leveraging data aggregation algorithm in LoRa networks. *Journal of Supercomputing*, 78(15), 16861–16875.
53. M. Malik, V. Dogra, R. Sandhu, R. Kumar, D. Ghai (2025). Topology in Network Technologies. Distributed and Parallel Computing, 39–56.
54. S. Gupta, Manorama, I. Snigdh (2023, June). An energy conserving MANET-LoRa architecture for wireless body area network. In: R. K. Shukla, A. Nayyar, A. K. Sangaiah, M. Z. Khan (Eds.), *International Conference on Data Analytics & Management* (pp. 603–615). Springer Nature Singapore.
55. V. K. A. Somayajula, D. Ghai, S. Kumar (2021, April). Land use/land cover change analysis using NDVI, PCA. *In 2021 5th International Conference on Computing Methodologies and Communication (ICCMC)* (pp. 849–855). IEEE .
56. S. Gupta, I. Snigdh (2022). A review on parameters that impact IoT application: An experimental evaluation. In: A. K. Singh, S. K. Saha, D. Gupta, A. Mohan (Eds.), *Microelectronics, Communication Systems, Machine Learning and Internet of Things: Select Proceedings of MCMI 2020* (pp. 203–213). Springer Nature Singapore.
57. S. Gupta, I. Snigdh, S. K. Sahana (2022). A fuzzy logic approach for predicting efficient LoRa communication. *International Journal of Fuzzy Systems*, 24(5), 2591–2599.
58. D. Ghai, D. Gera, N. Jain, (2016). A new approach to extract text from images based on DWT and K-means clustering. *International Journal of Computational Intelligence Systems*, 9(5), 900–916.
59. S. Gupta, U. Gupta, M. Sharma, K. Malik (Eds.). (2025). *Generative Intelligence in Healthcare: Transforming Patient Care with AI Creativity.* CRC Press.

12 Pros and Cons of Quantum Artificial Intelligence w.r.t. Applications

Narayanan Radha, Arumugam Deepika, Sundaramurthy Manju Priya, Natrajan Kavitha, and Ravindran Kiruthika

12.1 INTRODUCTION

Computational technology is a comparatively young science that works with calculations with the help of quantum mechanics. This area of computing is based on quantum mechanics, which is a theory that endeavors to explain the action of particles within atoms and sub-atomic particles. Quantum computers can solve computations that classical computers cannot in any way solve. One of the main characteristics is the possibility to carry out data storage and computational operations with the help of qubits, which are known for their ability to be at the same time both 0 and 1. This opportunity remains useful for making computations that require a lot of primitives to be made by quantum computers.

Many spheres of the economy, such as information science, medicine development, and cryptography, will highly benefit from the availability of quantum computing (QC). For instance, current encryption standards could be broken by quantum computers. However, the development of quantum computers is still in its infancy. The incompatibility issue is the largest barrier to QC. The process via which qubits lose their quantum characteristics as a result of interactions with their surroundings is known as decoherence. Because it can result in errors in calculations, this could be a serious issue [1–4].

12.1.1 Major Contribution to the Quantum World

This chapter is organized to deal with the research carried out in the field of quantum artificial intelligence (QAI) and its applications in various fields with respective pros and cons. Various machine learning algorithms employed for QAI are explained. This chapter is organized as follows: Section 12.2 explains the comparison of classical and quantum computers, and Section 12.3 discusses the advantages and disadvantages of quantum computers. Section 12.4 deals with QAI, Section 12.5 explains the various application domains and pros and cons of QAI, and Section 12.6 deals with the conclusion.

12.2 DIFFERENCE BETWEEN CLASSICAL AND QUANTUM COMPUTERS

Over the years, the development of computing has reached the focal point in which two different instruments exist—classical computers and quantum ones. Traditional computers, which for decades were the hallmark of current innovation, use bits—units of data that exist in two states: 0 or 1. They are used to solve a wide range of problems, from simple computations to complex simulations, based on the architectural foundation established by well-understood principles. On the other hand, quantum computers are based on the principles of quantum mechanics; they are characterized by the use of qubits that are in many states due to superposition. This ability, when combined with entanglement and quantum interference, makes it possible for quantum computers to solve certain algorithms much faster than classical computers. Outlining the major tenets of these two paradigms, as well as the potency and logistics of each, is the purpose of Table 12.1.

TABLE 12.1
Comparison of Classical and Quantum Computers

Classical Computer	Quantum Computer
A rapid parallel computing system that leverages the principles of quantum mechanics.	A high-speed parallel computer utilizing principles of quantum mechanics.
Information storage is in the form of bits.	Based on the direction of an electron spin, information storage is done in a Quantum bit.
Logic gates are used to process the information.	Quantum logic gates are used to process Information.
Classical physics governs circuit behavior.	Quantum mechanics governs circuit behavior.
Representation of Information is in 0 or 1.	Quantum computers use qubits [0, 1] simultaneously to run machines faster.
Boolean algebra is used to define operations.	Linear algebra over Hilbert space is used to define operations and is represented by unitary matrices with complex elements.
On copying or measuring signals, no restrictions exist.	More restrictions exist on copying and measuring signals.
CMOS is used to implement circuits.	Microscopic technologies are used to implement circuits.

DOI: 10.1201/9781003530800-12

12.3 ADVANTAGES AND DISADVANTAGES OF QUANTUM COMPUTERS

The pros of quantum computers are as follows:

a. Faster computations
b. Best for simulation
c. Accelerate every Google search
d. Perform strong encryption and effective cryptography
e. Used in radar manufacturing
f. These computers are good at artificial intelligence (AI) to make more decisions and to do better research.
g. QC is effectively used by machine learning to improve results.

The cons of quantum computers are as follows:

a. The minimum temperature must be maintained
b. Not available to the public
c. Risk to internet security.

12.4 QUANTUM ARTIFICIAL INTELLIGENCE

QAI is the combination of QC and AI in research and development. QAI leverages quantum entanglement and superposition to accelerate computations and improve machine-learning models. A wide range of industries, including healthcare, banking, climate research, transportation, and retail sales, could undergo a dramatic transformation because of its improved processing capacity, faster machine learning, and greater prediction skills [5,6].

QAI has the potential to develop large language models, neural networks, and machine learning approaches. A project called Google QAI aims to build a massive quantum computer that can do complex calculations with perfect accuracy. The program's objectives are to create superior QC gear and software and to pinpoint future applications for error-corrected quantum computers. Other businesses are also utilizing QAI.

12.5 APPLICATION DOMAINS OF QUANTUM ARTIFICIAL INTELLIGENCE (QAI)

QAI can be applied in various domains as follows:

a. Healthcare
b. Finance and economics
c. Logistics and supply chain
d. Telecommunication and networking
e. Energy sector
f. AI and machine learning
g. Automotive industry
h. E-commerce
i. Education

Figure 12.1 describes the application domains of QAI.

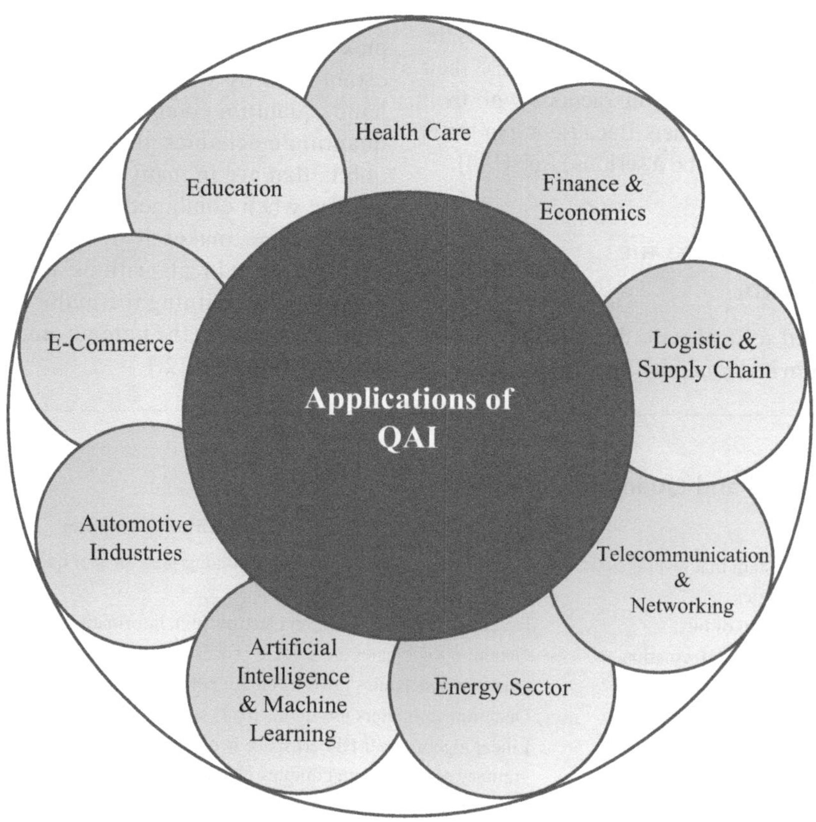

FIGURE 12.1 Application domains of QAI.

12.5.1 Healthcare

QAI in healthcare represents a cutting-edge intersection of QC and medical science, aiming to revolutionize various aspects of the field through advanced computational techniques.

i. **Drug Discovery and Development**: Drug development can be greatly accelerated by QAI through the quantum simulation of chemical and molecular interactions. In the rational drug design of different target molecules, conventional methods for drug discovery involve time-consuming and costly trial-and-error approaches. Quantum computers, as opposed to classical ones, have higher accuracy and faster simulation of interactions between molecules as well as their structures. This may well enhance understanding of how drugs behave in biological systems, and allow researchers to better predict the clinical benefits and potential sinister side effects of new compounds. Interconnected drug development cycles might be compressed as a consequence and bring about faster development of new treatments and potentially even a reduction in the cost of introducing new drugs to the market [7,8].
ii. **Personalized Medicine**: Advances in QAI can positively impact the enhancement of tailor-made treatment for a specific client, depending on his or her DNA and other personal health records. Proteomic and genomic data can be analyzed for correlation and syntropy by quantum systems, while this is difficult for classical systems to undertake. This could lead to more accurate prediction of patient-specific responses to drugs and support improved, tailored treatment regimens [9]. Personalized medicine takes into account each patient's genetic makeup and medical history in an attempt to treat diseases and minimize side effects by abandoning the use of one general therapy to accommodate every patient [10,11].
iii. **Medical Imaging**: QAI can be capable of enhancing the strategies of health imaging because the structure of the image process and analysis can be enhanced by QAI. Large amounts of data are created by high-definition image technologies, such as CT and MRI scans, that are used to diagnose, track, and assess diseases [12,13]. Large picture reconstruction and its analysis can be thought more quicker and accurate using quantum algorithms, contributing to higher quality diagnosis with the discovery of slight deviations. This increased capacity can lead to earlier and more accurate diagnosis, better disease mapping, or monitoring of the progress of illness or treatment outcomes [14,15].
iv. **Genomics and Proteomics**: Traditional techniques are less effective than the QAI approach in the data integration and analysis processes of various biological data structures in proteomics and genomics. Large amounts of genetic and protein data can be processed as QC and will offer new knowledge about relations between proteins, gene regulation, and the molecular bases of diseases. This may lead to identifying new disease markers, understanding the basis of various diseases, and identifying the possibility of producing precise treatments [16]. For example, there could be all new genetic findings for illnesses or an easier understanding of how proteins fold and work in the body at the level of QAI [17,18].
v. **Clinical Decision Support**: Since QAI can facilitate and interpret high data dimensions originating from clinical trials, patients' outcomes, and even Electronic Health Records (EHRs), it may help with the decision-making process. The information that cannot be searched for by conventional analytical procedures, trends, and correlations in data can be identified by quantum algorithms. This might assist clinicians in making sounder decisions on how best to treat their patients, design treatment regimens, and contain diseases. In particular, enhanced analysis of data can help to improve such important parameters as treatment regimes or clinical management guidelines for individual patients at QAI [15,19].

12.5.1.1 Pros of Quantum AI in Healthcare

The pros of QAI in healthcare are listed as follows:

i. QAI could accelerate the discovery of new drugs by simulating molecular interactions more accurately.
ii. It can improve patient outcomes by analyzing complex genetic and health data to create personalized treatment plans.

12.5.1.2 Cons of Quantum AI in Healthcare

The cons of QAI in healthcare are listed as follows:

i. Handling sensitive health data with QAI could raise privacy and security concerns.
ii. Current quantum technology may not yet be capable of addressing large-scale healthcare challenges effectively.

12.5.2 Finance and Economics

In the financial and economic domains, QAI has revolutionary possibilities through QC to improve multiple financial or economic procedures.

i. **Portfolio Optimization**: In the case of portfolio optimization, since QAI can conduct operations on frightfully large quantities of financial data at an unprecedented rate and precision, it would be a massive improvement. As financial data is usually of high dimensionality, conventional portfolio optimization implies a trade-off between the risk and expected return of a diverse set of assets, which is computationally expensive and challenging. With the help of considering various potential portfolio permutations, quantum algorithms, such as the Quantum Approximate Optimization Algorithm (QAOA), can address intricate optimization problems more effectively. It is also an opportunity to determine the most desirable compositions that can be made in the assets, greatly helping in the assessment of the desired returns compounded by risks. The presented results of the comparative analysis indicate that faster and more accurate portfolio optimization can have a positive impact on the final financial result and facilitate better decision-making of investors [17,20].
ii. **Risk Management**: By looking into large databases and complex risk parameters, QAI can enhance presenting and managing money risks. The use of QC carries higher precision in various economic situations and market conditions than the traditional way of modeling, thereby improving risk models. Financial institutions could indeed better understand and envisage several overall risks that may be linked to credit defaults, market fluctuations, and other forms of financial instability. Enhanced skills in the intervention can lead to appropriate hedging and exposure reduction strategies that make some of the financial structures more resilient.
iii. **Algorithmic Trading**: QAI is capable of augmenting algorithmic trading strategies and enhancing the speed at which they execute trades. Efficient and fast decision-making in trading activities is made possible by high-frequency trading owing to its ability to analyze large data in real-time. Since quantum algorithms can outperform their classical counterparts in pattern-matching problems, they can enhance the performance of trading algorithms. This may translate into better market assessment, improved trade strategy implementation, and perhaps, higher profits. New complex trading strategies that are hard to manage with the use of conventional computer methods may be achieved by the use of QC.
iv. **Financial Modeling**: QAI is capable of refining the efficiency of financial modeling for the same reason: It can provide models that simulate complex systems more accurately and in greater detail. Due to the limited ability of conventional computing modes, conventional finance models often need approximations and a certain level of simplification. QC can address more complex models, more terms, and interactions, and may give a more profound understanding of economic processes and market interactions. Better budgeting, risk appraisal, and improved projection might ensue from this, enabling more quintessential decision-making and strategies for both fiscal individualism and business enlargement [21,22].
v. **Fraud Detection**: In addition, using more efficient data analysis, QAI can establish better techniques to prevent fraudulent transactions. With the present large datasets characterized by patterns and diverse abnormalities that could lead to fraudulent activities, quantum algorithms can be implemented to enhance fraud detection systems' precision and speed. Quantum-based scam detection systems also provide faster and more accurate results by easily identifying all traces of suspicious activities by analyzing large amounts of transaction data in real-time [23,24]. This reduces the risk of losing money and increases security in general.

12.5.2.1 Pros of Quantum AI in Finance and Economics

The pros of QAI in finance and economics are listed as follows:

a. Quantum algorithms can optimize investment portfolios more effectively, considering numerous factors and scenarios.
b. Enhanced ability to model and manage financial risks by processing complex data sets faster.

12.5.2.2 Cons of Quantum AI in Finance and Economics

The cons of QAI in finance and economics are listed as follows:

a. Financial markets are highly volatile, and quantum-enhanced models may not always predict outcomes accurately.
b. The use of QAI in finance may face regulatory hurdles and compliance issues.

12.5.3 Logistics and Supply Chain

QAI may bring significant innovation to the field of logistics and supply chain management because it offers a higher potential for improving multiple tasks in this sphere.

i. **Route Optimization**: QAI could pose a huge opportunity in reorganizing the logistics for better optimization, untapped by conventional methods and models in analyzing and optimizing complex transport networks. The process of determining how to reach client destinations with the help of the least costly paths—considering distance, time, traffic, and delivery window constraints—is known as traditional route optimization. This problem is challenging for such transport networks, but quantum algorithms, including the QAOA, may simultaneously explore many solution paths. This capability can reduce fuel consumption, identify better routes, and ultimately reduce overall operating expenses. Another benefit of supply chains incorporating quantum-enhanced route optimization is that supply chains themselves can be made more adaptable and change-responsive, simultaneously shortening delivery times substantially and boosting the efficiency of overall logistics.

ii. **Inventory Management**: There will be an enhancement in forecasting and inventory control procedures is possible with the help of QAI that will enhance the overall inventory management. Demand forecasting, procurement of materials, and maintaining a perfect stock to meet customers' needs while minimizing costs form the core of inventory management. But to obtain a better estimation of demand, a quantum algorithm can analyze the trends in the industries, past sales data, and other relevant details. This may help reduce situations of understock or overstock, enable relevant businesses to keep the optimum stock, and make supply chain processes more efficient. Inventory management is beneficial to increasing profitability, reducing carrying costs, and enhancing customer satisfaction.

iii. **Supply Chain Optimization**: The supply chain could be improved by QAI because it optimizes decision-making when it comes to distribution and procurement. Static and dynamic complexity and the inefficiencies or other performance-impairing bottlenecks of complex Supply Chain Network (SCN) and their types can be solved with quantum algorithms. By choice of supplier, production, and distribution strategy, QAI is equally capable of enhancing the business of supply chain financial robustness and productivity. Thus, better relations between manufacturers, distributors, and suppliers may lead to shorter intervals and fewer disruptions. By managing the supply chain, better and more reliable functions can be produced at a lower cost.

iv. **Demand Forecasting**: Having sound demand forecasting is extremely important when it comes to supply chain management. QAI could improve demand forecasting by using a large dataset of past sales figures, industry trends, and factors from outside the organization, such as the current economic climate and the seasons. Some patterns and correlations are very hard for classical methods to identify, but can be detected using quantum algorithms. Reducing wastage and increasing the quality of service means that by improving demand forecasting, businesses can sell and purchase needed products and services in optimum quantities. This means that forecasting can help organizations carry out precise planning and effectively manage their operations and resources to compete well in the market.

v. **Risk Management**: By noting and minimizing such prospects of disturbance and risk, QAI can enhance supply chain risk management. Quantum algorithms can evaluate and assess potential consequences of various events such as supply chain disruptions, natural disasters, and geopolitical events. Companies may benefit from enhanced backup and more effective risk handling. Consequently, risk management can be quite helpful to create more resilient supply chains in the face of disruptions and other unanticipated events [25].

12.5.3.1 Pros of Quantum AI in Logistics and Supply Chain

The pros of QAI in logistics and supply chain are listed as follows:

a. Quantum algorithms can solve complex logistics problems like route optimization and inventory management more efficiently.
b. They have the potential to reduce operational costs through optimized supply chain and transportation networks.

12.5.3.2 Cons of Quantum AI in Logistics and Supply Chain

The cons of QAI in logistics and supply chain are listed as follows:

a. It is still in its early stages, and practical applications for logistics optimization are limited.
b. Adapting existing logistics systems to incorporate quantum solutions would be challenging.

12.5.4 Telecommunications and Networking

QAI seems to create new prospects of breakthroughs in telecommunications and networking through advanced network optimization and enhanced security.

i. **Network Optimization**: With improved telecoms network performance, management, and design, QAI has the potential to revolutionize network optimization. Network optimization is a process of refining various networking resources to provide higher levels of productivity and lower latency, ensuring reliable connectivity. Big complex network optimization problems are challenging, but the quantum approach, such as QAOA and quantum annealing, is more effective than the classical method.

The advantage of these algorithms is that they can analyze large amounts of information concerning traffic flows and the available capacities in Internet nodes and possible routes. It may lead to reduced operating expenses, differentiation in service delivery, and efficient consumption of network resources. Through quantum-enabled network optimization, network architectures can be real-time and dynamically configured, making it easier to provide solutions that can efficiently address changing traffic patterns and other conditions in the network system.

ii. **Traffic Management**: Through its authorities, QAI has the potential to enhance network information management and control. They are defined as the process of ensuring continuous end-to-end data, providing low delay, and effectively controlling traffic loads. The fact quantum algorithms deliver very precise traffic analysis and congestion prediction makes it possible to initiate anticipative changes to traffic routing and load distribution. It can lead to lower latency levels, optimized user experience, as well as improved networking standards. In highly trafficked circumstances, better traffic capability can also be useful in optimizing bandwidth standards as well as preventing traffic congestion.

iii. **Quantum Cryptography**: Quantum key distribution (QKD) offers a distinct model for network protection in quantum cryptology. Based on the principles of quantum mechanics, QKD designs secure communication lines that are invulnerable in concept. Unlike other cryptographic techniques, which depend on complex mathematical algorithms, QKD employs quantum entanglement and measurement to provide secure data transmission. This provides critical communication with an optimal shield against potential attack from adversaries who may have a capability in quantum technology. Adopting quantum cryptography with the present telecommunication networks may enhance data transfer security while protecting the technology from emergent cyber threats.

iv. **Discrete Data and Transmission**: QAI also opens up improvements in data compression and transmission in telecommunications networks. Efficient compression can produce quicker transmission, and more efficient utilization of bandwidth since less quantity of data needs to be delivered. Better data encoding and data compression methods that cannot be used with the traditional techniques can be explored by quantum algorithms. A reduction of network congestion and enhanced data transmission is possible through enhanced compression.

v. **Network Security and Threat Detection**: The use of QAI increases network security because of its ability to increase ability to identify and address threats. Traffic patterns in a network can be studied using quantum algorithms that can establish what is not usual and can be a sign of security threats, such as hacking or intrusion, among other things. The multilayered structure of quantum algorithms might improve the speed and accuracy of security issue identification through superior pattern recognition. With the help of quantum-enhanced machine learning, improvements to stronger security policies and measures against new emerging threats in cyberspace can also be developed.

12.5.4.1 Pros of Quantum AI in Telecommunications and Networking

The pros of QAI in telecommunications and networking are listed as follows:

a. It allows for instant communication across the globe, bridging geographical and time barriers.
b. It helps in converting voice, video, text, and data information in different modes such as voice, video, text, and data.
c. It serves as a communication tool that enhances organizational performance by providing cheap communication options such as mail, video calls, and cloud technologies.
d. It promotes technology development and the establishment of new technologies, industries, and services.
e. It provides access to a vast amount of information and educational resources online.
f. It offers immediate updates on news, weather, and other critical information.
g. It supports remote work and telecommuting, providing flexibility for employees and employers.
h. It enables connectivity through mobile devices, making it easier to stay connected on the go.
i. It facilitates social interactions and connections with friends, family, and communities worldwide.
j. It helps people connect with support groups and communities with shared interests or challenges.

12.5.4.2 Cons of Quantum AI in Telecommunications and Networking

The cons of QAI in Telecommunications and Networking are listed as follows:

a. It is vulnerable to hacking, data breaches, and cyber attacks that can compromise sensitive information.
b. Risks related to data privacy and surveillance can lead to potential misuse of personal information.
c. Heavy reliance on telecommunications can create vulnerabilities if systems fail or are disrupted.

d. Unequal access to technology can exacerbate social and economic inequalities.
e. High costs are associated with building and maintaining telecommunications infrastructure.
f. Ongoing costs for internet, mobile services, and data plans can be significant.
g. Data centers and network infrastructure consume substantial amounts of energy, contributing to environmental concerns.
h. Frequent updates and disposal of electronic devices contribute to electronic waste and environmental pollution.
i. It raises concerns about potential health effects from prolonged exposure to electromagnetic fields, although research is ongoing and inconclusive.
j. Troubleshooting and maintaining telecommunications systems can be complex and require specialized skills.
k. It can potentially interrupt service due to technical failures, maintenance, or other issues.

12.5.5 Energy Sector

QAI is poised to make a significant impact on the energy sector by optimizing grid management, advancing material discovery, and improving overall energy efficiency.

i. **Grid Management**: Energy grid management can be revolutionized by QAI by optimizing the balance between energy supply and demand. Contemporary energy grids are intricate networks that combine power from multiple sources, such as conventional fossil fuels and renewable energy sources like solar and wind. To maintain stability and effectiveness, managing this complexity necessitates making modifications in real-time. Large volumes of data from sensors and grid control systems can be analyzed by quantum algorithms to forecast demand, improve energy allocation, and oversee the integration of renewable energy sources. When compared to the existing model, QAI can reduce energy losses, enhance total efficiency, and ensure more reliable grids, mainly because the forecasts generated by the system enable more effective adjustments to be made.
ii. **Energy Storage**: There must be, for instance, supply and demand for electricity; there has to be energy storage since the source of electricity from natural resources is not constant. Through emulating and enhancing the properties of modern advanced batteries and other storage front-ends, QAI can accelerate the development of novel resources and capabilities for energy storage. Some of the material behaviors at the atomic scale can be effectively captured by quantum simulations as a tool to discover new compounds with improved performance characteristics. The availability and improved use of energy storage solutions also enable the development of a more reliable and stable energy ecosystem so that the integration of renewable energy sources can be made easier, and the reliance on fossil fuels can be minimized.
iii. **Material Discovery**: The energy field demands new materials to devise unique structures to power battery, fuel cell, and superconductor devices. Chemical and physical interactions could also be mimicked virtually by QAI to a far superior extent than any normally known approach to the discovery and design of new materials out there. It allows the scientists to create novel materials and customize the characteristics of mixtures and alloys in the form that cannot be achieved using the traditional processes. The use of QS, for example, can aid in finding other structures with a higher density of energy, electrical conductivity, or better toughness, which leads to the enhancement of other technologies in the production and supply of power.
iv. **Energy Efficiency**: QAI is capable of enhancing energy efficiency even in different industries such as refining industries up to the construction of energy management. Even complex systems such as manufacturing processes or HVAC systems in buildings can be predicted and optimized with the help of quantum algorithms. As a result, QAI can provide guidance on which measures should be taken to save maximum energy and minimize operating expenses. Efficiency of energy utilization is another factor that improves cost and also supports the sustainability dimension because it reduces energy use and greenhouse emissions.
v. **Predictive Maintenance**: Predictive maintenance is crucial in offering suitable service for energy structures such as power plants and power transmission lines. QAI can enhance preventive maintenance, where big data from sensors and monitoring systems can help predict equipment breakdowns before they occur. Quantum algorithms can process and analyze the data patterns, further allowing efficient and accurate maintenance planning. This can reduce the chances of unexpected downtimes, prolong the usability of the equipment, and keep energy systems running as expected.

12.5.5.1 Pros of Quantum AI in Energy Sector

The pros of QAI in the energy sector are listed as follows:

a. Efficient power distribution
b. Real-time demand response
c. Improved weather forecasting.
d. Optimal resource allocation
e. Better energy storage solutions
f. Development of advanced catalysts
g. Accurate pricing models

h. Risk management
i. Predictive maintenance
j. Process optimization

12.5.5.2 Cons of Quantum AI in Energy Sector

The cons of QAI in the energy sector are listed as follows:

a. Expensive technology
b. Maintenance and operational expenses
c. Early-stage technology
d. Lack of skilled professionals
e. Integration with existing systems
f. Scalability constraints
g. Vulnerability to quantum attacks
h. Regulatory compliance
i. High energy requirements
j. Resource-intensive manufacturing
k. Long-term benefits vs. short-term costs
l. Market volatility

12.5.6 Artificial Intelligence and Machine Learning

QAI is on the verge of revolutionizing AI and machine learning by introducing a major leap in computational capability. It enables faster computation, quicker prototyping of new algorithms, and improved fine-tuning of current models.

i. **Fast-Tracking Machine Learning Algorithms**: QAI is capable of providing a special outcome in the process of training as well as execution of machine learning algorithms. The traditional machine learning models bring down computational burdens and might take much time to solve when large datasets and complex calculations are used. QC involves the use of superposition and entanglement by looking at the numerous possibilities at the same time. It improves the handling of input data and accelerates the process of defining the combination in model configurations, hence enabling faster training of machine learning models. For instance, quantum algorithms, such as quantum support vector machines and QAOA, will solve the optimization problems better than other classical machine learning algorithms, thereby enabling models to converge faster and gain high performance [26].
ii. **Enhanced Data Analysis**: The traditional methods are outdone by QAI in managing large and complicated datasets in data analysis. Quantum algorithms are more effective to identify patterns as compared to traditional models of computer and particularly when identifying complex or challenging patterns. For instance, in both conventional techniques, principal component analysis—optimized using quantum mechanics—can be useful in better analysis of high-dimensional data and is also applicable to better feature extraction and reduction of dimensions. However, better data, enhanced data comprehension, enhanced decision making, and therefore elevated success rates of AI projects can be achieved [27,28].
iii. **Quantum Machine Learning Algorithms**: QAI allows for the creation of new machine learning; methods founded on quantum mechanics. Quantum neural networks and quantum Boltzmann machines, to give the example, provide a new way of approach to pattern recognition and learning. Quantum machine-learning algorithms of this kind intend to harness the benefits of quantum implementation power for attacks on quantum complexity which could result in more effective and robust strategies for solving hard machine learning problems. There could be one potential function of quantum neural networks in greater consumption of large extensive and high-dimensional data streams, where quantum neural networks are prospective in both speed and capacity [29].

12.5.6.1 Pros of Quantum AI in Artificial Intelligence and Machine Learning

The pros of QAI in AI and machine learning are listed as follows:

a. Solve complex problems quickly.
b. The features can be enhanced effectively.
c. High-dimensional data can be handled efficiently with improved performance.
d. Secure AI system in quantum cryptography.

12.5.6.2 Cons of Quantum AI in Artificial Intelligence and Machine Learning

The cons of QAI in AI and machine learning are listed as follows:

a. The availability of quantum hardware is limited.
b. Systems are error-prone and noisy.
c. Maintenance of the quantum computers is expensive.
d. Application areas for QAI are still unclear.

12.5.6.3 Optimization and Combinatorial Problems

Quite several complex AI and ML projects, including recommendations, appointments, and resource management, rely on optimality. Quantum optimization methods in QAI can effectively address the challenges like recommendations, scheduling, and resource management, etc. and provide optimal solutions. Grover's search and Quantum annealing; let's revert to combinatorial optimization, quantum algorithms can work on equal numbers of solutions simultaneously, thereby outclassing classical algorithms. That is why, in particular cases such as challenging scheduling problems, dynamic price setting, or personalized recommendation AI systems may work enhanced [30,31].

i. **Quantum Enhanced Generative Models**: Generative models are a subset of deep learning models developed for simulating complex natural patterns in the data. Such improvements empower generative models with QC capabilities to enhance their efficiency and effectiveness. Quantum enhancements are useful in generative models, which include variational autoencoders and generative adversarial networks. In this manner, quantum states can help to offer better and more diverse samples to promote improved performance in QAI of these models. For instance, quantum generative adversarial networks may yield synthetic data of higher variance or realism, which improves use cases of generative models, such as design creativity, drug design, and picture extraction. Realization of generative models with quantum support can liberate more horizons of data expansion and content generation [28,29].

The pros of QAI in optimization and combinatorial problems are listed as follows:

a. Enhanced computational power
b. Faster processing
c. Handling large datasets
d. Improved optimization algorithms
e. Enhanced model accuracy
f. Reduced training time

The cons of QAI in optimization and combinatorial problems are listed as follows:

a. Expensive technology
b. Complex infrastructure
c. Early-stage development
d. Scalability challenges
e. Immature ecosystem

12.5.7 Automotive Industry

QAI can bring a major change by directly influencing the development of new models, production methods, autonomous driving, and other aspects of car manufacturing.

i. **Autonomous Vehicles**: The effects of QAI on the advancement of autonomous vehicles include perception optimization, command adjudication, and handling capabilities. For effective functioning in real-time and making decisions, autonomy in driving heavily depends upon systems based on the data fed into them from the sensors (such as cameras, radars, and LiDARs). Complex data analysis, which in essence consists of large-scale data processing and pattern recognition issues, is handled more efficiently by quantum algorithms as compared to classical methods. Such results could complicate object recognition, create a more accurate vision of road conditions, and outline better decision-making for self-driving cars, due to quantum-enhanced machine learning models [32–34].
ii. **Vehicle Design and Simulation**: We believe that with QAI's ability to better model and optimize vehicle structures and systems on higher levels, significant changes can emerge for the automotive sector on multiple fronts. Recursiveness and modeling techniques are applied in conventional automotive design processes to evaluate effectiveness, reliability, and responsiveness. Specifically, new ways of more accurate modeling of multi-parametric interactions between materials, aerodynamics, and structural elements, as compared to traditional computational simulations obtained via the application of quantum simulations, are described. This makes it possible to fine-tune car designs more rapidly as well as accurately—all of which enhance safety, performance, and efficiency. Furthermore, high-value design enhancements for novel materials and manufacturing, which can increase vehicle performance, are other QC applications.
iii. **Supply Chain Optimization**: To equip the automotive sector to handle the manufacturing and distribution of automobiles and parts, there should be supply chain management. Supply chain management can be improved by evaluating complex information and decision-making related to supply, demand, manufacturing timeline, delivery schedule, etc. Routing for distribution-dependent product manufacturing and inventory controls capability demand paths, and even production schedules, can all be calculated by quantum algorithms at lower expense and faster rates of throughput. A better supply chain operation might minimize disruptions, afford automakers the capability to maneuver more effectively to market changes, and assure timely component and automobile delivery.
iv. **Predictive Maintenance**: From the standpoint of the automotive industry, predictive maintenance means monitoring vehicle systems and parts to prevent possible failures. Data collected from sensors and diagnostic tools is analyzed to identify patterns and deviations that could signify future issues, and QAI may enhance predictive maintenance. To reduce the chances of breakdowns and facilitate the practice of proactive checks, the quantum algorithms are capable of furnishing more accurate and timely details about the state of wear or complete failure of the component. Higher vehicle reliability, lower lost time, lower cost for maintenance, and improved connectivity have the

potential to be achieved through better use of predictive maintenance.

v. **Traffic Management and Route Optimization**: Optimization of automotive routes together with traffic regulation is another area where QAI can be useful—for single cars and advanced transportation systems. To increase route planning optimization and traffic flow, quantum algorithms can analyze historical data, current data on traffic situations, etc. This could lead to reduced congestion, shorter time consumed in commutation, and greater efficiency at large in transit. Automobile manufacturers should incorporate quantum traffic management systems in self-driving cars to improve the reliability and enhance the coordination capabilities of connected cars, thereby improving the driving experience.

12.5.7.1 Pros of Quantum AI in Automotive Industry

The pros of QAI in the automotive industry are listed as follows:

a. Efficient traffic flow
b. Real-time analysis

12.5.7.2 Cons of Quantum AI in Automotive Industry

The cons of QAI in the automotive industry are listed as follows:

a. Infrastructure costs
b. Data privacy

12.5.8 E-Commerce

In e-commerce, QAI transforms the global market by improving diverse features in various spheres of Internet shopping. Figure 12.2 describes the role of QAI in influencing e-commerce deals in various aspects of online retail, ranging from customer experience to logistics.

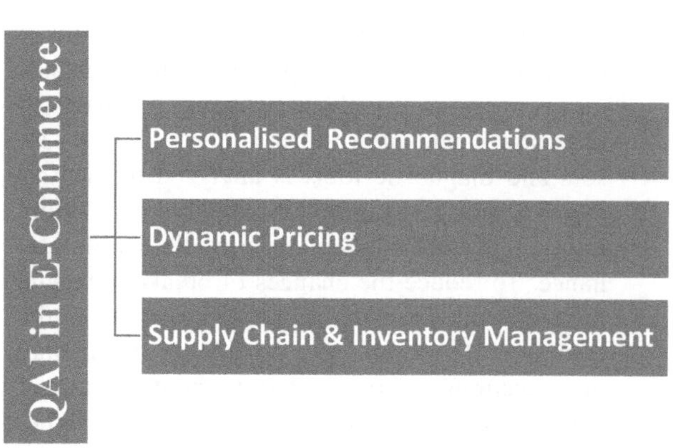

FIGURE 12.2 Influence of QAI in e-commerce.

i. **Personalized Recommendations**: Because QAI can accept large amounts of user data and preferences with unparalleled speed and accuracy, it can vastly enhance product suggestion systems. Traditional systems provide recommendations based on the use of functions that analyze user behavior and choice. The other kinds of data patterns and correlations that can be processed by the quantum algorithms are more sophisticated, such as quantum neural networks to generate the most appropriate suggestions. The showcasing of products that are more likely to reflect their taste and buying habits leads to better sales and strong customer interaction.

ii. **Dynamic Pricing**: Dynamic pricing means the prices are constantly changing depending on the supply and demand, stock, and competitors' actions. Due to the big data analysis and better estimates of price elasticity, QAI can develop flexible pricing strategies. To ensure that the firm's revenues and profits are optimal and retain competitiveness, quantum algorithms may change prices flexibly depending on the assessment of several pricing scenarios. Through this process, e-commerce platforms might enhance their standings within the market, hence elevating profitability. This is because they develop prices that adapt quickly to the market conditions and consumer behaviors.

iii. **Supply Chain and Inventory Management**: The sorts of inventories and supply chains that are functional for e-commerce companies are crucial to understand. QAI can also enhance procedures such as supplier relations, demand forecasting, and inventory control. Market conditions, the supply chain, and sales data are detailed and can be handled by quantum algorithms that minimize ways and understock or overstock. Improving supply chain management creates efficiency and reduces costs by ensuring products are on the shelves when customers expect them, resulting in high customer satisfaction.

iv. **Customer Service and Support**: Self-improving chatbots and virtual assistants will add capabilities of QAI that can help improve customer service and support. In the same way, quantum algorithms give improved accuracy and reliability that is pertinent to the questions that the clients ask and the mechanisms deployed to solve them. It may create improved customer satisfaction, faster pleasing of clients' difficulties, and generally more efficient PC handling of difficult queries. The case for enhancing and upgrading the customer service abilities will lead to happier and more loyal customers.

v. **Fraud Detection and Prevention**: Fraud prevention and detection have been become as an important issue in the most online stores to mitigate against fraudulent transactions and account creation.

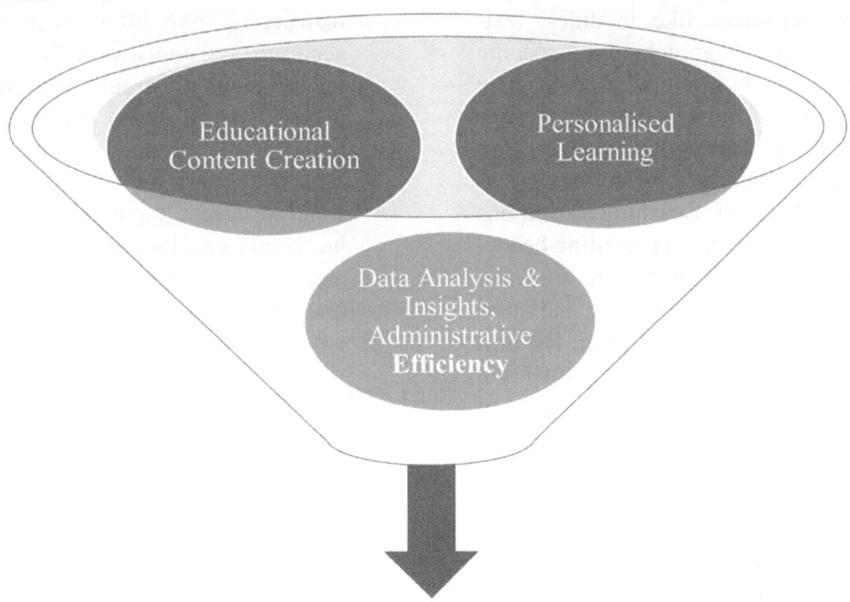

FIGURE 12.3 Impact of QAI on education.

QAI is better when it comes to the accuracy of analyzing transaction behavior and identifying frauds than classic rather improving fraud detecting systems. Better preventive measures can be achieved by using quantum algorithms that help identify small patterns and correlations that could be potentially fraudulent. Improving the fight against fraud can reduce costs, protect clients' data, and maintain e-commerce platforms stable.

vi. **Search Engine Optimization**: With the help of neural networks and optimization of searching algorithms and website content, QAI can improve the SEO process. To boost the ranks and visibility, quantum algorithms are effectively capable of evaluating a variety of parameters like user intentions, correlation of content with search queries, and search behaviors. This may lead to an improvement in the number of firms' e-commerce sites and web traffic, as well as successful SEO activities.

12.5.8.1 Pros of Quantum AI in E-Commerce

The pros of QAI in e-commerce are listed as follows:

a. QAI can enhance recommendation systems by analyzing consumer behavior and preferences more effectively.
b. Improves fraud detection mechanisms by processing transaction data more comprehensively.

12.5.8.2 Cons of Quantum AI in E-Commerce

The cons of QAI in e-commerce are listed as follows:

a. Not widely adopted.
b. Integrating quantum solutions into existing e-commerce platforms could be complex and costly.

12.5.9 Education

QAI could greatly reshape the education sector by improving personalized learning, streamlining administrative tasks, and advancing educational research. Figure 12.3 provides the impact of QAI on education.

i. **Personalized Learning**: QAI can transform the personalized learning process as it can provide personal experiences to students, products, and processes. Traditional adaptive learning systems adjust content through studies based on student's performance in the program. Expanded quantum analysis of students' data lets QAI enhance these systematic learning systems when analyzing more complex patterns in learning preferences, cognitive abilities, and engagement rates. Quantum-enhanced algorithms can give better recommendations for educational resources, learning activities, and teaching approaches that can eventually lead to efficient and personalized learning experiences. This can also improve the student results by identifying learning needs and providing tailored educational solutions to support each student effectively.

ii. **Educational Content Creation**: The creation of appealing educational materials is a process of creating a high-quality, engaging content with huge quantities of processed information. QAI can also create more content much more quickly by comparing published curricular requirements and other educational norms and expectations and by taking into account student feedback. This, in turn, implies that knowledge-related products such as electronic training tools, print and non-print teaching-learning resources like modules, textbooks, tests, etc., aimed at achieving specific learning outcomes, can be developed with the help of quantum algorithms. Moreover, it can assert relevance, coherence, and clarity to enhance NLP to increase the quality of instructional content.

iii. **Data Analysis and Insights**: Learning institutions often receive a lot of information regarding behavior, attendance, and performance from students. QAI eradicates large data set processing and interpretation complexities by accomplishing the task faster and with more precision. Using quantum algorithms, trends, correlation, and other pieces of information that cannot be discovered using classical methods may be obtained. This can help teachers and administrators to make informed decisions about the strategies used within the classroom, as well as regarding which students need more guidance, and where we should distribute resources accordingly. Effective data analysis can lead to better-targeted intervention and better planning of education [35–37].

iv. **Administrative Efficiency**: Scheduling, resource distribution, and enrolment are some areas in educational institutions where the implementation of QAI can be of added value. By applying quantum algorithms, scheduling can be enhanced using other constraints that include the preferences of the students, teachers' schedules, and available classrooms. Other possibilities for using quantum-enhanced optimization techniques include the optimal way of distributing textbooks, equipment, and support services. Anything that enhances administrative efficiency can translate to enhanced operational efficiency, reduced costs, and generally better management of education facilities.

v. **Enhanced Research Capabilities**: The progress of QAI's research functions can enhance educational research by providing novel approaches to understand and analyze existing educational processes. As for application, QC is useful when appearing in large-scale simulations and data-intensive research projects that are challenging for the classical approach. For example, cognitive processes for developmental purposes, educational instrument effectiveness, and teaching pedagogy impacts can be studied using quantum-enhanced algorithms. This might give a better understanding and stronger teaching skills consequently.

vi. **Tutoring and Support Systems**: QAI can enhance teaching and provide valuable resources, enabling virtual tutors and educational assistants to become more capable and effective. Quantum algorithms may open up more natural language processing and comprehension, so that virtual instructors may offer much more precise and accurate assistance that fits into the context of the problematic area being studied. This could mean that the hours spent in tutoring sessions prove more productive since students receive instant support with their assignments and personal progress feedback. Since internet access has been a crucial point in the lack of connections and support, students from remote or underdeveloped areas might prefer distance education with advanced virtual assistance.

12.5.9.1 Pros of Quantum AI in Education

The pros of QAI in education are listed as follows:

a. QAI enable highly personalized learning experiences by analyzing student performance data to tailor educational content and methods.
b. It could help in developing advanced educational tools, simulations, and interactive learning environments.

12.5.9.2 Cons of Quantum AI in Education

The cons of QAI in education are listed as follows:

a. The technology required for QAI is not yet widely available, limiting its application in educational settings.
b. Integrating QAI into educational tools would be expensive and complex.

12.6 CONCLUSION

As a pioneer AI concept, QAI is positioned to revolutionize many industries by leveraging the strong processing capabilities of QC. Its potential is very futuristic—ranging from optimized problem-solving algorithms, new solutions for drug problems, and enhanced and better security systems. Nevertheless, realizing these benefits is not straightforward. The current limitations related to technological complexity, resource demands, and knowledge required in quantum technology remain major barriers to its adoption. However, to avoid hitting the rocks on these ethical questions on privacy and security—as well as the many grey areas associated with the potential misuse of QAI—there is a pressing need for strong governance frameworks. This chapter finds that the researchers, practitioners, and policymakers need to adopt an innovation-friendly risk-conscious approach while dealing with the questions related to QAI. QAI is both promising and unpredictable, as seen by its challenges. Predictions about its impact should be beached in collaboration and cross-disciplinary work to ensure potential risks are addressed and its contributions to society are fully realized.

REFERENCES

[1] S. Abel, A. Blance, and M. Spannowsky, "Quantum optimization of complex systems with a quantum annealer," *Phys Rev A (Coll Park)*, vol. 106, no. 4, p. 042607, Oct. 2022, doi: 10.1103/PhysRevA.106.042607.

[2] Y. Wang, "Quantum Computation and Quantum Information," *Statistical Science*, vol. 27, no. 3, pp. 373–394, Oct. 2012, doi: 10.1214/11-STS378.

[3] C. H. Bennett and G. Brassard, "Quantum cryptography: Public key distribution and coin tossing," *Theor Comput Sci*, vol. 560, no. P1, pp. 7–11, Mar. 2014, doi: 10.1016/j.tcs.2014.05.025.

[4] P. Sangeetha and P. Kumari, "Quantum Algorithms for Machine Learning and Optimization," *2020 2nd PhD Colloquium on Ethically Driven Innovation and Technology for Society, PhD EDITS 2020*, Nov. 2020, doi: 10.1109/PHDEDITS51180.2020.9315301.

[5] K. P. B. Kanagarla, "Quantum Computing For Data Analytics," *SSRN Electronic Journal*, May 2023, doi: 10.2139/SSRN.5017531.

[6] B. Hanafi, M. Ali, and D. Singh, "Quantum algorithms for enhanced educational technologies," *Discover Education 2025 4:1*, vol. 4, no. 1, pp. 8-, Jan. 2025, doi: 10.1007/S44217-025-00400-1.

[7] F. Arute *et al.*, "Quantum supremacy using a programmable superconducting processor," *Nature 2019 574:7779*, vol. 574, no. 7779, pp. 505–510, Oct. 2019, doi: 10.1038/s41586-019-1666-5.

[8] S. McArdle, S. Endo, A. Aspuru-Guzik, S. C. Benjamin, and X. Yuan, "Quantum computational chemistry," *Rev Mod Phys*, vol. 92, no. 1, p. 015003, Mar. 2020, doi: 10.1103/RevModPhys.92.015003.

[9] Mehendale P, "Quantum Machine Learning: The Next Frontier in AI Pushkar Mehendale," *Journal of Scientific and Engineering Research*, vol. 10, no. 1, pp. 104–108, 2023, doi: 10.5281/ZENODO.13753380.

[10] J. C. L. Chow, "Quantum Computing in Medicine," *Medical Sciences*, vol. 12, no. 4, p. 67, Dec. 2024, doi: 10.3390/MEDSCI12040067.

[11] S. C. Fairburn, L. Jehi, B. T. Bicknell, B. G. Wilkes, and B. Panuganti, "Applications of quantum computing in clinical care," *Front Med (Lausanne)*, vol. 12, p. 1573016, Apr. 2025, doi: 10.3389/FMED.2025.1573016.

[12] J. Biamonte, P. Wittek, N. Pancotti, P. Rebentrost, N. Wiebe, and S. Lloyd, "Quantum machine learning," *Nature*, vol. 549, no. 7671, pp. 195–202, Sep. 2017, doi: 10.1038/NATURE23474.

[13] G. Carleo *et al.*, "Machine learning and the physical sciences," *Rev Mod Phys*, vol. 91, no. 4, p. 045002, Dec. 2019, doi: 10.1103/RevModPhys.91.045002.

[14] A. Elaraby, "Quantum medical images processing foundations and applications," *IET Quantum Communication*, vol. 3, no. 4, pp. 201–213, Dec. 2022, doi: 10.1049/QTC2.12049.

[15] V. Dunjko and H. J. Briegel, "Machine learning & artificial intelligence in the quantum domain: a review of recent progress," *Rep Prog Phys*, vol. 81, no. 7, Jun. 2018, doi: 10.1088/1361-6633/AAB406.

[16] P. W. Shor, "Polynomial-Time Algorithms for Prime Factorization and Discrete Logarithms on a Quantum Computer," *SIAM Journal on Computing*, vol. 26, no. 5, pp. 1484–1509, Jan. 1996, doi: 10.1137/S0097539795293172.

[17] E. Farhi, J. Goldstone, and S. Gutmann, "A Quantum Approximate Optimization Algorithm," pp. 1–16, Nov. 2014, Accessed: Dec. 29, 2025. [Online]. Available: https://arxiv.org/pdf/1411.4028

[18] L. K. Grover, "A fast quantum mechanical algorithm for database search," *Proceedings of the Annual ACM Symposium on Theory of Computing*, vol. Part F129452, pp. 212–219, Jul. 1996, doi: 10.1145/237814.237866.

[19] K. Nałecz-Charkiewicz, K. Charkiewicz, and R. M. Nowak, "Quantum computing in bioinformatics: a systematic review mapping," *Brief Bioinform*, vol. 25, no. 5, p. bbae391, Sep. 2024, doi: 10.1093/BIB/BBAE391.

[20] S. Ahmad, "The Intersection of Quantum Computing and AI in Supply Chain Optimization," Jun. 2024, doi: 10.2139/SSRN.5199680.

[21] T. D. Ladd, F. Jelezko, R. Laflamme, Y. Nakamura, C. Monroe, and J. L. O'Brien, "Quantum computers," *Nature*, vol. 464, no. 7285, pp. 45–53, 2010, doi: 10.1038/NATURE08812.

[22] I. Kerenidis, A. Prakash, and D. Szilágyi, "Quantum Algorithms for Portfolio Optimization," *AFT 2019 - Proceedings of the 1st ACM Conference on Advances in Financial Technologies*, pp. 147–155, Aug. 2019, doi: 10.1145/3318041.3355465.

[23] J. Preskill, "Quantum Computing in the NISQ era and beyond," *Quantum*, vol. 2, Jul. 2018, doi: 10.22331/q-2018-08-06-79.

[24] E. Grant, T. S. Humble, and B. Stump, "Benchmarking Quantum Annealing Controls with Portfolio Optimization," *Phys Rev Appl*, vol. 15, no. 1, p. 014012, Jan. 2021, doi: 10.1103/PhysRevApplied.15.014012.

[25] R. Orús, S. Mugel, and E. Lizaso, "Quantum computing for finance: Overview and prospects," *Reviews in Physics*, vol. 4, Nov. 2019, doi: 10.1016/j.revip.2019.100028.

[26] E. Farhi, J. Goldstone, S. Gutmann, and H. Neven, "Quantum Algorithms for Fixed Qubit Architectures," Mar. 2017, Accessed: Dec. 29, 2025. [Online]. Available: https://arxiv.org/pdf/1703.06199

[27] R. U. Rasool *et al.*, "Quantum Computing for Healthcare: A Review," *Future Internet 2023, Vol. 15*, vol. 15, no. 3, Feb. 2023, doi: 10.3390/FI15030094.

[28] M. Schuld, A. Bocharov, K. M. Svore, and N. Wiebe, "Circuit-centric quantum classifiers," *Phys Rev A (Coll Park)*, vol. 101, no. 3, p. 032308, Mar. 2020, doi: 10.1103/PhysRevA.101.032308.

[29] Y. Kwak, W. J. Yun, S. Jung, and J. Kim, "Quantum Neural Networks: Concepts, Applications, and Challenges," *International Conference on Ubiquitous and Future Networks, ICUFN*, vol. 2021-August, pp. 413–416, Aug. 2021, doi: 10.1109/ICUFN49451.2021.9528698.

[30] N. Thakur, D. Ghai, and S. Kumar, "Automatic imagery Bank Cheque data extraction based on machine learning approaches: a comprehensive survey," *Multimed Tools Appl*, vol. 82, no. 20, pp. 30543–30598, Aug. 2023, doi: 10.1007/S11042-023-14534-7.

[31] D. Ghai, S. Saxena, G. Dhingra, and S. L. Tripathi, "A comprehensive review on performance-based comparative analysis, categorization, classification and mapping of text extraction system techniques for images," *Multimedia Tools and Applications 2024 84:5*, vol. 84, no. 5, pp. 2327–2484, Oct. 2024, doi: 10.1007/S11042-024-20257-0.

[32] D. Ghai, H. K. Gianey, A. Jain, and R. S. Uppal, "Quantum and dual-tree complex wavelet transform-based image watermarking," *https://doi.org/10.1142/S0217979220500095*, vol. 34, no. 4, Jan. 2020, doi: 10.1142/S0217979220500095.

[33] R. Sandhu, D. Ghai, S. L. Tripathi, R. Kaur, K. Rawal, and K. Dhir, "Machine learning for cognitive treatment planning in patients with neurodisorder and trauma injuries," *Computational Intelligence and Deep Learning Methods for Neuro-rehabilitation Applications*, pp. 165–193, Jan. 2024, doi: 10.1016/B978-0-443-13772-3.00012-1.

[34] R. Sandhu, H. K. Channi, D. Ghai, C. Prabha, and H. Kaur, "From Stress to Success: Optimizing Brain Performance with Resilience," *https://services.igi-global.com/resolvedoi/resolve.aspx?doi=10.4018/979-8-3693-1785-3.ch013*, pp. 194–214, Jan. 1AD, doi: 10.4018/979-8-3693-1785-3.CH013.

[35] R. Sandhu, H. K. Channi, D. Ghai, G. S. Cheema, and M. Kaur, "An Introduction to Generative AI Tools for Education 2030," *https://services.igi-global.com/resolvedoi/resolve.aspx?doi=10.4018/979-8-3693-2440-0.ch001*, pp. 1–28, Jan. 1AD, doi: 10.4018/979-8-3693-2440-0.CH001.

[36] D. Ghai, S. P. Mishra, and S. Rani, "Supervised and unsupervised techniques for biomedical image classification," *Mining Biomedical Text, Images and Visual Features for Information Retrieval*, pp. 153–211, Jan. 2025, doi: 10.1016/B978-0-443-15452-2.00009-1.

[37] D. Ghai, S. L. Tripathi, S. Saxena, M. Chanda, and M. Alazab, "Machine learning algorithms for signal and image processing," *Machine Learning Algorithms for Signal and Image Processing*, pp. 1–473, Nov. 2022, doi: 10.1002/9781119861850.

13 Unravelling the Mysteries of Quantum Entanglement's Revolution in Computing and Communication

Mukesh Kumar and Sangeeta Prasher

13.1 INTRODUCTION

In the secretive realm of quantum physics, where particles behave like waves and uncertainty always exists, quantum entanglement emerges as a phenomenon that challenges classical logic and leaves scientists astounded. For decades, the idea has attracted physicists, as it holds opportunities for further exploration into the quantum world and leads to exciting advancements across multiple scientific and technological domains [1,2]. The present work explores the complex nature of quantum entanglement, traversing a path through one of the most revolutionary facets of contemporary physics. Examining the fundamental ideas and ancient origins of quantum entanglement is essential to comprehending its boundless potential. Entanglement is primarily concerned with interconnections between quantum particles, where the state of one instantly influences another, even across great distances [3–5].

Einstein's description of this interaction as "spooky action at a distance," illustrates the extent to which it diverges from conventional classical expectations of the physical world. By managing and harnessing these entangled states, scientists aim to develop powerful, formidable computing tools, simulations, secure communication, and sophisticated data analysis. A deeper knowledge of the principles enriches insights into quantum mechanics and also lays the groundwork for innovative technologies that could have the potential to shape the futuristic epoch of academic and scientific pursuits.

13.1.1 Historical Background

Reviewing the substantial historical advances in physics that occurred in the initial years of the 20th century is necessary for comprehension of the fundamental ideas of quantum entanglement. During these years, development in quantum mechanics caused an extensive improvement in our knowledge of physical science at the microscopic level, moving beyond the restrictions of classical Newtonian physics. The pioneering figures like Albert Einstein, Niels Bohr, and Erwin Schrödinger played an instrumental role in the quantum revolution, and their intellectual conflicts became a key element in conceptualizing quantum entanglement. It is a central concept in the realm of contemporary quantum physics, introduced by Einstein, Podolsky, and Rosen in 1935, now known as the EPR paradox [6,7]. In their exploration, the trio discussed the idealized system of two particles that had once interacted but then moved apart and still displayed correlations that challenged traditional explanations, which led to the violation of the speed-of-light limit. These correlations suggested that instantaneous measurement of the state of one particle would affect other particles irrespective of their spatial separation. The conclusion of non-locality raised philosophical concerns about the completeness of quantum theory. As a reaction, Niels Bohr responded by rejecting the EPR interpretation, asserting that the paradox observed was a misinterpretation of quantum mechanics and discussed the constraints of Heisenberg's uncertainty principle in measuring two physical properties simultaneously [8]. He stressed that quantum entangled particles do not possess specific properties until measured, and any effort to attribute well-defined properties would contradict the formalism of quantum theory. Even with Bohr's critique, the EPR paper ignited a dynamic debate among physicists and led to experimental investigations into entanglement. The EPR paradox motivated Schrödinger to delve into the physical implications of quantum mechanics. Schrödinger observed that two-particle EPR states do not allow an individual state to be assigned to their constituent subsystems, suggesting the emergence of "entanglement of predictions" for those subsystems [9].

He concluded that, until established through actual assessment, only a tentative description of the entangled particles existing in higher-dimensional space can be made available. This limitation suggests that even if the knowledge of the combined system can be optimal, information about the individual components of the system might be very limited or even absent. This paradox emphasizes the intricate nature of quantum mechanics, where knowing the whole may not necessarily require understanding its parts. Back in 1964, Bell adopted the conclusions of EPR as a working hypothesis and formalized it into the Local Hidden Variable Model [10]. This model suggests that

DOI: 10.1201/9781003530800-13

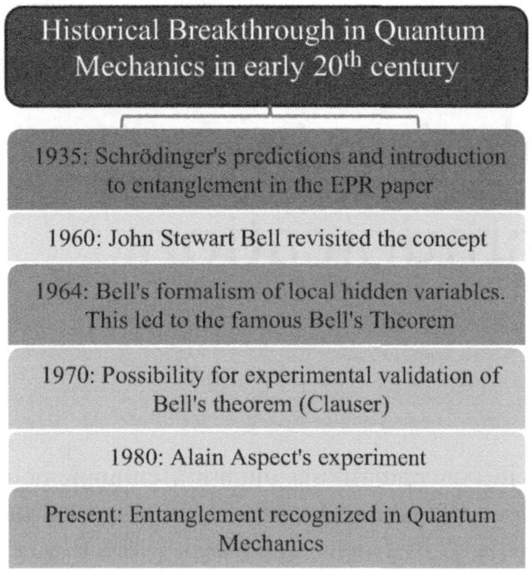

FIGURE 13.1 Key milestones in the acceptability of quantum entanglement and developments in entanglement-based applications.

a. The outcomes of measurements are predetermined by inherent properties of particles existing before and independently of the measurement process ("realism"),
b. Results observed at one location remain unaffected by actions taken at distant locations separated by spacelike intervals ("locality"), and
c. The configurations of local measurement devices are not limited by the hidden variables that govern the local outcomes ("free will").

Bell's formulation in 1964 marked a significant step in addressing the complex nature of quantum mechanics within a deterministic framework of entanglement. Over the subsequent decades, physicists developed imaginative experiments to evaluate the predictions of quantum mechanics. One famous experiment conducted by Alain Aspect in the 1980s tested Bell's inequalities and provided clear evidence for the existence of nonlocal correlations between entangled particles [11,12]. Through theoretical investigations and experimental tests, physicists have concluded that entanglement is a primary feature of quantum mechanics, with far-reaching applications in quantum computing, secure communication, and cryptographic systems [13–16]. A summary of the historical development that led to the recognition of quantum entanglement is presented in Figure 13.1.

13.2 UNDERSTANDING QUANTUM ENTANGLEMENT

Quantum entanglement was initially considered a theoretical loophole, but continuous advances in theory and experiment have established it as a real and measurable aspect of quantum mechanics. It has become even more useful in analysing the deeper concepts of quantum theory and the rapidly evolving landscape of quantum technologies. This section focuses on the complexities of quantum entanglement, focusing on the implications of entangled states, the hypothesis of non-locality and Bell's theorem. It also addresses the famous Einstein-Podolsky-Rosen (EPR) paradox that gave rise to debates about the completeness of quantum mechanics.

13.2.1 Entangled States

Entanglement occurs when two or more quantum states are correlated intrinsically, resulting in a situation where the configuration of one particle is intertwined with that of another, independent of the distance separating them [17–19]. The concept of entangled states is most easily understood by considering a quantum system made up of two basis vector qubits, represented by the up and down spin states of the electrons (Eq. 13.1) as $|0\rangle$ and $|1\rangle$, such that

$$|0\rangle = \begin{pmatrix} 1 \\ 0 \end{pmatrix} \text{ and } |1\rangle = \begin{pmatrix} 0 \\ 1 \end{pmatrix} \tag{13.1}$$

Any arbitrary vector $|\Psi_1\rangle$ can be expressed as a superposition of $|0\rangle$ and $|1\rangle$, as described in (Eq. 13.2).

$$|\Psi_1\rangle = \alpha|0\rangle + \beta|1\rangle \tag{13.2}$$

where α and β are the amplitudes of the state $|\Psi_1\rangle$ being found in the $|0\rangle$and $|1\rangle$, and the sum of their modulus squares (Eq. 13.3) must be normalized to one.

$$|\alpha|^2 + |\beta|^2 = 1 \tag{13.3}$$

This ensures that the inner product of the ket $|\Psi_1\rangle$ to itself is one. Now imagine a composite system comprising two qubits whose state kets are $|\Psi_1\rangle$ and $|\Psi_2\rangle$, belonging to Hilbert spaces H_1 and H_2, respectively. The ket of the composite system symbolized as $|\Psi\rangle$ is obtained through the Kronecker product of the kets of the constituent systems, as outlined in Eq. (13.4).

$$|\psi\rangle = |\Psi_1\rangle \otimes |\Psi_2\rangle \in H_1 \otimes H_2 \tag{13.4}$$

Here $|\Psi_1\rangle = \begin{pmatrix} \alpha \\ \beta \end{pmatrix} = \alpha\begin{pmatrix} 1 \\ 0 \end{pmatrix} + \beta\begin{pmatrix} 0 \\ 1 \end{pmatrix}$ and $|\Psi_2\rangle = \begin{pmatrix} \mu \\ \nu \end{pmatrix} = \mu\begin{pmatrix} 1 \\ 0 \end{pmatrix} + \nu\begin{pmatrix} 0 \\ 1 \end{pmatrix}$,

so that $|\Psi\rangle = \begin{pmatrix} \alpha \\ \beta \end{pmatrix} \otimes \begin{pmatrix} \mu \\ \nu \end{pmatrix} = \begin{pmatrix} \alpha\mu \\ \alpha\nu \\ \beta\mu \\ \beta\nu \end{pmatrix}$, where $\otimes$ symbolizes the tensor product.

The tensor product takes the dimensionality from 1×2 to 1×4 as each element of the first vector is being concatenated with the second vector. Since the ket of the two qubits system is a 4×1 dimensional matrix, there are a total of four basis vectors given by Eq. (13.5).

$$|00\rangle = \begin{pmatrix} 1 \\ 0 \end{pmatrix} \otimes \begin{pmatrix} 1 \\ 0 \end{pmatrix} = \begin{pmatrix} 1 \\ 0 \\ 0 \\ 0 \end{pmatrix}, |01\rangle = \begin{pmatrix} 0 \\ 1 \\ 0 \\ 0 \end{pmatrix},$$

$$|10\rangle = \begin{pmatrix} 0 \\ 0 \\ 1 \\ 0 \end{pmatrix}, |11\rangle = \begin{pmatrix} 0 \\ 0 \\ 0 \\ 1 \end{pmatrix} \quad (13.5)$$

Thus

$$|\psi\rangle = \alpha\mu \begin{pmatrix} 1 \\ 0 \\ 0 \\ 0 \end{pmatrix} + \alpha\nu \begin{pmatrix} 0 \\ 1 \\ 0 \\ 0 \end{pmatrix} + \beta\mu \begin{pmatrix} 0 \\ 0 \\ 1 \\ 0 \end{pmatrix} + \beta\nu \begin{pmatrix} 0 \\ 0 \\ 0 \\ 1 \end{pmatrix}$$

The general two-qubit composite ket can be characterized as a linear combination of basis kets of the space, as articulated in Eq. (13.6)

$$|\psi\rangle = \beta_{00}|00\rangle + \beta_{01}|01\rangle + \beta_{10}|10\rangle + \beta_{11}|11\rangle \quad (13.6)$$

where the amplitudes of $\beta_{00} = \alpha\mu, \beta_{01} = \alpha\nu$, $\beta_{10} = \beta\mu$, must satisfy the normalization condition given in Eq. (13.7).

$$\sum_{ij} |\beta_{ij}|^2 = |\beta_{00}|^2 + |\beta_{01}|^2 + |\beta_{10}|^2 + |\beta_{11}|^2 = 1 \quad (13.7)$$

The above mathematical formulations characterize the entanglement of two qubits if $\beta_{01} = \beta_{10} = 0$, which is obtained by applying a Hadamard gate to one qubit and then using that qubit as a control for a Controlled-NOT (CNOT) gate, with another qubit as the target (Figure 13.2).

Here Hadamard gate is a 2×2 matrix with $H_{11} = H_{12} = H_{21} = 1$ and $H_{22} = -1$ and CNOT gate is a 2×2 Pauli X matrix with matrix elements as $\sigma_{11} = \sigma_{22} = 0$ and $\sigma_{21} = \sigma_{12} = 1$. It should be highlighted that not all general states, expressible through Kronecker product of the constituent qubit kets, are entangled states. To illustrate the concept, consider a composite state of two qubits, denoted as $|\Psi\rangle$, expressible in terms of another product of $|\Psi_1\rangle$ and $|\Psi_2\rangle$. This tensor product is expressed as $|\Psi\rangle = |\Psi_1 \otimes |\Psi_2\rangle$. While this tensor product representation is valid for composite states, it does not encompass the entangled states. When two qubits become entangled, their composite state transcends the boundaries of conventional representation, and the amplitude of entangled states would have to satisfy specific constraints to be known as entangled states.

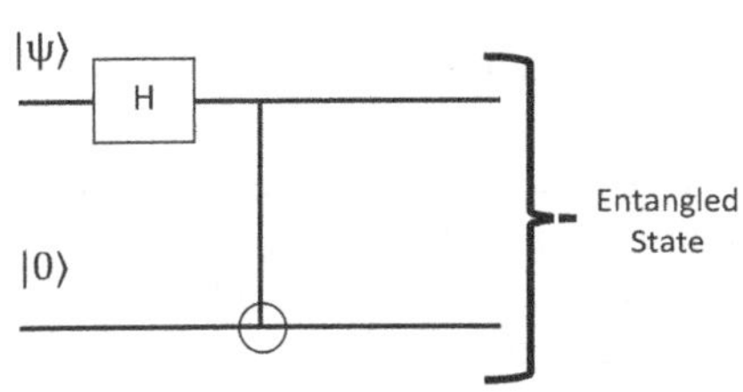

FIGURE 13.2 Generation of entangled state using Hadamard and CNOT gates.

13.2.2 EPR Paradox and Bell's Theorem

The Nobel Prize awarded in 2022 to Alain Aspect, John F. Clauser, and Anton Zeilinger represents not only a milestone in the scientific achievements of quantum theory but also a pivotal moment in our quest to resolve the ambiguities of the quantum realm, which were based on the fundamental experiments initiated by John Bell. To appreciate the revolution started by the work of Aspect, Clauser, and Zeilinger, it is necessary to reconsider the early 20th-century debate triggered by the EPR paradox. At its core, the paradox questioned the completeness of quantum mechanics, particularly its probabilistic description of physical phenomena. The state ket of the system, a mathematical entity representing all measurable quantities of a quantum system, is central to quantum mechanics. It is considered a linear combination of basis kets representing the system before measurement, but it collapses probabilistically upon observation into a definite state. Einstein argued that quantum mechanics is fundamentally incomplete due to its implications of the non-local connection between particles [20], which contradicted his conception of a universe governed by local interactions and objective reality—where properties of objects exist independently of measurement, as articulated in his renowned remark, "God does not play dice." They argued that when two particles are entangled, observing the state of one will immediately reveal information about the other, regardless of how far they may be. This implies that each particle must have its own set of properties, even when they are not measured. They called these hidden properties "elements of reality." To them, this implied that quantum mechanics, which deals in probabilities rather than certainties, might be missing something. They suggested there might be hidden variables—unknown factors—that predictably determine the consequences of measurements. These hidden variables would reinstate the determinism characteristic of classical physics that adheres to the idea that a complete understanding of the current state of a system allows the prediction of its future state with certainty. The theoretical underpinnings of the EPR paradox took a significant turn in the 1960s when John Stewart Bell revisited the concept [21]. Bell sought to clarify the conflict between the local hidden-variable theories and quantum mechanics by mathematically formalizing the implications of locality and realism. Local hidden-variable theories are based on the idea that the hidden variables influence the particles nearby, adhering to Einstein's principle of locality, which states that no action can travel faster than the speed of light. His groundbreaking contribution, Bell's theorem, proved through elegant mathematical reasoning that any local realistic theory must adhere to certain inequalities, referred to as Bell inequalities [10]. These inequalities represent a set of constraints that must be fulfilled by the entangled states that assume both locality (no faster-than-light influences) and realism (particles have pre-existing properties independent of measurement). In a simplified form, Bell's inequalities can be interpreted in the following way: In a local realistic theory, the correlations between measurements on entangled particles must fall inside a specific range. If experiments show correlations beyond this range, it will violate Bell's inequalities of local realism in favour of quantum mechanics and would impact the fundamental nature of reality. Experimental validation of Bell's theorem became possible through the innovative efforts of Clauser [22] and was later refined by Alain Aspect [11,12]. In the 1970s, Clauser [23,24] performed experiments to measure the correlation between entangled photons to prove that these correlations violated Bell's predictions. These experiments further demonstrated the predictions of quantum mechanics and were very important for subsequent advancements in quantum physics. Later, in the 1980s, Alain Aspect further attempted experiments to confirm Bell's theorems. Aspect's experiments [25] were designed to rigorously test Bell inequalities while addressing potential loopholes that could undermine the validity of previous results. These included loopholes related to the detection efficiency of experimental setups, the independence of measurement choices, and the locality of particle interactions. Aspect's meticulous experimental design and implementation successfully closed many of these loopholes, confirming beyond a reasonable doubt that quantum entanglement manifests non-local correlations that defy classical explanations. His work not only augmented the argument against local realism strongly, but also firmly established the basic ideas of quantum mechanics through experiments. Anton Zeilinger contributed significantly by demonstrating quantum teleportation [26,27], an advanced concept where entangled particles instantaneously share properties across vast distances, defying classical limits on information transfer. Unlike its science fiction counterpart, quantum teleportation involves transmitting quantum information rather than physical objects. Quantum teleportation is based on the phenomenon of entanglement, where two particles become linked so that measuring one immediately affects the state of the other, ignoring the distance between them. Bell's theorem and its experimental validations have significant implications and indicate that the classical concepts cannot describe the action of quantum particles. Quantum mechanics presents unpredictability and interconnectedness that challenge deterministic models and conventional notions of reality. The infringement of Bell inequalities implies that entangled particles do not conform to principles of locality and realism found in classical reality. This has led many researchers to admit that either realism must be abandoned, asserting that particles do not have definite properties until they are observed, or locality must be reviewed, indicating non-local impacts that transcend classical notions of causality. The consequences of the EPR paradox and Bell's experiments extend far beyond theoretical physics.

13.3 EXPERIMENTAL REALIZATIONS OF QUANTUM ENTANGLEMENT

Entanglement has been realized experimentally in many forms, including photons, electrons, and quark entanglements, paving the path for quantum communication and quantum teleportation. The phenomenon of quantum teleportation assists the transfer of quantum information devoid of the direct transmission of physical particles and requires entangled states. Entanglement was established in 1969, when John Clauser and his colleagues proposed the initial successful experimental demonstration of Bell's inequality [22]. They passed the laser light through a nonlinear crystal to produce entangled photon pairs. In this experiment, they observed that measuring the properties of one photon beam immediately reveals the corresponding property of the second photon. These observations offered convincing evidence that questioned the foundational theories of classical physics and established a foundation for future investigations into the phenomenon. Afterwards, in the 1990s, Spontaneous Parametric Down-Conversion (SPDC) became a popular method for generating entangled states [28]. In this process, a high-energy single photon is split into two low-energy entangled photons. In 1981, Alain Aspect, along with his research group, conducted a three-round series of experiments with entangled photons. In these experiments, they used an excellent source of entangled photons, and the experiment was designed to match Bell's original ideas to address the limitations found in earlier demonstrations of Bell's inequality. To improve the reliability of their findings, polarizing beam splitters were used to check that the phenomenon is purely quantum mechanical and to rule out the possibility of the photons influencing each other. Calcium atoms served as a medium for producing entangled photon pairs intricately connected by their polarization states. These entangled photons were then observed to have orthogonal polarization states using the detectors placed at a considerable distance from each other. In this experiment, researchers measured the coincidence rate, defined as the probability of both detectors detecting a photon at the same time. Measurements were taken across different configurations of the polarizing filters by rotating the plane of linearly polarized photons. Strong correlations between these entangled photons were observed against the statistical coincidence rates predicted by the constraints of Bell's inequality for a system of two classically entangled particles. The Aspect experiment consistently violated this limit and demonstrated that the correlations between the entangled photons exceeded the explanations provided by classical physics and offered compelling evidence for quantum entanglement. This achievement marked a significant advancement in comprehending the quantum realm of entangled states. After achieving the success for entangled photons, experiments were conducted to measure entanglement electrons, quarks, and neutrons, which solidified the presence of entanglement beyond photons. In 1984, the concept of quantum cryptography emerged through the seminal work of Bennett and Brassard [29]. Their work utilized the intrinsic randomness and non-local correlations. As a result, it enabled secure communication that is immune to eavesdropping attempts. The 1990s saw significant advancements in the manipulation and control of entangled states. Techniques such as parametric down-conversion gained prominence during this period. In 1993, Bennett and his colleagues introduced the notion of quantum teleportation [30], showcasing the remarkable potential of entanglement for transferring information. The process consists of three essential steps. First two particles are entangled, next a Bell's state measurement is conducted on one of the entangled particles, alongside the particle intended for teleportation. Finally, in the third step, an appropriate quantum operation is executed on the second entangled particle guided by the results of the measurement. The introduction of entanglement swapping by Zukowski et al. in 1993 [31] marked a significant advancement in the understanding of quantum entanglement. This innovative technique allowed for the establishment of entanglement between particles that had not interacted directly with one another. As a result, the possibilities for harnessing entanglement in various quantum systems expanded considerably. Through a series of entanglement measurements and classical communication, two initially unentangled particles can become entangled, effectively "swapping" their quantum correlations onto a third particle. The initial investigational demonstration of quantum teleportation was achieved at the University of Innsbruck in 1997 by a group headed by Dik Bouwmeester [27]. They successfully teleported the polarization state of a photon over a short distance. In 2000, scientists at the National Institute of Standards and Technology achieved entanglement between two beryllium ions, showcasing the precision and long coherence times offered by this method [31,32]. They used electromagnetic fields to confine the ions within a trap. Entanglement is generated by manipulating the internal states of the ions using laser pulses. This technique offers high precision and long coherence times. Subsequent advances in quantum computing led to the creation of multi-qubit entangled states, forming the foundation of current quantum processors. In 2017, a Chinese group at the University of Science and Technology, Shanghai, headed by Ji-Gang Ren, demonstrated entanglement preservation of two distant laser photons over record-breaking distances of over 1200 km [33]. They transmitted a data packet from Tibet to a satellite positioned in orbit above the Earth's surface. This scalability is crucial for future quantum networks. If the photons were transmitted through fibre-optic cables, rather than through space, interference of heat, vibration, and stochastic interactions with the medium would have disrupted the photons' connection. This achievement has pushed the boundaries of entanglement, leading to the study of particles with more complex properties, like the orbital angular momentum of photons, and has opened the door to exploring exotic quantum phenomena. In conclusion, the capability to create and manage entangled states is paramount for harnessing the full potential of quantum technologies. Spontaneous parametric down-conversion is a paramount technique for generating entangled pairs, but the invention of entanglement swapping broadens the possibilities offered by entanglement.

13.4 APPLICATIONS OF QUANTUM ENTANGLEMENT

The Aspects experiment opened many other doors of imagination for physicists and engineers. The concept that was initially regarded as an odd feature of quantum theory has undergone a substantial transformation. From being merely a philosophical curiosity, entanglement has appeared as a vital cog in emerging technologies. This transition packs profound implications for information processing, communication, and fundamental physics. Unveiling a realm of extraordinary potential, this concept serves as a gateway to a revolutionary scientific dimension known as quantum computing. This approach exploits the principles of quantum mechanics to propel computations to speeds unimaginable previously and vastly outperforming classical computers. Advancing from the binary framework of classical bits that can exist in one of the two states, 0 or 1, the qubits represented as $|0\rangle$ and $|1\rangle$ can exist in a superposition of both states, paving the way for innovations. The capability of entanglement of quantum states enables quantum computers to analyse multiple possibilities at once, greatly enhancing their processing speeds. As a result, they can efficiently navigate through gigantic data sets in parallel, improving cryptography and simulating quantum systems. This phenomenon enables quantum systems to process information in parallel, resulting in significantly faster performance for certain types of problems. Additionally, these qubits can "communicate" with one another, adapting their searches according to the overall computational progress. This permits the quantum computers to converge on the anticipated state more efficiently than independent processors. For instance, Grover's algorithm is designed to navigate through an unsorted database swiftly, provided the qubits are entangled. Success depends not only on increasing the number of processors but also on their ability to work together on the same problem, with deeper connections and the sharing of information to address problems more efficiently. An operation of a quantum computer could be illustrated with the help of a system of three qubits. While a classical computer with three bits can occupy only one of the eight states simultaneously, a quantum computer with three qubits in superposition can inhabit all eight states denoted as $|000\rangle$, $|001\rangle$, $|010\rangle$, $|011\rangle$, $|100\rangle$, $|101\rangle$, $|110\rangle$, and $|111\rangle$ concurrently. This attractive characteristic enables the quantum computer to scrutinize multiple latent outcomes simultaneously during calculations. Quantum gates are specialized operations designed to manipulate or transform the states to which they are applied into the requisite states. This parallelism is similar to performing the same operation on many classical bits at once, but accomplished through a single quantum operation. Similarly, Shor's algorithm uses entanglement to find the prime factors of large numbers swiftly, a task that is particularly challenging for a classical computing system, which typically works sequentially and finds it difficult to complete such calculations within a reasonable time frame.

13.4.1 Shor's Algorithm

Shor's algorithm, devised by Peter Shor in 1994 [34], is an imperative quantum algorithm. It demonstrates how quantum computing can exponentially speed up integer factorization compared to classical methods. This is achieved through techniques like the Quantum Fourier Transform and modular arithmetic. Integral factorization of large numbers is a time-consuming and costly undertaking for traditional computers, but it forms the basis of modern cryptography and security. The classical algorithms used for this process are General Number Field Sieve [35], and they counter an algorithmic runtime complexity as the numbers grow larger. It slows down the processing of traditional computers and becomes less practical.

Shor's algorithm, however, capitalizes on the theories of quantum mechanics and finds prime factors of large numbers much more quickly than classical methods. It can factorize an integer N in $O((\log N)^3)$ operations, called polynomial time. The key concept behind Shor's algorithm is to find the span of a modular exponential function. To start with, a random integer "a" that is co-prime and smaller than N is selected, and then the smallest integer r is found that meets the condition $a^r \equiv 1 \pmod{N}$. If r is even and $a^r \equiv -1 \pmod{N}$, then the factors of N can be calculated by calculating the greatest common divisor of $(a^{(r/2)} - 1, N)$ and $(a^{(r/2)} + 1, N)$. Shor's algorithm requires a quantum computer to prepare a superposition of many possible input values utilizing quantum gates. The process starts with preparing the initial state, then quantum gates carry out modular exponentiation and store the result in the output register, which filters the vast superpositions in the input register to a smaller, more focused superposition. Quantum Fourier Transform is then applied to identify the span, and classical post-processing extracts the factors from the identified span. Figure 13.3 presents a flowchart that outlines the key stages of Shor's algorithm. The algorithm starts by taking a large integer N as input and concludes with its prime factorization. Shor's algorithm poses a notable threat to current cryptographic standards; however, building a large-scale quantum computer capable of executing this algorithm on real-world encryption remains a formidable challenge. Secondly, quantum computations are prone to errors. Even small mistakes can lead to incorrect factorization. Shor's algorithm needs vigorous error correction techniques, which are still being developed for large-scale quantum computers.

13.4.2 Grover Algorithm

The Grover algorithm, developed by Lov Grover in 1996 [36], is an important quantum algorithm. It demonstrates the immense computational advantage that quantum systems hold over classical methods. This algorithm accelerates the process of solving unstructured search problems in comparison to classical analogues. Unstructured search is a task of finding a specific element within a collection of

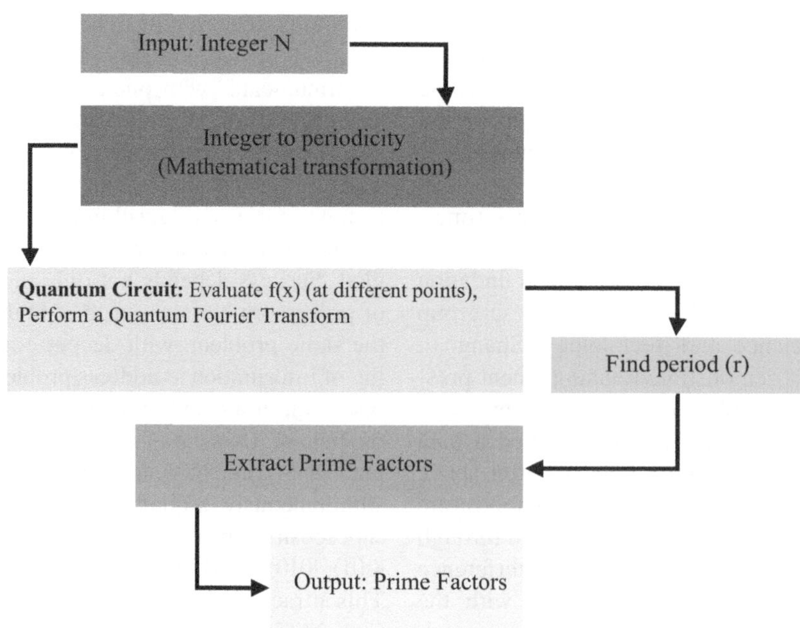

FIGURE 13.3 Flowchart of Shor's algorithm.

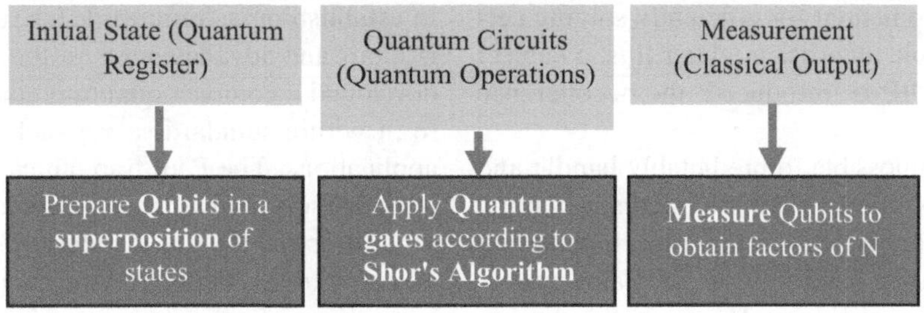

FIGURE 13.4 Block diagram to explain the working of Oracle's Gate.

items that are not sorted by any logical criteria. Classical computers use algorithms like linear search or binary search, in which each item is checked one by one diligently to sort it in a logical pattern or to locate an anticipated item. These algorithms take a long time when handling large data sets. Grover's algorithm could improve the efficiency of such searches with a quadratic speedup in comparison to classical methods, as it harnesses the idea of quantum entanglement to mark a major advancement in the field. In classical computing, finding an item in an unsorted list usually requires examining approximately half of the items, on average, and in the worst case, all the N entries. In contrast, Grover's algorithm can accomplish this task in roughly $\sqrt{N}$ steps. It operates on a superposition of all quantum states in the database and applies Grover's operation to amplify the amplitude of the desired target state. It utilizes quantum parallelism and interference to achieve the speedup. The superposition of all the available 2^N data entries is obtained by applying a Hadamard transformation on N qubits. This process effectively generates a quantum state that includes every item in the database. The subsequent phase involves constructing an oracle gate, as shown in Figure 13.4. The oracle gate is responsible for flipping the phase of the specified item(s), thereby enhancing their amplitudes. Subsequently, a reflection transformation is performed across the mean amplitude, which geometrically aligns the amplitudes of all states more towards the specified item(s) [37]. The Grover operator consists of a series of quantum operations that amplify the probability of getting the desired outcome while diminishing the probability of being in any other state. It uses the information from the oracle to achieve this amplification. Finally, the qubit with high probability is measured, and this measurement collapses the superposition to find the target state (the desired item in the database). The flowchart for Grover's algorithm is represented in Figure 13.5 and has significant implications for cryptography. It facilitates faster attacks on specific cryptographic operations, including symmetric key searches and hash functions. Unlike classical brute-force methods that require 2^n operations, where 'n' is the key length, Grover's algorithm can achieve the same outcome in approximately $2^{(n/2)}$ operations. Such advancements underscore the importance of post-quantum cryptography in countering the vulnerabilities posed by quantum threats. Numerous optimization problems are concerned with

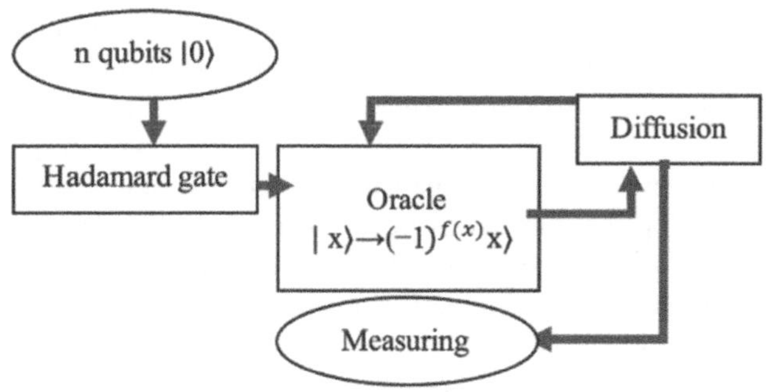

FIGURE 13.5 Flowchart of Grover's algorithm.

determining the most suitable solution amidst an extensive set of possibilities. By leveraging Grover's algorithm, it is capable of accelerating the process of solving these problems, showcasing potential advantages in domains such as logistics, operations and time management, and capacity planning. Grover's algorithm offers speedup but requires a complex and resource-intensive oracle in some cases, reducing its practical advantage. Practical implementation demands stable, error-corrected quantum hardware due to inherent noise, errors, and decoherence in quantum systems. This algorithm is poised to revolutionize search algorithms once large-scale, fault-tolerant quantum computers become a reality.

13.5 QUANTUM ENTANGLEMENT AND INFORMATION PROCESSING

A quantum computer leverages key principles of quantum mechanics, including superposition and entanglement, to tackle complex computational challenges more efficiently than classical computers. Notable applications include factoring large numbers with Shor's algorithm and searching extensive databases with Grover's algorithm. The computational process begins by initializing the system into a defined quantum state, followed by executing a series of targeted quantum operations as dictated by the chosen algorithm. Finally, a measurement of the resulting quantum state provides the solution. Quantum information processing (QIP) was initially proposed by Feynman and Deutsch [38,39], who extended the classical concept of a bit to the quantum realm, introducing the quantum bit, or qubit. Deutsch's concept of quantum parallelism is emphasized to gain insight into the potential for efficiently solving certain classically intractable algorithms. After this, a subject central to the field of QIP is introduced: the decoherence phenomenon.

At first, it seemed impossible to predictably handle and process quantum states due to their probabilistic nature. This made using quantum algorithms for computation impractical, and quantum computing was seen as a curiosity rather than a useful technology. However, the discovery of Shor's and Grover's algorithms for factorizing large numbers and a quicker search for desired target states from an unstructured database, respectively, demonstrated that quantum computing possesses far more practical implications. These developments spawned a worldwide pursuit for the development and implementation of quantum computers. They also opened new possibilities for cryptography, optimization, and machine learning. The ongoing research to develop quantum hardware and software points to a promising future of quantum computing. This technology has the potential to revolutionize various industries. QIP relies on entangled photon systems for efficient long-distance quantum communication. The entangled states are generated with the help of nonlinear crystals. These crystals possess multiple degrees of freedom such as polarization, spatial mode, orbital-angular-momentum, frequency, and time-bin for generating entangled photons. In experiments, researchers typically select entanglement in one typically chosen degree of freedom for their studies. These photons are used to accomplish tasks like quantum key distribution (QKD) [40], quantum secret sharing [41,42], and quantum secure direct communication [43–45]. In this section, the quantum computers working on the idea of ion trapping are discussed as they represent a promising method for developing large-scale quantum computers. They exhibit high-fidelity operations and long qubit coherence time and utilize individual charged atoms as qubits. The core idea behind this technology is to use electromagnetic fields to suspend ions in empty space, providing them a controlled environment where qubits can be manipulated and observed. In these computers, first the ions are created by removing an electron from the neutral atom, then these ions are trapped in an ion trap, generally known as Paul trap. These traps use oscillating electric fields to confine these ions in a limited area. These ions are used to process quantum information through the Coulomb force. The functionalities of an ion trap quantum computer rely upon the proficient utilization of laser beams to drive the ions in the desired initial state, which induces coupling between the qubit states for single-qubit operations, or between the internal qubit states and the external motional states, enabling entanglement between qubits. The development of ion trap quantum computing began in 1995, when Ignacio Cirac and Peter Zoller laid out the theoretical blueprint of storing quantum information using trapped ions. David J. Wineland at the National Institute of Standards and Technology, Colorado, demonstrated the first quantum logic gate—a controlled NOT gate tailored to the trapped ions system. It resulted in establishing a framework for further experimental realizations and advancements in the field. The scientists have developed a compact quantum computing system designed to fit within standard server racks, necessary for practical applications. The Paul trap, an electrodynamic quadrupole ion trap, serves as a crucial component in the development of ion trap quantum computers. This device was originally invented in the 1950s by Wolfgang Paul for mass spectroscopy. It was honoured with a Nobel Prize for its innovative design because it overcame the limitations posed by Earnshaw's theorem, which states that it is impossible to stabilize charged particles in three-dimensional space using only static electric fields. The Paul trap makes use of an oscillating electric field to form a dynamic potential well, permitting stable confinement of ions, as described by the Mathieu equations. Recent advancements have achieved controlled entanglement of up to 32 particles in a single trapped-ion system. This success demonstrates the expanding capabilities of ion trap quantum computers, and further refinements are possible to improve the processing power and efficiency of these computers. However, increasing the number of qubits in ion trap quantum computers may lead to several challenges in preserving quantum coherence and might take longer to execute algorithms. The addition of each ion complicates the system, making precise control and manipulation increasingly difficult. This is because the motional states of the ions (vibrations along the equilibrium position of trapped ions) increase as more ions are added, which complicates the execution of quantum operations and enhances the risk of errors. Additionally, integrating more than ten ions to a single trap introduces further complications because they experience the repulsive electric field of neighbouring ions as well. Also, as the number of ions increases, the probability of collisions and other interactions between them increases, potentially disrupting their trajectories and influencing their behaviour within the trap [46]. To challenge this, investigations have been carried out to check the possibility of connecting multiple smaller traps to form a better quantum network. Although this concept has been under discussion for more than 20 years, achieving practical implementation remains intangible. Transporting ions between different zones of the trap presents another technical hurdle. The electric fields required for trapping also add complexity to the integration of multiple traps on a single chip as they generate heat in the system. Hence realization of a quantum computer that fits within a standard server rack becomes unreasonable. Thus, it could be concluded that expanding ion trap quantum computers to support more qubits without losing performance or control is difficult.

13.6 QUANTUM ENTANGLEMENT IN QUANTUM CRYPTOGRAPHY

Quantum entanglement has found another remarkable application in quantum cryptography. This area is dedicated to developing secure communication protocols that are inherently resistant to eavesdropping. Traditional cryptographic methods rely on the complexity of mathematical algorithms to ensure security. These systems assume that encoded communications cannot be deciphered without access to the key. However, the advent of quantum computing algorithms offers a fundamentally different approach. It possesses the capability to exploit many of the cryptographic schemes to negotiate the security of encrypted messages. Quantum cryptography addresses these vulnerabilities by utilizing the unique properties of entanglement. One prominent example is QKD. In QKD, two parties exchange cryptographic keys using entangled photons. Any attempt to intercept or measure these photons disturbs their quantum state. This disturbance immediately alerts the communicating parties to the presence of an eavesdropper [41,42]. The no-cloning theorem reinforces security, as it is impossible to produce identical copies of an unknown quantum state. As a result, quantum cryptography can achieve high security and privacy that are inaccessible using classical methods. Notwithstanding robust theoretical foundations, practical utilization of quantum entanglement in cryptography encounters considerable challenges. One of the main difficulties lies in preserving quantum coherence over long distances and for extended periods. Entangled states can be disrupted by various environmental factors, such as thermal fluctuations and electromagnetic interference, resulting in compromising the integrity of quantum operations, and hence more efforts are required to overcome these obstacles. Progresses in quantum optics, superconducting qubits, and error correction protocols are being tracked to tackle these issues. Quantum error correction (QEC) is essential for conserving entanglement. These techniques detect and correct errors caused by environmental interactions or hardware imperfections. Continuing discoveries in this expanse is indispensable in the realization of robust quantum cryptographic systems.

13.6.1 Quantum Error Correction (QEC)

QEC is utilized to reduce disruptions caused by environmental interference, such as decoherence and quantum fluctuations [50], but it faces unique challenges due to quantum states' delicate nature. QEC must reduce quantum disturbance and support the unique properties of quantum states, such as superposition and entanglement. In classical systems, errors are blocked by duplicating bits and comparing results. Quantum systems, however, focus on protecting individual qubits in an entangled state, allowing errors to be detected and fixed without directly interfering with quantum information. The process involves three steps: encoding a logical qubit redundantly across multiple qubits, conducting specialized measurements called syndrome measurements to identify errors and applying recovery operations to correct the identified errors. In this method, ancilla qubit entangled with the original qubit helps to verify and recognize the error. Once the syndrome is measured, the classical computing analyses it and decodes the original qubit, making the quantum computing reliable. Thus, a QEC works on the principle of copying a single ancilla qubit's information across several qubits, allowing the system to identify and correct bit-flip errors. Techniques like the Shor code, the first QEC method developed by Peter Shor, can correct single-qubit errors, including bit-flip errors (X errors), phase-flip errors (Z errors), and combinations of both (Y errors) [47]. The Steane code goes further, addressing both bit-flip and phase-flip errors by distributing quantum data across seven entangled qubits [48]. These methods rely heavily on entanglement to protect information, ensuring quantum computers can function despite inevitable environmental noise. Beyond computing, QEC's impact extends to fields like drug discovery, as it allows quantum computers to function despite the expected errors. Quantum computers are more reliable and quicker in molecular dockings and simulations and, hence, could outpace classical systems in modelling complex interactions. Similarly, materials science might benefit from QEC as new materials with tailored properties might be designed, revolutionizing industries from energy to manufacturing. While challenges remain, QEC bridges the gap between theoretical quantum mechanics and practical applications to unlock fault-tolerant quantum systems.

13.7 FUTURE DIRECTIONS AND CHALLENGES

Quantum entanglement, though comprehensively studied in theoretical frameworks, has not yet been realized in practice due to its noteworthy limitations. Amongst the paramount hurdles is the requirement to develop scalable techniques to generate, control, and detect entangled states across various physical systems. Addressing these challenges requires innovative approaches that bridge the gap between theoretical and practical implications. As quantum computing systems grow larger to manage a greater number of qubits, maintaining the integrity of entanglement becomes exponentially more difficult. This difficulty stems from the fragile nature of quantum states, which can be easily disturbed by their surroundings, a phenomenon referred to as quantum decoherence. When decoherence takes place, entanglement quickly deteriorates, compromising the effectiveness of QIP. To mitigate these issues, researchers are developing advanced error correction techniques and improved isolation methods. Moreover, integrating quantum and classical computing systems, despite its potential, adds another layer of complexity. Classical computers excel at specific tasks and remain central to current technological infrastructure, making it essential to design interfaces that create smooth interfaces between quantum and classical platforms to communicate and work together synergistically. Achieving this goal requires not only innovative hardware but also new algorithms and software capable of bridging the gap between the two computing paradigms and operating within quantum environments. Moreover, the investigation of entanglement in complex systems, such as many-body quantum systems and new quantum materials, could reveal unexpected quantum phenomena and lead to breakthroughs in quantum simulation, metrology, and sensing. Understanding the functioning of entanglement in these settings may unlock new capabilities in precision measurement and quantum-enhanced technologies. As developments unfold, building scalable quantum networks is seen as a crucial step toward realizing the quantum internet, which could offer ultra-secure communication through quantum cryptography. The potential of entanglement in precision sensing and measurement may even surpass what is possible with classical devices. Although technical challenges remain, ongoing advances in quantum physics and engineering continue to push the boundaries and explore the limits of quantum mechanics, setting the stage for a future where quantum entanglement is not just a theoretical marvel but a practical asset in our technological toolkit. The journey from laboratory research to everyday applications is complex and demanding, yet the progress achieved so far suggests a future where quantum entanglement becomes a practical tool, driving innovation and expanding the horizons of technology and discovery.

13.8 CONCLUSION

Quantum entanglement stands as a fascinating idea that continues to be a captivating concept that persistently draws the attention of scientists and innovators. Its potential extends far and wide, with consequences that could revolutionize information processing, to creating secure communication methods and deepening understanding of the universe. As research in this field continues to advance, there is still much to uncover, and the societal impact could become even more significant. Technologies based on entanglement, such as advanced quantum computers and highly secure encryption systems, aim to leverage the fundamental principles of the universe for practical ends. Getting entanglement-based technologies to their full potential will not be easy, but future advancements will lead to major tech breakthroughs and deeper insights into reality. The exploration of quantum entanglement not only holds the potential to reshape scientific knowledge but also transform society. Looking forward, research in this area may blur the distinction between the possible and impossible, ultimately revealing the secrets of the quantum sphere.

REFERENCES

1. Green, E. J. (2002). Review of quantum evolution: How physics' weirdest theory explains life's biggest mystery. *The Quarterly Review of Biology*, *77*(4), 442–442. doi:10.1086/374429.
2. Kinch, S. S. (2001). *Quantum Mechanics and Modern Fiction*. Proquest Dissertation and Thesis, 3037511, The University of Texas at Austin.
3. Alet, F., Hanada, M., Jevicki, A. et al. (2021). Entanglement and confinement in coupled quantum systems. *Journal of High Energy Physics*, *34*. doi:10.1007/JHEP02(2021)034.
4. Brown, W. (2019). Unified physics and the entanglement nexus of awareness. *NeuroQuantology*, *17*(7), 40–52. doi:10.14704/nq.2019.17.7.2519.
5. Cirac, J. I., Perez-Garcia, D., Schuch, N., & Verstraete, F. (2021). Matrix product states and projected entangled pair states: Concepts, symmetries, theorems. *Reviews of Modern Physics*, *93*(4), 045003. doi:10.1103/RevModPhys.93.045003.
6. Einstein, A., Podolsky, B., & Rosen, N. (1935). Can quantum-mechanical description of physical reality be considered complete? *Physical Review*, *47*(10), 777. doi:10.1103/PhysRev.47.777.
7. Grossi, M., Di Meglio, A., & Vallecorsa, S. (2024). Spooky quantum action: From thought experiments to real world quantum technology application. In: M. Streit-Bianchi & V. Gorini (Eds.), *New Frontiers in Science in the Era of AI* (pp. 35–50). Springer.
8. Bohr, N. (1935). Quantum mechanics and physical reality. *Nature*, *136*(3428), 65–65. doi:10.1038/136065a0.
9. Schrödinger, E. (1935, October). Discussion of probability relations between separated systems. *Mathematical Proceedings of the Cambridge Philosophical Society*, *31*(4), pp. 555–563. doi:10.1017/S0305004100013554.
10. Bell, J. S. (1964). On the Einstein Podolsky Rosen paradox. *Physics Physique Fizika*, *1*(3), 195.
11. Aspect, A., Grangier, P., & Roger, G. (1981). Experimental tests of realistic local theories via Bell's theorem. *Physical Review Letters*, *47*(7), 460.
12. Aspect, A., Dalibard, J., & Roger, G. (1982). Experimental test of Bell's inequalities using time-varying analyzers. *Physical Review Letters*, *49*(25), 1804.
13. Paneru, D., Cohen, E., Fickler, R., Boyd, R. W., & Karimi, E. (2020). Entanglement: Quantum or classical? *Reports on Progress in Physics*, *83*(6), 064001.
14. Horodecki, R., Horodecki, P., Horodecki, M., & Horodecki, K. (2009). Quantum entanglement. *Reviews of Modern Physics*, *81*(2), 865–942.
15. Friis, N., Vitagliano, G., Malik, M., & Huber, M. (2019). Entanglement certification from theory to experiment. *Nature Reviews Physics*, *1*(1), 72–87.
16. Dakic, B., & Brukner, C. (2009). Quantum theory and beyond: Is entanglement special? arXiv preprint arXiv:0911.0695.
17. Latorre, J. I., & Riera, A. (2009). A short review on entanglement in quantum spin systems. *Journal of Physics A: Mathematical and Theoretical*, *42*(50), 504002.
18. Esfeld, M. (2004). Quantum entanglement and a metaphysics of relations. *Studies in History and Philosophy of Science Part B: Studies in History and Philosophy of Modern Physics*, *35*(4), 601–617.
19. Khang, A., & Rath, K. C. (Eds.). (2024). *The Quantum Evolution: Application of AI and Robotics in the Future of Quantum Technology*. CRC Press.
20. Wiseman, H. M. (2006). From Einstein's theorem to Bell's theorem: A history of quantum non-locality. *Contemporary Physics*, *47*(2), 79–88.
21. Bertlmann, R. (2017). Bell's universe: A personal recollection. In: R. Bertlmann & A. Zeilinger (Eds.), *Quantum [Un]Speakables II: Half a Century of Bell's Theorem* (pp. 17–80). Cham: Springer.
22. Clauser, J. F., Horne, M. A., Shimony, A., & Holt, R. A. (1969). Proposed experiment to test local hidden-variable theories. *Physical Review Letters*, *23*(15), 880.

23. Freedman, S. J., & Clauser, J. F. (1972). Experimental test of local hidden-variable theories. *Physical Review Letters*, *28*(14), 938.
24. Clauser, J. F., & Horne, M. A. (1974). Experimental consequences of objective local theories. *Physical Review D*, *10*(2), 526.
25. Aspect, A., Grangier, P., & Roger, G. (1982). Experimental realization of Einstein-Podolsky-Rosen-Bohm Gedankenexperiment: A new violation of Bell's inequalities. *Physical Review Letters*, *49*(2), 91.
26. Bouwmeester, D., & Zeilinger, A. (2000). The physics of quantum information: Basic concepts. In: D. Bouwmeester, A. K. Ekert, & A. Zeilinger (Eds.), *The Physics of Quantum Information: Quantum Cryptography, Quantum Teleportation, Quantum Computation* (pp. 1–14). Springer.
27. Bouwmeester, D., Pan, J. W., Mattle, K., Eibl, M., Weinfurter, H., & Zeilinger, A. (1997). Experimental quantum teleportation. *Nature*, *390*(6660), 575–579.
28. Keller, T. E., & Rubin, M. H. (1997). Theory of two-photon entanglement for spontaneous parametric down-conversion driven by a narrow pump pulse. *Physical Review A*, *56*(2), 1534.
29. Bennett, C. H., Brassard, G., Crépeau, C., Jozsa, R., Peres, A., & Wootters, W. K. (1993). Teleporting an unknown quantum state via dual classical and Einstein-Podolsky-Rosen channels. *Physical Review Letters*, *70*(13), 1895.
30. Zukowski, M., Zeilinger, A., Horne, M., & Ekert, A. (1993). " Event-ready-detectors" Bell experiment via entanglement swapping. *Physical Review Letters*, *71*(26), 4287–4290.
31. Holzscheiter, M. H. (2002). Ion-trap quantum computation. *Los Alamos Science*, *27*, 264–283.
32. Wineland, D. J. (2002). Trapped ions and quantum information processing. In: F. De Martini & C. Monroe (Eds.), *Experimental Quantum Computation and Information* (pp. 165–196). IOS Press.
33. Yin, J., Cao, Y., Li, Y.-H., Liao et al. (2017). Satellite-based entanglement distribution over 1200 kilometers. *Science*, *356*, 1140–1144. doi:10.1126/science.aan3211.
34. Shor, P. W. (1994, November). Algorithms for quantum computation: Discrete logarithms and factoring. In: *Proceedings 35thAnnual Symposium on Foundations of Computer Science*, Santa Fe, New Mexico, pp. 124–134. IEEE.
35. Shor, P. W. (1999). Polynomial-time algorithms for prime factorization and discrete logarithms on a quantum computer. *SIAM Review*, *41*(2), 303–332.
36. Grover, L. K. (1996, July). A fast quantum mechanical algorithm for database search. In: *Proceedings of the 28*th *Annual ACM Symposium on Theory of Computing*, Philadelphia, PA, USA, pp. 212–219.
37. Karthikeyan, S., Akila, M., Sumathi, D., & Poongodi, T. (Eds.). (2024). *Quantum Machine Learning: A Modern Approach*, 1st ed. Chapman and Hall/CRC. doi:10.1201/9781003429654.
38. Feynman, R. P. (1982). Simulating physics with computers. *International Journal of Theoretical Physics*, *21*(6/7), 467–488.
39. Deutsch, D. (1985). Quantum theory, the Church–Turing principle and the universal quantum computer. *Proceedings of the Royal Society of London. A. Mathematical and Physical Sciences*, *400*(1818), 97–117.
40. Briegel, H. J., Dur, W., & Cirac, J. I. et al. (1998). Quantum repeaters: The role of imperfect local operations in quantum communication. *Physical Review Letters, 81*, 593.
41. Bennett, C. H., & Brassard, G. (1984). Quantum cryptography: Public key distribution and coin tossing. In: *Proceedings of IEEE International Conference on Computers, Systems and Signal Processing,* Bangalore, India, pp. 175–179. IEEE, New York.
42. Ekert, A. K. (1991). Quantum cryptography based on Bell's theorem. *Physical Review Letters, 67*, 661–663.
43. Long, G. L., & Liu, X. S. (2002). Theoretically efficient high-capacity quantum-key-distribution scheme. *Physical Review A, 65*, 032302.
44. Deng, F. G., Long, G. L., & Liu, X. S. (2003). Two-step quantum direct communication protocol using the Einstein-Podolsky Rosen pair block. *Physical Review A*, *68*, 042317.
45. Deng, F. G., & Long, G. L. (2004). Secure direct communication with a quantum one-time pad. *Physical Review A*, *69*, 052319.
46. Haddadfarshi, F., & Mintert, F. (2016). High fidelity quantum gates of trapped ions in the presence of motional heating. *New Journal of Physics*, *18*, 123007. doi:10.1088/1367-2630/18/12/123007.
47. Shor, P. W. (1995). Scheme for reducing decoherence in quantum computer memory. *Physical Review A*, *52*(4), R2493–R2496.
48. Steane, A. M. (1996). Error correcting codes in quantum theory. *Physical Review Letters*, *77*(5), 793–797.

14 Quantum Artificial Intelligence for Environmental Management

Manjushree Nayak and N Toyaad Kumar Reddy

14.1 INTRODUCTION

Quantum computing is an important advancement in computing because it uses ideas from quantum physics to process data differently from classical computers. The fundamental ideas behind quantum computing are quantum parallelism, entanglement, and superposition [1]. Because of superposition, a quantum bit, commonly called a qubit, is able to be in several different states at once, unlike a classical bit that can only be 0 or 1. With this feature, quantum computers can handle different computations at the same time, which allows them to solve big problems much faster than standard computers. A qubit's state does not depend on how far it is from another, and therefore, entanglement, which Einstein labeled as "strange behavior at a distance", occurs between qubits when they become highly entangled. This is a key property for both quantum communication algorithms and protocols. With quantum parallelism, quantum computers can assess a function for many inputs at the same time because of superposition, which makes computations much faster for specific types of problems. It was in the early 1980s that David Deutsch and Richard Feynman began thinking about using quantum systems for computing, marking the beginning of the development of quantum technology. Peter Shor designed a quantum method to factor large numbers in 1994, and it was nearly ten times faster than the most popular algorithms, proving that quantum technology might advance work on both cryptography and optimization [2]. Scientists continued making progress in quantum computing in the following years, focusing on both theoretical advances and hands-on experiments. In 1998, IBM built the first two-qubit quantum computer. Google, IBM, and other businesses had managed to build quantum computers with 50 qubits by the early 2020s. Google achieved quantum supremacy in 2019 by running a calculation on its 53-qubit Sycamore processor in 200 s, which would have taken the world's strongest supercomputer 10,000 years [3]. Remember that certain tasks are better handled by either classical or quantum computers. Most of the speed and success in routine tasks performed by classical computers are based on the use of binary logic. Information is handled and represented in digital systems with bits and pre-defined algorithms. On the other hand, quantum computers perform their calculations using quantum mechanics. They work well in some machine learning tasks, the study of quantum systems, and solving optimization problems. Nevertheless, quantum computers are expected to provide the best performance in certain tasks, and they will generally work alongside conventional computers. This involves designing computer systems that can complete activities like language translation, interacting with people via speech, visual perception, and making decisions, each requiring human intelligence. Since it was first introduced in the 1950s, artificial intelligence (AI) has advanced substantially as researchers explore many ways to construct smart robots [4]. Deep learning uses complex networks of algorithms to analyze data, and machine learning allows algorithms to learn with experience, just like the brain, which are key concepts in AI. Technology embedded by AI is used in many areas such as advanced game algorithms, medical diagnostics, self-driving cars, and virtual assistants Alexa and Siri [4]. One very interesting area of research involves the shift from classical AI to quantum AI (QAI). Classical AI has improved substantially over recent decades, mainly because of deep learning and the availability of large data. However, the more difficult tasks these systems try to handle, the less efficiently and less quickly they perform their jobs. QAI is designed to enhance AI algorithms and potentially overcome some of these problems using the special features of quantum computing. Quantum machine learning might process significant amounts of data at a greater speed than standard techniques can. Using quantum artificial neural networks, which have qubits instead of neurons, may allow them to discover more complex patterns and relationships in data. Many QAI researchers are focusing on quantum-enhanced optimization for machine learning, quantum generative models, and quantum reinforcement learning. Some scientists suggest that quantum calculations of algorithms such as principal component analysis and support vector machines can run much more quickly than the same algorithms using current systems [5]. Even so, we should recognize that QAI is at an early phase, and developing quantum algorithms and hardware systems is not an easy task. With quantum computing becoming more accessible, we should expect to see more AI involved in financial modeling, medical studies, and predicting climate conditions. The combination of AI and quantum computing can lead to major shifts in how we handle difficult problems in many fields. Further research in AI and Big Data could result in important advancements that could change technology over the next few decades.

DOI: 10.1201/9781003530800-14

14.2 QUANTUM GATES AND CIRCUITS

Just as logic gates are important in today's computers, quantum gates are the basic components in quantum computing circuits. Unlike conventional gates, quantum gates are able to transform quantum states and work with qubits differently [1].

Hadamard (H) Gate: Superposition is formed for a qubit by putting it in a state halfway between |0⟩ and |1⟩. In the two-qubit gate, the first qubit is initialized, and the second qubit is set to the state |1⟩. , a condition necessary for entanglement to occur. Using (*S*) and π/8 (*T*) gates causes a phase change in a quantum system, which is important for several quantum algorithms.

Some gates are combined correctly to create different sequences for quantum computers. Classical circuits cannot be reversed, but quantum circuits can, which means the input can be calculated from the output [1].

14.2.1 Correction of Quantum Errors

It is particularly hard to protect quantum states, which are extremely fragile and easily disturbed, in quantum computing. A method named quantum error correction (QEC) was designed to preserve quantum data from being affected by decoherence and other kinds of noise [6]. Redundancy in QEC comes from encoding the main logical qubits into several physical ones, which allows for error detection and correction without changing the quantum state.

14.2.2 Important QEC Codes

Large and reliable quantum computers can only be built with the help of effective and practical QEC methods [6]. Surface codes benefit from being able to cope with high error levels and having only local interactions, setting a path to large quantum computers. Stabilizer codes such as Shor and Steane form a large category of QEC codes.

14.3 QUANTUM ALGORITHMS

Quantum computers are built to use quantum algorithms, which are known to be faster than classical algorithms for some sets of problems. Many significant quantum algorithms have been created. For example, Shor's algorithm deals with finding prime factors and performing discrete logarithms that are important for cryptography [2]; Grover's technique allows for a quadratic (much faster than conventional methods) exploration of unstructured problems [7]; HHL algorithm are used for linear equation systems, which perform more efficiently than traditional approaches for specific cases [8]; The quantum FFT transform is an important part of various quantum algorithms because it is the quantum variation of the discrete Fourier transform [1]. It was found that these algorithms can be processed quickly by quantum computers, but they still face difficulties when it comes to building them on noisy quantum machines [1].

14.4 QUANTUM SIMULATION

Quantum computing can be used for simulating molecules, which can be important in fields like materials science and medicine. Classical computers do not work well in simulating quantum systems since the computing resources have to grow exponentially as the system gets larger [9]. Unlike classical computers, quantum simulators generally handle quantum states and dynamics, which might help increase the efficiency of simulating complex systems. As a result, new and improved products, services, and systems might be created. These applications include: (1) drug discovery, made possible through a better understanding of drug–molecule interactions; (2) materials science by making new materials that have certain features; and (3) chemistry, by explaining why chemical reactions work as they are designed and finding ways to improve them. Quantum simulations have already been shown by researchers on a small scale, and this field is expected to achieve quantum advantage early on [9].

14.5 ANNEALING AT QUANTUM LEVEL

A type of quantum computing known as quantum annealing is used to address optimization problems. Global optimization using quantum fluctuations is the principle of Mehta's approach [10]. It is especially useful for tackling problems that require finding the best combination, such as with the traveling salesman or choosing a portfolio. D-Wave Systems has launched quantum annealers equipped with thousands of qubits; however, the extent to which these quantum systems provide a practical advantage over classical computers remains an active area of debate. Their flexibility isn't as strong as quantum gates yet, but quantum annealers could be used in areas like logistics and finance before gates [10]. All of these points explain how promising quantum computing is, and how hard it still is to master. Closer study and experimentation in these subjects may cause quantum computing to become more widely used in various areas ahead.

14.6 QUANTUM ARTIFICIAL INTELLIGENCE (QAI) AND QUANTUM COMPUTING INTERSECTION

The intersection between QAI and quantum computing is also important. Because of the union of AI and quantum physics, we have a potential new field known as QAI. Concepts from quantum mechanics, including superposition, entanglement and quantum tunneling, are used in QAI to increase and speed up algorithms and processes [5]. QAI is working to solve problems in traditional AI by using the potential of quantum computers in solving tough computational and visual tasks [11]. Handling massive data sets and difficult optimization issues is one main edge that QAI has over standard AI. Using several states at once, quantum computers make it possible to carry out operations that regular computers cannot do [12]. It is most important in machine learning where data includes many dimensions or where you have to use a large number of samples, much like in finance, finding new drugs, and studying the climate [13]. There are still many experiments and new frameworks being created, and the field of QAI is only just beginning. Even so, the industry is fast-changing because major tech firms and universities are investing heavily in developing quantum technologies [14]. There is a strong possibility for QAI to be useful in areas such as cryptography, optimization, and simulations, which can transform both logistics and healthcare [15]. Quantum algorithms have a key role in the growth of QAI. One of the main quantum algorithms in AI is Grover's method that can speed up searching by a factor of two compared to traditional methods, while the Quantum Approximated Optimization Algorithm uses a quantum computer to help optimize combinatorial problems [16]. By applying this approach to AI, the complexity and performance of pattern recognition and data classification are improved [17]. Key subjects in QAI research are quantum neural networks and QAI models. They attempt to make computer processes faster and learning easier using quantum events. Quantum Support Vector Machines (QSVMs) are built to increase classification accuracy on different datasets [18]. Using quantum gates instead of neurons allows quantum neural networks to represent data in more efficient ways [19]. Studies carried out so far have proved QAI to be effective, but these have been quite limited in scope. A quantum annealer is used to optimize traffic flow as an example, and this has been found to provide better results than using classical approaches [20]. In finance, a case study was done with a quantum-inspired algorithm for managing a portfolio, and it demonstrated promising results as far as risk-adjusted returns [21].

With advances in quantum error correction and quantum hardware improvements, the scope for QAI applications is likely to increase immensely. Researchers expect advances in fields like encryption and drug research, where quantum simulations may speed up the identification of novel substances. In similar cases, quantum algorithms could both strengthen and potentially break current encryption methods [22].

It's crucial to remember that many barriers still stand in the path of developing practical QAI systems. These include resolving the shortcomings of existing quantum machines, such as short coherence durations and high error rates, creating applications and programming paradigms tailored to the quantum world, and creating more secure and scalable quantum hardware [3]. Figure 14.1 shows a quantum circuit

```
from qiskit import QuantumCircuit, Aer, transpile, assemble
from qiskit.visualization import plot_histogram
import matplotlib.pyplot as plt
def create_bell_state():
    # Create a quantum circuit with 2 qubits and 2 classical bits
    qc = QuantumCircuit(2, 2)
    # Apply a Hadamard gate to the first qubit
    qc.h(0)
    # Apply a CNOT gate with control qubit 0 and target qubit 1
    qc.cx(0, 1)
    # Measurement
    qc.measure([0, 1], [0, 1])
    # Use Aer's qasm_simulator
    simulator = Aer.get_backend('qasm_simulator')
    # Compile the quantum circuit for the simulator
    compiled_circuit = transpile(qc, simulator)
    # Run the quantum circuit on the qasm simulator and get the results
    job = simulator.run(compiled_circuit, shots=1024)
    result = job.result()
    # Get the results
    counts = result.get_counts(qc)
    # Plot the results
    print("Counts:", counts)
    plot_histogram(counts)
    plt.show()
# Run the function
create_bell_state()
```

```
Counts: {'00': 499, '11': 525}
```

FIGURE 14.1 A quantum circuit that carries out a fundamental quantum operation, like generating a Bell state and then measuring the qubits with output.

that performs a basic quantum operation, such as creating a Bell state, and then measuring the qubits with output.

The steps involved in the intersection of AI and quantum computing are listed as follows:

Step 1: Import Qiskit and visualization libraries.
Step 2: Take two qubits and two classical bits in a quantum circuit.
Step 3: Include the Bell state, a CNOT gate, and a Hadamard gate.
Step 4: To observe the qubits, add measurement operations.
Step 5: Get the qasm_simulator backend.
Step 6: Optimize the circuit for simulation.
Step 7: Execute the circuit on the simulator and obtain results.
Step 8: Extract measurement results from the simulation.
Step 9: Print and plot the results using a histogram.

Despite these obstacles, there is still a lot of interest and funding opportunities in QAI research. QAI has the potential to expand the capabilities of AI and provide answers to problems that are currently intractable with traditional approaches as quantum technologies develop and become more smoothly integrated with standard computer infrastructures [23].

14.7 QUANTUM COMPUTING FOUNDATIONS AND ADVANCES IN MACHINE LEARNING

Quantum computing has shown a paradigm shift in computing power that uses the concepts of quantum physics to handle data in ways that conventional computers cannot. Fundamental to quantum computing are quantum bits, or qubits, which are capable of representing multiple values at once and existing in superposition states [1]. Together with quantum entanglement, this fundamental characteristic enables quantum computers to perform certain tasks ten times quicker than their traditional counterparts [8]. Quantum gates are the fundamental components of quantum circuits because they control qubits to carry out operations. Common quantum gates include the Hadamard gate for superposition phases, the rotation gate for phase shifts, and the CNOT gate for entanglement [24]. Quantum programs are built using combinations of these gates so they can address certain issues faster than classical algorithms [25]. It is very important to maintain the coherence of qubits in quantum computing because they are easily disrupted by other influences. Quantum computers can be built to be reliable and large enough only with the help of error-correction methods [26]. You can find current quantum hardware using topological qubits, superconducting circuits and trapped ions, each having different pros and cons [27]. Mixing machine learning with quantum computing has made AI capable of handling many issues more effectively. Certain tasks, for example, data clustering and classification, may see tremendous improvements in speed due to QAI [28]. Using quantum support vector machines, there have been suggested results in making things easier for computers and more accurate in classifying datasets that are very high-dimensional [29]. Neural networks using quantum techniques give scientists a new direction to pursue in AI. Quantum networks make use of quantum superposition to check all the inputs at the same time, which may help in training more efficiently [30]. Even without using quantum hardware, such algorithms help traditional machine learning by using quantum principles in solving optimization problems [31]. New research in quantum reinforcement learning uses quantum algorithms to manage the balance between trying out new actions and using the best ones in complex decision-making [32]. Using similar methods might be useful in financial modelling, robotics, and game theory [33]. By describing data with quantum feature maps and kernel methods, high-dimensional Hilbert spaces can offer a way to recognize patterns that are usually hard to spot with traditional techniques [34]. Quantum computing benefits in data representation could help improve technology for finding images and understanding languages [35].

It is important to keep in mind that many of these advancements have only been demonstrated on small-scale quantum mechanical systems or are still theoretical. Applying these techniques to real-world, practical problems are becoming more challenging as quantum hardware develops [12]. As the field develops, the combination of machine learning and quantum computing could enhance AI and possibly address issues that are currently unsolvable using only traditional techniques [5].

14.8 UTILIZING QAI IN MANAGEMENT OF THE ENVIRONMENT APPLICATIONS

Because QAI offers previously unheard-of processing power and efficiency, quantum environmental management could undergo a radical change to QAI. Resource optimization is one of the main uses for quantum algorithms, which can resolve challenging optimization issues far more quickly than traditional techniques [36]. QAI, for example, can be used to optimize systems for managing waste, lowering expenses, and their impact on the environment at the same time. Han and Kim [37] claimed that a quantum-inspired approach could enhance garbage collection routes by as much as 20% when compared to traditional techniques, which could result in a notable decrease in carbon emissions.

In the field of pollution control, QAI can enhance our ability to model and predict the spread of pollutants in air, water, and soil. Large volumes of environmental quantum machine learning techniques can examine data to identify patterns and improve forecast accuracy. One recent application, by Zhu et al. [38], used a quantum-enhanced neural network to predict air quality with 15% improved accuracy over standard models, with potential implications in improving early warning systems of hazardous events of air pollution.

14.8.1 Climate Modeling

Some applications of QAI can transform climate modeling. The classical climate models have computational limits when it comes to the inclusion of fine-scale phenomena and dealing with the risk involved in complex weather systems, even though they are sophisticated. It has been conjectured that quantum computing will be able to surmount these restrictions because it can operate on exponentially larger state spaces [39]. A quantum algorithm for reproducing molecular dynamics was proposed in a breakthrough study by Kassal *et al.* [40]. This approach has the potential to significantly enhance our understanding of atmospheric chemistry and its links to climate change. The algorithm could offer exponential speed-up on traditional techniques, possibly allowing more precise and detailed climate prediction. Figure 14.2 illustrates a simple machine-learning model and a classical version of a quantum algorithm to predict weather patterns.

The following is a list of the steps involved in the QAI and how it is used in climate modeling:

Step 1: Create artificial weather data, including wind speed, humidity, and temperature.
Step 2: Create artificial labels, such as a condensed "storm intensity" forecast.
Step 3: Separate the training and test sets of data.
Step 4: Train a simple classical machine learning model (multilayer perceptron)
Step 5: Predict storm intensity on the test set
Step 6: Hypothetical quantum-enhanced model prediction (for illustration, we'll assume a 30% improvement in accuracy)
Step 7: Calculate and print the mean squared error for both models
Step 8: Plot the predictions vs true values

Classical Model MSE: 1.10

Quantum-Enhanced Model MSE: 0.54

This includes the mean squared error for both models and a plot comparing the predictions of the classical and quantum-enhanced models to the true storm intensity values. This simplified example helps illustrate the potential improvement in prediction accuracy that QAI could bring to climate modeling.

When we have more extreme weather events because of climate change, QAI could help us develop better models for them. Martinez-Amaya et al. [41] have recently outlined ways quantum machine learning can be used to make hurricane and tropical storm forecasts better. By using quantum methods, the model predicted where hurricanes would head with 30% greater accuracy than traditional techniques, which helped people prepare and prevented losses.

14.8.2 Ecosystem Dynamics

The study of how ecosystems respond to feedback, stress, and changes. Knowing and observing ecosystem processes is very important for the protection of biodiversity and for

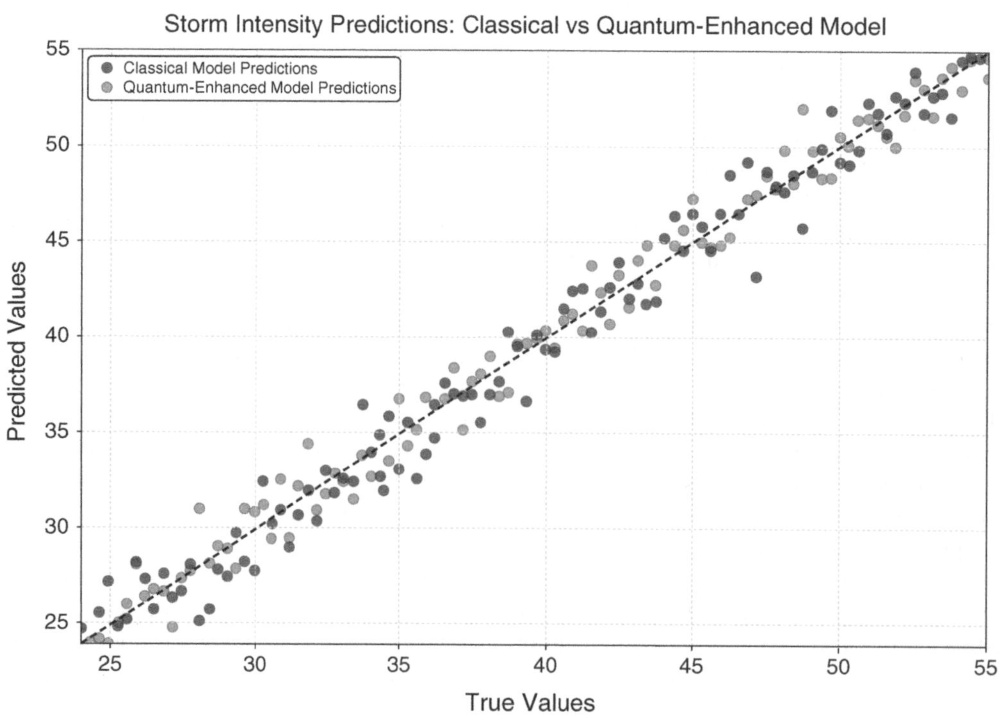

FIGURE 14.2 Classical version of a quantum algorithm and a simple machine learning model to predict weather patterns.

conserving resources. QAI introduces new advantages in ecological computing by permitting the processing of elaborate, multidimensional ecological information. Singh et al. [42] demonstrated how to use a quantum-like approach for modeling the distribution of species. With their method, scientists found that predictions about species and climate change were 25% more accurate than usual, which could make forecasting easier. QAI may greatly improve our knowledge of how food webs and ecosystems respond to change. In their paper, Akbar and Saritha [43] theorized that quantum algorithms may be better at describing complicated processes within ecosystems than traditional approaches. Therefore, this could mean we can better predict how environments might respond to things like extinctions or the presence of new species. Another use for QAI is to supervise and care for forest ecosystems. Scott [44] recently used a quantum-inspired technique to improve how forests are inventoried. Using their method, researchers found that 40% less sampling was needed to get accurate results, which may allow forest management to become both more efficient and less costly. Figure 14.3 illustrates that using a quantum-inspired algorithm tends to improve the predictions used in modeling species distribution.

The following is a list of the steps involved in QAI and how it is applied in ecosystem dynamics:

Step 1: Create artificial ecological data, such as environmental variables like elevation, temperature, and precipitation.
Step 2: Create artificial labels (such as species presence or absence).
Step 3: Separate the training and test sets of data.
Step 4: Train a classical machine learning model (multilayer perceptron)
Step 5: Predict species distribution on the test set
Step 6: Hypothetical quantum-inspired model prediction (for illustration, we'll assume a 25% improvement in accuracy)
Step 7: Calculate and print the mean squared error for both models
Step 8: Plot the predictions vs true values

In conclusion, these applications demonstrate the enormous potential of QAI in the management of the environment, climate simulation, and ecosystem dynamics, even though many of them are still in the conceptual or early experimental stages. We can anticipate seeing more real-world applications of these concepts as quantum technology develops, which could result in important advances in our comprehension, forecasting, and control of intricate environmental systems.

14.8.3 Resource Optimization

By using these algorithms, challenging problems related to resource allocation can be solved, and the damage to nature can be lessened. Because of using entanglement and superposition from quantum systems, these algorithms examine more solutions than traditional approaches [45]. Using quantum algorithms in supply chain optimization may help cut energy use and protect the environment. Kaswan [46] showed that using quantum annealing for transportation route optimization in a supply chain can decrease fuel usage and related emissions by around 25% as compared

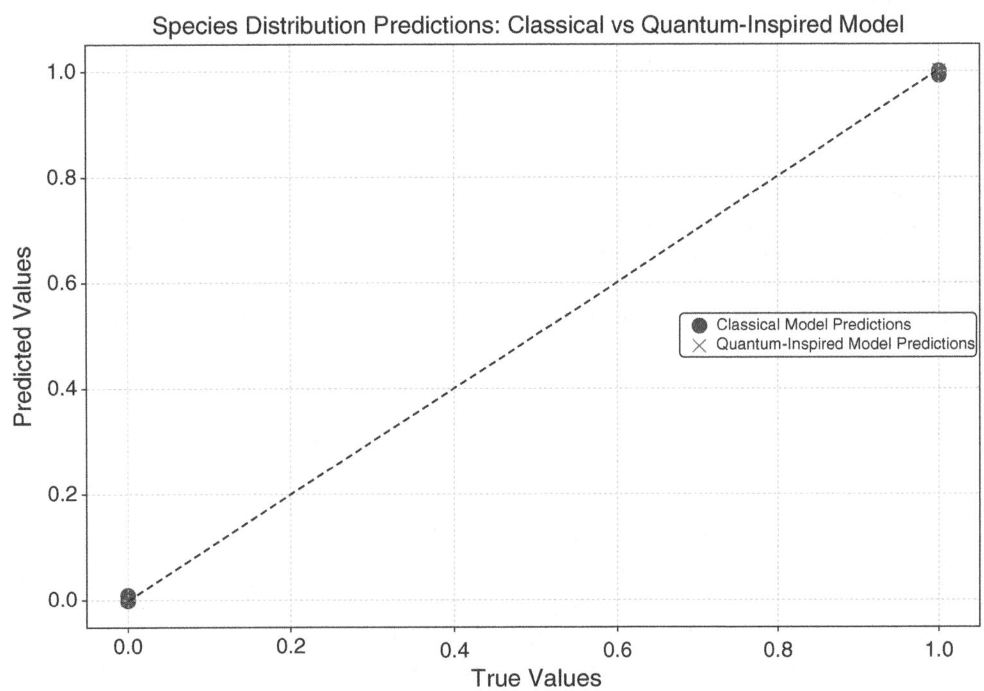

FIGURE 14.3 Demonstrating how a quantum-inspired algorithm could improve the prediction accuracy for species distribution modeling.

to the results obtained by conventional algorithms. This approach could be very beneficial in sectors where logistics are difficult to manage such as the food industry and manufacturing. Another area where quantum algorithms could help a lot is renewable energy optimization. Ajagekar and You [47] presented a Quantum Approximated Optimization Algorithm method for optimum placement and management of wind turbines . With their quantum-enhanced approach, they saw a 20% boost in energy from solar cells, which may bring renewable energy to people faster. In the same way, Shah et al. [48] applied a mixture of quantum and classical methods to improve solar panel placement and noted up to 15% better energy capture efficiency. Quantum computing makes it possible to reduce greenhouse gas emissions in many industries. The approach of quantum annealing was used by Perdomo-Ortiz et al. [23] to handle the problem of carbon collection and sequestration management. Due to quantum methods, the placement of carbon capture centers and routes was optimized which may lead to implementing them at 30% less cost and removing a greater amount of CO2. Using quantum techniques could reduce energy use in the building industry, which uses a lot of energy globally.

A quantum-inspired algorithm was proposed to optimize building energy management systems. The results demonstrate the substantial impact that quantum computing could have on urban sustainability, which had the potential to cut energy consumption by up to 18% when compared to traditional control systems.

Additionally, waste management system optimization, a crucial component of environmental sustainability, shows promise with quantum algorithms. Recently, Han and Kim [37] applied an evolutionary algorithm, based on quantum mechanics, to the optimization of urban solid waste collection routes. Their approach proved to be 22% better than conventional optimization methods and it reduced transportation costs, as well as minimized fuel costs and associated emissions. Although most of these applications remain conceptual or at an early experimental level, they indicate the huge potential of quantum optimization methods in solving difficult environmental problems. With the improvement in quantum hardware and its availability , more usable applications of these methods may be on the way, leading to significant improvements in resource allocation efficiency and a reduction of environmental impact in many industries.

14.9 CURRENT CHALLENGES IN QAI

In the area of environmental management, scientists are trying to resolve several technical issues about the QAI. These are hardware constraints and algorithm development issues, among others, that need to be resolved before QAI can achieve its potential in real-world use cases [49]. Among the most significant issues in QAI is creating reliable quantum algorithms that may surpass the traditional methods of environmental analysis and decision-making problems. Theoretically, searching techniques by Grover and other quantum phase prediction methods have a potential application, whereas in practice, they remain challenging to convert into practical environmental problems [12]. Researchers are exploring hybrid quantum-classical algorithms as a near-term solution. For instance, Cao et al. [50] proposed a hybrid approach for optimizing water distribution networks, demonstrating a 30% improvement in solution quality compared to classical methods.

Another significant obstacle in the creation of useful QAI applications is quantum error correction. Because quantum states are delicate, they can be affected by noise from the environment and decoherence, which could result in computational errors [6]. The trustworthiness of quantum calculations depends on sophisticated error-correcting methods, especially for long-running environmental simulations. Recent work by Fowler et al. [26] on surface code shows the potential for fault-tolerant quantum computing with quantum error correction, potentially enabling more reliable QAI applications in the future.

The realization of useful QAI applications in environmental management also depends on hardware developments. The size and complexity of issues that can be handled by current quantum processors are restricted by their qubit count and coherence times [27]. With their own advantages and disadvantages, researchers are investigating a variety of hardware architectures, including superconducting qubits, trapped ions, and topological qubits. In recent years, Arute et al. [3] demonstrated quantum supremacy using a 53-qubit processor, which was a major step toward more potent quantum hardware.

Interdisciplinary collaboration is key to advancing QAI for environmental applications. Environmental scientists, quantum computing experts, and policymakers must work together to identify high-impact problems and develop tailored quantum solutions [9]. For example, a collaborative study by Rahman et al. [51] brought together climate scientists and quantum algorithm experts to develop a quantum-enhanced method for simulating atmospheric dynamics, potentially improving long-term climate predictions.

Several potential breakthroughs on the horizon could significantly impact environmental management. Algorithms developed by Biamonte et al. [5] are promising for working with complex environmental data sets quickly and accurately. Because of these improvements, we could use better climate models, manage our environment more successfully, and handle pollution better. Changing theoretical research in QAI into real-world applications for environmental management goes through a number of key stages. To begin with, researchers should look for issues in the environment where getting a quantum edge is anticipated soon [23]. Following this, running quantum algorithms alongside classical algorithms for these problems will be key in proving real benefits [52]. Making these solutions address actual environmental problems will also depend on more advanced hardware and effective quantum software [53]. It looks promising that QAI will support the environment, but efforts and research will be necessary to continue.

With better quantum computing hardware and lower error rates, we will likely see more practical QAI in climate modeling, ecosystem management, and making the best use of resources [15], but it's clear that much work remains to achieve QAI's full potential. Many practical challenges still need to be solved, yet the recent growth in hardware, error correction, and quantum algorithms is making it possible for QAI to play a major role in the environment. These new tools might have a major impact on addressing current environmental issues.

14.10 APPLICATIONS IN THE REAL WORLD AND CASE STUDIES

Using quantum computational intelligence is a new field with great potential for taking care of the environment. Although some applications are only being discussed, studies and experiments are demonstrating that this technology is already helpful. One good example comes from the industry of water resource management. Working with quantum computing company D-Wave Systems, researchers at UC Berkeley used quantum annealing to solve problems in water distribution networks [54]. The main goal was to lower pumping costs while keeping up with the water needs for a detailed network. Using the quantum-inspired algorithm, the company showed up to 20% savings on operating costs in tests. The case study illustrates that QAI has the ability to greatly enhance how resources are used in important infrastructure systems. In climate modeling, an important breakthrough by Rahman et al. [51] applied quantum technology to model how the atmosphere moves. By joining quantum and classical methods, the researchers were able to improve their ability to predict weather by 25% compared to standard techniques. It could help produce more predictable climate forecasts for future periods, which is important for making policy and adaptation choices. QAI is also being studied to help protect biodiversity. Singh et al. [42] developed an algorithm, influenced by quantum ideas, for modeling where species exist. Compared to conventional machine learning, their methods improved predictions of species' reactions to climate change by 30%. By being able to predict better, scientists may offer more concentrated and successful help to conservation groups. QAI is proving to be productive in finding better ways to use renewable energy. Senderovich et al. [55] used quantum computing in a case study to help optimize where wind farms are built.

When compared to conventional optimization techniques, their quantum-enhanced method produced a 15% increase in total energy output. This development could accelerate the transition to renewable energy sources by improving the profitability and efficiency of wind farms [49].

Applications of QAI in the real world are also beginning to appear in monitoring and pollution control. Quantum machine learning algorithms were used in a pilot project by the Environmental Systems Research Institute and quantum computing startup QC Ware [56] to analyze satellite imagery in order to identify and forecast patterns of air pollution. When compared to classical methods, the quantum-enhanced approach demonstrated a 40% reduction in processing time, which could allow for near-real-time pollution monitoring and a quicker reaction to environmental threats. Research and development efforts are still focused on the viability and scalability of QAI solutions. Even though the qubit count and coherence times of current quantum hardware are constrained, continuous advancements are progressively broadening the range of problems that can be solved. An important step toward more potent quantum systems that can address more significant environmental challenges is IBM's recent announcement of a 433-qubit quantum processor [57].

It's important to keep in mind that a number of obstacles stand in the way of widespread practical implementations after laboratory experiments. Quantum error correction is still a developing field and is crucial to reliable large-scale quantum computations [58]. Furthermore, it is still difficult to create software tools and user-friendly interfaces that allow environmental scientists to use quantum algorithms without having extensive knowledge of quantum physics [53]. Notwithstanding these obstacles, QAI has a significant potential impact on environmental management. According to a thorough analysis by Ajagekar and You [36], quantum computing could optimize energy, transportation, and industrial processes, lowering global carbon emissions by as much as 7% by 2030. The revolutionary potential of QAI in tackling climate change and other environmental issues is highlighted by this projection. Future research, interdisciplinary cooperation, and gradual integration with current systems are all part of the roadmap for applying QAI in environmental management. More useful applications of quantum advantage are expected in domains like resource optimization, ecosystem management, and climate prediction as quantum hardware and algorithms advance [15].

In conclusion, even though QAI is still in its early stages, the case studies and new applications show how much potential it has for environmental management. Powerful new tools to tackle some of the most urgent environmental issues of our day should be made available by technological advancements. To fully realize this potential, though, consistent research funding, the creation of useful quantum software applications, and close cooperation between environmental specialists, policymakers, and quantum scientists would be necessary.

14.11 IMPLICATIONS FOR ETHICS AND SOCIETY

The use of quantum computational intelligence in environmental management raises a few ethical issues and possible societal implications, which must be considered. Since this powerful technology is becoming increasingly competent in making decisions that affect our environment and by extension, the lives of human beings, there is a strong need to make sure that it is created and applied in a responsible manner. Ethical considerations in QAI under environmental management have multiple aspects. One of the primary concerns is the likelihood of bias in quantum computing algorithms, leading to unfair or harmful environmental evaluations. It is stated that the complexity and secrecy of quantum systems may exacerbate the problem of accountability and transparency in AI ethics [59]. As a way of resolving this problem, they propose the development of ethical frameworks and guidelines specific to quantum technology. Another ethical factor is fair access to QAI technologies. Dhuliya et al. [60] recommend that it is possible that the benefits of QAI in environmental management will be skewed toward the wealthy nations or companies, and this will increase the inequality in environmental conservation and climate resilience experienced in the world. To ensure its ethical implementation, it would be necessary to ensure fair access to QAI technologies and their benefits at different geographical locations and socioeconomic strata. The potential misuse of QAI in environmental management also raises ethical questions. One example is the optimization of resource extraction in environmentally delicate regions which could be carried out by quantum simulations, and might favor financial returns at the expense of the environment. According to Coeckelbergh, this form of abuse has to be prevented with strong governance frameworks to ensure that QAI applications serve Sustainable Development Goals (SDGs) [61]. These ethical dilemmas should be dealt with through a diversified approach. Guidelines proposed by Floridi et al. [62], named quantum ethics by design, ensure that moral aspects are considered during the very creation of QAI systems. Such an approach could help to minimize potential risks and ethical dilemmas prior to their realization in practice. The social impact of QAI in environmental management can be extensive with a profound effect. QAI can also play an immensurable role in creating a more sustainable future by enhancing our ability to predict climate behaviors, manage resource efficiency, and simulate complex environmental structures. Perdomo-Ortiz et al. [23] state that QAI can totally change our approach to mitigation and adaptation measures to climate change, and maybe avert catastrophic environmental effects; however, technological development is not sufficient to achieve this potential. The key to the success of QAI technologies adoption and use is publicity and involvement. The gap between the quantum technologies and the scientific knowledge of the masses is sometimes considerable, according to Moller and Vuik [63]. The only way to build trust and acceptance of QAI applications in environmental management is by closing this gap via an effective science communication and public engagement program. Education is also necessary in order to get society ready to enter the quantum era. To provide the next generation of environmental managers with the means by which they may utilize QAI to its fullest potential, efforts like those proposed by Hughes et al. [64] are proposing to integrate ideas of quantum computing into the curricula of environmental sciences. QAI impacts on society beyond the environmental impacts to include workforce and economic issues. The QAI technologies can evolve job markets and skill prerequisites in the environmental fields. A recent transition to a quantum-empowered environmental management premise relies on predicting and getting ready for these changes via workforce preparation programs and policies [65].

Moreover, the success of QAI to effectively participate in a sustainable future is also dependent on its capacity to be interlinked with the broader sustainability policies and initiatives. Vinuesa et al. [66] emphasize the importance of aligning the AI (and, subsequently, QAI) development with the UN SDGs . In their argument, they state that although AI technologies have the potential to support the attainment of all 17 SDGs, in case they are not managed, they may also render some of them more difficult to attain [67–74]. Lastly, there are diverse and complicated moral and social implications of QAI in environmental management. Although the technology seems incredibly promising as a means of improving sustainability and preserving the environment, its ethical questions, fair access, and possible social ramifications must be considered thoroughly to develop and employ the technology responsibly. The concerted effort by scientists, policymakers, ethicists, and the general population will be required to harness the full potential of QAI in the future, reduce risks, and ensure that the benefits of QAI are fairly distributed across society.

14.12 CONCLUSION

To recap it all, QAI applied to environmental management is a highly prospective area of interest, which could essentially alter how we approach some of the most compelling ecological issues in modern times. As we have detailed, QAI offers computational power and novel solutions to long-standing environmental problems never heard of before, whether in the optimization of resources and the dynamics of ecosystems or in modeling the climate. To conclude the key points, we have seen how QAI could enhance our ability to better model and predict climatic patterns, which may transform our approach to adaptation and mitigation of climate change. Quantum algorithms promise to help manage ecological systems by unraveling complex ecological interactions and predicting species responses to perturbations in their environment. What is more, the possibility of QAI to streamline resource placement, as well as minimize environmental effects, can contribute to greener operations of various companies. The list of challenges that still need to be addressed is considerably long and must be mentioned to use QAI fully in environmental management. These are both more technical, such as scaling quantum hardware and quantum error correction, but also more general, such as providing fair access to QAI technology and addressing possible ethical dilemmas. In order to overcome such obstacles, long-term investment and research on quantum approaches and their implementation in environmental science will be required. The role of the interdisciplinary collaboration, in this regard, could hardly be overestimated. The gaps between computer science, environmental science, and quantum physics need to be closed to come up with workable QAI applications [5]. All legislators, business stakeholders, as well as the general population, should be part of this partnership so that QAI innovations can be created and used in a manner that is righteous and in line with the norms and values of society.

This takes us to the idea of potentially having a future in which highly accurate long-term forecasts made possible by quantum-enhanced climate models enable proactive climate adaptation measures, with QAI playing a vital role in maintaining a healthy planet. QAI would be able to maximize resource distribution across the world by making sure there is fair access to resources and waste and environmental destruction are minimized. Quantum algorithms could guide conservation in ecosystem management with an accuracy that has never been heard of, maintaining biodiversity and ensuring the maintenance of an ecological balance. Nevertheless, this vision cannot be implemented with technological development only. Vinuesa et al. [66] argue that much attention should be paid to ensure that the development of QAI is aligned with the wider sustainability agenda and ethics. This implies that the positive aspects of QAI should be shared with all sections of society and its uses should be controlled by the philosophy of sustainability and environmental justice. Including QAI in the sustainable environmental practice will likely be a challenging and satisfying process. It will require patience as some of the most important applications may not be achieved fully for years or decades to come. But it is a voyage worth making, considering the possible payoff in environmental conservation, climatic adaptation, and resource productivity. The funding of quantum research and development will be a priority in the future, ensuring an enhancement in the proficiency of environmental sciences and quantum literacy. Also of significance will be the setting of governance structures and ethics to warrant the proper development and application of QAI techniques in environmental management. QAI is a very strong instrument in the common quest to build a sustainable future, although it is not a magic wand for all the environmental problems. Using the exceptional powers of artificial Quantum technology and intelligent machines can totally transform the way humans perceive and interact with the natural world. We are on the verge of this environmental management revolution, and we have to cautiously and ethically steer its evolution so as to make sure that it is beneficial to the human race and the earth that we inhabit.

REFERENCES

1. Nielsen, M. A., & Chuang, I. L. (2010). *Quantum Computation and Quantum Information.* Cambridge University Press.
2. Shor, P. W. (1994). Algorithms for quantum computation: Discrete logarithms and factoring. In: *Proceedings 35th Annual Symposium on Foundations of Computer Science,* Santa Fe, NM, USA, pp. 124–134.
3. Arute, F., Arya, K., Babbush (2019). Quantum supremacy using a programmable superconducting processor. *Nature,* 574(7779), 505–510.
4. Russell, S., & Norvig, P. (2020). *Artificial Intelligence: A Modern Approach.* Pearson.
5. Biamonte, J., Wittek, P., Pancotti, N., Rebentrost, P., Wiebe, N., & Lloyd, S. (2017). Quantum machine learning. *Nature,* 549(7671), 195–202.
6. Lidar, D. A., & Brun, T. A. (Eds.). (2013). *Quantum Error Correction.* Cambridge University Press.
7. Grover, L. K. (1996). A fast quantum mechanical algorithm for database search. In: *Proceedings of the Twenty-Eighth Annual ACM Symposium on Theory of Computing,* Philadelphia, Pennsylvania, USA, pp. 212–219.
8. Harrow, A. W., Hassidim, A., & Lloyd, S. (2009). Quantum algorithm for linear systems of equations. *Physical Review Letters,* 103(15), 150502.
9. Georgescu, I. M., Ashhab, S., & Nori, F. (2014). Quantum simulation. *Reviews of Modern Physics,* 86(1), 153.
10. Hauke, P., Katzgraber, H. G., Lechner, W., Nishimori, H., & Oliver, W. D. (2020). Perspectives of quantum annealing: Methods and implementations. *Reports on Progress in Physics,* 83(5), 054401.
11. Schuld, M., Sinayskiy, I., & Petruccione, F. (2015). An introduction to quantum machine learning. *Contemporary Physics,* 56(2), 172–185.
12. Preskill, J. (2018). Quantum computing in the NISQ era and beyond. *Quantum,* 2, 79.
13. Dunjko, V., & Briegel, H. J. (2018). Machine learning & artificial intelligence in the quantum domain: A review of recent progress. *Reports on Progress in Physics,* 81(7), 074001.
14. Gibney, E. (2019). The quantum gold rush. *Nature,* 574(7776), 22–24.
15. Mohseni, M., Read, P., Neven, H., Boixo, S., Denchev, V., Babbush, R., ... & Martinis, J. M. (2017). Commercialize quantum technologies in five years. *Nature,* 543(7644), 171–174.
16. Farhi, E., Goldstone, J., & Gutmann, S. (2014). A quantum approximate optimization algorithm. arXiv preprint arXiv:1411.4028.
17. Wittek, P. (2014). *Quantum Machine Learning: What Quantum Computing Means to Data Mining.* Academic Press.
18. Rebentrost, P., Mohseni, M., & Lloyd, S. (2014). Quantum support vector machine for big data classification. *Physical Review Letters,* 113(13), 130503.
19. Killoran, N., Bromley, T. R., Arrazola, J. M., Schuld, M., Quesada, N., & Lloyd, S. (2019). Continuous-variable quantum neural networks. *Physical Review Research,* 1(3), 033063.
20. Neukart, F., Compostella, G., Seidel, C., von Dollen, D., Yarkoni, S., & Parney, B. (2017). Traffic flow optimization using a quantum annealer. *Frontiers in ICT,* 4, 29.
21. Rosenberg, G., Haghnegahdar, P., Goddard, P., Carr, P., Wu, K., & de Prado, M. L. (2016). Solving the optimal trading trajectory problem using a quantum annealer. *IEEE Journal of Selected Topics in Signal Processing,* 10(6), 1053–1060.
22. Aspuru-Guzik, A., Dutoi, A. D., Love, P. J., & Head-Gordon, M. (2005). Simulated quantum computation of molecular energies. *Science,* 309(5741), 1704–1707.
23. Perdomo-Ortiz, A., Benedetti, M., Realpe-Gómez, J., & Biswas, R. (2018). Opportunities and challenges for quantum-assisted machine learning in near-term quantum computers. *Quantum Science and Technology,* 3(3), 030502.

24. Barenco, A., Bennett, C. H., Cleve, R., DiVincenzo, D. P., Margolus, N., Shor, P., ... & Weinfurter, H. (1995). Elementary gates for quantum computation. *Physical Review A*, 52(5), 3457.
25. Montanaro, A. (2016). Quantum algorithms: An overview. *NPJ Quantum Information*, 2(1), 1–8.
26. Fowler, A. G., Mariantoni, M., Martinis, J. M., & Cleland, A. N. (2012). Surface codes: Towards practical large-scale quantum computation. *Physical Review A*, 86(3), 032324.
27. Kjaergaard, M., Schwartz, M. E., Braumüller, J., Krantz, P., Wang, J. I. J., Gustavsson, S., & Oliver, W. D. (2020). Superconducting qubits: Current state of play. *Annual Review of Condensed Matter Physics*, 11, 369–395.
28. Schuld, M., & Petruccione, F. (2018). *Supervised Learning with Quantum Computers*. Springer.
29. Havlíček, V., Córcoles, A. D., Temme, K., Harrow, A. W., Kandala, A., Chow, J. M., & Gambetta, J. M. (2019). Supervised learning with quantum-enhanced feature spaces. *Nature*, 567(7747), 209–212.
30. Beer, K., Bondarenko, D., Farrelly, T., Osborne, T. J., Salzmann, R., Scheiermann, D., & Wolf, R. (2020). Training deep quantum neural networks. *Nature Communications*, 11(1), 1–6..31. Moll, N., Barkoutsos, P., Bishop, L. S., Chow, J. M., Cross, A., Egger, D. J., ... & Tavernelli, I. (2018). Quantum optimization using variational algorithms on near-term quantum devices. *Quantum Science and Technology*, 3(3), 030503.
32. Dong, D., Chen, C., Li, H., & Tarn, T. J. (2008). Quantum reinforcement learning. *IEEE Transactions on Systems, Man, and Cybernetics, Part B (Cybernetics)*, 38(5), 1207–1220.
33. Levit, A., Crawford, D., Ghadermarzy, N., Oberoi, J. S., Zahedinejad, E., & Ronagh, P. (2017). Free energy-based reinforcement learning using a quantum processor. arXiv preprint arXiv:1706.00074.
34. Schuld, M., & Killoran, N. (2019). Quantum machine learning in feature Hilbert spaces. *Physical Review Letters*, 122(4), 040504.
35. Lloyd, S., Mohseni, M., & Rebentrost, P. (2014). Quantum principal component analysis. *Nature Physics*, 10(9), 631–633.
36. Ajagekar, A., & You, F. (2019). Quantum computing for energy systems optimization: Challenges and opportunities. *Energy*, 179, 76–89.
37. Han, K. H., & Kim, J. H. (2002). Quantum-inspired evolutionary algorithm for a class of combinatorial optimization. *IEEE Transactions on Evolutionary Computation*, 6(6), 580–593.
38. Zhu, J., Zhang, Z., Gu, W., Zhang, C., Xu, J., & Li, P. (2025). Air Quality Prediction Using Neural Networks with Improved Particle Swarm Optimization. *Atmosphere*, 16(7), 870.
39. Daskin, A. (2020). A quantum approach to climate modeling and prediction. *Climatic Change*, 162, 1729–1748.
40. Kassal, I., Jordan, S. P., Love, P. J., Mohseni, M., & Aspuru-Guzik, A. (2008). Polynomial-time quantum algorithm for the simulation of chemical dynamics. *Proceedings of the National Academy of Sciences*, 105(48), 18681–18686.
41. Martinez-Amaya, J., Longépé, N., Nieves, V., & Muñoz-Marí, J. (2023). Improved forecasting of extreme hurricane events by integrating spatio-temporal CNN-RF learning of tropical cyclone characteristics. *Frontiers in Earth Science*, 11, 1223154.
42. Singh, M., Dhara, C., Kumar, A., Gill, S. S., & Uhlig, S. (2022). Quantum artificial intelligence for the science of climate change. In *Artificial Intelligence, machine learning and blockchain in quantum satellite, drone and network* (pp. 199–207). CRC Press.
43. Akbar, S., & Saritha, S. K. (2021). Quantum inspired community detection for analysis of biodiversity change driven by land-use conversion and climate change. *Scientific Reports*, 11(1), 14332.
44. Scott, C. T. (1998). Sampling methods for estimating change in forest resources. *Ecological Applications*, 8(2), 228–233.
45. Rieffel, E. G., & Polak, W. H. (2021). *Quantum Computing: A Gentle Introduction*. MIT Press.
46. Kaswan, K. S. (2024). Quantum Computing for Supply Chain Optimization. In *Quantum Computing and Supply Chain Management: A New Era of Optimization* (pp. 1–32). IGI Global.
47. Ajagekar, A., & You, F. (2020). Quantum computing assisted deep learning for fault detection and diagnosis in industrial process systems. *Computers & Chemical Engineering*, 143, 107119.
48. Shah, N., Shah, A. A., Leung, P. K., Khan, S., Sun, K., Zhu, X., & Liao, Q. (2023). A review of third generation solar cells. *Processes*, 11(6), 1852.
49. Badawy, R., Heßler, A., Albayrak, S., Hirsch, B., & Yassine, A. (2014). Quantum-inspired evolution for smart building energy management in future power networks. EngOpt2014, 226.
50. Cao, Y., Zhang, Y., Zhao, Y., Wang, C., & Niu, Z. (2025). Interactions and Integrated Optimization between Secondary Water Supply Devices and Drinking Water Distribution Systems: a Review. *Water Resources Management*, 1–15.
51. Rahman, S. M., Alkhalaf, O. H., Alam, M. S., Tiwari, S. P., Shafiullah, M., Al-Judaibi, S. M., & Al-Ismail, F. S. (2024). Climate change through quantum lens: Computing and machine learning. *Earth Systems and Environment*, 8(3), 705–722.
52. Aaronson, S., & Chen, L. (2021). Complexity-theoretic foundations of quantum supremacy experiments. *Communications of the ACM*, 64(6), 107–115.
53. LaRose, R. (2019). Overview and comparison of gate level quantum software platforms. *Quantum*, 3, 130.
54. Rocha, C. R., Renaud, N., Leijnse, K., van Beek, S., & Castro-Gama, M. (2025). Quantum Simulation and Optimization of Water Distribution Networks. arXiv preprint arXiv:2507.06862.
55. Senderovich, A., Zhang, J., Cohen, E., & Beck, J. C. (2022). Exploiting hardware and software advances for quadratic models of wind farm layout optimization. *IEEE Access*, 10, 78044–78055.
56. QC Ware. (2021). *QC Ware and Esri Partner to Bring Quantum Machine Learning to ArcGIS Users*. QC Ware.
57. IBM. (2022). IBM unveils 433 qubit quantum processor and next-generation IBM quantum system two. *IBM Newsroom*. IBM.
58. Terhal, B. M. (2015). Quantum error correction for quantum memories. *Reviews of Modern Physics*, 87(2), 307.
59. Perrier, E. (2021). Ethical quantum computing: A roadmap. arXiv preprint arXiv:2102.00759.
60. Dhuliya, P., Rana, D. S., Goyal, S., Kukreti, S., & Pundir, S. (2024, November). Quantum Computing for Sustainable Development: A Framework for Environmental and

Social Impact. *In 2024 International Conference on Advances in Computing, Communication and Materials (ICACCM)* (pp. 1–7). IEEE.
61. Coeckelbergh, M. (2020). *AI Ethics*. MIT Press.
62. Floridi, L., Cowls, J., Beltrametti, M., Chatila, R., Chazerand, P., Dignum, V., Luetge, C., Madelin, R., Pagallo, U., Rossi, F., Schafer, B., Valcke, P., Vayena, E. (2018). AI4People—An ethical framework for a good AI society: Opportunities, risks, principles, and recommendations. *Minds and Machines*, 28(4), 689–707.
63. Möller, M., & Vuik, C. (2017). On the impact of quantum computing technology on future developments in high-performance scientific computing. *Ethics and Information Technology*, 19(4), 253–269.
64. Hughes, C., Isaacson, J., Turner, J., Perry, A., & Sun, R. (2022). Teaching quantum computing to high school students. *The Physics Teacher*, 60(3), 187–189.
65. Gharavi, H., Granjal, J., & Monteiro, E. (2024). Post-quantum blockchain security for the Internet of Things: Survey and research directions. *IEEE Communications Surveys & Tutorials*, 26(3), 1748–1774.
66. Vinuesa, R., Azizpour, H., Leite, I., Balaam, M., Dignum, V., Domisch, S., Felländer, A., Langhans, S.D., Tegmark, M. and Fuso Nerini, F. (2020). The role of artificial intelligence in achieving the Sustainable Development Goals. *Nature Communications*, 11(1), 233.
67. Ghai, D., Saxena, S., Dhingra, G., & Tripathi, S. L. (2024). A comprehensive review on performance-based comparative analysis, categorization, classification and mapping of text extraction system techniques for images. *Multimedia Tools and Applications*, 1–158.
68. Ghai, D., Gianey, H. K., Jain, A., & Uppal, R. S. (2020). Quantum and dual-tree complex wavelet transform-based image watermarking. *International Journal of Modern Physics B*, 34(04), 2050009.
69. Sandhu, R., Channi, H. K., Ghai, D., Cheema, G. S., & Kaur, M. (2024). An introduction to generative AI tools for education 2030. In: R. Doshi, M. Dadhich, S. Poddar & K. K. Hiran (Eds.), *Integrating Generative AI in Education to Achieve Sustainable Development Goals* (pp. 1–28). IGI Global.
70. Soewu, T., Kaur, H., Sandhu, R., Sandhu, P., Ghai, D., Dhir, K., & Tripathi, S. L. (2025). Machine learning models for text and image processing. In: S. Dash, S. K. Pani & W. P. dos Santos (Eds.), *Machine Learning Models and Architectures for Biomedical Signal Processing* (pp. 153–177). Academic Press.
71. Ghai, D., Tripathi, S. L., Saxena, S., Chanda, M., & Alazab, M. (Eds.). (2022). *Machine Learning Algorithms for Signal and Image Processing*. John Wiley & Sons.
72. Ghai, D., Rawal, K., Dhir, K., Tripathi, S. L. (Eds.). (2024) *Artificial Intelligence Techniques for Sustainable Development*. CRC Press.
73. Faiz, M., Sandhu, R., Akbar, M., Shaikh, A. A., Bhasin, C., & Fatima, N. (2023). Machine learning techniques in wireless sensor networks: Algorithms, strategies, and applications. *International Journal of Intelligent Systems and Applications in Engineering*, 11(9s), 685–694.
74. Arora, C., & Sandhu, R. (2024, January). Adoption of quantum NLP for improved healthcare system. In: A. K. Bairwa, V. Tiwari, S. K. Vishwakarma, M. Tuba & T. Ganokratanaa (Eds.), *International Conference on Computation of Artificial Intelligence & Machine Learning* (pp. 51–59). Springer.

Index

For Product Safety Concerns and Information please contact our EU representative GPSR@taylorandfrancis.com Taylor & Francis Verlag GmbH, Kaufingerstraße 24, 80331 München, Germany